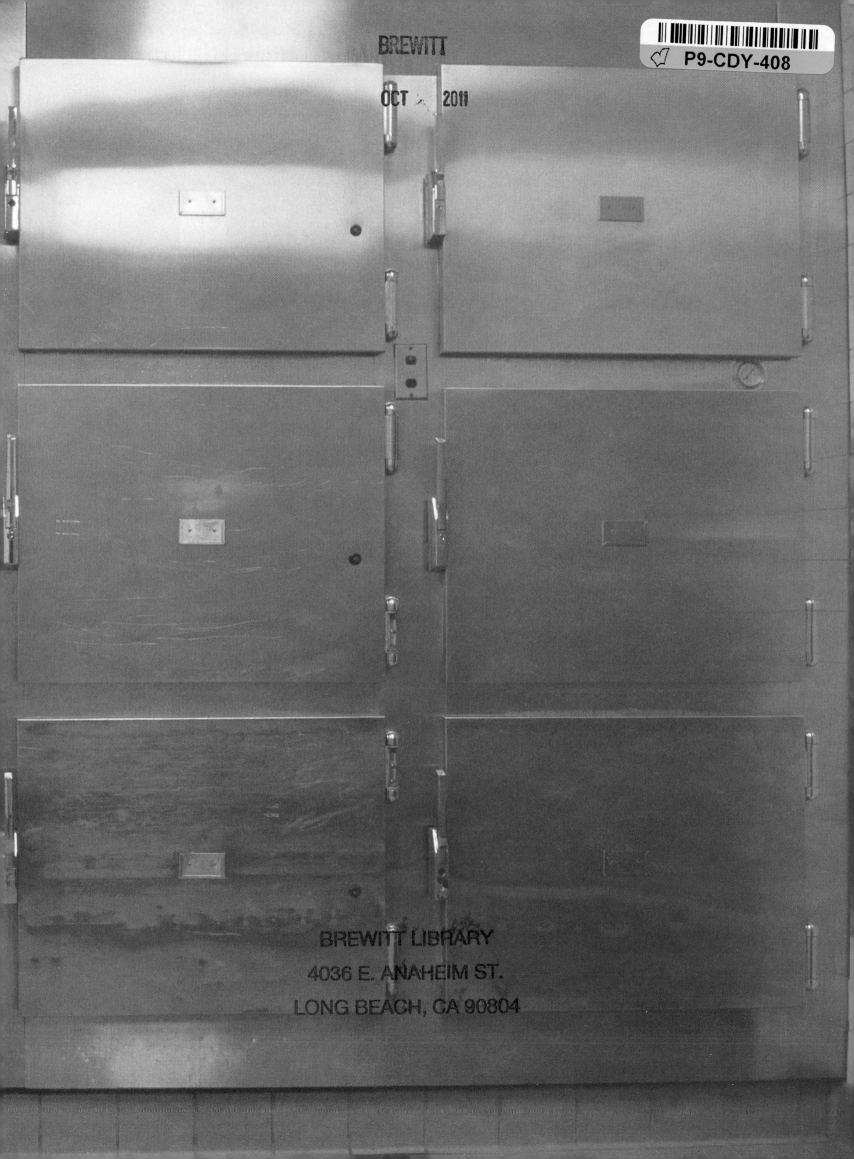

BREWITT

OCT 2011

P9-CDY-408

BODY
IN QUESTION

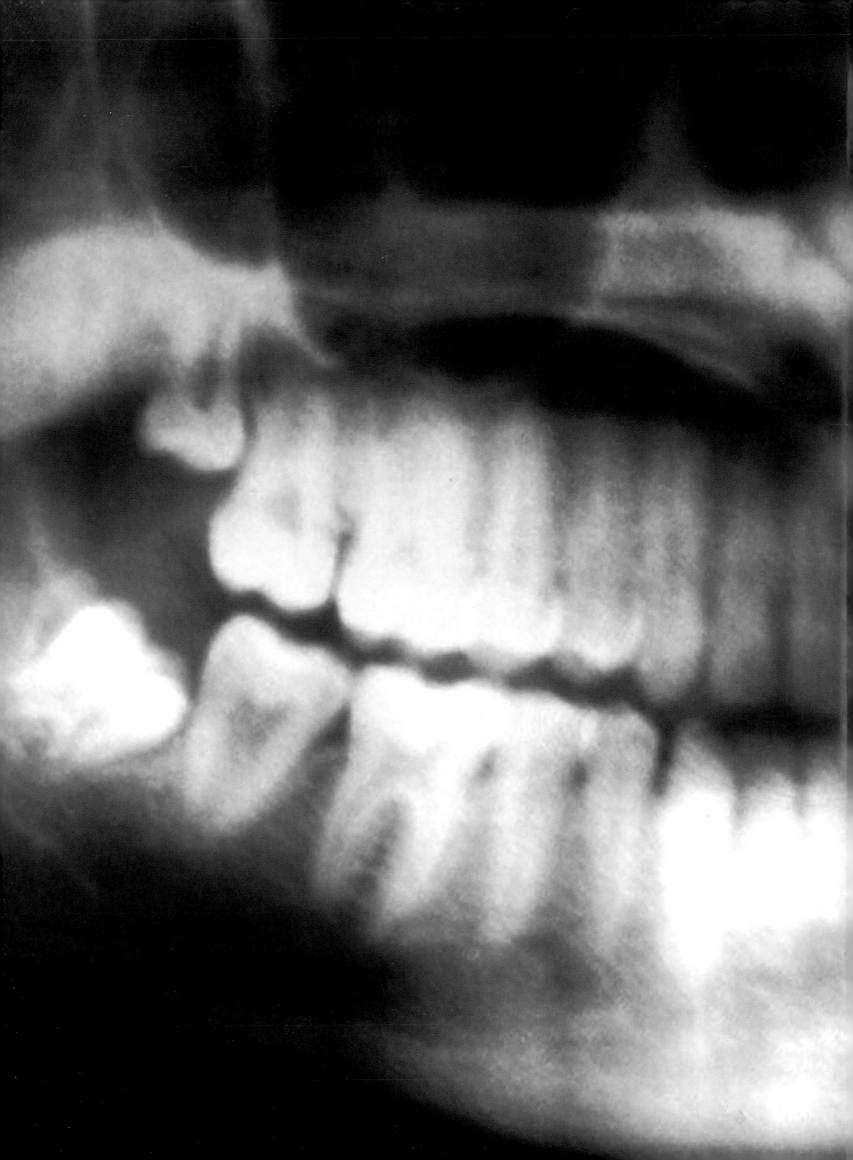

BODY
IN QUESTION

EXPLORING THE CUTTING EDGE IN FORENSIC SCIENCE

BRIAN INNES

FOREWORD BY **RONALD L. SINGER, M.S.,**
PRESIDENT, AMERICAN ACADEMY OF FORENSIC SCIENCES

STERLING

ACKNOWLEDGMENTS

Any complicated book of this sort requires the participation of numerous people with expertise in diverse fields. The publishers would like to acknowledge the contributions of the following individuals, without whose help this book would still be an unsolved crime (in no particular order): photographer Tyler Cancro, whose fearless camera work provided unflinching but compassionate images of the autopsy process; the New York City Medical Examiner's Office and the staff—particularly resident pathologist Xin Min Zang, resident neurologist Hope Wu, and mortuary technician Dorian Acosta—who initiated Tyler into the autopsy process and allowed him to intimately document some of the amazing work the NYC ME's staff does every day; the Sacramento Police Department, especially Captain Joe Valenzuela, Public Information Division, who helped us immensely by explaining police procedure at a crime scene and gave us the confidence to create evidence for the fictional case of Jane Doe; Dr. Ronald Singer, crime lab director of the Tarrant County ME's office, who provided a wonderful foreword for this book and the encouragement we needed to finish the case; Dr. Neal Haskell, a forensic entomology consultant who provided the remarkable photographs documenting the entomological demolition of a corpse on the Body Farm; the talented publishing staff at 122 Fifth Avenue, including art director Kevin Ullrich, photography director Christopher Bain, assistant photography director Lori Epstein, copy editor Erikka Haa, and digital imaging specialist Daniel Rutkowski; the tireless and extremely patient cast at Amber Books, including project editor Michael Spilling, design manager Mark Batley, picture manager Natasha Jones, and designer Zöe Mellors; and the California State Library, whose resources were cheerfully made available to us.

CONTENTS

FOREWORD

For a long time, forensic scientists toiled in the shadows of the criminal justice system. Though the discipline provided invaluable information to the investigator, the general public was seldom aware of the critical role played by the men and women who had dedicated themselves to the application of science to the investigation of crime. To the casual observer, the exploits of a detective attempting to crack a case using deduction, interrogation, and meticulous attention to detail is far more compelling than the (no-less-essential) contributions of the scientist in the lab trying to accomplish the same goal using test tubes and microscopes. Similarly, for that portion of the public with an interest in science, the discoveries of research scientists at universities or large drug companies are more fascinating (not to mention better publicized) than the innovative applications developed by forensic scientists, using (for the most part) already discovered techniques. In many ways, we in the field have been isolated by the very nature of the job, which involves long hours of painstaking work in the laboratory—in short,

the kind of work that rarely affords the opportunity for us to appear in the public eye.

Two nearly simultaneous events have changed all of that, however: The use of DNA technology in forensic investigations and the trial of O.J. Simpson.

The use of DNA technology is considered by many to be the single most significant advancement in criminal investigation since the introduction of fingerprinting techniques some hundred years earlier, and its advent gripped the public imagination. Like fingerprints, DNA has the potential to absolutely link an individual to a crime scene. Unlike fingerprints, however, DNA is found in almost every part of the body, so anything of biological origin left behind at a crime scene can, theoretically at least, yield a DNA profile (commonly referred to as a "DNA fingerprint") of the perpetrator. The fact that the DNA molecule quite literally holds the blueprint to who and what we are only added to its mystique. As a result, people became interested in not only how DNA technology could be used to help solve crimes, but also how science in general played a part in the overall process.

For the first time, the public became overwhelmingly curious to see how doctors, dentists, engineers, chemists, anthropologists, and other people of science contribute their talents to providing information pertaining to the investigation of criminal acts, the identification of unknown persons, or to the unraveling of historic events. Forensic scientists were no longer just "geeks in the lab" (or worse), but were now bona fide investigators who happened to use science instead of interrogation in the pursuit of answers.

At roughly the same time, O.J. Simpson was brought to trial for the murder of his ex-wife, Nicole Brown Simpson. The media coverage surrounding that trial brought the courtroom into the homes of people around the world, and generated widespread interest in the workings

"Every contact leaves a trace."
—EDMOND LOCARD,
L'ENQUETE CRIMINELLE ET LES METHODES SCIENTIFIQUE (1920)

of the judicial system and in the forensic process—an interest that continues to this day. In the United States, a widely viewed television network now offers gavel-to-gavel coverage of major trials, and the demand for books about crime, criminals, and the criminal justice system is at an all-time high. At this writing, the hottest shows on any television network center around either the courtroom or the crime scene. The public is no longer satisfied with motion pictures and television programs that soft-pedal the scientific process, instead demanding more realism and better science in popular depictions of investigative procedure.

Nor is this general interest relegated to popular culture. Courses in forensic science have become ubiquitous in colleges and universities across the country, and are even appearing on high school schedules. I personally receive several e-mails and phone calls a week from people ranging from middle school students to adults with college degrees inquiring about how to enter the field of forensic science. And, indeed, never has there been so much to learn! As the technology in the laboratory becomes more sophisticated, the information that can be derived from evidence continues to increase at an exponential rate, raising the demand for trained forensic scientists. Today, for instance, DNA profiles can regularly be obtained from a single hair left at a crime scene; electronic databases exist now that make it possible for computer-assisted searches of biological, fingerprint, and firearm evidence to be completed in minutes, whereas it would have taken weeks, or simply been impossible, only a few years ago; and information stored on computer hard drives can be deciphered even after having been erased. And these are just a few isolated examples of the enormous scientific evolution underway.

Within the next few years, techniques that are now in the research phase will be introduced into case work that will allow physical characteristics of the perpetrator, such as sex, hair, and eye color, to be predicted on the basis of biological evidence. The utilization of computers in the analysis of data will increase tremendously, as will the amount of information forensic scientists are able to obtain from physical evidence. At the same time, the amount of sample required to obtain the information will continue to decrease. In short, the "science" in forensic science will continue to become more sophisticated and precise.

Into this mix comes *Body in Question: Exploring the Cutting Edge of Forensic Science*. This book is an extremely readable, comprehensive, and easily understood

> *The public is no longer satisfied with motion pictures and television programs that soft-pedal the scientific process, instead demanding more realism and better science in popular depictions of investigative procedure.*

introduction to the broad scope of forensic science today. Using both real and fictional cases as examples, it takes the reader through each of the various aspects of forensic science, providing insight into the history, technology, and application of each particular specialty. Brian Innes uses his skills as a writer to tell an intriguing story, scientific in nature, that is sure to captivate and enlighten anyone curious about what forensic science is all about.

If *Body in Question* piques your interest in forensic science to the point that you would like more detailed information on the subjects discussed, or if you are interested in making a career of some aspect of the science, be sure to visit the website of the American Academy of Forensic Sciences at www.aafs.org. Founded in 1948, this 6,000-member international organization is composed of the best forensic scientists from more than sixty countries. The AAFS website provides information about the current state of the art of forensic science, advice about career possibilities, and links to numerous other websites that the reader may find useful.

Edmond Locard, one of the founders of modern forensic science, said that every contact leaves a trace. Contact with *Body in Question* should leave the reader with considerably more than that.

—Ronald Singer, President,
American Academy of Forensic Sciences

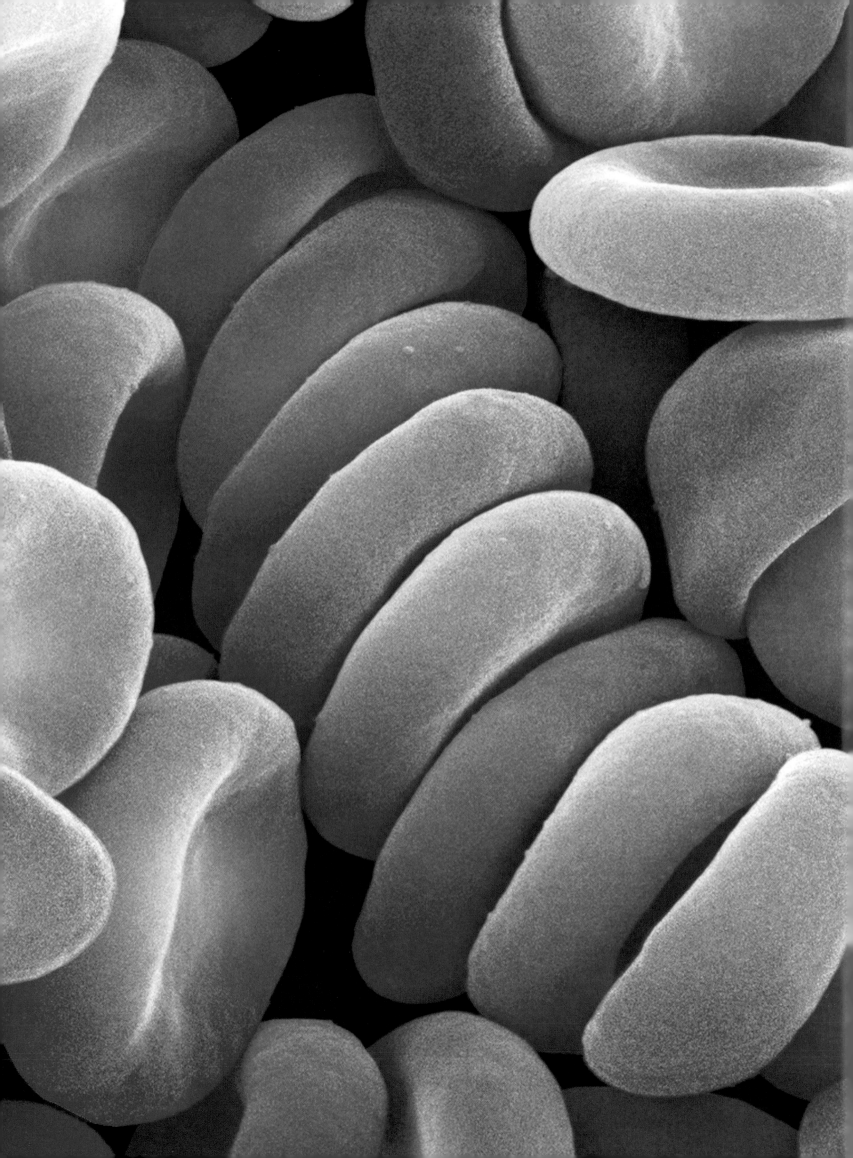

BEYOND REASONABLE DOUBT

Without the application of forensic science in the investigation of crime—and particularly violent crime—countless criminals around the world would have gone unapprehended, and innumerable mysteries would remain unsolved. The link between the science and its role in the investigation, not to mention the prosecution, of crime is suggested by the very meaning of the word *forensic*: "connected with the courtroom." Indeed, the law requires the forensic expert—in the broadest meaning of this term— to establish "beyond reasonable doubt" the physical details of a crime, in the expectation that these details will be presented as crucial evidence in court.

*"The times have been,
That, when the brains were out,
the man would die,
And there an end;
but now they rise again ..."*
—WILLIAM SHAKESPEARE, *MACBETH*

FACING PAGE THIS COLORED SCANNING ELECTRON MICROGRAPH (SEM) SHOWS RED CELLS—ERYTHROCYTES— OF HUMAN BLOOD AT A MAGNIFICATION OF 4,850. THEY PLAY AN ESSENTIAL PART IN THE IDENTIFICATION OF THE DIFFERENT BLOOD TYPES. HOWEVER, OF ALL THE CELLS IN THE BODY, THEY ARE THE ONLY ONES THAT DO NOT CONTAIN DNA.

Despite its significance today, the science of forensic investigation is scarcely two centuries old. What follows is a (necessarily) brief survey of the immense strides that were taken during the first one hundred years. In the early days of forensic evidence, when an inquiry was held into the circumstances in which a person had been found dead this evidence comprised little more than the details of the cause of death and an estimate of the time at which it had occurred. For this reason, most of the early forensic experts were physicians or surgeons, and the subject is still sometimes referred to as medical jurisprudence. However, many other kinds of expert are now also involved in forensic matters: the expert in firearms or other weapons, the fingerprint expert, the analytical chemist, the serologist, and the forensic anthropologist—to name only a few. In fact, there is not a single area of science or technology that has not been called upon for advice in the investigation of a crime and the subsequent presentation of a case in court. In recent years attention has also been turned to the psychology of the criminal—although this is usually used to assist the investigation rather than as firm evidence that a court will accept.

A HIT OR MISS AFFAIR

The development of forensic science has progressed hand in hand with the gradual increase in the sophistication of scientific investigation in general. Previously—before the invention of instruments capable of measuring physical forces such as electricity, or the establishment of chemical analysis and the isolation of pure chemical compounds, for

CHINESE PIONEERS

The Chinese are credited with the earliest attempts to apply practical techniques to crime investigation, which were described in a mid-thirteenth-century book by Sung Tz'u, *Hsi Yuan Lu* (*The Washing Away of Wrongs*). Although many of its suggestions were totally unscientific, the book also contained some useful advice—such as how to distinguish drowning (characterized by water in the lungs) from strangulation (which was revealed by pressure marks on the throat and damaged cartilage in the neck). There was advice on the examination of decomposed bodies, and a warning against making too hasty an assumption concerning what appeared to be wounds. Above all, the *Hsi Yuan Lu* stressed the importance of trace evidence at a crime scene: "The difference of a hair is the difference of a thousand *li*," it cautioned, a *li* being a Chinese mile.

One case described in the book is of a farmer found by the roadside slashed to death. The local headman ordered everybody to bring their sickles to him for examination. "The weather was hot," wrote Sung Tz'u, "and the flies flew about and gathered on one sickle." "The sickles of the others have no flies," said the headman to the owner. "Now you have killed a man … so the flies gather." Wrote Sung Tz'u: "The bystanders were speechless, sighing with admiration. The murderer knocked his head on the ground and confessed."

established by the Bishop of Bamberg twenty-six years earlier and was applied throughout the Holy Roman Empire. The Caroline Code specified that expert medical advice should be obtained, for the guidance of judges, in cases of suspected murder, wounding, poisoning, hanging, drowning, infanticide, and abortion.

Unfortunately, medical practice at this time remained grounded in superstition rather than science. As late as the mid-seventeenth century, at a trial in Norwich, England, for example, the eminent physician Dr. Thomas Browne gave expert testimony describing how the vomiting of pins and nails was the result of the Devil's work. This was at a time when practical investigation in the physical sciences was making great advances: The telescope and the microscope had been invented, the possibility that light traveled in waves was being discussed, the mathematics of astronomy was developed, and Sir Isaac Newton was soon to put forward his theories on gravitation. Medical science, however, lagged far behind physical science for nearly a further two centuries.

BELOW ONE OF THE GREATEST SURGEONS OF ALL TIME, AMBROISE PARÉ WAS AN EARLY STUDENT OF FIREARM WOUNDS. THE CHIEF IMPROVEMENTS INTRODUCED BY PARÉ WERE A REFORM IN THE TREATMENT OF GUNSHOT WOUNDS AND THE REVIVAL OF THE PRACTICE OF TYING OFF ARTERIES AFTER AMPUTATION. ON ACCOUNT OF HIS HUMANITARIAN ACTIVITY HE WAS HELD IN SPECIAL REGARD AMONG SOLDIERS. HIS MOTTO, AS INSCRIBED ABOVE HIS CHAIR IN THE COLLÈGE DE ST-COSME, READ: *JE LE PANSAY ET DIEU LE GUARIST* (I TREATED HIM, BUT GOD HEALED HIM).

example—practical science had been very much a hit-or-miss affair, largely devoted to observation but without the equipment to establish an explanation of the observation. The investigation of violent crime in particular also suffered from the fact that dissection of the human body (except that of an executed criminal) was, in most circumstances, illegal.

For centuries, in most criminal inquiries, it was sufficient to observe that a dead body was indeed a dead body. If some kind of a wound were visible, that was obviously the cause of death; if the body were found in water, it was a case of drowning. As for finding a culprit, the authorities had to rely first of all upon suspicion of a motive, and then upon circumstantial evidence: An identified person had been seen near the scene of the crime, or was known to have threatened the life of the dead person, or was the only one in the vicinity to possess the strength, the appropriate weapon, or some other means of murder. And, frequently, the authorities had to resort to the use of torture to obtain a confession.

An important judicial development came in 1533, when Holy Roman Emperor Charles V published his *Constitutio Criminalis Carolina* (the *Caroline Code*), which followed a similar code

ANATOMY ACTS

As schools of anatomy were gradually instituted in Britain, the demand for human bodies grew, but there were no legal means of obtaining them. So-called resurrectionists clandestinely exhumed buried corpses from their graves and secretly sold them to anatomy teachers.

The scandal culminated in the execution of William Burke, in Edinburgh, Scotland, in 1829, for his part in the trade. Burke and his accomplice, William Hare, instead of bothering to dig up dead bodies, had murdered sixteen lone travelers and then sold them to Dr. Robert Knox, a leading anatomist. The sixteenth victim was the first to be reported missing, and the police were able to trace the body to Dr. Knox's cellar. Hare turned king's evidence, and so escaped execution.

A result of this case was the passing of the Anatomy Act in 1832, permitting the use of unclaimed bodies—such as those of persons who had died in the "poor wards" of hospitals—by specially licensed teachers. In the commonwealth of Massachusetts a similar law had been passed the previous year, and the example was soon followed in other U.S. states.

BELOW IN THIS PAINTING, ENGLISH PHYSICIAN WILLIAM HARVEY (STANDING, RIGHT) DEMONSTRATES TO KING CHARLES I (SEATED, LEFT) HIS THEORY OF THE CIRCULATION OF THE BLOOD. BY STUDYING ANIMALS GIVEN TO HIM BY HIS ROYAL EMPLOYER, HARVEY DEVELOPED AN ACCURATE THEORY OF HOW THE HEART AND CIRCULATORY SYSTEM OPERATE. HE PUBLISHED HIS THEORIES IN HIS BOOK *ON THE MOTION OF THE HEART AND BLOOD IN ANIMALS* (1628).

There were, happily, enterprising individuals who made vital discoveries regardless. The French surgeon Ambroise Paré (1510–90), who was largely self-taught, has been named one of the three greatest surgeons of all time. He took a particular interest in firearm wounds, tracing the position of bullets in the bodies of victims and so determining the direction from which they had come. His nearest contemporary was the Belgian anatomist Andreas Witing (1514–64)—known as Vesalius—whose teaching at the University of Padua made that institution preeminent in the study of anatomy for more than a century.

In 1616, the English physician William Harvey, who had spent four years studying at Padua, finally successfully established the connection between the beating of the heart and the continuous circulation of blood throughout the body. Over the next two centuries, anatomy, in association with surgery or medicine, was taught in most of the universities of Europe, but in Britain the discipline was adopted very slowly.

It was not until 1770 that Scottish obstetrician William Hunter (1718–83) established—at his own expense—a school and museum of anatomy in London. Hunter and his brother John (1728–93), together with English physiologist William Hewson (1739–74), taught there; Benjamin Franklin was a frequent visitor, and he later persuaded Hewson's widow and children to move to Philadelphia, where a number of their descendants became eminent physicians.

Two earlier pupils of the Hunters, William Shippen and John Morgan, had established a school of medicine in Philadelphia in 1765, teaching anatomy and surgery; this was to become a famous part of the University of Pennsylvania.

Gradually, the number of cases in which physicians and surgeons were able to assist the investigating authorities with expert advice increased. By the end of the eighteenth century, two landmark works had been published: *Traité de Médécine Légale et d'Hygiene Publique* (*A Treatise on Forensic Medicine and Public Health*) by French physician T.E. Fodéré, and *The Complete System of Police Medicine* by German expert Johann Peter Franck.

BEYOND REASONABLE DOUBT?

The scientific method is—or should be—a rigorous one. In ideal terms, it involves the postulation of a theory, followed by the performance of an experiment that is designed to disprove that theory. If the results of the experiment—and of others that follow—fail to disprove the theory, there are solid grounds (but still with reservation) for believing that the theory is sound, and therefore represents the truth.

Unfortunately, it must be said that most forensic investigation is directed largely to supporting theory: "We have reason to believe that this is the blood of John Doe, and the tests we have carried out prove that it is his."

However, in fairness to current forensic invesitigation, it should be pointed out that time and cost considerations limit the practical number of tests, which are generally far from exhaustive. Which, of the varying and wide range of tests available, is the one that might exclusively establish that this is *not* the blood of John Doe?

So, what does it mean to say, "beyond reasonable doubt"? In practice, the law accepts that identity has been established provided an agreed number of points of similarity can be demonstrated in a range of forensic evidence. But many innocent persons have been convicted on the results of investigations and analyses that were carelessly carried out, and were designed only to "prove" guilt (see the Innocence Project, Chapter Six).

Unfortunately, there are also cases in which it was established eventually that supposed forensic experts had confused or contaminated the samples on which they had worked, or even—perhaps under pressure from the authorities to secure a conviction—deliberately falsified their findings. Consequently, an element of doubt often remains.

CASE STUDY
TWO CASES: SCIENCE ENTERS THE COURTROOM

One of the earliest cases in what has since become the scientific study of firearm fatalities—nowadays commonly known as ballistics—was recorded in 1784, in Lancaster, England.

Edward Culshaw was found shot dead with a pistol, and examination of his gunshot wound revealed a small wad of paper that had been rammed down the barrel of the pistol to keep the ball and powder in place. When the wad was unrolled and cleaned, it was found to be a piece torn from a musical ballad sheet. The rest of the ballad sheet, exactly matching the torn fragment, was found in the pocket of a man named John Toms, who had been suspected of the murder. The evidence was presented in court, and was judged sufficient for the conviction and execution of Toms—one of the first cases in which true scientific investigation was employed.

Another early English case was heard in Warwick in 1816. A young servant girl had been sent on a brief errand, but did not return. The next morning her body was found drowned in a shallow pool, but bearing the marks of violent assault. There were signs of a struggle in the mud at the edge of the pool, together with scattered grains of wheat and chaff—and the imprint from a corduroy trouser leg that had been patched with a piece of similar material. The grains and chaff led the investigators to suspect a local farm laborer, who had been threshing the previous day. And one knee of his trousers had been patched in a way that exactly matched the imprint in the mud. Although he tried to prove an alibi, he was found guilty.

Cases such as these are interesting in the context of the history of forensic science, but they depended more on fortunate observation rather than formal and rigorous investigation. The specific application of scientific method really began in what was, in fact, one of the most difficult areas of investigation: the question of poisoning.

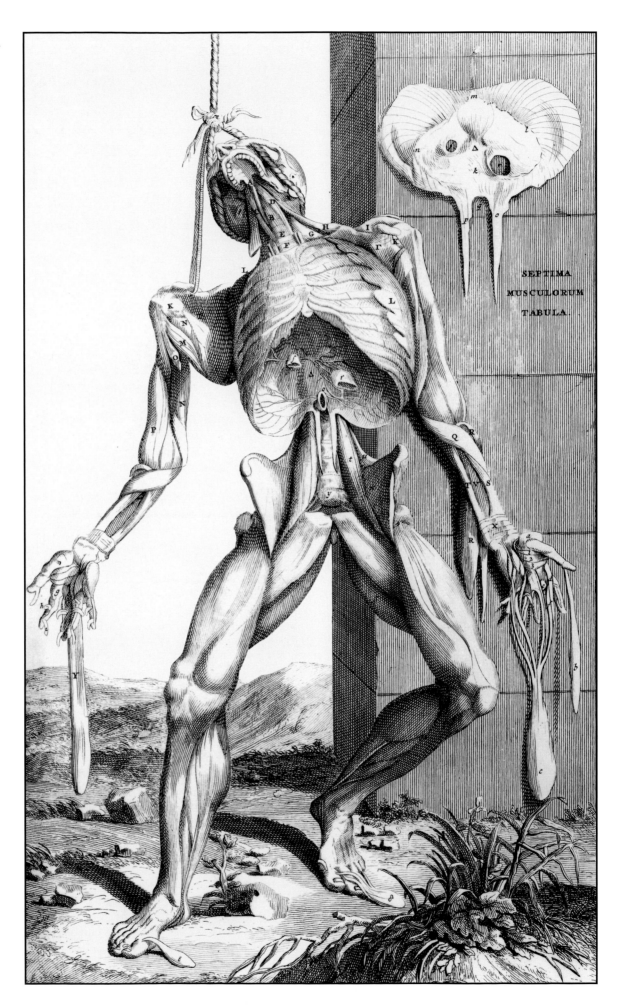

RIGHT THE PUBLISHED WRITINGS OF VESALIUS, THE GREAT ANATOMIST, BECAME FAMOUS FOR THEIR METICULOUS ENGRAVINGS OF DISSECTED BODIES. HERE, THE MUSCLES OF THE ARMS AND THORAX ARE LAID OPEN, EACH LABELED FOR PRECISE IDENTIFICATION.

SEPTIMA
MUSCULORUM
TABULA.

TOXICOLOGY

Throughout many centuries, murder by poison was frequently suspected but impossible to prove—as Phineas Foote put it early in the seventeenth century, it was the "coward's weapon." To the ancient Greeks, the herb *Aconitum napellus*—monkshood or wolfsbane—was known as stepmother's poison; the citizens of Imperial Rome were forbidden to grow it in their gardens. The use of poison became so common in Rome, in fact, that many of the richer people employed food tasters, whose job was to sample all the dishes of a meal—and occasionally to exhibit suspicious symptoms, or even fall dead—before their patrons would take a mouthful.

There are many known natural poisons, mostly of plant origin. The Greek philosopher Socrates, accused of "corrupting Athenian youth," was allowed a drink of hemlock extract to gain an honorable death; and Livia, wife of the Roman emperor Augustus, was widely feared for her possession of a chest of poisonous potions. In the fifteenth century, members of the Borgia family—notably Lucrezia—were rumored to have poisoned many of their enemies. There existed no apparent way, however, to prove the presence of a poison in a dead body.

More recently, the mineral arsenious oxide—popularly known as arsenic—became readily available as a poison for rats and other vermin. For four or five centuries it was the commonest substance employed for murder. Its faintly sweet taste was undetectable when it was added to food, and its lethal effects were usually attributed to acute gastric disease. (Indeed, as late as 1975, when Marie Hilley of Anniston, Alabama, used arsenic to kill her husband, his death was certified as "infectious hepatitis.") It was not until 1836 that a simple and definite test for the presence of arsenic in a dead body became available.

The development of this test involved the work of several chemists over a period of some

ABOVE A RELATION OF THE CARROT FAMILY, HEMLOCK IS A HIGHLY POISONOUS PLANT. THE IMPRISONED GREEK PHILOSOPHER SOCRATES (c. 469–399 BC) WAS OFFERED A DRINK OF THE PLANT EXTRACT TO ACCORD HIM AN HONORABLE DEATH.

sixty years. In 1775, the great Swedish chemist Carl Wilhelm Scheele discovered that when arsenious oxide was treated with nitric acid and zinc granules, it evolved a poisonous gas, which was subsequently named arsine. Shortly thereafter, German chemist Johann Metzger showed that if arsenious oxide were heated with charcoal a mirrorlike deposit would condense on a cold plate held above. This was, in fact, the element arsenic. This procedure became known as the Metzger test.

The first recorded forensic application of this discovery came in 1810, in Berlin. Dr. Valentine Rose took the stomach contents of a suspected victim of poisoning, dried the liquid to a white powder, and heated it with charcoal to obtain the characteristic mirror. His technique proved sufficient evidence against a domestic servant who had poisoned several of her employers.

Finally, in 1832, an elderly English farmer, George Bodle, was alleged to have been poisoned by his grandson John. James Marsh, a former assistant to the eminent scientist Michael Faraday, was asked to demonstrate at trial that the dead man's coffee had contained arsenic. Using Metzger's method, he did so, but failed to persuade the jury, who found John Bodle not guilty. Frustrated, Marsh determined to find a way of producing clearly demonstrable evidence. He went back to Scheele's initial discovery, and so developed the famous "Marsh test." Treating the suspect matter with sulfuric acid and zinc, he passed the arsine that was evolved through a narrow glass tube, which was heated over a short distance. The arsenic mirror formed farther along the tube; any undecomposed gas was burned at the end of the tube and formed a second mirror on a porcelain plate. As little as 0.02 milligrams of arsenic could be detected in this manner, and in 1836 Marsh was awarded the Gold Medal of the Society of Arts for his technique.

The man who made the first forensic use of the Marsh test was Mathieu Orfila (1787–1853). Born on the Spanish island of Minorca, he had won a scholarship to Barcelona University, and then went to Paris to earn his medical degree. There he attempted to demonstrate the then currently accepted tests for various poisons, and found them completely unreliable. "The central fact that struck me," he later wrote, "had never been perceived by anyone else ...

toxicology does not yet exist." Orfila published his first *Treatise of General Toxicology* in 1813; his abilities were quickly recognized, and he was appointed professor of medical jurisprudence at Paris University in 1819. Called upon to give evidence in a number of poisoning cases, he asked himself whether arsenic present in the soil of cemeteries might find its way into buried bodies and so confound the findings of a toxicologist. Learning of the reliability of the Marsh test, he successfully showed that arsenic could not enter a sealed coffin; and he also showed, by numerous experiments, that great care should be taken to ensure that arsenic did not contaminate the reagents that were used in the test. Orfila soon had the opportunity to demonstrate his findings. This was in the case of Marie Lafarge (see below).

ABOVE THE EMINENT SPANISH PHYSICIAN MATHIEU ORFILA, WHO FOUNDED THE SCIENCE OF TOXICOLOGY IN THE EARLY NINETEENTH CENTURY. HE IS PARTICULARLY FAMOUS FOR HIS WORK ON ARSENIC POISONING.

CASE STUDY
MARIE LAFARGE

In December 1839, twenty-two-year-old Marie Lafarge, née Capelle, recently married to middle-aged Charles Lafarge, an ironmaster in the Limousin area of France, sent a cake to her husband, who was away on business in Paris. He became violently ill, and when he returned home he again fell sick. His wife fed him herself, and on January 14, 1840, he died. Suspicious, his relatives asked a local pharmacist to test Charles's food, and he reported that he had found arsenic.

Marie's trial for murder opened in September 1840—but experts for the prosecution announced that they had been unable to find arsenic in Charles Lafarge's organs, though foodstuffs taken from his home contained "enough to poison ten persons." Mathieu Orfila was asked to resolve the problem. He questioned closely the experts and tested the reagents they had used. Finally, in a locked room of the courthouse, Orfila successfully performed the Marsh test on Lafarge's exhumed remains, demonstrating that the experts had bungled their analyses.

Giving evidence, Orfila said, "I shall prove, first, that there is arsenic in the body of Lafarge; second, that this arsenic comes neither from the reagents with which we worked nor from the earth surrounding the coffin; also, that the arsenic we found is not the arsenic component that is naturally found in every human body." Marie Lafarge was found guilty.

LEFT MARIE LAFARGE, TWENTY-TWO YEARS OLD AND ONLY RECENTLY MARRIED, POISONED HER HUSBAND IN 1839. SHE WAS FOUND GUILTY, AND EVENTUALLY SENTENCED TO PRISON WITH HARD LABOR.

The ready availability of arsenic-containing rat poison, and its widespread employment in murder, led many countries to pass "Arsenic Acts" to control its sale, but it continued to be used in homicide throughout the nineteenth century—which has been dubbed the golden age of poisoning—and well into the twentieth.

In addition, the development of the science of chemistry resulted in the isolation of a constantly increasing range of other pure poisons, both extracted from plants and prepared by synthesis.

Aconitine (the active ingredient of wolfsbane), nicotine, strychnine (from the nux vomica tree), chloroform, potassium antimony tartrate, or "tartar emetic"—all of these, and many more, which were first produced in chemical laboratories but soon to be found on the shelves of pharmacists and physicians, were used in notorious cases of murder by poison.

The direct result of this was that, as fast as new poisons were made available, analytical chemists had to set about ways of detecting them—particularly when they were required to give evidence in a case of suspected homicide. In many cases, fortunately, the physical effects of a particular poison had been observed; nevertheless there were without doubt many instances of murder in which the death was attributed to natural causes such as heart failure or acute gastric disease.

The problem persists to the present day—there are now well over 100,000 chemical substances classified as poisonous, and the question remains for the toxicologist: What to look for?

ABOVE THE COMMON—BUT EXTREMELY POISONOUS—FLOWERING PLANT ACONITE, KNOWN ALSO AS MONKSHOOD OR WOLFSBANE. ROMAN CITIZENS WERE BANNED FROM GROWING IT IN THEIR GARDENS.

RIGHT BEFORE THE PASSING OF THE VARIOUS ARSENIC ACTS IN THE MID-NINETEENTH CENTURY, EVEN YOUNG CHILDREN COULD LEGALLY BE SOLD ARSENIC AND OTHER POISONS BY PHARMACISTS, OR EVEN AT DRY GOODS STORES.

In 1876, British doctor George Lamson married a younger woman, a Miss John who, with her brothers, had inherited a share of her parents' estate. Lamson soon exhausted his wife's money, and turned his attention to her crippled eighteen-year-old brother, Percy. On December 3, 1881, he visited the youth at his school in Wimbledon, south London, bringing with him some ready-cut cake. Ten minutes after Lamson had left, Percy was taken violently ill, and he died later that night.

Lamson was arrested, and inquiries revealed that he had bought a quantity of aconitine on November 24, 1880. To this day, there is no simple chemical test for the drug, and at that time the only way of detecting it was by a tingling sensation, known as aconitia, that it produced in the mouth. Giving evidence at Lamson's trial, Dr. Thomas Stevenson of Guy's Hospital reported that he had

made extracts from the dead youth's organs. "Some of this extract I placed on my tongue," he said, "and it produced the effects of aconitia." Lamson was found guilty, and confessed shortly before his execution.

Englishman Edwin Bartlett, forty years old, had been married to his thirty-year-old wife, Adelaide, for eleven years when, on New Year's Day, 1886, he was found dead in bed. At autopsy, a large quantity of chloroform was found in his stomach, though no traces could be discovered in his mouth or throat. Adelaide was tried for murder, and testimony was given that a young minister, Rev. George Dyson—strongly suspected, but without evidence, of being her lover—had purchased quantities of chloroform from pharmacists in the days before Edwin Bartlett's death.

The prosecution was unable to propose how the poison had been administered. Chloroform will blister the mucous membrane when taken by mouth. Had Adelaide somehow found a means of introducing a rubber tube into her husband's stomach? In view of insufficient evidence, Adelaide was acquitted. After the trial, leading surgeon Sir James Paget allegedly commented, "Now she's acquitted, she should tell us, in the interests of science, how she did it." But Adelaide kept the secret to herself.

ABOVE DR. GEORGE LAMSON, WHO POISONED HIS YOUNG BROTHER-IN-LAW PERCY JOHN WITH ACONITINE IN 1876. LAMSON HAD LEARNED OF THE DIFFICULTY OF DETECTING THE POISON WHILE A MEDICAL STUDENT.

LEFT ADELAIDE BARTLETT, WHO WAS TRIED FOR THE MURDER OF HER HUSBAND, EDWIN, WITH CHLOROFORM IN 1886. EXPERT WITNESSES WERE UNABLE TO EXPLAIN HOW SHE COULD HAVE ADMINISTERED THE POISON, AND SHE WAS ACQUITTED.

HUMAN DIMENSIONS

As human bodies and skeletons became more readily available for research in the nineteenth century, close attention was turned to what could be gathered from observation and measurement. This approach took two directions: Anatomists concerned themselves principally with what could be deduced of the previous appearance of the living body, such as age and sex; while anthropologists were more interested in racial types—and the possibility, as Charles Darwin had proposed, that humankind had evolved from ape-like ancestors. The investigation of the human skeleton has now made it possible to declare, with a notable degree of accuracy, both the sex and the age—and in many cases the racial type—of a dead body, whatever its state of decomposition. (This application of anatomy will be dealt with in detail in the next chapter.) The study of anthropology, together with other anatomical investigations, led, in due course, to the forensic theories of anthropometry. In the meantime, a question that had exercised thinkers for centuries was whether the psychological nature of a person—and, in particular, their criminal propensities—could be deduced from their physical appearance, their physiognomy.

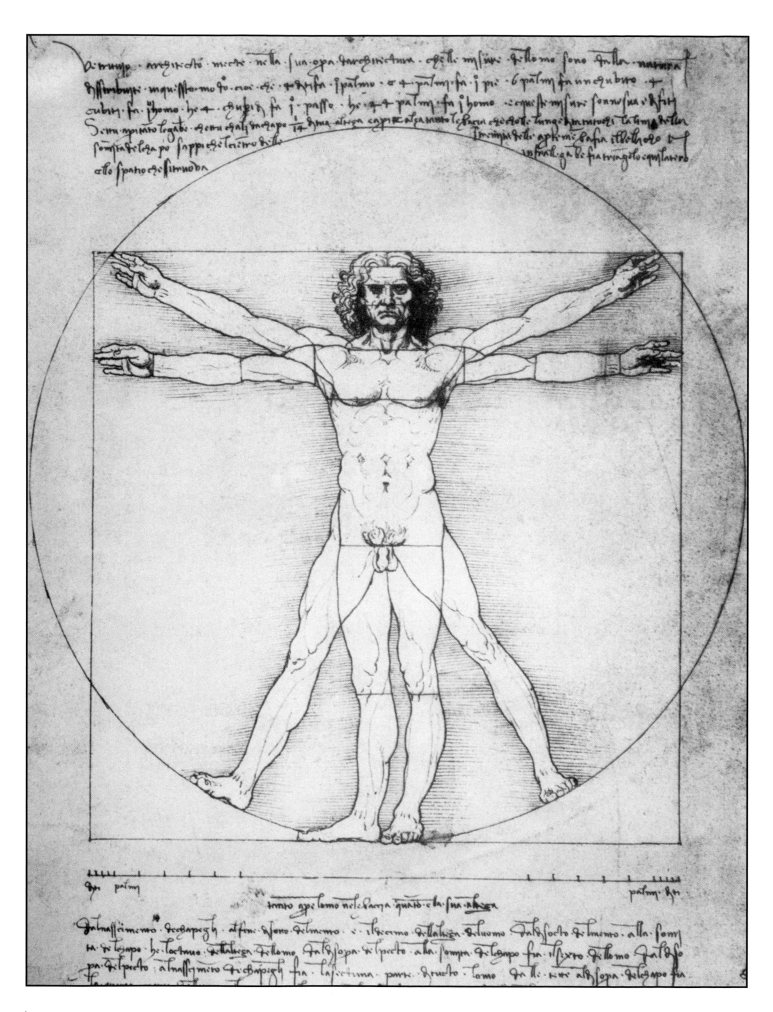

In 1533, Frenchman Barthélemy Coclés published his book, *Physiognomonia*, illustrated with many woodcuts to illumine his theory that a person's nature could be determined from their external features, such as the forehead, mouth, eyes, teeth, nose, or hair. As one of his followers, David l'Agneau, wrote:

> Those with a high forehead are lazy and ignorant, and if it is fleshy and sleek they are wrathful, and if with this they have prick ears, they are still more wrathful.... Those who have little foreheads are bustling and foolish, as are they likewise who have them great and narrow. Those with long foreheads are docile and gentle and of good sense; those who have them, as it were, square and pleasant are magnanimous and strong....

This concept, that a person's external appearance could reveal the internal workings of the mind, was very well expressed by poet and playwright William Shakespeare, in his play *Julius Caesar* (1599):

> Let me have men about me that are fat;
> Sleek-headed men and such as sleep o'nights;
> Yond' Cassius has a lean and hungry look;
> He thinks too much: such men are
>   dangerous ...
> Seldom he smiles, and smiles in such a sort
> As if he mock'd himself, and scorn'd his spirit,
> That could be mov'd to smile at anything.
> Such men as he be never at heart's ease,
> Whiles they behold a greater than themselves,
> And therefore are they very dangerous.

PHRENOLOGY

A person's outward appearance remains, of course, an essential part of medical diagnosis, but very gradually the thinking of Western philosophers began to influence physicians, as it became accepted that the human brain was the principal seat of the emotions as well as "mental diseases"—a theory that had first been put forward, two thousand years earlier, by the Greek "father of medicine," Hippocrates. The possibility of discovering specific parts of the brain that determined a person's character (an

RIGHT A CHINA HEAD, LABELED
WITH THE AREAS OF THE SKULL
THAT PHRENOLOGISTS
BELIEVED REPRESENTED THE
"ORGANS" OF THE BRAIN.
HEADS SUCH AS THIS CAN
STILL BE FOUND IN ANTIQUE
DEALERS' SHOPS. THIS ONE
IS A RELATIVELY MODERN
CREATION, PRODUCED BY
THE FOWLER COMPANY IN
ENGLAND. THE COMPANY WAS
LARGELY RESPONSIBLE FOR
THE PUBLICATION OF POPULAR
BOOKS ON ASTROLOGY
DURING THE EARLY TWENTIETH
CENTURY.

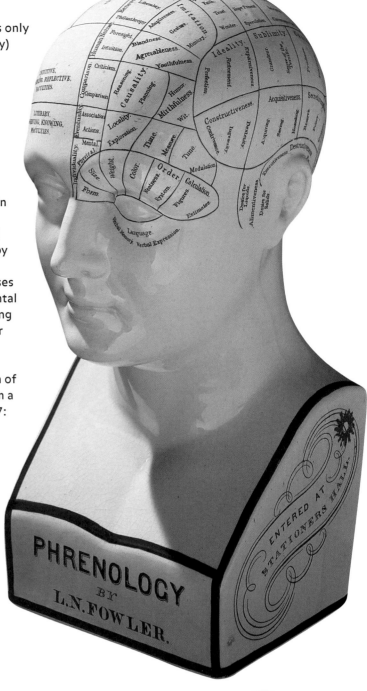

area of neurological research that has only recently been developed scientifically) was advanced by Austrian physician Franz Joseph Gall (1758–1828). Gaining the name of *phrenology*, the theory was regarded with suspicion by much of the medical profession, but it captured the popular imagination.

Gall was a fashionable practitioner in Vienna, and he put forward the proposition that the brain was composed of thirty-three "organs," and that their position and developed size could be discovered by feeling the external "bumps" of the cranium. He distinguished three classes of organ: those controlling fundamental human characteristics, those governing "sentiments," such as benevolence or mirthfulness, and those of a purely intellectual nature, such as the appreciation of size or the realization of cause and effect. As this excerpt from a poem titled *The Craniad* put it in 1817:

BELOW THE ITALIAN PHYSICIAN CESARE LOMBROSO. HIS RESEARCHES LED HIM TO PROPOSE THAT THE EXTERNAL CHARACTERISTICS OF A PERSON COULD INDICATE THE PROBABILITY OF THEIR BEING A "CRIMINAL MAN."

In every human character there be
Organs and faculties full thirty-three,
Distinct in kinds, and differing in extent—
But natural, constant, marked and permanent.
Within some heads they're large, in others small,
But all possess them, and possess them all.
They act in various ways, alone, combined.
And hence the varied character of mind.

The "organs" that Gall claimed to have identified included those of murder, theft, and cunning, as well as one that attracted particular attention: the human "desire for procreation." Both Gall and his disciple J.K. Spurzheim (1776–1832)—who later named a further four "organs"—were compelled to leave Austria because of conflict with current medical opinion there, but their theories attracted widespread popular attention in France, Britain, and the United States. In Edinburgh, Spurzheim gave a public dissection of a human brain, pointing out the position of the various "organs"; and in America so-called practical phrenologists traveled the country from fair to fair, claiming that they could cure both mental and physical disease. Heads made of porcelain, with the areas representing the specific emotions delineated, can still be found in antiques dealers' shops, and modern reproductions are available in many "novelty" shops. Persons who seriously believed in phrenology continued to practice until well into the twentieth century—this author had his "bumps read" as a child—but the next significant advance in the study of criminal characteristics was, in effect, a return to the principles of physiognomy.

Cesare Lombroso (1836–1909) was an Italian physician who, after serving as an army surgeon in the war of 1866 between Austria and Italy, was appointed professor of mental diseases at the University of Padua. Wondering whether there was a structural difference in the brains of those who were insane, he began to carry out dissections on the brains of mentally ill patients who had died.

His research, however, did not result in any positive findings; but then, in 1870, he heard of the work of famous German pathologist Rudolf Virchow. Virchow reported that he had discovered unusual features in the skulls of some criminals, which resembled those of prehistoric mankind or even some species of animals.

Lombroso immediately took up a physiognomic study of criminals in the local jails, and soon he was fortunate in being able to perform an autopsy on the body of an executed brigand. In the structure of the skull he found a single unusual feature, which, he decided, resembled one found in the skull of a rodent:

BELOW AN EARLY NINETEENTH-CENTURY SATIRICAL VIEW OF THE THEN CURRENT CRAZE FOR PHRENOLOGY. APPLICANTS FOR A POST AS SERVANT ARE HAVING THEIR "BUMPS READ" TO DETERMINE THEIR SUITABILITY FOR EMPLOYMENT.

FACT FILE

THE CRIMINAL MAN

Cesare Lombroso on the physiognomy of criminal types:

"In Assassins we have prominent jaws, widely separated cheekbones, thick dark hair, scanty beard, and a pallid face.

"Assailants have brachycephaly [a rounded skull] and long hands; narrow foreheads are rare among them.

"Rapists have short hands … and narrow foreheads. There is a predominance of light hair, with abnormalities of the genital organs and of the nose.

"In Highwaymen, as in Thieves, anomalies of skull measurement and thick hair; scanty beards are rare.

"Arsonists have long extremities, a small head, and less than normal weight.

"Swindlers are distinguished by their large jaws and prominent cheekbones; they are heavy in weight, with pale, immobile faces.

"Pickpockets have long hands; they are tall, with black hair and scanty beards."

"At the sight of that skull, I seemed to see, all of a sudden, lighted up as a vast plain under a flaming sky, the problem of the nature of the criminal—an atavistic being who reproduces in his person the ferocious instincts of primitive humanity and the inferior animals."

He hailed this as "a revelation" and pursued his research with enthusiasm. In 1876, Lombroso was appointed professor of forensic medicine at Turin, and in the same year he published the results of his investigations in a book, *L'Uomo Delinquente* (*Criminal Man*). From his observations, he divided his cases into "occasional criminals," who were driven to crime by circumstances, and "born criminals," who regularly committed crimes because of some hereditary defect that was apparent in their physical appearance. These "atavistic" individuals were distinguished by their "primitive" features: long arms, acute eyesight (like that of birds of prey), heavy jaws, and "jughandle" ears. A later book, *Criminal Anthropology* (1895), summarized the results of Lombroso's study of 6,034 living criminals.

BERTILLONAGE

Cesare Lombroso's first book came under widespread and bitter attack from other forensic experts, and he was accused—with considerable justification—of oversimplification. He subsequently modified his approach and, toward the end of his life, admitted that the "criminal type" could no longer be distinguished simply by physical characteristics.

Meanwhile, advances had been made in the field of anthropometry. The leading light of the Paris Anthropological Society at that time was Dr. Louis Adolphe Bertillon, who spent his time comparing and classifying the dimensions and shape of the skulls of different races. His son Alphonse (1853–1914) at first showed little interest in his father's work; then, in 1879, Alphonse found a post as a junior clerk in the records office of the Paris Prefecture of Police. He soon realized that one of the great problems facing the police was the definite identification of known criminals when they were rearrested, and he remembered that one of his father's friends, Belgian statistician Lambert Quetelet, had said that no two persons shared exactly the same combination of physical measurements. Bertillon put forward a proposal to his superiors, and in due course—after he had persisted for several years—he was allowed to set up a system of measuring all those who were arrested in connection with a crime.

Bertillon made measurements of the length and breadth of the head and of the right ear, the length from the elbow to the end of the middle finger, the lengths of the middle and ring fingers, the length of the left foot, the total height and that of the trunk, and the distance between the tips of the middle fingers when the arms were outstretched. All these were entered, together with eye color, on a card, which was filed in one of 243 specific drawers in his cabinet. Bertillon calculated that the probability that two individuals should be alike in all these eleven measurements was one in more than 4 million.

Bertillon had already begun to add photography to his records, cutting up

pictures of convicted criminals and selecting specific identifying details. He then established a standard procedure of taking full-face and profile portraits, which remains police practice to this day. He carried his interest even further, taking photographs of murder scenes, a number of which still survive.

LEFT ALPHONSE BERTILLON, THE FRENCH CRIMINOLOGIST WHO ESTABLISHED THE USE OF PHYSICAL MEASUREMENTS TO IDENTIFY RECIDIVIST CRIMINALS. HIS SYSTEM OF "BERTILLONAGE" WAS ADOPTED BY THE FRENCH AND OTHER POLICE FORCES, UNTIL IT WAS SUPERSEDED BY THE TECHNIQUE OF FINGERPRINTING.

CASE STUDY
DUPONT, ALIAS MARTIN

Between November 1882 and February 1883, young Alphonse Bertillon painstakingly put together a file-card system of 1,600 records, cross-referencing with measurements he made of arrested criminals. On February 20, 1883, after only three months, he scored his first success. A man calling himself "Dupont" was brought to him, and, after taking the man's physical measurements, Bertillon began to sort through his files. At last, in triumph, he picked out a single card: "You were arrested on December 15 last year!" he cried. "At that time you called yourself 'Martin.'" News of Bertillon's success made headlines in the Paris newspapers. By the end of the year, he had positively identified some fifty recidivists, and during 1884 he identified more than three hundred. What quickly became known as "Bertillonage" was soon adopted by police and prison authorities throughout France.

RIGHT IN THE COURSE OF DEVELOPING HIS SYSTEM OF PHYSIOGNOMY, ALPHONSE BERTILLON INTRODUCED THE RELATIVELY NEW TECHNIQUE OF PHOTOGRAPHY. THIS PROCEDURE IS MAINTAINED TO THE PRESENT DAY: ALL OVER THE WORLD, POLICE CONTINUE TO TAKE "MUG SHOTS," PROFILE AND FULL-FACE, OF INDIVIDUALS WHOM THEY HAVE ARRESTED. HERE, SIDE- AND FRONT-VIEW PHOTOGRAPHS DEMONSTRATE THE DIFFERENCE BETWEEN TWO SIMILAR-LOOKING SUSPECTS IN A CASE OF MISTAKEN IDENTITY IN 1920S PARIS.

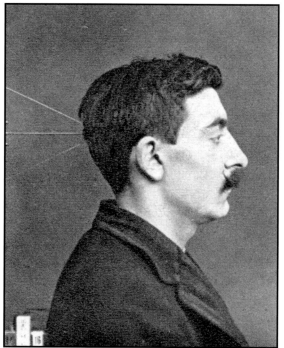

PORTRAIT PARLÉ

Another of Alphonse Bertillon's innovations was what he called the portrait parlé (the "portrait in words"). This comprised a set of brief formulae describing the shape of facial features such as the nose, eyes, mouth, and jaw, together with such identifying marks as scars or prominent warts, which he added to his records.

Even today, this remains the basis on which Identikit and other more modern visual-identification systems—such as Video-Fit—have

been developed, and which still forms part of the training of detectives in many countries throughout the world.

Bertillon has often been credited with the adoption of fingerprinting. However, although he frequently added criminals' prints to his records, he persisted in his belief in his initial system of measurements, and it is known that on more than one occasion he failed to recognize the identity of prints in his records.

And, as the police of other countries developed fingerprinting during the early years of the twentieth century, the French and all others eventually lost interest in Bertillonage.

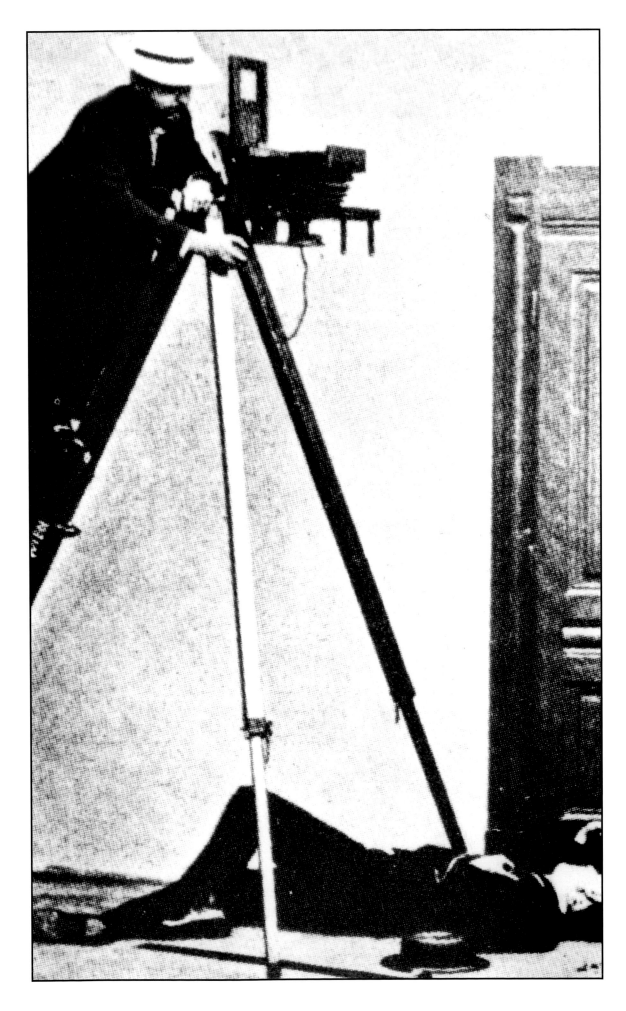

LEFT ALPHONSE BERTILLON'S INTEREST IN PHOTOGRAPHY LED HIM TO DEVELOP SPECIAL CAMERA TECHNIQUES FOR THE INVESTIGATION OF CRIME. HIS "LADDER CAMERA" ENABLED HIM TO OBTAIN PHOTOGRAPHS OF THE WHOLE BODY OF A MURDER VICTIM AS IT LAY WHERE IT HAD FALLEN. HE ALSO TOOK MANY OTHER PICTURES OF CRIME SCENES, AND WAS A PIONEER IN THIS APPROACH TO CRIME INVESTIGATION.

LEFT AN INSTRUCTIONAL CLASS
FOR DETECTIVES BEING HELD IN
THE HEADQUARTERS OF THE
PARIS POLICE. A CHART ON THE
LEFT LISTS THE IMPORTANT
ELEMENTS OF ALPHONSE
BERTILLON'S PORTRAIT PARLÉ;
TYPICAL PHOTOGRAPHS ARE
DISPLAYED IN THE CENTER,
AND THE INSTRUCTOR ON THE
RIGHT IS DESCRIBING THE
IDENTIFICATION OF DIFFERENT
TYPES OF NOSE.

FINGERPRINTS

The skin of the inner surface of the hands, and on the soles of the feet, is noticeably different from that of the rest of the body. From the fingertips to the wrist, and from the toes to the heel, it is hornier and covered with a pattern of "papillary" ridges. These are formed during the fourth and fifth months of the development of the fetus in the womb, and no changes in the pattern occur after birth. It changes only in size, as the hands and feet grow, and (as far as is known) no two individuals—even otherwise "identical" twins—possess patterns that are exactly alike.

The credit for the recognition that the patterns on the fingertips—and, indeed, on the whole hand—were unique to each individual, and could be used to identify that individual, must be shared by two British men working in faraway lands during the nineteenth century: Dr. Henry Faulds (1843–1930), in Japan, and William Herschel (1833–1917), in British India.

Illiterate persons had used the print of their thumb to sign legal documents for centuries, but the significance of the pattern of ridges went unrecognized. The first recorded scientific observation of their existence was made by an English physician, Dr. Nathaniel Grew, in 1684; and in 1788, J.C.A. Mayer published an illustrated book on anatomy, in which he stated that "the arrangement of skin ridges is never duplicated in two persons." In 1823, Jan Evangelista Purkyne (1787–1869), a professor at the University of Breslau, Poland, noted that finger-ridge patterns could be classified into various categories. But all three were academically minded scientists, unconcerned with questions of identification, and there is no evidence that either Herschel or Faulds had ever heard of their work.

In July 1858, Herschel, aged only twenty-five, was appointed administrator of a rural area of Bengal, India. Within weeks, he decided to undertake the construction of a new road, and negotiated a contract for materials with a local man, Rajyadhar Konai. Justifiably cautious, Herschel decided "to try an experiment by taking a stamp of his hand ... to frighten Konai out of all thought of repudiating his signature thereafter." This first experiment excited Herschel's curiosity, and not long afterward he testified to a Commission of Inquiry into the abuse of contracts: "I can suggest a signature of exceeding simplicity, which it is all but impossible to deny or to forge. The impression of a man's finger on paper cannot be denied by him...."

The commission ignored Herschel's suggestion, however, and, eager to prove his point, he began to make a collection of inked fingerprints and to study how they differed. In 1877, he was appointed a senior magistrate of a district not far from Calcutta, responsible for the courts, the jail, and the payment of government pensions. Rightly suspecting that many pensions were being claimed by imposters in the name of persons who were no longer alive, he introduced the use of a print of the right, first, and middle fingers on receipts. He then extended the practice to all legal documents in his area, and finally gave orders for prints to be taken of all convicted criminals, so that their identity would be unquestionable. In 1879, Herschel retired from the Indian Civil Service and returned to England, taking his collection of fingerprints with him—and made a disconcerting discovery.

BELOW A portrait of the anthropologist Sir Francis Galton, who followed up William Herschel's initial research into fingerprinting, and published the first detailed study of the technique.

CASE STUDY
IDENTIFYING THE CULPRIT

Quite by chance, in 1878, Dr. Henry Faulds found that the supply of medicinal alcohol at his hospital was being rapidly depleted; it was clear that it was being stolen by someone as a drink. Then he found a measuring beaker that had been used as a glass, and on it the imprint of sweaty fingers. Searching his collection of prints, he quickly identified the culprit—one of his own students.

Shortly afterward, a burglar attempted to enter the hospital by climbing a whitewashed wall, and left the sooty imprint of his hand. The police accused one of Faulds's staff, but he was able to show them that the print was detectably different from that of the suspect. Later, another man was arrested, and confessed, and Faulds demonstrated that his matched the print left on the wall.

DACTYLOGRAPHY

In December 1873, Henry Faulds and his newlywed wife had traveled to Japan, to establish the first Scottish Medical Mission there. While he ran his hospital outside Tokyo, Dr. Faulds also began to take an interest in a mound of prehistoric refuse at nearby Omari,

and discovered fragments of ancient pottery that bore the fingerprints of their makers. He wondered whether present-day pottery would reveal similar markings and, searching local markets, discovered that "one peculiar pattern of lineations would appear with great persistency, as if the same artist had left her sign-mark on her work."

At first, Faulds took an interest in fingerprints as a way of distinguishing racial

CASE STUDY
THE ROJAS MURDERS

In 1891, in La Plata, Argentina, the deputy chief of police, Juan Vucetich, set up an Office of Identification and Statistics. Initially, he employed Alphonse Bertillon's anthropometric system, but soon read of Sir Francis Galton's work in a French journal and became immediately enthusiastic about its possibilities, taking the fingerprints of arrested criminals who were brought before him. He even developed his own crude system of classification.

A year later, in the coastal town of Necochea some two hundred miles south of La Plata, Francisca Rojas ran screaming from her home, crying, "He killed my children!" The two children, a six-year-old boy and a four-year-old girl, lay in bed with their heads smashed in. Rojas named one of her rejected suitors as the perpetrator, but even after torture he protested his innocence. Inquiries revealed that Rojas also had a lover, who hated her children, and it seemed possible that she

might have killed them to secure his affections. To add to this suspicion, both of the men were found to have alibis. Summoned from La Plata, Inspector Eduardo Alvarez searched Rojas's home meticulously, without finding incriminating evidence. He was about to leave, when he spotted the bloody imprint of a thumb on a door. Recalling the work of his superior, Vucetich, he cut out the wood from the door and arrested Rojas. At the Necochea police station, he demonstrated to Rojas that her own thumbprint exactly matched the bloody one—and she confessed.

This is the first recorded use of a modified form of Galton's system in the identification of a criminal. Vucetich rapidly refined his classification methods, and he described them at the Second Scientific Congress of South America in 1901. Within a few years, Vucetich's system had been adopted by nearly every country in South America.

types; he began to collect prints—not of only one or two, as William Herschel had done, but of all ten fingers of both Japanese and Europeans. He wrote to scientists around the world, requesting examples, but received almost no response. "Some thought I was an advocate of palmistry," he later complained.

Faulds then set out to investigate whether fingerprints always remained the same. He and his students shaved the skin from their fingertips, and found that, without exception, the papillary ridges returned in exactly the same pattern. They tried "pumice-stone, sandpaper, emery dust, various acids, caustics, and even Spanish fly," and in every case the ridges reappeared unchanged. He wrote a letter to the British scientific journal *Nature*, published in October 1880, in which he suggested that "bloody fingerprints or impressions on clay, glass, etc." could be used for "the scientific identification of criminals." He named his technique dactylography.

The letter provoked little interest, except for a reply from William Herschel, newly arrived back in England, who lodged a claim that his own use of fingerprints in India antedated that of Faulds in Japan.

Despite many attempts to interest chiefs of police forces around the world, as well as a long-running dispute with Herschel, Faulds did not achieve recognition of his discoveries until long after his death: He died, poor and embittered, near Birmingham, England, half a century later. Herschel, on the other hand, gained the support of the brilliant English physician and anthropologist, Sir Francis Galton.

Carrying out research, like many other anthropologists, into racial types, Galton set up an anthropometric laboratory at the South Kensington International Health Exhibition in 1884, where visitors could be examined for height and weight, length of limbs, strength of pull, force of blow, keenness of hearing, and color discrimination. This laboratory, moved to other premises when the exhibition closed, existed for some eight years.

In 1888, Galton paid a visit to Alphonse Bertillon in Paris, and was at first impressed with his techniques, but, upon returning to England, he came across the Faulds-Herschel correspondence in *Nature* and lost interest in Bertillonage. (In fact, it was probably Galton who persuaded Alphonse Bertillon to add fingerprints to his records.) Galton wrote to Herschel, who sent him his papers. Visitors to the laboratory were now asked also to provide their fingerprints, and Galton, after reading of the work of Jan Evangelista Purkyne, set about trying to find a way of classifying them. This was difficult, as the patterns contained dozens of variables, but he observed eventually that nearly all the prints in his growing collection contained a small triangular area where the ridges ran together. He named this a delta, and distinguished four types of print: those with no delta, those with a delta to the right, those with a delta to the left, and those with several deltas. A set of prints from all ten fingers could then be divided into more than sixty thousand classes. Galton published his results in his book, *Finger Prints*, in 1892.

Meanwhile, in British India, Herschel's innovation of taking fingerprints had gradually fallen into neglect. When young Edward Henry (1850–1931) was posted as assistant magistrate in Herschel's former district in 1873, however, he must have become acquainted with the method. Appointed inspector general of Bengal police in 1890, Henry at first relied upon anthropometric records, making them a routine element of police practice—but he went on to add an imprint of the left thumb to them. In 1893, he read Galton's book, and, in 1894, on leave in England, he visited Galton and conferred with him.

Returning to India, Henry reported to the government of Bengal: "The substitution of

In August 1897, Hriday Nath Ghosh, manager of a tea garden in northern Bengal, was found dead in his bedroom, with his throat cut. His safe and dispatch box had been rifled, and several hundred rupees taken. Suspicion fell upon a number of persons, but principally on Kangali Charan, a former cook in the household, who had previously been sentenced to six months in jail for stealing from the same safe.

Among the papers in the dispatch box police found an almanac, with two prints in blood on its cover. Because Edward Henry's officers had taken Charan's fingerprints upon his previous conviction, a match was soon found.

Although Charan had moved several hundred miles away, he was found and brought to Calcutta, where his right thumbprint was again taken. The three matching prints were placed before the court in his trial for murder and theft.

The judge and his two assessors agreed "beyond question" that the cook had been in Ghosh's room, and "the presumption that he committed the theft was irresistible."

They decided that it would be unsafe to convict Charan of murder, however, as no one had been a witness to the crime. Kangali Charan was sentenced to two years hard labor for the theft.

finger impressions for measurements, if a satisfactory system of classifying them can be devised, would yield even better results than we are now getting." He stated: "The accessories, a piece of tin and some printer's ink, are inexpensive and procurable everywhere; the impressions are self-signatures, free from possible errors of observation and transcription; any person of ordinary intelligence can learn to take them with a little practice after a few minutes' instruction."

With the cooperation of two of his Indian officers, Henry was able to show in 1897 that he had developed a workable system of classifying the prints of all ten fingers. His classification differed from that of Galton and Juan Vucetich. Henry identified five clearly distinguishable types of pattern: arches (A); "tented" arches

(T); radial loops—loops inclined toward the radius bone on the outside of the arm (R); ulnar loops, inclined toward the inner ulnar bone (U); and whorls (W). To these he added a sub-classification by deltas. Henry wrote: "The deltas may be formed by either (a) the bifurcation of a single ridge, or (b) by the abrupt divergence of two ridges which have hitherto run side by side." He then counted the number of ridges between the centerpoint of the delta and the next identifiable arch, loop, or whorl.

A committee that met in Henry's office on March 29, 1897, reported: "We are of opinion that the method of identification of habitual criminals by means of finger-prints ... may be safely adopted as being superior ..."—and the signatories added their fingerprints to the report. Within months, the government of Bengal had established the first national

1

2

3

4

5

6

7

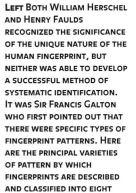
8

Left Both William Herschel and Henry Faulds recognized the significance of the unique nature of the human fingerprint, but neither was able to develop a successful method of systematic identification. It was Sir Francis Galton who first pointed out that there were specific types of fingerprint patterns. Here are the principal varieties of pattern by which fingerprints are described and classified into eight broad types:
1 Plain arch
2 Tented arch
3 Simple loop
4 Central pocket loop
5 Double loop
6 Lateral pocket loop
7 Plain whorl
8 Accidental

THE STRATTON BROTHERS

On June 27, 1902, a burglar entered a house in south London, and stole some billiard balls. The investigating officer noticed some dirty finger marks on a newly painted windowsill, and he informed the Fingerprint Department. Detective Sergeant Charles Collins photographed the clearest, the mark of a left thumb, and began the task of searching through their criminal records. Eventually, the print of Harry Jackson, a forty-one-year-old laborer, came to light, and he was arrested.

Now came the difficulty of having the evidence accepted in court. Although this was a relatively minor case, an experienced counsel, Richard Muir, was retained for the prosecution. He spent hours with Collins, learning about the newly introduced system, and in opening the case he carefully explained to the jury how it had proved so successful in India. Collins himself then demonstrated how fingerprints were identified, and submitted his photographs. The jury was impressed, and even the defense did not contest the fingerprint evidence. Jackson was found guilty.

In this way the acceptability of fingerprints as evidence was established in the English courts. Less than three years later, they were accepted in a trial for murder. On March 27, 1905, Thomas Farrow, manager of a paint shop in Deptford, south London, was found battered to death; his wife was similarly beaten, and she died four days later.

A cash box under her bed had been rifled, and a sweaty right thumbprint was discovered on its inner tray. Inquiries led to two local petty criminals, Alfred and Albert Stratton, and the print was found to be Alfred's. Richard Muir again led the prosecution, and Collins—now a detective inspector—presented his detailed photographs and charts. (Interestingly, Henry Faulds was part of the defense team, but Alfred Stratton's lawyer did not call him to give evidence.)

In his summing up, the judge suggested that the jury might not like to act on the fingerprint evidence alone; however, despite this recommendation, they pronounced the Stratton brothers guilty.

fingerprint bureau in the world to employ Henry's system.

In England, a committee chaired by Charles Troup had been appointed in 1893 to look into ways of identifying habitual criminals. After hearing the evidence of Galton, they recommended a modified form of Bertillonage, but combined with fingerprint matching. They further stated that they would have recommended fingerprints alone as the most reliable way of identifying recidivists—if only a practicable means of classification existed. In 1900, when it became apparent that this combined system was not working as well as expected, a second committee was appointed. Henry was summoned from India, and he brought with him the proofs of a book he had

written, *Classification and Uses of Fingerprints*. The committee was suitably impressed, and in 1901 Henry was recalled, and he was appointed assistant commissioner of the Metropolitan Police, in charge of the Criminal Investigation Department (CID).

Henry immediately set about organizing a Fingerprint Department, recruiting three officers who had previously become skilled in anthropometry. One of these was Detective Sergeant Charles Collins. Collins had developed an interest in photography, and he realized that this could be employed to record fingerprints at the site of a crime. He very soon had his first success (see left).

FINGERPRINTING IN THE UNITED STATES

The Edward Henry system of fingerprint analysis spread rapidly to many of the world's police forces. In the United States, a mild interest in thumbprints as a means of identification had gone no further, in view of the absence of a satisfactory system of classification. Faulds's letter to *Nature* in 1880 was discussed briefly at the 1881 International Medical Congress, and possibly inspired Mark Twain's tale, "A Thumb-Print and What Became of It," in his *Life on the Mississippi* (1883). In the same year, a California detective, Harry Morse, suggested that immigrant Chinese laborers should be registered by their thumb marks. His proposal was ignored, but Franklin Lawton, superintendent of the San Francisco Mint, was sufficiently interested to ask the well-known landscape photographer Isaiah W. Taber to begin photographing thumbs. By 1888, however, the matter was no longer considered relevant, Congress having banned the entry of all Chinese laborers.

Then, in 1904, Detective Sergeant John Ferrier of the Fingerprint Branch was among British police officers sent to guard the British Royal Pavilion at the St. Louis World's Fair and Exposition. While there, he gave a number of demonstrations of the Henry system. In his book *Crooks and Crime*, Ferrier recalled:

"I was introduced to a police official of high position in New York who ... scoffingly remarked: 'Scotland Yard has nothing on us, we are more ahead than sleepy old England.' I ascertained that he was sailing for England the following week, and persuaded him to let me take two sets of his finger impressions. One he kept, the other I marked and sent to Scotland

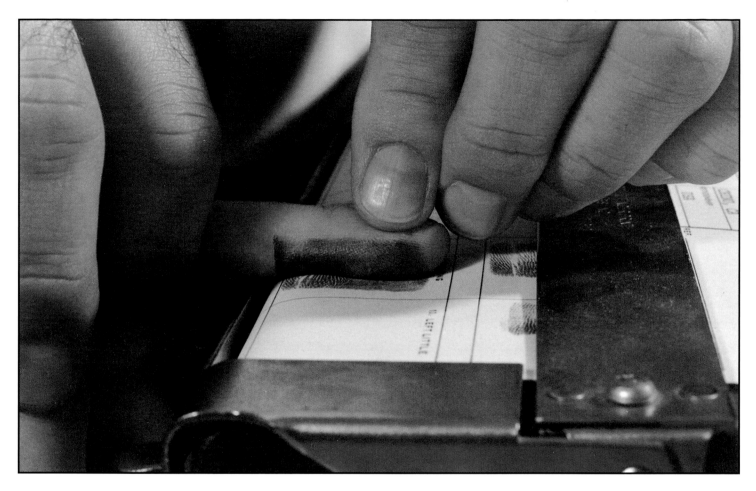

Yard.... About a month later the American officer called at the Yard and refused to disclose his identity, but produced his fingerprints and said: 'Here are my fingermarks; tell me who I am.' To his astonishment he had within two minutes placed in his hands the two sets of his fingerprints. He was so impressed ... that on his return to the United States he soon converted other skeptics and established a fingerprint department in New York."

At about the same time, the United States Department of Justice allocated a sum—"not to exceed $60"—to set up an identification system of fingerprinting at Leavenworth prison in Kansas. Sing Sing and other prisons in New York State followed suit in 1905, and St. Louis police adopted the technique the following year.

The U.S. Army, Navy, and Marine Corps began to fingerprint both officers and enlisted men, and it soon became obvious that all these separate records should be coordinated. The Department of Justice accepted the task, but gave the work of cataloging to Leavenworth—where it soon emerged that the inmates employed in the duty were sometimes altering the records to their own advantage. It was not until 1924, when J. Edgar Hoover was appointed director of the Federal Bureau of Investigation, that the sorting of the records—by then numbering more than 800,000—was begun.

ABOVE THE ROLLED FINGERPRINT OF A SUSPECT IS TRANSFERRED ONTO A RECORD CARD. A PRINT OF EACH FINGER AND THUMB IS TAKEN. ALTHOUGH THIS REMAINED REGULAR PRACTICE FOR DECADES, MODERN COMPUTER SYSTEMS CAN SCAN FINGERS AND HANDS FASTER AND MORE ACCURATELY, AND STORE THE PATTERNS IN A DATABASE.

CASE STUDY
THOMAS JENNINGS

The acceptability of fingerprints as evidence was established in United States law in 1911. On the night of September 19, 1910, Clarence Hillier encountered an intruder on the stairs of his Chicago home. He grappled with the man, and both fell to the foot of the stairs, where Hillier was shot twice and died within a few seconds.

Shortly afterward, four police officers stopped a man named Thomas Jennings, discovered a loaded revolver in his pocket, and, not satisfied with his explanation, immediately detained him. At that time, they had no knowledge that a murder had been committed nearby.

When Hillier's home was examined, the impression of four left-hand fingers was found on the newly painted railing. They were soon identified as those of Jennings, and, at his trial for murder, four experts agreed that the identification was sound. Jennings appealed to the Illinois Supreme Court on the grounds that fingerprint evidence was inadmissible, but his appeal was rejected and his death sentence confirmed.

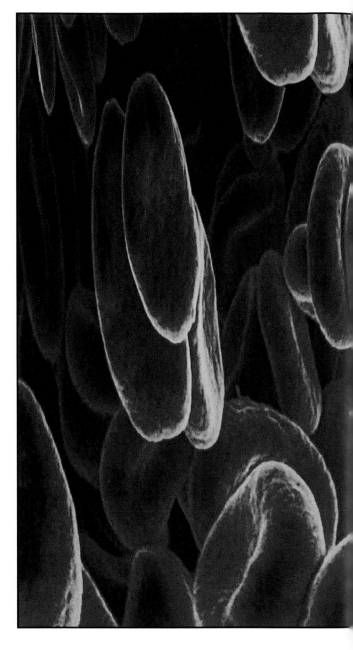

BLOOD TYPING

The transfusion of blood has a long history. It had its beginnings in the 1650s, when the young Christopher Wren (later the famous architect of St. Paul's Cathedral in London) invented the first crude hypodermic—a sharpened slender quill attached to a bladder. In 1668, Dr. Jean Denys of Montpellier, France, was ordered to cease his experiments when one of the patients he had been treating with sheep's blood died. In England, about 1814, Dr. James Blundell successfully transferred blood from one dog into another drained dog, but when he used sheep's blood the dog quickly died. Four years later he tried human blood transfusion: Some of his patients recovered, but others died. There was clearly something in some blood that was not compatible with others.

The first clue came in 1875, when German physiologist Leonard Landois took the red blood cells from one animal and mixed them with the serum—the clear blood liquid—from another species. The red cells clumped together ("agglutinated"): This was obviously what had happened in unsuccessful transfusions.

In 1900, an assistant professor at the Institute of Pathology and Anatomy in Vienna, Austria, Karl Landsteiner (1868–1943), discovered that there were different types of human blood, and that mixing blood of two different types resulted in agglutination. At first he identified three types, which he labeled A, B, and C (subsequently labeled O). Shortly afterward, one of Landsteiner's colleagues discovered a fourth type, which did not agglutinate either A or B, and it was labeled AB.

The red blood cells carry substances—known as antigens—that help to produce antibodies to fight infection. Put briefly, it is the meeting of two incompatible antigens that causes agglutination. Landsteiner's 1909 classification of the four basic blood groups can be tabulated as follows:

A: antigen A present, antigen B absent
B: antigen B present, antigen A absent
O: both antigens absent
AB: both antigens present

This means that, in blood transfusion, an A person can be given either A or O blood, a B

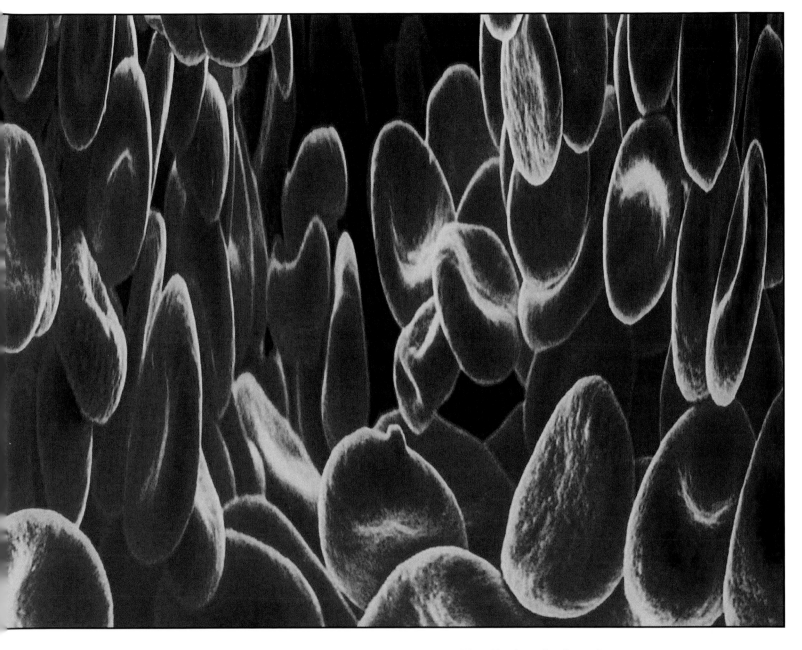

person can be given either B or O blood, an AB person can be given any of the three types, but an O person can be given only O blood. The proportions of each group vary from one population to another. In Britain, for example, the proportions are approximately as follows: A, 42 percent; B, 8 percent; O, 47 percent; and AB, 3 percent. In the United States they are: A, 39 percent; B, 13 percent; O, 43 percent; and AB, 5 percent.

Landsteiner, recognizing that these were hereditary characteristics derived from a person's parents, was the first to suggest that testing for blood group could be important in questions of paternity. He was not to foresee, however, the great value of the system in criminal investigation.

In 1901, German biologist Paul Uhlenhuth (1870–1957) designed a test to distinguish human blood from that of other animals and, in the same way, to identify the animal species. His contemporary, Belgian physiologist Jules Bordet (1870–1961), working at the Pasteur Institute in Paris, had discovered that if a laboratory animal was injected with milk or egg white it developed a specific antibody against it, and if its blood was then mixed with milk or egg white, a cloudy precipitate—named precipitin—was produced.

Paul Uhlenhuth found that he could obtain the same effect by injecting a rabbit with, say, chicken's blood, and then separating the serum from the rabbit's blood and adding a drop of chicken's blood, resulting in the formation of precipitin.

The mechanism was similar to the agglutination of red blood cells, and he was soon able to produce a range of serums specific to a wide range of animal species. Within a few months, Uhlenhuth was able to apply his test in

ABOVE THIS COMPUTER-ENHANCED IMAGE OF A SCANNING ELECTRON MICROGRAPH (SEM) SHOWS HEMOGLOBIN, THE PIGMENT OF THE RED BLOOD CORPUSCLES. IT TAKES UP OXYGEN FROM THE LUNGS AND TRANSPORTS IT, THROUGH THE ARTERIES AND CAPILLARIES, TO EVERY PART OF THE BODY. WHEN THE BLOOD IS STARVED OF OXYGEN, ASPHYXIATION RESULTS.

On July 2, 1901, the disemboweled and dismembered bodies of two young brothers were found scattered in woodland on the island of Rügen, off the Baltic coast of Germany. Suspicion fell upon a traveling carpenter, Ludwig Tessnow, and dark stains were discovered on his boots and clothing. He protested his innocence, claiming the stains were wood dye, but the examining magistrate recalled a newspaper report of a similar case. Several hundred miles away, in Osnabrück, two young girls had been similarly butchered, and among those questioned was—Ludwig Tessnow. Three weeks before the Rügen murders, a farmer had found seven of his sheep hacked to pieces, and had seen a man running from his meadow. This man he now identified as Tessnow. A report of Paul Uhlenhuth's work had recently been published, and the magistrate ordered Tessnow's clothing to be sent to him for analysis. A month later, Uhlenhuth reported that some of the stains were sheep's blood, but others were human. Tessnow, who became known as the Mad Carpenter, was found guilty.

a murder case, that in which Ludwig Tessnow was found guilty.

Landsteiner's fundamental groups remain vital in the decision as to which blood to use for transfusion, but many more specific factors in blood have since been discovered, and they are invaluable in the identification of the source of bloodstains in criminal investigation. Landsteiner was awarded the Nobel Prize in 1930, as Jules Bordet had been in 1919.

BALLISTICS

In 1835, Henry Goddard of the Bow Street Runners (the precursors of England's first police force) investigated what appeared to be a burglary at a house in Southampton, Hampshire. The butler of the house claimed that, waking to find the burglar in his room,

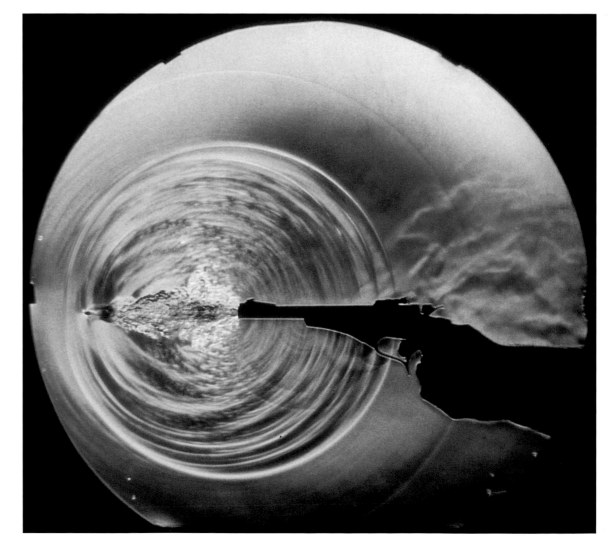

RIGHT THE PROPULSIVE CHARGE DRIVES A BULLET FROM THE MUZZLE OF A PISTOL AT MORE THAN 540 YARDS (500 METERS) PER SECOND. THIS PHOTOGRAPH DRAMATICALLY DEMONSTRATES THE SHOCK WAVE GENERATED BY A BULLET'S FLIGHT AS IT SPINS OUT OF THE BARREL; IT ALSO REVEALS HOW PARTICLES OF THE CHARGE CAN BE PROPELLED BACK ONTO THE SHOOTER'S HAND.

he had been shot at. Goddard dug out the bullet from the headboard of the butler's bed and compared it with bullets from the man's own pistol. All showed the same flaw: a small bump produced by an imperfection in the mold from which they had been cast. This was perhaps the first case in which "the butler did it," and he confessed that he had staged the "burglary." It was also a landmark in the study of what has come to be known as ballistics.

A murder case in France in 1869 was investigated with a rather different—and significantly scientific—approach. Analysts determined the melting point, the various components of the metal, and the weight of a bullet taken from the victim's skull, and established an exact similarity with other bullets found in the suspect's possession. However, ballistics examiners have found a readier—and even more exact—method of identifying not only the bullet but also the gun from which it has been fired.

Since early in the nineteenth century, most gun barrels—with the exception of smoothbore shotguns—have been rifled. Spiral grooves, left-hand or right-hand, are cut by tool into the bore of the barrel to spin the bullet and provide greater accuracy. The uncut areas of the barrel between these grooves are called lands. Bullets are made very slightly larger than the bore of the barrel, to ensure a close fit, and so the lands produce visible grooves along the length of the bullet.

Each manufacturer has one or more ways of rifling gun barrels, and every one is distinctive. Examination of the scored grooves on a bullet can quickly determine the make of gun. In addition, as one gun after another is rifled on the same machine, the tools become slightly worn, or even damaged. These imperfections will produce faint, but distinguishable, scratches—known as striations—on the bullet, parallel to the grooves cut by the lands, and so can lead to the identification of a specific weapon.

The first application of these observations in a murder case was made in 1889 by Alexandre Lacassagne, professor of forensic medicine at the University of Lyon, France. On a bullet recovered from the victim's body, he matched seven grooves on the bullet to the rifling in the barrel of a gun in a suspect's possession. Following up this technical approach to firearm identification, Dr. A. Llewellyn Hall published his landmark book, *The Missile and the Weapon*, in America in 1900.

Such was the state of forensic science at the beginning of the twentieth century. Since then, the elements of forensic investigation described above have undergone revolutionary developments, and the application of modern scientific discoveries and the swiftly evolving technology of the information age have put a miraculous array of sophisticated tools at the fingertips of the modern crime scene investigator. All these tools and techniques—the analytical equipment available to the toxicologist and the examiner of trace fragments, the growing precision of forensic anthropology, the refinements in fingerprint detection and identification, and the instruments used in ballistics examination—will be detailed in the following chapters, together with even more recent and important advances (for instance, DNA typing and forensic entomology).

CASE STUDY
BEST

Dr. A. Llewellyn Hall's book, *The Missile and the Weapon*, came to the attention of eminent American jurist Oliver Wendell Holmes. In 1902, Holmes was hearing the trial of a man named Best, accused of murder with a revolver. Holmes called in a gunsmith to examine the weapon, as well as the bullet taken from the corpse. The gunsmith fired a bullet from Best's gun into a box packed with cotton wool; then, with a magnifying glass, he demonstrated to the court the similarity of markings on the two bullets. In his judgment, Holmes recorded: "I see no other way in which the jury could have learned so intelligently how a gun barrel would have marked a lead bullet fired through it."

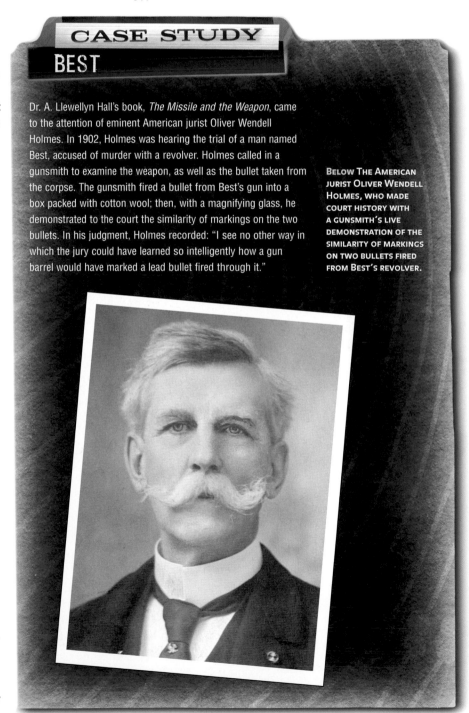

BELOW THE AMERICAN JURIST OLIVER WENDELL HOLMES, WHO MADE COURT HISTORY WITH A GUNSMITH'S LIVE DEMONSTRATION OF THE SIMILARITY OF MARKINGS ON TWO BULLETS FIRED FROM BEST'S REVOLVER.

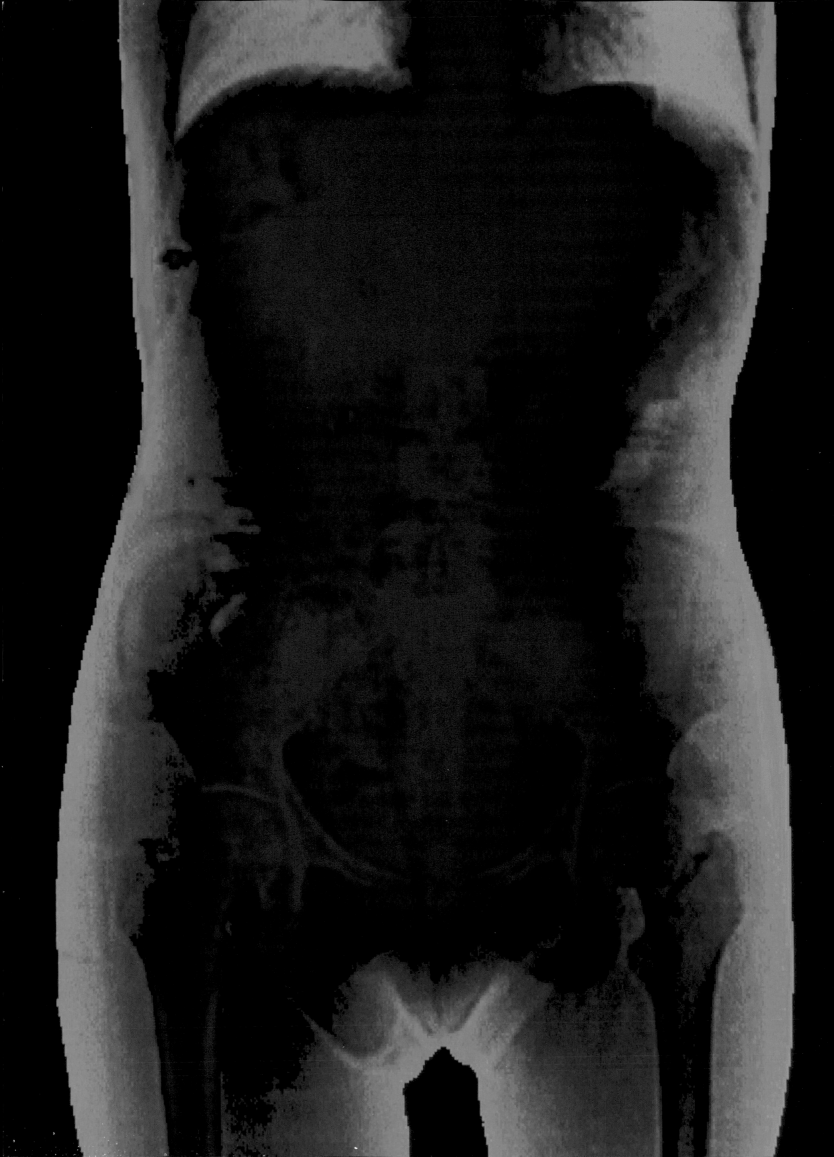

2

WHO WAS JOHN – OR JANE – DOE?

The remains of what was once a living human being have been found. Of course, the discovery could be anywhere: The body may be somewhere in the dead person's home, perhaps in bed, an outhouse, a cupboard, or even under the floorboards or in the attic. Or, it could be in the home of another person altogether. Perhaps the discovery was made in a public building, such as a hotel, store, or social club, or in a deserted house, factory, or storage facility. Or the corpse may be outdoors: lying in the open, or perhaps hidden in undergrowth or partially covered by an attempt at burial, or even stuffed into a plastic garbage bag. The place in which the body is discovered almost always provides clues as to the cause of death.

*"Here's a corpse in the case,
with a sad swell'd face
And a Medical Crowner's
a queer sort of thing!"*

—REV. RICHARD BARHAM
A LAY OF ST. GERGULPHUS

FACING PAGE A COLORED X-RAY OF THE TORSO AND ABDOMEN OF A FEMALE SUBJECT REVEALS THE CHARACTERISTIC STRUCTURE OF THE PELVIS. IT IS BROADER AND SHALLOWER THAN THAT OF A MALE, AND THE CAVITY— THROUGH WHICH THE CHILD IS DELIVERED—IS ALSO NOTICEABLY LARGER.

The body may be newly dead, in one of several stages of decomposition, or mummified or skeletonized. It may be whole, or dismembered; outdoors, pieces may have been scattered over a wide area by scavenging animals. The probable cause of death may be immediately apparent—wounds from gunshot or some other weapon, or a ligature of some sort around the throat—or the person may appear to have drowned, or died in a fire or explosion. The body may be clothed, or naked; articles of clothing and other personal belongings may or may not be found, either with the body or some distance away. All of these details will inform the direction of the investigation to come and will provide invaluable clues to the many experts whose combined efforts will be brought to bear on solving the question of what happened to the victim.

THE CORONER

All and each of these circumstances can raise a wealth of questions. Who was this person? Was the death natural or unnatural? What was its cause? When and where did it occur? Is this a case of accidental death, suicide, manslaughter, or murder? And, in these latter cases, who were the person or persons responsible for the death? These are questions that must be addressed, and if possible answered, by the Coroner's Office.

It is the duty of a coroner to rule on the identity of the dead person and—with or without a jury, according to circumstances—to give his or her opinion on the cause of death. The office of coroner is an ancient one, first developed in England in the twelfth century. The name was originally "crowner" or "coronator," reflecting the fact that the coroner represented the power of the king within the local jurisdiction, and could therefore rule on all questions of property—which, in cases of questionable death, was obviously of great importance.

Gradually—as the supreme rule of the king was delegated to appointed representatives—the powers of the coroner became more circumscribed, and during the seventeenth century, when the English system of law was also established in America, the office of coroner became similar to what it remains to be at the present day. William Penn is said to have appointed the first coroner in the British colonies.

In Scotland, the duties of a coroner are performed by an appointed legal officer, the Procurator Fiscal. In Canada, coroners have been appointed by Order in Council. Other European countries have no corresponding

system. In Europe, suspicious deaths are notified to the police or the local public prosecutor; in many countries, an autopsy must be authorized by the examining magistrate. And there is no holding of a public inquest at which a jury delivers its verdict.

For a considerable time the office of coroner in the United States was almost always an elected one, established in each county. Politically appointed, the coroner did not necessarily have any medical, or even legal, experience: He (at that time it was invariably a male prerogative) was often the local mortician, but might equally well be a local mayor's brother, or someone with his ambitions set on the state legislature. As late as the 1960s, in a rural county of southern California, the local butcher was also for a time the coroner. The commonwealth of Massachusetts was the first to abolish the office of coroner, in 1877, and replace it with the post of medical examiner. Medical examiners, unlike coroners, had to be medically qualified—though not necessarily in pathology.

The coroner system proved to be wide open to abuse. At the beginning of the twentieth century in New York City, for example, the coroner was paid $11.50 to examine a body and declare it dead; he received $10 if he declared that a suicide was a natural death; and, for $50,

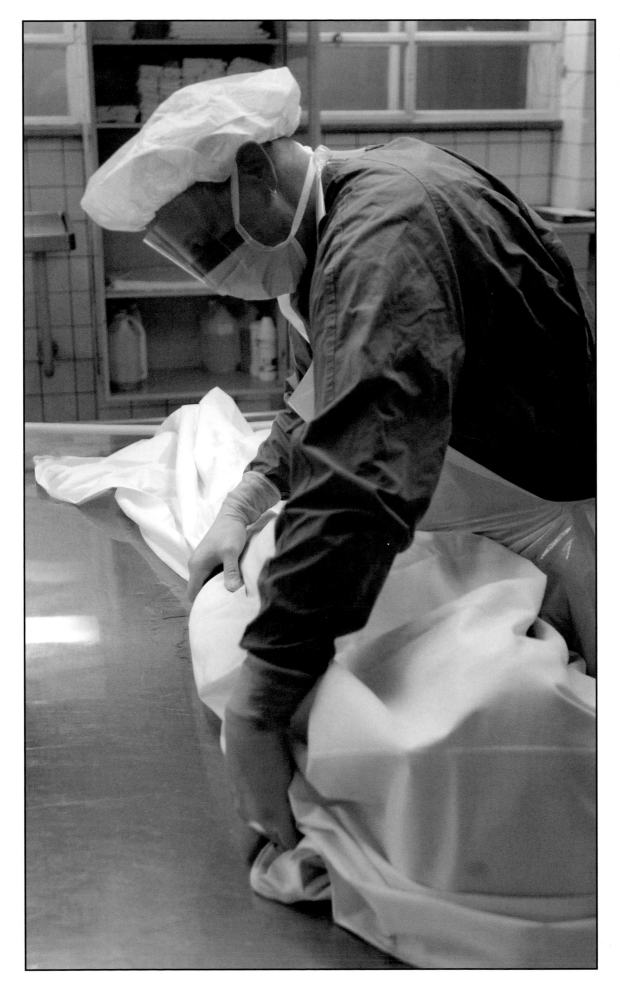

LEFT HERE, A DANISH
CORONER EXAMINES A BODY IN
A MORTUARY IN COPENHAGEN.
THE BODY IS CAREFULLY
STORED AND COVERED: WHEN
AN UNIDENTIFIED VICTIM IS
EXAMINED IN A MODERN
MORTUARY, STRICT
PRECAUTIONS ARE TAKEN TO
AVOID ANY CONTAMINATION
OF WHAT COULD PROVE TO BE
VITAL TRACE EVIDENCE.

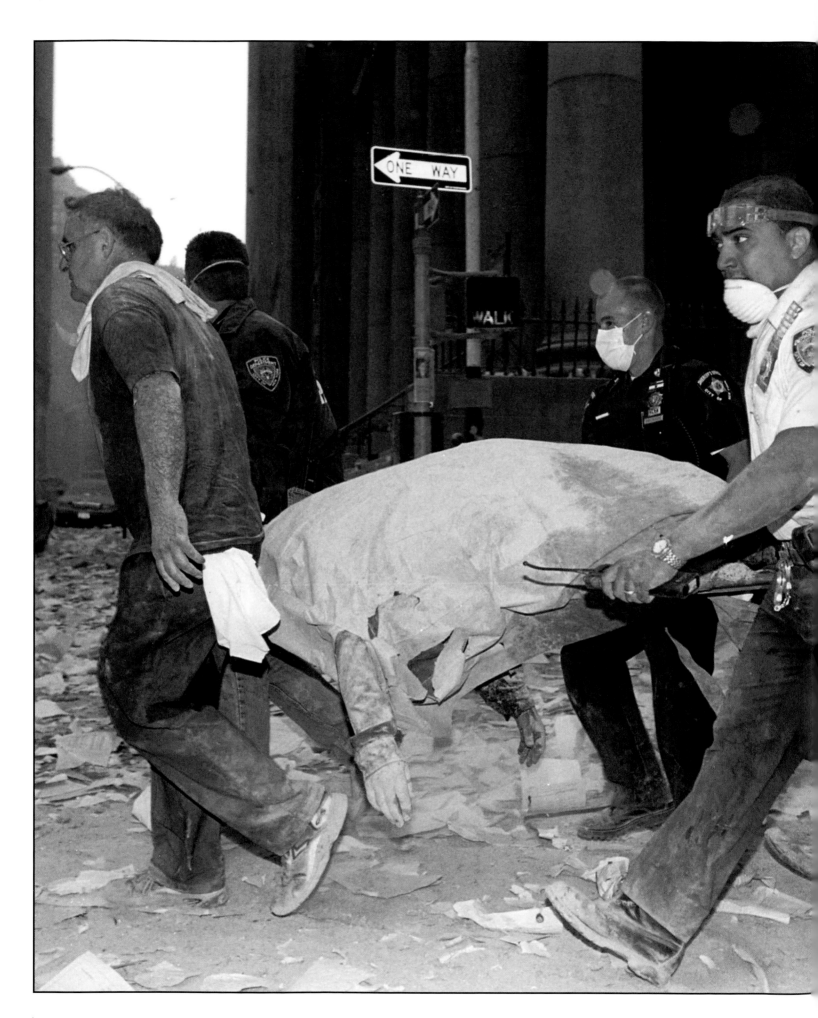

he would announce that a homicide was a natural death. In 1918, Mayor John Purroy Mitchel, in order to deal with these corrupt practices, finally replaced the office of coroner with the appointed post of medical examiner, which had to be filled by someone who was not only a physician but also a pathologist with autopsy experience. Other cities gradually followed suit.

Even today, the United States still operates two parallel systems: Most heavily populated areas employ medical examiners, but some states, or the counties within them, continue to have coroners. There are existent coroners' associations, for example, in California, Washington State, and Ohio.

IDENTIFICATION

The first, and most important, question to be answered about a person "found dead" is what is his or her identity.

If the corpse is discovered soon after death, identification is frequently easy. In most cases the body is within, or close to, the location where the person had lived. Neighbors may have expressed concern that they had not seen the deceased for several days, or relatives may have reported the person missing. In such cases, a view of the body—generally of no more than the face—is sufficient. Sometimes, particularly if the face has been rendered unrecognizable, it may be necessary for a physical peculiarity (a deformity, a tattoo, or a distinguishable pattern of moles or warts, for example) to be identified. Personal items on or near the body (particularly identity documents, but also other identifiable items such as billfolds, purses, clothing, or jewelry) can help substantiate the identification. Informal family photographs—rather than retouched studio portraits—can also be of assistance.

Problems naturally arise, however, when the person is not immediately identifiable. This may be because they were unknown in the vicinity, or because their recognizable features have been obliterated by violence, the effects of fire or water, or the natural processes of decomposition. If the body is dismembered, either following a homicidal attack or a disaster such as an aircraft crash—and, most particularly, after the destruction of the World Trade Center on September 11, 2001—investigators may be faced with the overwhelming difficulty of matching up disparate parts. And, finally, if the body has been reduced to a skeleton only an expert anatomist can provide clues to establishing identity.

LEFT RESCUE WORKERS CARRY A DEAD BODY FROM THE WRECKAGE OF THE WORLD TRADE CENTER, FOLLOWING THE COLLAPSE OF THE TWIN TOWERS ON SEPTEMBER 11, 2001. IN THE IDENTIFICATION OF VICTIMS—MANY OF WHOM WERE DISMEMBERED IN THE EXPLOSION OR BADLY BURNED IN THE FIRE—THE AVAILABILITY OF DNA TYPING WAS INVALUABLE.

INITIAL EXAMINATION

At autopsy, the medical examiner will first describe the external condition of the body to determine its probable appearance in life. This may prove difficult, however, when it is in an advanced state of decomposition, or has been recovered from water, or from a fire, explosion, or major disaster. The body is weighed, and an estimate of height is made by measurement—but changes in body length very often occur after death. The state of general nourishment is also observed. If possible, a rough estimate of age is also made at this time.

The color and type of hair, including facial, body, and pubic hair, is recorded, if any remains, and the color of the eyes is particularly important. Molds of the deceased's upper and lower jaw are made, as well as a report on any visible dental peculiarities. Characteristic skin blemishes, congenital defects, external evidence of surgery or old injuries, tattoos, piercings, and evidence of specific industrial practice, such as calluses on the hands—all these must be looked for before internal examination of the body begins.

Modern forensic examiners can call on a number of investigative approaches in the search for the identity of an unknown person. Briefly summarized, these are, in no specific order:

- The external condition of the body.
- Skin and hair characteristics/coloration.
- Fingerprints.
- Dental characteristics.
- Evidence of surgical intervention or disease.
- Bone and skull structure.
- Blood typing.
- DNA analysis.
- Facial reconstruction on the skull.

All these methods presuppose, of course, that independent data exists, somewhere, that will match the findings of the investigators.

SKIN AND HAIR

It might be thought that the skin coloration of a recently dead body would be a simple indication of its racial type. It is not that simple, however. For example, the face of a corpse that has spent some days in the water before rising to the surface is likely to be so swollen and darkened by the onset of decomposition as to be unrecognizable, even to close relatives.

On the other hand, there are certain differences in the proportional sizes of bones that are described later, which can be indicative of race. Also, unless it has been destroyed by fire or chemical means, hair can outlast all but the skeleton and the teeth, and an examination of its structure may provide some positive clues to the race and also the sex of the body in question.

Human hair is easily distinguished from animal hair, except for that of some ape species. Growing from follicles in the skin, it has three parts: the bulb or root, the shaft, and the tip. Under a low-power microscope, its cross section is also seen to be in three parts: the outer sheath (the cuticle), which is formed of tiny overlapping scales pointing toward the tip; the cortex, which contains the granules of pigment that give the hair its natural color; and the central medulla, in which the cells may be "continuous" or "interrupted." Most humans have an interrupted medulla, or even no medulla at all, just a hollow tube. This is particularly true of female scalp hair. The Mongoloid racial types—those of northern and eastern Asia, Malaysians, Inuit, and some Native Americans—usually have a continuous medulla.

According to where it grows on the human body, hair has different characteristics, divisible into the following six types:

Scalp hair—generally circular in cross section, with ends frequently split or sheared off as the result of hairdressing.
Eyebrows and eyelashes—also circular in section, but with tapering tips.
Beard or moustache—stiffer, curlier than scalp hair, and often triangular in section.
Axillary (underarm) hair—oval in section.
Body hair—oval or triangular in section, usually curly.
Pubic hair—springy, and oval or triangular in section. Female pubic hair tends to be shorter and coarser than that of a male.

There are, of course, exceptions to this classification, complicated by the increase in interracial marriage. While Caucasian types

have hair that is mostly oval to round in section, Afro-Caribbean hair tends to be nearly flat to oval. Caucasians show the greatest variety in hair color, and their hair is usually straight or wavy, with fine pigment granules evenly distributed in the cortex. African hair is likely to be kinky, with dense pigment unevenly distributed, while Mongoloid types have straight black hair.

During life, the scalp hair grows at an average rate of 0.1 in. (2.5 mm) per week, the male beard considerably faster, and the body hair more slowly. Growth ceases at death—despite the popular belief that the beard, and even the hair of the head, continues to grow after death. This apparent postmortem "growth" is due to the skin, particularly that of the face, shrinking.

MODERN FINGERPRINT IDENTIFICATION

The most important improvement on Edward Henry's classification system was made by Detective Chief Inspector Harry Battley at New Scotland Yard in 1927. By then, the Fingerprint Branch records held many thousands of file cards, and the task of searching them was daunting.

Faced with crime scenes at which only a single print could be found, Battley set out to develop a classification that would identify every individual fingerprint. He designed a special fixed-focus magnifier, provided with a glass base engraved with seven concentric circles, with radii from 0.12 in. (3 mm) to 0.6 in. (15 mm). These were identified by the letters A to G. Placing the glass over what appeared to be the center of the print (the "core"), it was easy to classify the delta by the engraved circle in which it was found.

Ten separate collections, one for each digit, were formed. Each was then subdivided into nine classifications: arch, tented arch, radial loop, ulnar loop, whorl, twinned (double) loop, lateral pocket loop (with a tiny whorl at its center), composite,

and accidental (similar to a twinned loop, but with one loop enclosing a tiny pocket). Within these classes each print was filed according to the classification of its delta.

This Single Fingerprint System has remained the basis of all modern fingerprint analysis. It rapidly proved its efficacy. Between 1923 and 1925, New Scotland Yard had succeeded in solving only seventy crimes by means of fingerprints. From 1928 to 1929, more than 360 successful fingerprint identifications were effected by the new system.

Until recently, the search for a fingerprint match among the millions of files available was a long and tedious process, exacerbated by their steadily increasing number; now, however, the vast backlog of print characteristics is being steadily transferred to computers, which can search and compare a database of thousands of prints in a matter of seconds. The taking of prints has also been made more rapid and efficient by the use of computerized scanners, which scan each finger and record the information as digital data that can be linked directly to the database.

BELOW WITH THE ADOPTION OF COMPUTERIZATION, DIGITALIZED FINGERPRINTS CAN BE RAPIDLY COMPARED. IN THIS SYSTEM EMPLOYED BY THE FRENCH POLICE, THE COMPUTER HAS IDENTIFIED THE NECESSARY NUMBER OF "POINTS OF SIMILARITY" BETWEEN TWO PRINTS, AND HAS REGISTERED THE IDENTIFICATION AS A "HIT."

FINGERPRINTS

It is now almost a century since the police and the legal profession agreed on the probability that no two people can possess identical fingerprints—and so far no evidence has emerged to question this belief, though in 1927 there was a minor panic among police authorities all over the world when an English physiologist wrote a paper on the study of identical twins. He reported that certain elements of their fingerprints seemed to be "mirror images" of each other, but a national newspaper published a story with the headline: "Extraordinary Twins: Fingerprints Identical." As a result, New Scotland Yard ("New" following the establishment of new premises in 1890) received a flood of letters seeking reassurance—a reassurance that they were fortunately able to give. The British medical journal *The Lancet* confirmed that the physiologist's paper had not claimed that the

LEFT IN THIS 1940S PHOTOGRAPH, TRAINEE AGENTS OF THE FEDERAL BUREAU OF INVESTIGATION RECEIVE INSTRUCTION ON THE PRINCIPLES OF FINGERPRINT IDENTIFICATION.

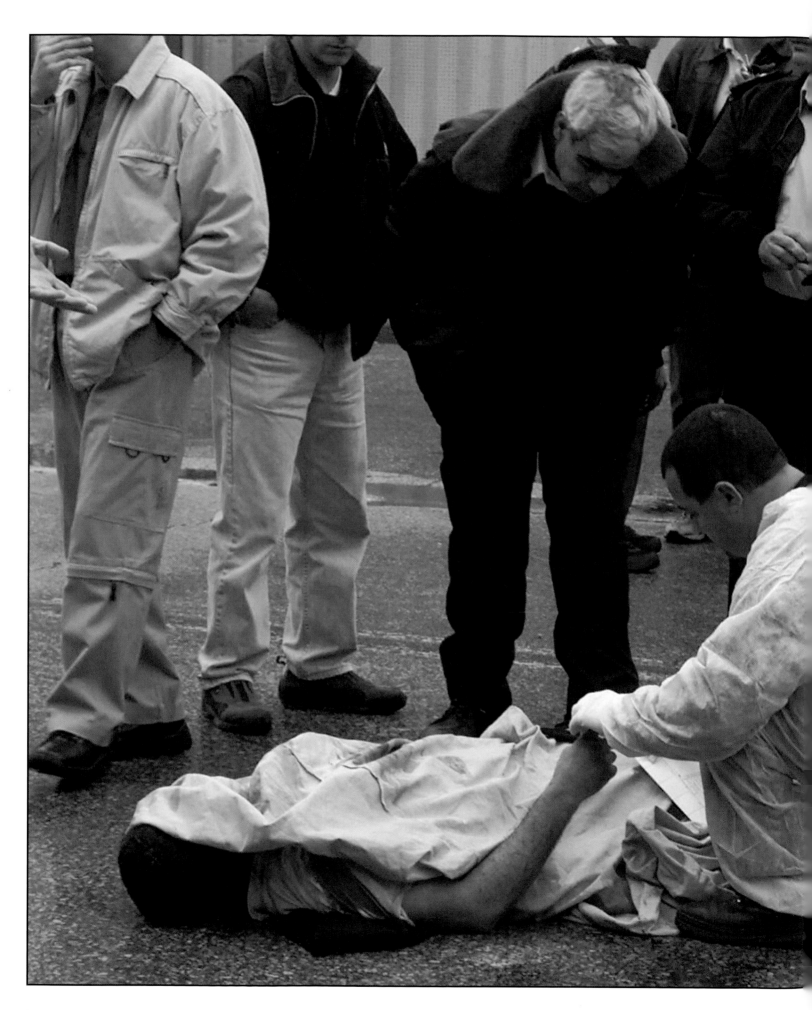

LEFT ISRAELI POLICE TAKING FINGERPRINTS, ON THE SPOT, FROM A DEAD PALESTINIAN IN JANUARY 2002. HE HAD BEEN SHOT DEAD BY SECURITY FORCES AFTER DRIVING OVER A POLICEMAN NEAR TEL AVIV, AFTER BREAKING THROUGH A MILITARY ROADBLOCK BETWEEN THE WEST BANK AND ISRAEL.

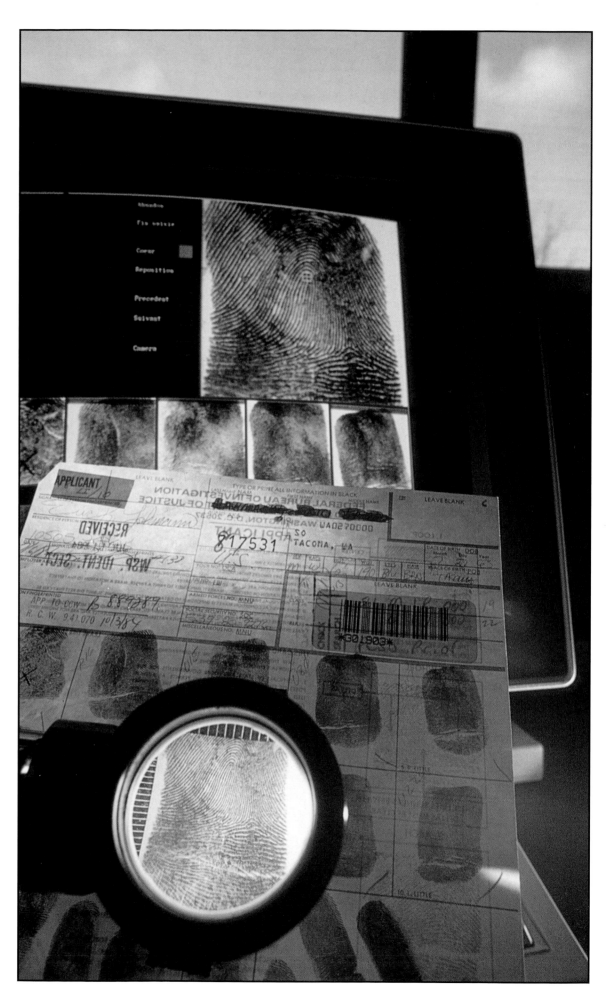

RIGHT EXISTING FINGERPRINT RECORDS MUST BE TRANSFERRED ONE BY ONE TO BE DIGITIZED BY COMPUTER. HOWEVER, ONCE THE PRINTS ARE CONVERTED TO A DATABASE, THE COMPUTER CAN FIND A MATCH WITHIN SECONDS.

fingerprints of twins were identical, and the scare was soon dismissed. When the body of an unknown person is examined, therefore, one of the first actions is to take a set of fingerprints. Prints of the palms of the hands, and the feet, are also frequently taken, in consideration of the possibility that they might be matched with prints found on premises (in a bathroom for example) that are believed to be the person's home. Many official agencies and military organizations, particularly in the United States, require the filing of fingerprints, together with other identifiable characteristics, of all personnel. There are also, of course, police archives—and, in the United States, those of the FBI—which should contain the prints of everybody found guilty of a crime (and, sometimes illegally, of many other people) in the past one hundred years.

In principle, taking the prints of a corpse's fingers is a routine process, very similar to what is done in life. On occasion, however, problems have arisen in which considerable ingenuity has had to be exercised. In 1938, the decomposing, legless body of a woman was discovered in the sea off the coast of Cornwall, England, and the action of sand and shingle had worn her fingertips completely smooth. Chief Superintendent Frederick Cherill of New Scotland Yard, who was at that time the leading British fingerprint expert, succeeded in peeling off the skin of the hands—just as one would a pair of close-fitting gloves—to reveal the pattern, in reverse, on the underside.

Once the fingerprints have been obtained, they must be compared with any found at other locations, and also with those in official files. At the same time, the discovery of fingerprints, other than those of the dead person, at the scene of what may be considered a suspect death must be treated with the utmost caution—there are numerous reasons fingerprints may be found in a particular place. Ideally, the prints of everyone who has had access to the scene should be taken, in order to eliminate them from the inquiry.

Investigators are expected to wear latex gloves at all times, so as not to contaminate the evidence; although frequently those first on the scene—police officers and ambulance crews—are so concerned with the possibility that the victim might still be alive that they cannot take full precautions.

Once they are satisfied that the person is dead, however, all personnel should be withdrawn, and the area should be sealed off. Ideally, any further investigation should be suspended until the arrival of the medical examiner or police pathologist, as well as the crime scene investigation team.

DENTAL CHARACTERISTICS

The teeth can survive much longer than the bones of the skeleton can, and will even endure destructive events such as an intense fire. They can provide an indication of the age of the corpse, and in the hands of an odontologist the casts that are taken can prove a very important means of identification. He or she will probably also take X-ray photographs of the victim's jaws to determine the stage of tooth development, any dental work that has been carried out, and the deterioration that occurs with age.

In young persons, the assessment of age can often be made within a relatively brief period of time. In babies and youngsters, the stage of development of the first or second teeth—though there can be distinct variability in certain cases—can provide a fairly accurate indication, and X-rays of the jaw will reveal which teeth are still developing. The third molars—the "wisdom" teeth—do not generally emerge until the late teens or early twenties.

In older persons, all of whose teeth have emerged, it is possible to make a rough estimate of age from the degree of wear, the

BELOW A COMPUTERIZED SCAN OF A COMPLETE SET OF PERMANENT TEETH IN THE LOWER JAW. THREE MOLARS ARE THE LARGEST TO BE SEEN ON EITHER SIDE. THE THIRD MOLARS IN EACH JAW, COMMONLY KNOWN AS WISDOM TEETH, ARE THE LAST TO EMERGE, AND OFTEN DO NOT APPEAR AT ALL.

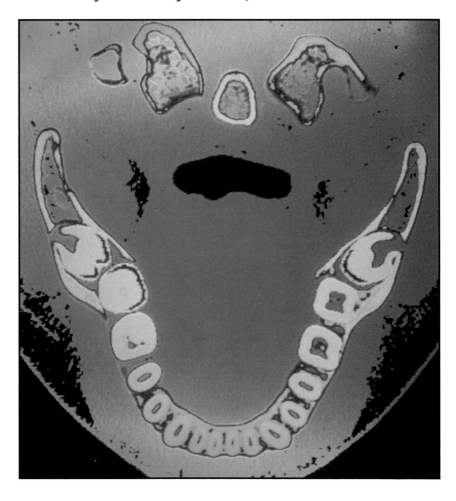

thickness of the dentine layer, etc.—very much as the age of horses and other animals is judged. During the 1950s, Professor Gosta Gustafson of Sweden introduced a six-point system of recording these visible changes.

Professor Gustafson stressed that his classification should be used only by experienced odontologists, and it provides, in any case, only an approximation. The examiner rates each stage of change on a scale of 1 to 4. In a controlled study of the system, one case was rated at 1.5, indicating an age between 14 and 22; the actual age was 18. In another case, the changes were rated at 12, giving an estimated age of between 66 and 76; the actual age was 68.

CASE STUDY
THE *NORONIC* FIRE

On the night of September 7, 1949, fire swept through the cruise ship *Noronic*, tied up in Toronto harbor. When the inferno was finally brought under control, 118 passengers had perished. Among these, dental records provided the sole means of identification of twenty persons, they were the principal clue to identity in another twenty, and they were of great value in the identification of a further nineteen.

In another case of fire, at a hotel near Voss, Norway, in 1959, twenty-four people were burned to death. Of these, six were identified only by dental records, including X-rays, and another nine by their teeth together with objects found with their bodies.

Other important points to note are the coloration of the teeth, their spacing, their size, any that are missing, and the type of bite—that is, whether the upper teeth close slightly outside the lower teeth, which is normal, or whether they close noticeably outside or inside the lower teeth. An odontologist will also record other peculiarities, such as crooked or gappy teeth, and markings due to the habits or occupation of their owner. For example, a pipe smoker is likely to have stained and worn teeth, and a tailor may have a groove on the surface of two facing teeth, due to the habit of biting thread. Professor Gustafson even claimed that he could distinguish the player of a brass instrument from a woodwind player by the effect on their teeth. When it is apparent that the dead person used a full or partial denture, this may perhaps be found at the home of a missing person, or with relatives. If it fits, identity is almost certainly established.

Most people in developed countries now pay regular visits to their dentist, who keeps detailed records of fillings, extractions, bridges, and dentures, together with a note of any deformities or peculiarities. He or she may also take more than one series of X-ray photographs. It has been estimated that there are, throughout the world, some two hundred different systems of recording this data, but all provide a relatively easy, and almost totally reliable, means of identification. This can prove very important where there are victims of a mass disaster.

BLOOD

The analysis of a person's blood type can reduce the process of identification to within considerably narrow limits. This technique can also be of great significance when blood that is not that of the victim—and is most likely that of the attacker—is found at the scene of a violent crime. Originally, as described in Chapter One, only four major types of human blood were known, but more recent research has identified more than twenty different components.

In 1927, Karl Landsteiner, who had immigrated to the United States, discovered two secondary blood groups, which were named MN and P. During 1939 to 1940, he made another important distinction. In some 85 percent of white race subjects, the red cells were agglutinated by the serum of laboratory rabbits that was treated with the blood of Macasus rhesus monkeys. In the following year, Landsteiner's former colleague, American immunologist Philip Levine (1900–1987), showed that this was the cause of "hemolytic disease of the newborn," due to the incompatibility of the rhesus-negative blood of the mother, which effectively destroyed the rhesus-positive blood of the fetus.

In 1949, two British scientists discovered that it was possible to distinguish between male and female body cells, particularly the white blood cells. The nucleus of female cells contains a body—named the Barr body—that will take up a dark stain. Male cells do not contain this Barr body. Further research has identified a wide range of proteins and enzymes in blood, all of which can be detected specifically.

In making a positive identification, it is, of course, necessary to know the proportions of these different substances that occur in a given population. For example, if blood of type B occurs in some 13 percent of the population, the protein haptoglobin in 49 percent of these, and the enzyme adenylate kinase in 7 percent, the probability of a person possessing these three blood types is 13 x 49 x 7 = 4,459 in 1 million, that is, between 4 and 5 in every 1,000.

The development of DNA analysis is increasingly superseding this approach to blood typing, though it remains a valuable confirmatory technique. In the identification of the victims—whose bodies were almost totally disintegrated—of the collapse of the twin towers of the World Trade Center in New York on September 11, 2001, DNA proved to be the only means of naming them in the majority of cases.

On October 2, 2001, the National Institute of Justice called a meeting, a "summit of genetic experts," in New York. Representatives of five laboratories who would be carrying out the DNA analysis were present, and a Kinship and Data Analysis Panel (KADAP) was set up a few days later. Among the members of this panel was Dr. Charles Brenner, who was instrumental in the development of a suitable computer program.

The first two successes involved identical twins, but after some thirty further identifications the program began to run dry: What was needed was further data on family relationships, and the discovery of more victims. Then, even as the panel was discussing the problem, an American Airlines aircraft crashed in Queens on November 12. Study of the data on the victims—most of whom were identified within a few weeks—made it possible to improve the computer software, and to identify many more WTC body fragments.

On May 30, 2002, excavation of the WTC site was officially concluded. On June 18, 2003, New York's chief medical examiner, Charles Hirsch, announced the identification of the 1,500th victim. He said that his goal was to reach 2,000—but this could well depend on the further development of DNA technology. More victims would remain forever unidentified because the fire and explosion had completely destroyed their DNA.

BELOW INVESTIGATORS IN PROTECTIVE SUITS AND MASKS STAND OVER A CONVEYER AS THEY EXAMINE DEBRIS FROM THE WRECKAGE OF THE WORLD TRADE CENTER AT THE FRESH KILLS LANDFILL FACILITY, NEW YORK CITY, JANUARY 14, 2002. ALL THE DEBRIS FROM THE WORLD TRADE CENTER DISASTER SITE IS TAKEN THERE, WHERE INVESTIGATORS SEARCH FOR EVIDENCE AND REMAINS OF VICTIMS. THE VICTIMS' REMAINS ARE SEPARATED OUT SO THAT THEY CAN BE IDENTIFIED—A PAINSTAKING PROCESS INVOLVING THE USE OF DNA TYPING, DENTAL RECORDS, AND VARIOUS FORENSIC TECHNIQUES.

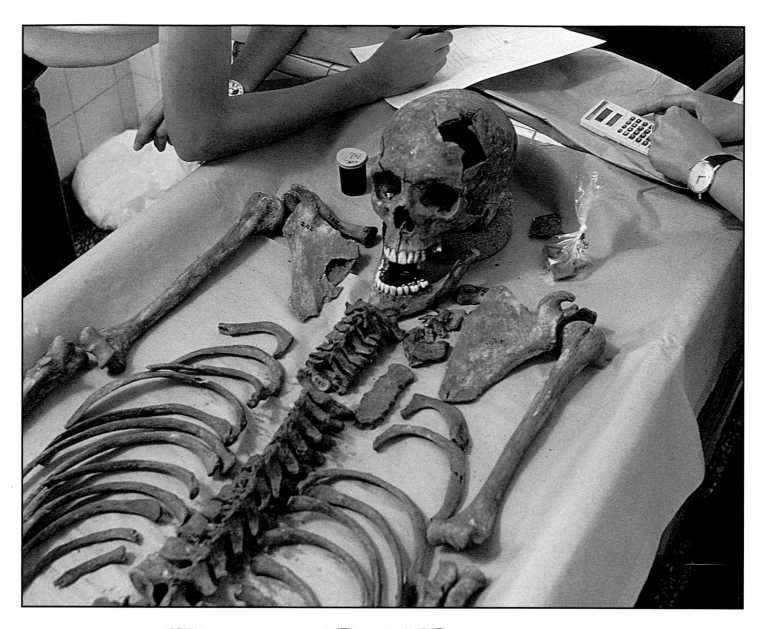

SKULL AND BONES

In the morgue, the medical examiner or pathologist can be faced with a number of alternatives: The corpse may be newly dead, in one of a number of stages of putrefaction, or skeletonized. The body begins to decompose from the moment of death; facial features become unrecognizable within days, the tissues gradually liquefy and are consumed by insects, until finally all that is left is an array of bones.

The problem becomes even more complicated if these bones have been scattered—whether as a result of the activities of scavenging animals or dismemberment by a psychopathic killer. And, in the case of a disaster such as an explosion or aircraft crash, a forensic anthropologist, whose task is to distinguish between disparate body parts, must be called in. In the course of identification

procedures, the most important indicators of the sex of a skeleton are the pelvis and the skull. The female pelvis, which is designed for the bearing of children, is broader and shallower than the male's. The pelvic cavity—through which the infant is delivered—is visibly larger; pathologists give its usual diameter as the spread of a thumb and forefinger, while the cavity of the male is approximately the spread of the fore and middle fingers. There are also minor differences in the size and shape of other pelvic bones, and scored markings on the female pelvis can indicate whether she had borne a child.

Differing characteristics in the male skull usually begin to develop only after the age of fourteen, and determining the sex of a younger child is difficult. There are, however, distinct differences between the skulls of male and female adults. In the female skull the orbit (the eye socket) is rounded, but it tends to be more rectangular in males. The nasal cavity of a woman is rather pear-shaped, while a man's is

CASE STUDY
THE ROMANOV FAMILY

Following the Russian Revolution of 1917, Tsar Nicholas II was forced to abdicate, and he and his family, and their physician and servants, eleven people in all, were eventually imprisoned in a house in Yekaterinburg, Siberia. On the night of July 16, 1918, all were executed by firing squad—though a rumor persisted that the tsar's daughter Grand Duchess Anastasia had escaped, and a woman, Anna Anderson, claimed to be the duchess throughout her life.

Six months later, investigator Nicholas Sokolov announced that he had found pieces of evidence from the presumed burial site of the bodies, a deserted mineshaft, but concluded that they had been soaked in sulfuric acid and then doused in gasoline and consumed by fire.

This was the accepted story for seventy years, but in April 1989 a Russian filmmaker announced that he had discovered skulls at a site five miles away from that identified by Sokolov. In July 1991, President Boris Yeltsin authorized the excavation of the site: Some one thousand bone fragments were unearthed, and assembled into four male and five female skeletons. Using photographic superimposition, Russian scientists identified the skulls, and concluded that those of Tsarevitch Alexei and Grand Duchess Maria were missing. This was consistent with the account of the chief executioner, Yakov Yurovsky, that he had burned two of the bodies.

There was considerable disagreement about these findings, however. An invited American team, led by William Maples of the University of Florida, examined the bones and teeth, and suggested that one of the missing bodies was that of Anastasia.

In September 1992, Russian DNA expert Pavel Ivanov carried the bones to England, where he began work on them with Peter Gill of the British Forensic Science Service. Their analysis confirmed that five of the bodies were definitely related, three being female siblings. Tsarina Alexandra was identified by comparison with a sample provided by her grandnephew, the Duke of Edinburgh. The identification of the tsar proved much more difficult. Eventually, permission was obtained to open the tomb of his brother, Grand Duke Georgij, who died in 1899, and Ivanov was able to prove a perfect match. At the same time, Anna Anderson's claims were finally dismissed by DNA analysis.

ABOVE THE ROMANOV IMPERIAL FAMILY. CLOCKWISE, FROM THE LEFT: GRAND DUCHESS MARIA; TSAR NICHOLAS II; GRAND DUCHESSES OLGA, TATIANA, AND ANASTASIA; THE TSAR'S WIFE, TSARINA ALEXANDRA; AND THE YOUNG TSAREVITCH (PRINCE) ALEXEI.

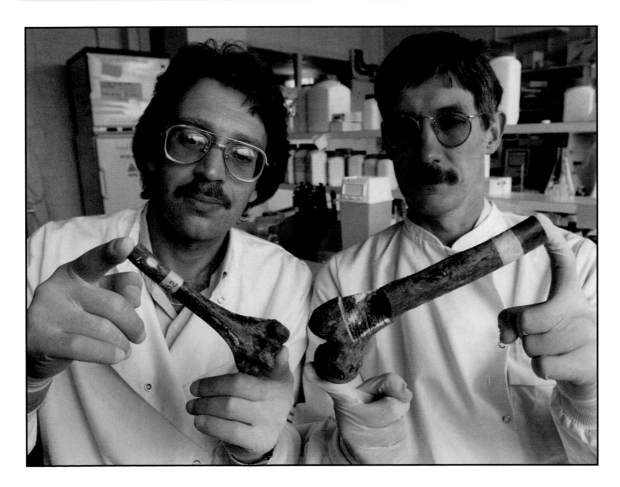

LEFT DR. PAVEL IVANOV AND DR. PETER GILL HOLD UP A FEMUR AND HUMERUS FROM WHAT WAS LATER PROVED TO BE THE BODY OF TSARINA ALEXANDRA ROMANOV. THE BONES HAVE BEEN LABELED TO ENSURE THAT THERE IS NO CONFUSION ABOUT THEIR SOURCE.

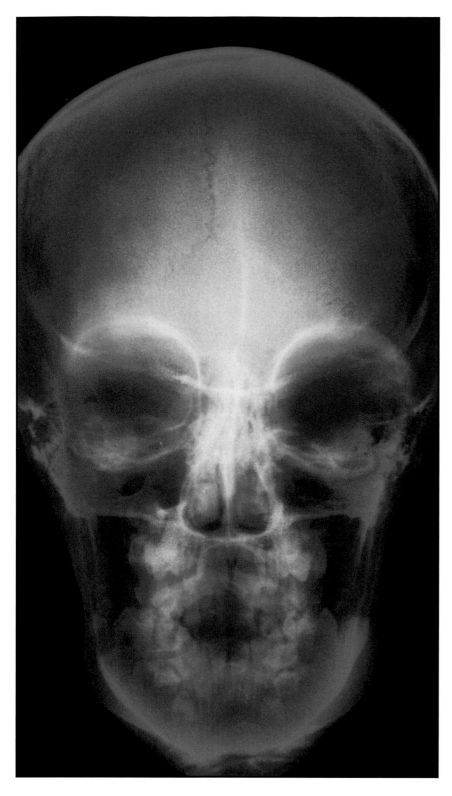

indicative sex characteristics of the pelvis and skull.

When it comes to judging the age of a body, the skull can provide the strongest clues, though an estimate can be made even when only a few bones are available. In a newborn child, the ends of the long bones of the arms and the legs are attached to the appendages by cartilage (epiphysis). Gradually, the two fuse together. This process continues up to the age of some thirty years, and can be detected visually or by X-ray examination, and the different stages of fusion can provide an estimate of age that is accurate to within two or three years. Beyond the age of thirty, however, changes in bone structure, and the onset of such diseases as arthritis, will provide an estimate no closer than a bracket of ten years.

The skull can similarly indicate the stages of development that occur with age. The skull of the newborn is flexible, to make birth easier, and is made up of a number of pieces marked by "sutures," which join up in stages. The frontal suture is the first to close, generally quite early in life. Other sutures usually begin to close between the ages of twenty and thirty, but some may remain open, or partially closed, up to the age of some sixty years. The last suture does not close completely until age seventy or later.

To summarize: Estimates of age based solely upon the skull and bones can be reasonably accurate—within two or three years—up until the mid-twenties, but become progressively imprecise in later life.

The minimum stature of the body—likely to be about 1 in. (2.5 cm) less in death than it is in life—is calculated by laying out the bones on a specially marked "ostiometric board," which permits more accurate measurement than using a measuring tape and calipers would. Even if the whole skeleton is not available, the calculation can be made from the length of the long bones alone. The rules for this calculation were first proposed by the French pathologist Rollet in 1888, and have changed little in principle. The length of the adult humerus (the upper-arm bone) is reckoned to be roughly 20 percent of the total stature, the femur (the thighbone) is 22 percent, and the spine is 35 percent.

Obviously, these calculations rely on the assumption that most bodies are in a fairly constant proportion; dwarves and unusually tall persons—to say nothing of young children—are likely to deviate significantly from the norm. It has also been noticed that, while most people reach their maximum stature at about eighteen years, American whites now do not finish growing until the age of twenty-three.

The normal stature, and the relative proportion of the limbs, can also vary greatly

longer and narrower, like a teardrop. The jaw of the female is rounded, the male's more angular, as well as generally larger and heavier. Furthermore, the female forehead does not slope backward as much as the male's does, and usually lacks a pronounced brow ridge above the eyes.

Although male bones—particularly of the arms and legs—tend on the whole to be heavier than those of females, this is a distinction that can be made only in comparison with the more

In November 1889, Alexandre Lacassagne, the professor of forensic medicine at the University of Lyon, France (see Chapter One), had a dramatic success. A naked body was discovered in a sack on a riverside some nine miles (15 km) from Lyon. It was badly decomposed, but was that of a man, apparently dark haired, who had been strangled. A further clue was the discovery of the remains of a trunk, which smelled strongly of rotting flesh and had, presumably, originally contained the sack. A label showed that the trunk had been sent from Paris to Lyon some four months previously, on July 27.

The disappearance of a forty-nine-year-old man named Gouffé had been reported to the police in Paris on that date. He was known as very much a ladies' man, and this might have been the motive for his murder. However, his brother-in-law, who was summoned to Lyon, said that he could not identify the corpse, because Gouffé's hair was chestnut in color. The body was accordingly buried as "unknown."

It was only later, when one of the investigating officers washed a sample of the hair, that its true color was revealed. The corpse was exhumed, and Lacassagne examined the skeleton. He reported that the victim had walked with a limp—as Gouffé had done—and that his teeth indicated that he was aged about fifty.

Finally, the hair from the corpse was compared under the microscope with hair from Gouffé's hairbrush, and shown to be identical. With the identity of the "unknown" now established, it was not long before his killer was tracked down, found guilty, and executed by guillotine.

with different racial types. This is not a reliable distinction, however, and the shape of the skull and pelvis are better—if only rough—guides.

Bones sometimes turn up unexpectedly during excavations for building or highway construction, and in such cases it is important to make an approximate estimate of their age, as they may be evidence of an unnatural death. Complete reduction to a skeleton has been known to occur within three or four weeks; in normal conditions, however, a buried body will not be completely skeletonized in much less than two years, and shreds of cartilage and other tissue may still adhere to the bones.

BELOW IN THE MORGUE, THE BODIES OF VICTIMS, BOTH KNOWN AND UNIDENTIFIED, ARE STORED IN A BANK OF REFRIGERATED CABINETS. THESE ARE THE BODIES OF UNCLAIMED VICTIMS OF THE FATAL HEATWAVE IN FRANCE IN AUGUST 2003.

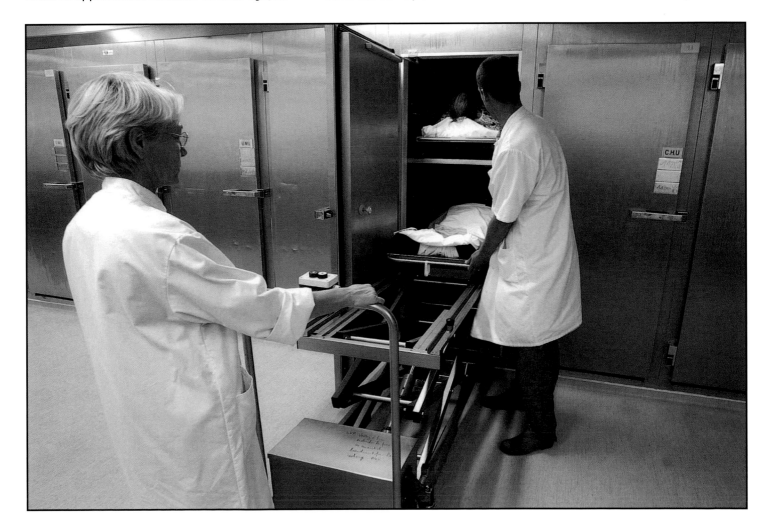

RIGHT THE EXCAVATED
SKELETON OF THE VICTIM OF
AN ANCIENT CHINESE
SACRIFICIAL RITE, MANY
CENTURIES OLD. ALTHOUGH,
IN NORMAL CONDITIONS, THE
BONES OF A SKELETON BECOME
BRITTLE WITHIN FORTY OR
FIFTY YEARS, THEY MAY BE
PRESERVED FOR THOUSANDS
OF YEARS IN DRY SAND. BONES
SUCH AS THESE CAN BE DATED
TO WITHIN A REASONABLE
TIME BRACKET BY THE
MEASUREMENT OF THE
RADIOACTIVE DECAY OF THEIR
C-14 CONTENT. A SKELETON
MORE THAN FIFTY YEARS OLD,
HOWEVER, IS GENERALLY OF
LITTLE INTEREST TO THE
FORENSIC INVESTIGATOR: EVEN
IF IT REVEALS EVIDENCE OF A
CRIMINAL ATTACK, THE
PERPETRATOR IS UNLIKELY STILL
TO BE ALIVE. ON THE OTHER
HAND, ARCHAEOLOGISTS HAVE
EXHUMED THE SKELETONS OF
MORE THAN ONE HISTORICAL
FIGURE AND SUCCESSFULLY
DEMONSTRATED HOW THEY
DIED USING THE LATEST
FORENSIC TECHNIQUES.

Bones remain heavy, and slightly greasy to the touch, for a number of years, but after forty or fifty years the surface becomes dry and brittle, and the bones begin to crumble. This is very much a generalization—in dry sand, for example, three-thousand-year-old bones have been found in good condition, while in a wet and acidic environment they may dissolve away within only twenty years.

If the bones are more than fifty years old, they are unlikely to be of forensic interest, as there is little hope of finding the perpetrator of a crime. There are a number of techniques that have been developed to date bones. The best known is radiocarbon dating, but this is of interest only to archaeologists, as the radioactive decay of C-14 is relatively slight over the first hundred years.

Most chemical analyses of older bones are equally unhelpful for forensic purposes—with the exception of the detection of blood pigments and antibody reactions, which can persist for the first five years or so. Much more important is the possible discovery of artifacts with the remains, which are a surer indication of the time at which the body was buried.

THE O'HARE DISASTER

One of the leading practitioners of a relatively new means of identification, forensic anthropology, is Dr. Clyde Snow. He spent a number of years at the Civil Aeromedical Institute of the U.S. Federal Aviation Authority (FAA), where he carried out research into what happens to the bodies of persons involved in aircraft crashes. He has said that he prefers to call his specialty osteobiography: "There is a brief but very useful and informative biography of an individual," he says, "contained within the skeleton—if you know how to read it." This "biography" can include evidence of former injuries, indications of unusual trades, and—in the case of females—faint signs of their sexual history.

In 1979, Snow resigned from the FAA to concentrate on forensic inquiries. He was consulted in many international investigations, including the examination of the exhumed remains of the Nazi concentration camp experimenter

BELOW THE SHATTERED FUSELAGE OF AMERICAN AIRLINES FLIGHT 191, WHICH CRASHED AT O'HARE INTERNATIONAL AIRPORT, CHICAGO, ON MAY 25, 1979. THE BODIES OF ALL 271 PERSONS ABOARD WERE SCATTERED IN PIECES, AND THIS PRESENTED A MAJOR PROBLEM OF IDENTIFICATION FOR THE INVESTIGATORS.

Dr. Joseph Mengele in Brazil, the identification of "disappeared" victims in Argentina, Bolivia, and Guatemala, and the excavation of mass graves in the former Yugoslavia. But one of the most challenging cases of his career was the identification of the victims of the crash at O'Hare International Airport, Chicago, in 1979.

On the sunny afternoon of May 25, American Airlines Flight 191, with 271 persons on board, took off from Chicago on an everyday flight to Los Angeles. At only 200 ft. (61 m), the left engine assembly and part of the leading edge of the left wing broke away, but the aircraft continued to climb until, at 325 ft. (99 m), it rolled steadily to the left and plunged to the ground, exploding in a mass of flame. All those on board, and two on the ground, were killed instantly. The explosion scattered their bodies in pieces, and the fire consumed clothing and documents that might otherwise have given a clue to their identity. One of the firemen who rushed to the scene reported: "We didn't see a single body intact ... just trunks, hands, arms, heads, and parts of legs. But we couldn't tell whether they were male or female, whether they were an adult or a child, because they were all charred."

The Cook County medical examiner, Robert Stein, established a morgue in one of O'Hare Airport's huge aircraft hangars, and assembled a team of more than a hundred expert investigators, who flew in from all over the country. Among the earliest arrivals was Lowell Levine, consultant odontologist to the New York City Medical Examiner's Office, who had been on holiday in Florida when he heard the news and had immediately left for Chicago. It was essential to identify the victims to settle their estates and prove insurance claims. Twenty dentists worked on the 273 dismembered bodies, and they were among the first to secure successful identification.

Within a few days, many more of the passengers and aircrew had been named by pathological examination, fingerprints, and personal jewelry, but there remained nearly fifty who defied identification. At this point, Levine suggested to Stein that Clyde Snow should be called in.

Snow arrived, having been told that he would probably be needed for only a few days; in fact, he remained in Chicago for five weeks. He soon weeded out the bones of birds and animals that had been gathered up during the field searches, and then requested a radiographer, John Fitzpatrick, who was able to make a number of further matches. In recording their findings, the investigators had to handle "thousands and thousands of little bits of paper," and Snow suggested that a computer could make their task much easier. With the aid of a programmer from American Airlines, everything that was known about the still-unidentified victims, together with their anthropological and other data, was entered.

Working in shifts with Fitzpatrick, Snow succeeded, in those five weeks, in identifying twenty more victims. But the remaining twenty-nine were never fully identified.

FACIAL RECONSTRUCTION

Undoubtedly the most dramatic of techniques for the identification of dead persons from their skulls is facial reconstruction. In forensic investigation it is regarded as a relatively modern development, but it has a long history. As early as 1895, the Swiss anatomist Wilhelm His acquired a skull that was believed to be that of Johann Sebastian Bach, and on this he

CASE STUDY
GERASIMOV'S FIRST CRIMINAL SUCCESS

In 1939, Mikhail Gerasimov was given his first forensic investigation. Scattered bones had been found in a wood near Leningrad (now St. Petersburg), which at first appeared to be the remains of someone killed and eaten by wolves. When Gerasimov examined the skull, however, he found marks that suggested the victim had been attacked with a hatchet.

Uncompleted bone formation, open skull sutures, the absence of wisdom teeth, and only slight wear on those still in the jaw indicated that the individual had been twelve to thirteen years of age. A developed bony ridge above the eye sockets and a relatively large jaw suggested that the victim was probably a boy. Added to this was the fact that some reddish-blond hairs still adhered to the scalp, and had been cut short only days

before death occurred. As he gradually remodeled the head, Gerasimov revealed a snub-nosed, chubby-cheeked boy, with a high forehead, thick upper lip, and slightly projecting ears. To complete the picture, he added short red-blond hair.

While this work was proceeding, the police had been searching their missing persons files. They found a record of a boy whose parents believed that he had run away to the city some six months before.

Photographs of the reconstructed head were mixed with some thirty photos of similar-looking boys, and then shown to the father, who recognized his son immediately. Further inquiries traced the boy's movements, and eventually led to the arrest of his murderer.

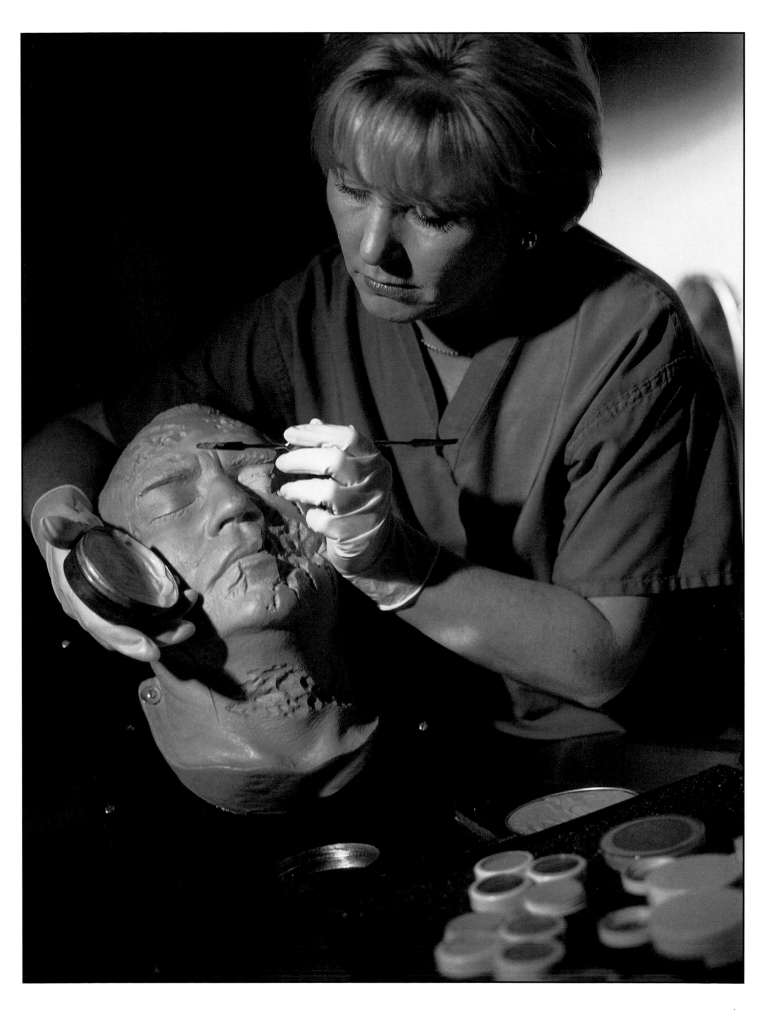

RIGHT A NEAR-CONTEMPORARY
PORTRAIT OF THE RUSSIAN
TSAR IVAN IV— "THE
TERRIBLE." HE WAS
NOTORIOUS FOR HIS ILL
TEMPER AND CRUELTY.

sculpted a face that was accepted as a good likeness (though he had a couple of unconfirmed portraits of the composer to aid him). In 1916, an unidentified skeleton was discovered in a cellar in Brooklyn, New York. A police anatomist mounted the skull on a roll of newspaper for a neck, and fitted it with brown glass eyes; he then covered it with flesh-colored plasticine, which was finally finished off by a sculptor. Local Italian residents immediately identified the likeness as that of Domenico la Rosa, who had disappeared a year or two earlier.

In 1927, aged only twenty, Mikhail Gerasimov (1907–70) took charge of the archaeology department at the Irkutsk museum in Russia. Even before his appointment, Gerasimov had spent two years measuring and dissecting the heads of corpses, studying the thickness of the flesh on various parts of the skull and how this was affected by the structure of the muscles. With this research in hand, he began to experiment, building up sculptors' clay on the ancient skulls in his care. As he later wrote:

"The essence of the program was that not only definite information about the thickness of the soft parts must be found, but also morphological features of the skull which could

RIGHT MIKHAIL GERASIMOV
PUTTING THE FINISHING
TOUCHES, IN 1953, TO HIS
RECONSTRUCTION OF THE
FACIAL FEATURES OF IVAN THE
TERRIBLE. HE PARTICULARLY
NOTED "THE MOUTH, WITH ITS
DROOPING CORNERS AND
EXPRESSION OF DISGUST."

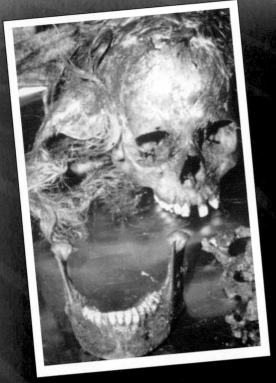

ABOVE THE SKULL OF "LITTLE MISS NOBODY," AS IT WAS DISCOVERED IN 1989 BY BUILDING WORKERS IN CARDIFF, SOUTH WALES.

ABOVE THE COMPLETED RECONSTRUCTION, WITH HAIR ALSO MODELED IN CLAY. THE FACE WAS SOON RECOGNIZED BY A SOCIAL WORKER AS THAT OF KAREN PRICE.

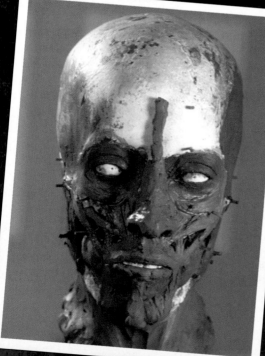

ABOVE EARLY STAGES IN THE FACIAL RECONSTRUCTION ON THE SKULL. MODELING CLAY HAS BEEN USED TO BUILD UP THE PRINCIPAL MUSCLES.

In 1989, building workers digging drains in Cardiff, south Wales, uncovered a skeleton firmly tied in plastic bags inside a rolled carpet. Examination by pathologists, an odontologist, and a forensic entomologist established that the remains were those of a young girl, aged about fifteen, who had been buried at some time between 1981 and 1984. But there were no clues to the victim's identity, and the frustrated police dubbed her Little Miss Nobody.

The assistance of Richard Neave was called on. He spent two days making the reconstruction, producing a strikingly lifelike head of the young girl. Photographs were taken and distributed to the press and television networks. Within two days a social worker reported that they resembled a former client, one Karen Price. Her dental records were found, and the odontologist confirmed the identification. As a final proof, DNA was extracted from the victim's bones and checked against that of Karen Price's parents.

The sad story of young Karen Price was soon established. A runaway from home, she had taken up prostitution; in a row over her refusal to pose for pornographic photographs, her pimp and the doorman from a local bar had killed her. They were both found guilty of murder in February 1991.

serve as clues for the reconstruction of the different parts of the face—nose, mouth, eyes and so forth."

By 1935, Gerasimov's experiments bore fruit. He showed that he could produce facial reconstructions of persons unknown to him, which proved closely similar when compared subsequently with their photographs. The success of his work was recognized, and in 1950 he was appointed to the Laboratory for Plastic Reconstruction, then newly established by the USSR Academy of Sciences.

In April 1953, Gerasimov was a member of a special commission, which was given permission by the Soviet Ministry of Culture to open the sarcophagus of Tsar Ivan ("the Terrible") IV in the Kremlin, Moscow. When the body was revealed, still dressed in the remnants of a monk's habit, a few traces of eyebrow and beard hair were seen to be attached to the skull. Ivan's long bones showed clear evidence of crippling arthritis, and most of his adult teeth had only emerged in his fifties—a very painful experience that explained the irrational rages and cruelty that had earned him the name of "the Terrible."

As Gerasimov began his task of reconstructing the face of the tsar, every stage was filmed and photographed. As he wrote:

> The most revealing portrait was that of the face without any hair. It seemed to hide nothing—the form of the low forehead, the peculiarities of the supraorbital area [the ridge above the eyes], the size and outline of the symmetrical orbits which conditioned the external specific appearance of the eyes. The mouth, with its drooping corners and expression of disgust, was determined by the shape of the dentition. The face was hard, commanding, undoubtedly clever, but cruel and unpleasing, with pendulous nose and clumsy chin.

After nearly four hundred years, the Russians at last knew what their infamous tsar had looked like. Gerasimov's work became famous throughout the world, and his example was soon followed by others. At present, one of the world's leading practitioners of the technique is Richard Neave of the medical faculty of Manchester University, England. Much of Neave's work has been devoted to archaeological remains, as described in the book *Making Faces* (1997) that he wrote with John Prag, but he has also been involved in criminal investigation. Although Neave's method of reconstruction is simple in principle, it requires

expert anatomical knowledge. First of all, casts of the skull are made in a firm but flexible plastic, both as it is received, to preserve a record of any adhering tissue, and again after it has been cleaned. The eye sockets are then filled with balls of polystyrene, and, at what are known to be important anatomical points, small holes are bored into the cast, and thin wooden pegs are inserted to represent the expected thickness of the flesh at these points. The muscles and surrounding flesh are built up with modeling clay, so as just to cover the pegs. The cheeks and brow are rounded out, and the thin flesh of the scalp is applied in strips. Shaping the nose and ears is a difficult process that requires the accumulated experience of the sculptor. Artificial hair is added to the eyebrows, and, finally, a wig or more artificial hair completes the reconstruction.

A more recent method makes use of computerized technology. The skull is mounted on a turntable, then scanned by a laser beam as the table turns. This provides three-dimensional information on the exact shape and size of the skull, which is fed into a computer. The computer compares this information with a databank assembled from measurements of skull shape and tissue thickness made on the heads of living persons, then produces a digital likeness. When a skull or dismembered head is suspected to be that of a known missing person, and a photograph of that person is available, a rather different technique can be used. It consists of superimposing the photograph on a same-scale photograph of the skull—or an X-ray of the head—and was pioneered by Professor John Brash of Edinburgh University, Scotland, in 1936.

Between September 29 and November 4, 1935, a number of dismembered body parts, wrapped in newspaper and pieces of clothing, were discovered in the waters of a stream near Moffat in Scotland. Among the remains were two heads and the limbs of two bodies. The corpses had been expertly dismembered, and the murderer had taken pains to remove parts that could lead to identification. The eyes were missing from one skull, and the eyes, nose, tongue tip, lips, and several teeth were missing from the other. Most of the fingertips had been cut away, and the hands were mutilated—but one hand remained, from which some faint fingerprints could be obtained.

Painstakingly, Professor John Brash of Edinburgh University, working with Professor John Glaister of Glasgow University's department of forensic medicine, sorted the remains, and they eventually put together the bodies of two females. Although they were badly decomposed, it proved relatively easy to establish the approximate time at which the bodies had been thrown into the stream: A piece of newspaper from the *Sunday Graphic* was dated September 15, and some body fragments had probably been washed downstream by a spate on September 19. The newspaper proved to be from a special edition that was distributed only in the Lancaster and Morecambe area of Lancashire, England, and the police therefore directed their inquiries to people reported missing in that area at the critical time.

One of these missing people was Mary Jane Rogerson, a maid in the Lancaster household of Indian-born Dr. Buck Ruxton. He had reported her disappearance, as well as that of his wife, Isabella, but had raised suspicions by his varying explanations of how they came to be missing. On October 12, he was formally charged with the maid's murder; carpets in his house were found to be bloodstained, there were traces of human fat and tissue in the drains, and some of the items of clothing used to wrap the body parts were identified by Mary Jane Rogerson's mother. To clinch the matter, fingerprints obtained from the remaining hand were positively identified as Rogerson's.

But the question remained: Was the other body that of Isabella Ruxton? Professor Brash obtained a photograph of the missing wife, and he photographed the unidentified skull from the same angle and at the same scale. When the two photographs were superimposed, they fitted exactly. Buck Ruxton was found guilty of both murders.

With the increasingly impressive range of investigatory techniques available, forensic examiners are now very often able to establish the identity of a dead person. There are still problems to be overcome, of course; whatever the data that can be obtained from the corpse, it is still essential to obtain provable confirmatory data from other sources, such as the supposed victim's home, dentist, physician, or members of the immediate family. Many cases remain unsolved, particularly when facial reconstruction is the only clue to the identity of the deceased, and nobody—not even confirmed family members—can, or will agree to, recognize it.

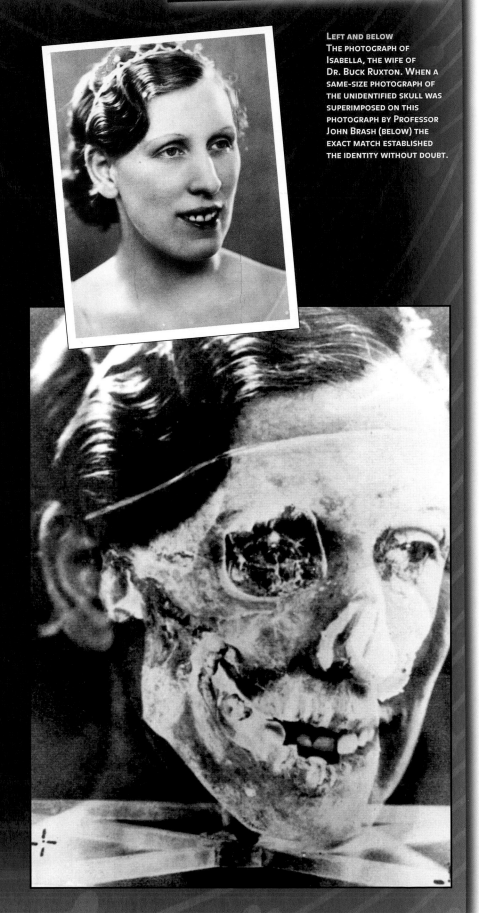

LEFT AND BELOW
THE PHOTOGRAPH OF ISABELLA, THE WIFE OF DR. BUCK RUXTON. WHEN A SAME-SIZE PHOTOGRAPH OF THE UNIDENTIFIED SKULL WAS SUPERIMPOSED ON THIS PHOTOGRAPH BY PROFESSOR JOHN BRASH (BELOW) THE EXACT MATCH ESTABLISHED THE IDENTITY WITHOUT DOUBT.

What follows is fictional, but is typical of the painstaking investigations that may have to be carried out to establish the identity of an unknown body—a John or Jane Doe—and to find the clues that can lead to the arrest of the victim's killer.

PART 1

A GRUESOME DISCOVERY

Late in the afternoon of October 20, 2001, two boys were exploring a stretch of woodland not far from the Santa Ana Freeway southeast of Los Angeles, California. Suddenly, they were horrified to spot what looked like the bones of a human leg lying partly concealed by undergrowth. They were tempted to pick the up the remains, but decided not to; instead, they hurried to their homes nearby, where one of the boys' parents immediately telephoned the local sheriff's office. Sheriff's Deputy Brendan O'Malley arrived shortly in his cruiser, and the two boys led him to the site of their discovery. Light was fading fast, and O'Malley shone his flashlight: "Looks like human bones to me, too," he grunted. With a long roll of tape marked "Police Line Do Not Cross" he enclosed an area with a radius of some 50 yards (45.7 m) round the bones; as they had clearly been in their current position for a considerable time and there was little likelihood of their being moved overnight, further investigation was left until the following morning.

At first light, a small team—which soon came to be named the "Skeleton Crew"—began to assemble on the edge of the woodland, parking their cars in line along the dirt road. Apart from Sheriff Aral Verdian and his two deputies—O'Malley and Jose Rodriguez—the team comprised John Burton, investigating officer, Deputy Coroner Dr. Alvin Hackenbacker, and a photographer.

The northwest perimeter of the crime scene— hard to believe such a nice place could hide such a dark secret. →

9

Here's the carpet that contained the rest of the Jane Doe skeleton. Not much of a burial site!

3

This is the wallet as it looked lying on the ground. It had nothing in it and may have been new when it was dropped.

Followed by Burton and the photographer in single file, Hackenbacker ducked under the tape and led the way to the center of the enclosed area, Burton scanning the ground to the left and right as he went. After the photographer had taken shots from several angles, Dr. Hackenbacker pulled on a pair of latex gloves and picked up one of the bones. "I'd say this is definitely a human femur," he said, "and this here's a tibia. Score marks of teeth on both, likely a coyote or some such feeding on the flesh. But where's the rest of the body?" He glanced at Burton: "You're going to need a full search team here."

By 10 a.m., the dirt road along the woodland's edge was crowded with vehicles; a hastily assembled search team of deputies and civil aides gathered round John Burton, while a scattering of sightseeing locals hovered in the background. Burton held a clipboard marked in small squares, on which a rough circle representing the enclosing police tape had been drawn. "At this point," he told the team, "we don't have a crime on our hands, just a search for an unidentified body. But I want you to treat it like a crime scene—who knows what we may discover?" He directed his team around the perimeter of the tape, and slowly, making a "fingertip" search in latex gloves, they began to work toward the center.

Only a few minutes had passed when a cry of "Bingo!" came from Rodriguez on the far side of the circle.

"Everybody stay where you are!" shouted Burton, and, circling the tape to where Rodriguez had begun his search, he moved cautiously forward to where the deputy stood beside a tree, excitedly waving his arms. At the deputy's feet, another leg bone was sticking partially out of the shallow earth, together with a corner of what appeared to be carpet.

"Hell!" said Burton. "Looks like we've got ourselves a burial and a likely homicide here," and he marked the point on his clipboard grid. "Continue your search," he shouted to the team. "You'll be looking principally for bones—but make sure you don't miss any other trace evidence."

An hour later, a collection of small foot bones had been discovered, each of which was placed in an evidence bag marked with the point on Burton's grid corresponding to where they had been located. In addition, at some distance from the burial a leather wallet was found, overgrown with weeds. As the wallet was carefully bagged and labeled, Burton noted that it was weathered and had been nibbled by beetles. He carefully noted the location on his map of the crime scene.

Meanwhile, more experts were summoned by radio: the county crime scene investigation officer, Tamara Gregory; the assistant medical examiner, Dr. Jane Kurosawa; a photographer with a video camera; and an anatomist from the local hospital, Ivan Vrba, who was the last to arrive.

3

SUSPICIOUS CIRCUMSTANCES

An unidentified corpse may well not have suffered an unnatural

death. A dead body may be found in bed in a hotel or rooming

house, for example, and,

if there are no apparent signs of

violence or poisoning, the medical

examiner or pathologist's task will

most likely be no more than that of

establishing the cause of death

(see Chapter 5). However, the immediately apparent

circumstances at the scene, or the detailed examination of the corpse

carried out at autopsy, may reveal something suspicious that suggests the

death is not natural. The findings of the medical examiner will therefore

immediately lead either to an inquiry into a possible suicide or to a

homicide investigation.

> *"Suspicion always haunts
> the guilty mind;
> The thief doth fear each
> bush an officer."*
>
> —WILLIAM SHAKESPEARE,
> *HENRY VI, PART 3*

FACING PAGE THE METICULOUS COLLECTION OF THE SMALLEST ITEM OF TRACE EVIDENCE AT THE SCENE IS VITAL WHENEVER THERE IS THE SLIGHTEST SUSPICION THAT A CRIME MAY HAVE BEEN COMMITTED. HERE, A FORENSIC SCIENTIST LIFTS FINE FIBERS FROM THE DOOR OF A CAR INVOLVED IN AN ACCIDENT. THEY MAY HAVE COME FROM THE CLOTHING OF THE PERSON ALLEGED TO HAVE BEEN STRUCK BY THE CAR.

When a corpse is found in the open, it may be that the person has collapsed and died naturally, they may be a victim of cold and died of hypothermia, or they may have committed suicide. On the other hand, they may have suffered a homicidal attack—in which case the signs generally will be obvious—or may have been killed elsewhere and dumped where they are discovered. Cases that appear to be of a drowning or a suicidal fall from a height must be treated with great care: "Did she fall, or was she pushed?" Bodies discovered in the aftermath of a fire or explosion evoke similar questions: Was this an accident, or was the fire and/or explosion started by another person? Was the victim alive or dead before the event?

All these possibilities must be considered in the course of the examination of the body and the site where it is found.

AT THE SCENE

Whatever the circumstances in which a body is discovered, the possibility that the pathologist's ultimate findings will establish an unnatural death must be borne in mind. Ideally, the police or sheriff's officers will be the first on the scene, and should seal off the immediate area. A qualified physician should examine the corpse with as little disturbance as possible, merely to confirm that death has occurred. He or she will take notes on the general appearance and disposition of the body—but it should not be moved until photographs have been taken, of both the corpse and its surroundings.

After the dead person has been removed to the morgue, the scene of the death should

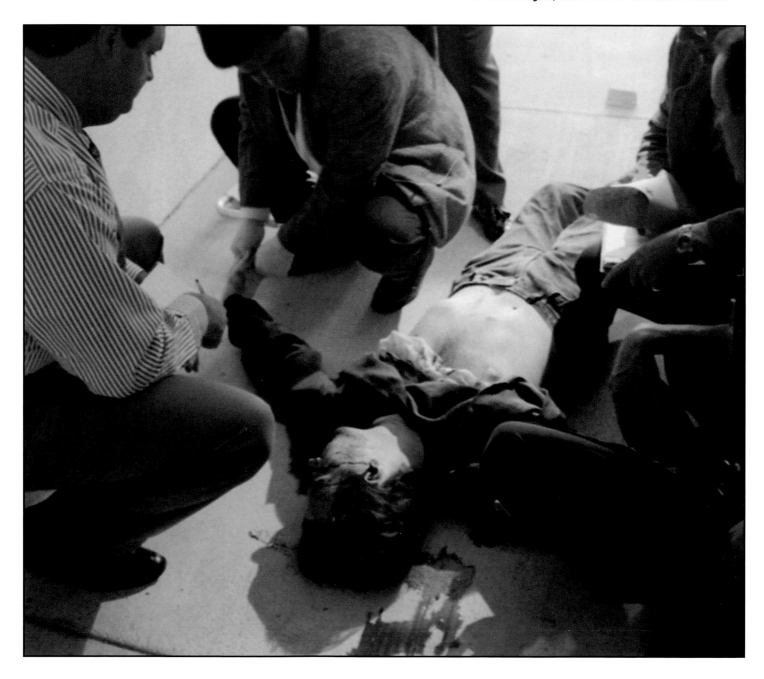

DR. EDMOND LOCARD

Dr. Edmond Locard studied medicine and law at the University of Lyon, France, and eventually became an assistant to Professor Alexandre Lacassagne, one of the pioneers of criminology. He remained in that appointment until 1910, when he established his own criminal investigation laboratory. Gradually, the French police came to recognize the value of his work, and Locard successfully helped them to solve many cases. One of his discoveries was that the number of tiny pores that lies along the papillary ridges of the fingertips is as characteristic as the fingerprints themselves—they have been described as "fingerprints within fingerprints." Continuing his research throughout much of his long life, Locard published, between the ages of fifty-four and sixty-two, a massive seven-volume *Treatise of Criminology*.

An admirer, from his childhood, of Sir Arthur Conan Doyle's stories of Sherlock Holmes, he was delighted to be known as the Sherlock of France. One of the strangest accounts of his experiences concerns a visit that Conan Doyle made to Locard's collection of criminal cases. The British author stopped before a photograph, and exclaimed: "But that is Jules, my former

chauffeur!" It was a picture of Jules Bonnot, the notorious terrorist and leader of *la bande á Bonnot*, who—by an odd coincidence—had taken up crime after leaving Sir Arthur's employ and had used stolen cars in driving about France to commit robberies and murders.

BELOW ONE OF THE FIRST TO PUT FORENSIC INVESTIGATION ON A FORMAL FOOTING WAS THE FRENCH SCIENTIST DR. EDMOND LOCARD. HERE, HE EXAMINES A REVOLVER FROM HIS COLLECTION OF CRIME-RELATED WEAPONS.

remain sealed until the autopsy findings are known. If there is even the slightest evidence that the case is one of homicide, a meticulous examination of the crime scene should begin as soon as possible, so that all trace material, some of which may rapidly deteriorate, can be found. Above all, strict precautions should be taken to ensure that the scene is not contaminated by "foreign" material, owing to the carelessness of those allowed access to the site.

Dr. Edmond Locard (1877–1966) expressed the fundamentals of crime examination in a brief phrase that is the guiding principle of all

investigators: "Every contact leaves a trace." That is, every criminal unwittingly leaves something of himself at a crime scene, and unwittingly carries something away. Trace evidence at the scene, or on the person or belongings of a suspect, is of the greatest importance in the solving of a crime.

The crime scene investigator (CSI in the United States, SOCO—scene of crime officer—in Great Britain) starts by drawing up a grid, on which every item of trace evidence will be marked in place. He begins by noting the most obvious evidence: materials used to conceal the

body, a discarded weapon, spatters and pools of blood, broken articles, or—in the open—car tire tracks, marks on trees caused by contact with the car, footprints, or scattered clothing. Then a more meticulous "fingertip" search must be made by his team of helpers, who look for signs of a struggle, empty cartridge cases, stray bullets, fibers and hairs, unusual dust, and fragments of all kinds—in fact, anything that "should not be there." If the body has lain for some time exposed to the air, or in a shallow grave, there will be maggots and other insects present, or traces of former insect infestation, which will be examined later by a forensic entomologist.

If the crime scene is indoors, the team will look for signs of forced entry as well, such as overturned furniture or broken articles. Often, a murderer or brutal assailant will try to "stage" the scene to look like an attempted burglary, and this must be allowed for in careful assessment of the events. Also, blood spattering is much easier to observe indoors than it would be on

trees and undergrowth in the open. Every stage that changes the overall appearance of the scene, such as the removal of the body to the mortuary, should be photographed, together with the discovered traces, *in situ*, and a video record is frequently made. Each piece of physical evidence is picked up, either with

latex-gloved fingers or forceps, and placed in an individual plastic bag or box, which is labeled with the time and location, and initialed by the officer who discovered it. This is essential: All trace evidence must be logged as it passes from hand to hand in the process of examination, or the defense may query the "chain of custody" and suggest that it has been tampered with. After photographs of footprints or tire tracks have been taken, casts are made, whenever possible.

Although fingerprints can last for a long time, the fingerprint expert should look for them as soon as possible. It is also vital that the prints of all those who had access to the crime scene are taken—some may not have worn latex gloves, and their prints must be eliminated from the inquiry; if prints are found that are not identified as such, they will provide essential evidence that can lead to the perpetrator of the crime. Palm prints should be taken as well, as many are likely to be found at a crime scene, often on such surfaces as door and fence posts, and they must be either eliminated or sent on for possible identification.

THE INVESTIGATION OF FINGERPRINTS

The first successes in fingerprint identification came with those that were visible: in sweat, blood, and other media, or impressed in a plastic surface such as paint or wax—all of which could be photographed. It was soon discovered, however, that invisible ("latent") prints could be detected on many smooth surfaces.

Latent prints are formed by traces of sweat, either from the fingertips themselves or unconsciously transferred from the face or another part of the body. On contact, they are made up of 99 percent water, the rest being a complex mixture of many substances that will vary not only from person to person, but also from hour to hour in the same individual. Even when all the water has evaporated, this remaining 1 percent can persist for a long time. The print, depending on other factors, may be effectively permanent: Latent prints have been obtained from objects removed from ancient tombs.

The search for latent prints depends on their being "developed" to make them visible. The basic method has not changed greatly since it was first introduced. The fingerprint expert dusts with a fine powder all those surfaces that might yield a result. He or she uses either a very soft brush or an insufflator—a fine-puffing-spray device. Prints on glass, silver, or dark surfaces

are dusted with a light-gray powder; those on light-colored, nonabsorbent surfaces are dusted with black powder. Fluorescent powders are also used; illuminated with ultraviolet light, the latent prints show up clearly.

A more recent device is the Magna-Brush™, which employs magnetic powders: The tiny particles adhere to the ridges of the print, and any excess is removed from the surrounding areas by the magnet in the body of the brush. There is disagreement, however, over whether or not this is effective on ferrous surfaces. Another method makes use of molybdenum disulfide, a chemical that is often employed as an ingredient in lubricants. Fine particles are suspended in a detergent solution and adhere to the grease in the print; this "wet" process can be used with success, for example, on water-soaked firearms.

ABOVE A MAGNETIC BRUSH USED TO REVEAL FINGERPRINTS ON SURFACES THAT ARE NOT SUITABLE FOR CONVENTIONAL DUSTING. BECAUSE THE BRUSH LACKS BRISTLES, WHICH MAY SMEAR THE PRINT, THE TECHNIQUE YIELDS SHARPER RESULTS ON SURFACES SUCH AS PLASTIC. THE ORIGINAL MAGNA-BRUSH™ WAS DEVELOPED BY AMERICAN FORENSIC SCIENTIST DR. HERB MACDONNELL.

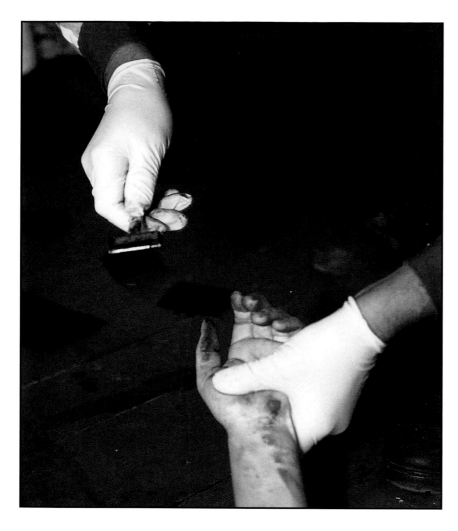

doorknobs, can be lifted in a similar way, using a special flexible rubber tape.

Prints on such semi-porous material as cardboard or wood must be developed in a different way. For many years, the standard technique was to use silver nitrate, which reacts with the salt in sweat, or iodine vapor, which reveals the grease. Nowadays, the usual method is to spray the material with a solution of the chemical ninhydrin. It had been known for some years that ninhydrin would react with amino acids when, in 1954, Swedish researcher Svante Odén established that it would successfully reveal the amino acids in sweat. The sprayed surface is then dried in an oven at 176°F (80°C) for a few minutes, and any latent prints will develop as a pinkish-purple coloration.

Latent fingerprints on human skin—notably important in cases of rape—will survive for only about two hours. However, they can be lifted by the use of the high-gloss paper Kromecote, which is then dusted in the usual manner. Subsequently, an attempt can be made to dust the skin itself, and the Magna-Brush™ is reported to be the most effective in such cases. Specialized X-ray illumination techniques have also been developed; however, they are still in an experimental stage.

The search for fingerprints in the time-honored way can be a lengthy process, as the entire crime scene must be examined. Two recent discoveries have made the fingerprint expert's task considerably easier. One such discovery, made by accident, is that prints exposed to the fumes of superglue (cyanoacrylate) will show up white on a darker surface. They can then be dusted, then lifted or photographed. This technique is particularly useful for examining an enclosed space, such as a cupboard or car's

When latent prints were first discovered, these developed prints were then photographed; now, they are usually "lifted" onto transparent adhesive tape, which can then be mounted on a transparent film or a card of a suitable color, ready for analysis and, it is to be hoped, identification. Prints on curved surfaces, such as

CASE STUDY
VALERIAN TRIFA

In 1975, the United States Department of Justice sought a deportation order against Valerian Trifa (right), a former archbishop of the Romanian Orthodox Church. It was alleged that, on entering the United States, he had concealed his former membership in the Iron Guard, Romania's pro-Nazi party during the 1940s. Trifa denied this, but in 1982 the West German government discovered, among the state archives, a postcard that Trifa appeared to have written to a high-ranking Nazi official. The Germans naturally refused to allow the FBI to use any fingerprint-detection technique that would alter this important historical document in any way. However, examination by laser light very soon revealed Trifa's thumbprint, and he was deported in 1984.

interior. The second discovery, also accidental, was made by researchers in a Canadian laboratory, who found that laser beams would reveal latent prints. Controlled laser illumination, unlike powders or chemicals, does not affect the evidential object, and—unexpectedly—it appears to be more effective on older prints.

The usual method of taking fingerprints, whether from a living or dead person, has scarcely altered in the century since Edward Henry introduced his system. On a standard fingerprint form, two sets of prints are recorded, each finger being inked in turn, using either a roller or an inkpad. The first set are "rolled" prints, in which the finger is rolled completely from edge to edge, so that the ridge patterns extending round the curve of the finger are recorded. The second set are "plain" prints, taken without any rolling action. This is a precaution, mainly to ensure that the prints are obtained in the same correct sequence—arrested suspects have been known to offer their fingers in the wrong order, or even offer the same hand twice, to confuse subsequent examination.

The fingers of a dead body are not rolled because of the danger of smudging them, and a print of each finger is taken separately by rolling a piece of thin card against it. This card is then attached at the appropriate place on the fingerprint form. There is no difficulty in fingerprinting a corpse after its rigidity has relaxed. While it is still rigid, however, the fingers are likely to be clenched into the palm; although it is often suggested that tendons in the hand should be cut so that the fingers can be straightened, it is in fact only necessary to bend the wrist backward against the forearm, whereupon the fingers straighten themselves.

This standard method of fingerprint-taking is gradually being superseded by the use of scanning equipment, which inputs digital information directly into a computer where it can be compared with millions of records in a database, and can produce a match—if one exists—in as little as ten minutes.

Palm prints are also being recorded in increasing numbers—although far fewer than that of fingerprints. A landmark case occurred

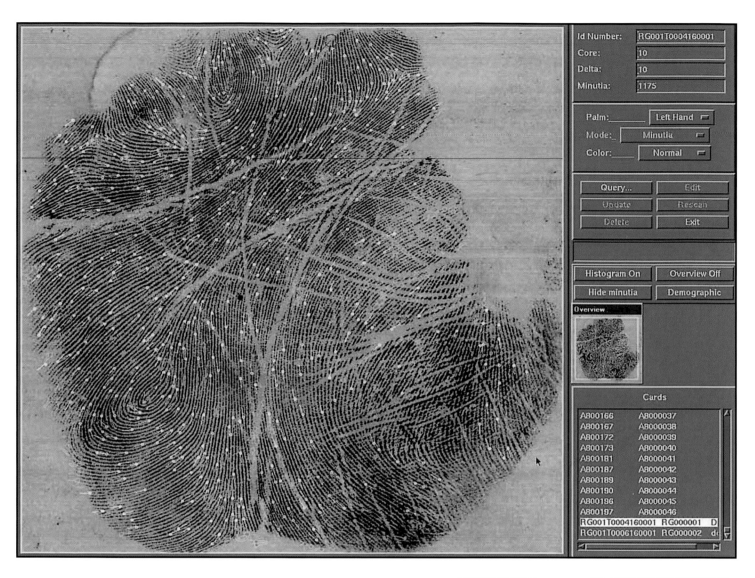

Id Number: RG001T0004160001
Core: 10
Delta: 10
Minutia: 1175

Palm: Left Hand
Mode: Minutia
Color: Normal

Query... Edit
Update Rescan
Delete Exit

Histogram On Overview Off
Hide minutia Demographic

Overview

Cards

A800166	A8000037
A800167	A8000038
A800172	A8000039
A800173	A8000040
A800181	A8000041
A800187	A8000042
A800189	A8000043
A800190	A8000044
A800196	A8000045
A800197	A8000046

RG001T0004160001 RG000001 D
RG001T0006160001 RG000002 d

ABOVE FINGERPRINTS—AND PALM PRINTS—CAN NOW BE SCANNED AND DIGITALIZED BY COMPUTER AND QUICKLY ANALYZED. IN THIS PALM PRINT OF A MALE LEFT HAND, THE POSITION OF THE CORE AND ITS RELATED DELTA HAS BEEN IDENTIFIED.

FACING PAGE USING AN ULTRAVIOLET LIGHT SOURCE TO PRODUCE FLUORESCENCE, AN FBI OPERATIVE EXAMINES A METAL CAP ON WHICH A FINGERPRINT HAS BEEN DEVELOPED BY THE USE OF FUMES FROM SUPERGLUE TO WHICH A DYE HAS BEEN ADDED.

in London in 1955. The body of Mrs. Elizabeth Currell was found on a golf course north of the city; she had been battered to death with the heavy iron tee-marker from the nearby seventeenth hole, on which police found a partial palm print in blood. At that time, the files at New Scotland Yard contained some 6,000 palm prints, but—as expected—no match could be found. The police therefore decided that their only course was a mass printing operation of all males who lived or worked in the vicinity.

Over two months, house-to-house teams took nearly 9,000 palm prints in the area. Those given the task of matching the prints worked week-on/week-off, to reduce fatigue and the possibility that a match might be missed. At last, print No. 4,605 was identified; it had been obtained several weeks earlier from eighteen-year-old Michael Queripel. At first, Queripel insisted that he had come across Mrs. Currell's body during a walk over the golf course, but he eventually confessed. He escaped capital punishment (at that time still the penalty for murder in Britain) by a quirk of fate—he had been aged only seventeen on the date of the murder.

GLOVE PRINTS

Many criminals, knowing how easily their fingerprints can give them away, wear gloves while committing a crime—but this can frequently prove a valueless precaution. In one classic case, a burglar wore a pair of latex gloves while breaking into a post office in Manchester, England. He stripped them off as he left, however, and carelessly discarded them. Turning the gloves inside out, the police fingerprint expert was able to obtain a perfect set of prints from the inner surface. In another case, a burglar took a new pair of gloves with him to the scene of the crime, then threw away the manufacturer's paper band that had surrounded them—leaving behind a good set of his prints on the paper. Cases such as these are the result of luck rather than scientific method. However, during the 1960s, Gerald Lambourne, later head of the Fingerprint Branch at New Scotland Yard, began to study the identification of prints from gloves. As he wrote in his book *The Fingerprint Story* (1984):

On December 19, 1987, the skeletal remains of a middle-aged woman were discovered in the foundations of a residential building in Los Angeles. Examination of the bones revealed that she had died of multiple stab wounds. The upper part of her body had been buried in poured concrete, which, as it flowed over her, had left a clear cast of her head and torso. Using the head cast, the composite artist of the LAPD's Scientific Investigation Division was able to produce a lifelike drawing of the victim. After this drawing was screened on TV, a viewer produced for the police a photograph that closely resembled it, and the "Jane Doe" was provisionally identified as Adrienne Piraino.

The victim's arms were crossed over her body and had left visible cavities in the concrete where her hands had been. Parts of the concrete were particularly smooth in texture, and it seemed possible that identifiable fingerprints could be obtained from it. Operatives of the police Latent Print Division carefully poured a silicone-rubber mix into the mold of each hand and obtained sufficient ridge detail from the fingers and palm. Piraino had previously made an application for employment, at which time her fingerprints had been taken, and she was positively identified from these. The casts also dramatically revealed cuts and stab wounds on the hands and fingers, caused as Piraino attempted to defend herself from her attacker.

The concrete in which the victim had been buried also yielded pieces of clothing and other pieces of trace evidence. Most important of these was a partially disintegrated cigarette packet, which had been crumpled and discarded. Members of the LAPD Comparative Analysis Unit painstakingly assembled the fragments, and discovered the name of the manufacturer, Liggett & Meyers. Gradually, they were able to determine the style, color, and general appearance of the package. A representative of Liggett & Meyers was able to inform them that the fragments were from an "L&M Long" soft pack, which had been introduced in test marketing only in their western region: California, Arizona, New Mexico, Colorado, Nevada, Idaho, Montana, Wyoming, North and South Dakota, Washington, Oregon, and Utah.

The test product was launched in March 1974 and withdrawn in March 1975, when the packet design was changed. The scope of the inquiry was quickly narrowed down even further when it was found that the dimensions of the tax stamp, which had been affixed by the local retailer, were consistent with those used in California.

The relatively narrow time frame of a single year, and the localization of the tax stamp, led investigators to a suspect who was known to have had access to the building at that time. Other items of trace evidence helped to clinch the matter.

RIGHT MODERN EQUIPMENT FOR FINGERPRINT DETECTION IS INCREASINGLY SOPHISTICATED, AS THIS PHOTOGRAPH FROM SANDIA NATIONAL LABORATORIES, ALBUQUERQUE, NEW MEXICO, SHOWS. THE RESEARCHER IS USING THE LAMP IN HIS RIGHT HAND TO ILLUMINATE A SET OF PRINTS ON THE GLASS IN FRONT OF HIM, WHICH FLUORESCE. THE SPECIALIZED GLASSES "BLINK" RAPIDLY, REGULARLY SYNCHRONIZING WITH THE FLASHING OF THE LAMP, SO THAT THE PRINTS ARE EASY TO DETECT.

"A glove soon becomes impregnated with grease and dirt. Even during the putting on and removal of a glove, a layer of perspiration is placed on it. Consequently, when it comes in contact with a smooth, hard surface, a layer of this grease is ... deposited, in much the same way as an unprotected finger will leave a fingerprint.... Each glove can be individualized in many ways: the material it was made from, hand-stitched, knitted, molded, its embossing, perforations; the creases and contours formed when it is worn constantly; the accidental damage caused by the wearer."

After more than ten years of research, Lambourne was able to show in court that a glove print could be positively identified. In January 1971, a man was arrested on suspicion of trying to break into premises in Pimlico, London, and a glove print was found on a newly broken window.

Lambourne examined the lifted print: "I was satisfied that it had been made by a left-hand glove. The texture of the print indicated a glove with a suede finish, the surface of which had been damaged." The suspect was in possession of a pair of sheepskin gloves with a suede finish, and surface damage on the left-hand glove

exactly matched the print. Although the prisoner pleaded guilty at trial, Lambourne was permitted to explain his evidence to the court, thus establishing a precedent in English law.

It might be thought that domestic rubber gloves, which are produced in the hundreds of thousands by an identical manufacturing process, would reveal no signs of individuality. Lambourne, however, secured the cooperation of a manufacturer and examined a large batch. As he successfully showed:

"Such gloves are made, inside out, on porcelain formers. The grip pattern is indented in the former. This is dipped in a tank containing latex which adheres to it.... Slight uneven adhesion of the latex can mutilate what should be a regular pattern. Air bubbles can occur in the pattern area when the former is dipped into the latex, or a piece of latex from a previous glove can contaminate a portion of the pattern. All of these factors can be detected in a glove print. The user of such gloves would not be aware of these slight variations, which are only revealed under magnification."

The results of Lambourne's findings are now employed by police forces and forensic institutions all over the world.

BELOW FINGERPRINTS CLEARLY REVEALED ON A NEOPRENE GLOVE BY THE USE OF MAGNETIC DUSTING. MANY BURGLARS WEAR GLOVES WHILE BREAKING INTO AND RANSACKING A HOME, THEN FOOLISHLY DISCARD THEIR GLOVES AT THE SCENE, UNAWARE THAT THEY HAVE LEFT THE INCRIMINATING EVIDENCE BEHIND.

FOOT AND TIRE PRINTS

Prints of the naked foot are as individual as fingerprints and may be of help in the identification of an unnamed corpse, but they are seldom found at the scene of a crime—at least in the developed world. There have, however, been cases in which a burglar has removed his shoes and socks—fitting the socks over his hands to avoid leaving fingerprints—and left clear prints of his feet to be identified!

Prints left by shoes and boots, on the other hand, are often found at a crime scene, and can

be matched in due course with a pair owned by a suspect. If they are impressed in mud, sand, or similar material (snow presents obvious technical difficulties, but even these can be overcome), a cast is made in plaster of paris or silicone rubber. Prints visible on a dusty floor are photographed. Sometimes, housebreakers may kick in a door, leaving a clear, dusty print on its surface, particularly if they are wearing rubber-soled footwear.

The work of the forensic investigator is frequently complicated by the fact that every person at the crime scene is likely to leave their own footprints, every one of which must be matched for elimination. Then comes the task of meticulously examining any unidentified print: first, for evidence of the manufacturer (which,

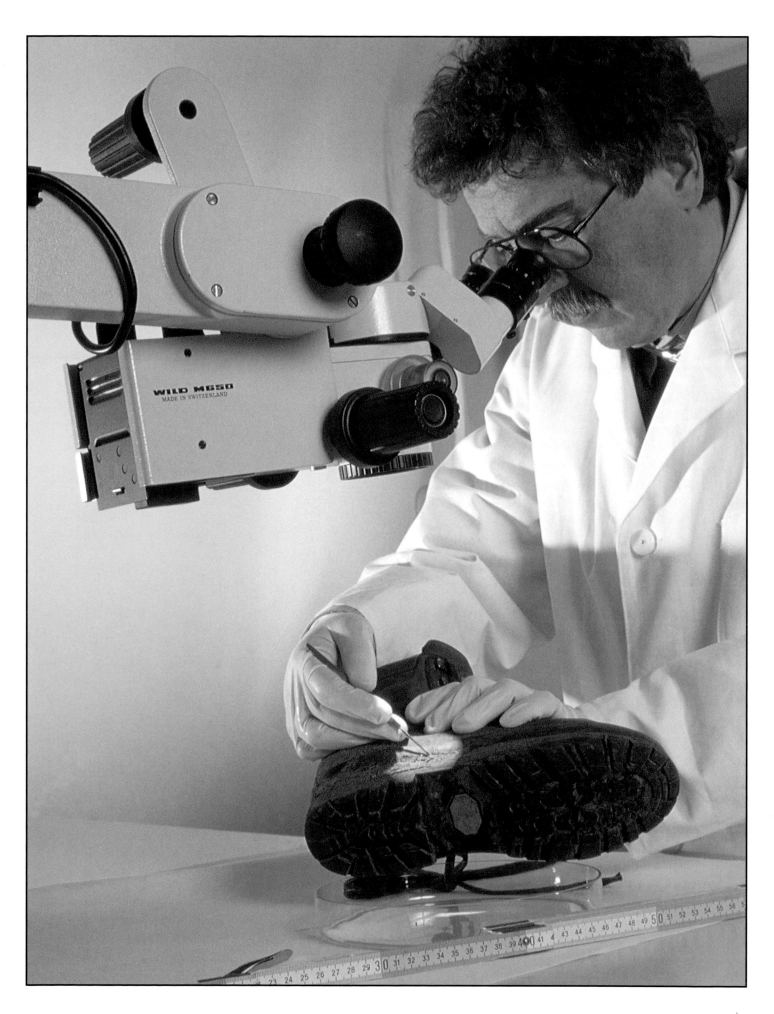

in the case of sneakers, may be relatively simple), then for specific signs of wear and damage. In some cases, the nature of the prints can even provide an indication of the way the criminal walks, as well as any deformities and injuries from which he or she suffers.

Prints of car tires or those of other vehicles can take several different forms. They may be direct impressions in earth, clay, mud, sand, snow, or other material at the crime scene, in which case casts are taken as with footprints. Alternatively, they may be transfer prints from a pool of blood, oil, or spilt paint, or from a patch of mud, and will be photographed.

In the case of hit-and-run incidents or traffic accidents, the prints may appear as clear, bruising impressions on the flesh of the victim. Tracks left at the scene by a moving vehicle or a bicycle will be clear enough only if the vehicle has moved in other than a straight line; otherwise, the print of the rear tire, or tires, will be superimposed onto the tracks of the front wheels.

If the tire has left transfer prints from a thick material, such as mud, examination at the scene can sometimes provide a measure of the depth of tread, but this evidence is difficult to preserve. However, impressions from which a cast can be made will give an accurate picture not only of the tread, but also of the degree of wear, and—if tracks of both front tires are found—of any imbalance in the loading of the vehicle. Uneven setting of the suspension can also be detected, as well as "scrub" due to improper alignment of the front wheels.

The tread is the principal factor in identifying the tire. Every manufacturing company has its own distinctive patterns, together with specific differences for cars, trucks, motorcycles, and bicycles. The forensic investigator can refer to his files and quickly identify the type and make of tire. Often, it is possible to narrow down the inquiry even further, as particular types of tires are fitted only to a specific range of vehicles.

ABOVE A WORKER AT THE FRENCH *INSTITUT DE RECHERCHE CRIMINELLE* COMPARES A PLASTER CAST OF A TIRE PRINT OBTAINED FROM A CRIME SCENE WITH INFORMATION PROVIDED BY A MANUFACTURER. THIS CAN LEAD NOT ONLY TO IDENTIFICATION OF THE MODEL OF THE CAR CONCERNED, BUT ALSO TO A PARTICULAR BATCH SUPPLIED TO A RELATIVELY SMALL NUMBER OF RETAIL OUTLETS.

CASE STUDY
THE UNUSUAL OVERSHOE

Beginning in 1945, a series of domestic break-ins occurred in New York State. In the first two cases, the thief left fingerprints, but no match could be found in the police files. In 1946, police discovered the print of an unusual overshoe in the yard of a burgled house, and made a cast. In August 1947, a sneaker print was found, and a few days later an identical print turned up, together with fingerprints that matched those discovered in 1945.

After a gas station was robbed in Seneca Falls, New York, in November 1947, a member of the public gave the police the license plate number of a car that had been parked nearby. The owner was traced; he admitted his involvement in the robbery, and also implicated his uncle. A search of the uncle's house uncovered both the overshoes and the sneakers, and his prints matched those already on record. Both men eventually confessed to more than fifty burglaries in the vicinity.

BLOOD AND OTHER BIOLOGICAL FLUIDS

Traces of blood at the scene of a crime usually can be seen as a sure indicator that violence has occurred, even if the body of a victim is not immediately discovered; moreover, the blood may be that of the perpetrator, accidentally injured by a knife, broken glass, or some other sharp object, or in the course of a struggle. It is obviously essential to identify the blood, in case it may provide a lead to the perpetrator.

Particularly indoors, the blood may be immediately obvious as pools of liquid, large dried stains, or spatters on the surroundings. Alternatively, there may be signs that an attacker has washed away all visible blood. In this case, the search for stains must therefore be directed to places that are out of sight, or which may have been neglected during the cleanup, such as drawer interiors and doorknobs, draperies, and upholstery. Sinks and drains, into which the attacker may have emptied pails, often yield traces. If a room's floor has been washed, blood could still be found in cracks between boards or tiles, or beneath the edges of a floor covering.

The first question to be answered on the spot is: "Is this blood?" Where only minute spots of blood are present, or if the perpetrator has attempted to clean up the scene, there are several chemical tests that will detect mammalian blood—but confirmation that this is

CASE STUDY
VIJAY COOPPEN

The body of Jini Cooppen was discovered in a yard in Brixton, south London, on March 31, 1990. She had been strangled, but there were no signs of a struggle at the scene, and it seemed probable that she had been murdered elsewhere and her body dumped where it was found. Particularly important, therefore, were the car tire marks visible nearby.

Investigation showed that the vehicle had a Dunlop tire on the front left-hand wheel and a Goodyear on the other front wheel. Suspicion fell on the victim's husband, Vijay Cooppen, whose Volvo had three Dunlop tires and one Goodyear, newly fitted on March 30. Comparison of the Volvo's two front tires showed an exact match with the tracks found at the scene, but this in itself was considered insufficient evidence for a trial. The police therefore set about tracing the batch of tires from which Cooppen's Goodyear had come.

The manufacturers reported that there were only twelve molds used to make this particular type and size of tire, with only two that could have produced the specific pattern of tread. Most of the tires from these molds had been exported to the Netherlands, and only a few went to British fitters. The possibility that another Volvo, with a Dunlop on its left-hand wheel and a new Goodyear of this type on the right, could have been in south London on the night in question was judged to be extremely unlikely. The case was finally closed when Cooppen's young son told police that his father had been away from home at the critical time.

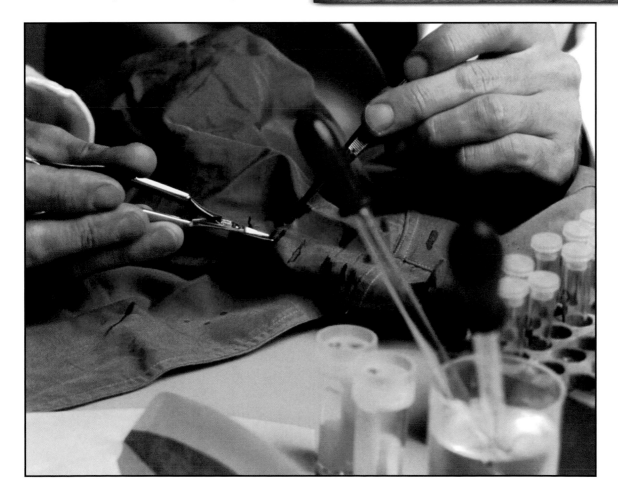

LEFT A FORENSIC EXAMINER, USING FORCEPS AND MINIATURE SCISSORS, TAKES THREADS FROM AN ITEM OF BLOODSTAINED CLOTHING. THE AREAS OF FABRIC THAT ARE STAINED WITH SPOTS OF BLOOD WILL ALSO BE CUT OUT FOR ANALYSIS IN THE SEROLOGICAL LABORATORY.

in fact human blood will have to await serum tests in the laboratory.

Samples for ABO blood group and related typing must be obtained and preserved as soon as possible because blood rapidly begins to deteriorate. Barry A.J. Fisher, director of the Scientific Services Bureau of Los Angeles County sheriff's department, underlines this fact: "It is a certainty that wet or damp bloodstains packaged in airtight containers, such as plastic bags, will be useless as evidence in a matter of days." Many legal systems require that evidence that could prove the innocence of a defendant should be made available to the defense for independent assessment; if sampled blood has deteriorated to a point at which it can no longer be typed, even a positive identification by the police forensic scientist may not be accepted by the court.

Blood that is still in liquid form is the best for laboratory analysis. If there are pools, the recommended procedure is to take about 2 ml (.00007 oz.) with a clean disposable pipette, then to place it in a test tube with an equal quantity of saline solution. Even if the investigator, or an accompanying forensic scientist, brings the necessary equipment to the crime scene, this sample must be in the laboratory within twenty-four hours. An alternative method is to take a sample with a piece of absorbent material, such as filter paper, a cotton-wool bud, or cotton

fabric. This is placed in a test tube or similar container—which must be left unstoppered so that the sample slowly dries in the air without deterioration.

Most blood found at crime scenes, however, has already dried. A relatively fresh stain will usually be of a reddish-brown color and is likely to be glossy on the surface—unlike stains caused by rust, tobacco, coffee, etc., which have often been at first mistaken for blood. The color and glossiness, however, will depend on the material on which it is found and how long it has been there. If it is flaky, it can be removed with a thin blade and scraped onto a clean piece of paper. Smears and spatters are collected on moistened cotton squares or filter paper, which are then transferred to unstoppered test tubes. For purposes of laboratory comparison, control specimens from unstained adjacent areas should also be taken.

Bloodstained objects that can be removed from the crime scene are sent to the laboratory as they are. As before, great care must be taken in their packaging, and items such as bloodstained clothing should, if possible, be allowed to dry in the air before being placed separately in wrapping paper or paper bags. If carpets and mattresses have been soaked in blood, it is usually sufficient to cut out a representative piece. Every item should, of course, be numbered and initialed.

During the 1970s in Oregon, an elderly widow, Ellen Anderson, was severely beaten about the head. Fortunately, she survived and was able to testify at trial. She named a young woman, Leslie Harley, who helped the widow with housework, ran errands for her, and acted as an unpaid companion, as her assailant. When Harley learned that she would not be adequately provided for in Mrs. Anderson's will, she seized a poker from the fireplace in the dining room and struck her; then, striking again and again, she pursued the widow into the living room, up the stairs, and into the bedroom. Blood spatter was found in all these places, including on the bedroom ceiling.

The defense claimed that Mrs. Anderson had fallen and struck her head on the fireplace. Harley said that she had then helped the widow to her bedroom, and had offered to telephone doctors from a list that was kept by the bed. She insisted that the blood on the ceiling came from the victim's shaking her head again and again as each doctor's name was suggested.

Dr. Herbert MacDonnell was retained by the prosecution. He realized that the bloodstains in the bedroom could not have been caused by Mrs. Anderson shaking her head—even if she had done so with such sufficient violence that the drops reached the ceiling, they would have been in a crisscross pattern. Those drops, he said, "radiated from the area directly above the pillow, with their angles of impact to the ceiling becoming more acute the farther they were away from the area above the pillow. The shift in angular impact was evident by the increasing length-to-width ratio of those bloodstains that were farthest from their convergence above the pillow."

To make his evidence clear to the trial jury, MacDonnell decided to provide a practical example on film. He found a longhaired young nurse to volunteer to play the part of the victim, and soaked her hair in fresh pig's blood. No matter how vigorously the nurse shook her head, no blood drops reached the ceiling. Then, still on film, MacDonnell dipped a short broom handle in blood and repeatedly struck a pillow on a table, resulting in patterns on the ceiling that were closely similar to those found in the widow's bedroom. Leslie Harley was found guilty.

Out of doors, the search for blood as evidence, as well as recovering the traces, is much more difficult. Pools of blood will have soaked into the dirt, and samples must be dug up. There may be splashes on surrounding trees or undergrowth, which have to be found, as the possibility that they have come from the assailant must always be considered. In all such cases the victim's bloodstained clothing will be analyzed, in order to distinguish their blood from any other traces found at the scene.

BLOOD PATTERNS

The pattern of spots of blood at the scene can often provide evidence of what occurred during the course of the crime. The first formal classification of blood traces was made some seventy years ago by the Scottish pathologist Professor John Glaister. He defined six basic types: drops, splashes, spurts, pools, trails, and smears, as follows.

Drops are found on horizontal surfaces and are effectively circular in shape, but modified according to the height from which they have fallen. From a height of up to some 20 in. (50 cm) they are almost round; from greater heights they begin to spray out around the edges, and individual fine drops may radiate even farther.

Splashes are due to blood flying through the air to hit a surface at an angle. This is most likely to occur when the victim is struck more than once with a moving weapon, but it may also be due to a longhaired victim swinging her blood-soaked head. The bloodstain is shaped like an exclamation mark, and the direction of its elongation indicates the way it has traveled through the air.

Spurts result from the continuing pumping of the heart while the victim is still alive. If a major blood vessel is severed, its pressurized spurt can travel a considerable distance, even as far as the walls and ceiling of a room, and frequently soaks the clothing of the assailant.

Pools form around the body of a badly bleeding victim. There may be more than one, indicating that he or she has attempted to move from one place to another, or has been dragged from another location.

Trails reveal that a bleeding body has been moved. If the body is dragged, the trail will be smeared; if it is carried, there will be a trail of blood drops.

These simple distinctions, based on observation, have remained the basis of crime scene interpretation, but in recent years much more detailed research has been carried out by practical work in forensic laboratories. In particular, the pattern of spatter—Glaister's "splashes"—has been studied experimentally.

Very soon after leaving their source, drops of blood take on a spherical shape, due to their surface tension. When they strike a surface, the traces they leave can depend not only on the nature of the surface—whether it is smooth or textured—but also on their speed, as well as

FACING PAGE MEDICAL STAFF ATTEND TO THE WOUNDED VICTIM OF A SHOOTING IN A PARIS STREET IN 1994. FORENSIC INVESTIGATORS WILL EXAMINE THE BLOOD PATTERNS LEFT ON THE STREET TO DETERMINE THE TYPE OF WEAPON USED AND THE LIKELY POSITION OF THE SHOOTER.

the direction in which they were moving. Low-velocity blood, such as that which has dripped or was moving at less than 6.5 ft. (2 m) per second, results in a spatter size greater than 0.1 in. (3 mm) in diameter. Medium-velocity blood, moving between 6.5 and 26 ft. (2 and 8 m) per second due to a beating or stabbing, generally forms smaller spatters, often not much more than 0.04 in. (1 mm) in diameter. Gunshots—particularly to the head—explosions, and severe mechanical accidents produce a mist of blood traveling at high velocity, and the spatters are less than 0.04 in. (1 mm) in diameter.

In cases of beatings with a blunt instrument, as Glaister has noted, blood will also be thrown from the weapon. The spatter traces are smaller than they would be from low-velocity drops—the greater the force used, the smaller the spatter. And, because the blood is being thrown, the spatter forms straight or slightly curved trails, and the spatter is relatively uniform in size. Depending on the angle at which they strike a surface, the drops will form the "exclamation mark" described by Glaister, although sometimes a smaller drop will detach itself and land ahead of the main drop, forming a "tadpole." Using photographs of the various blood trails, a computer program can indicate both the point from which the trails originated and that point's height above the ground.

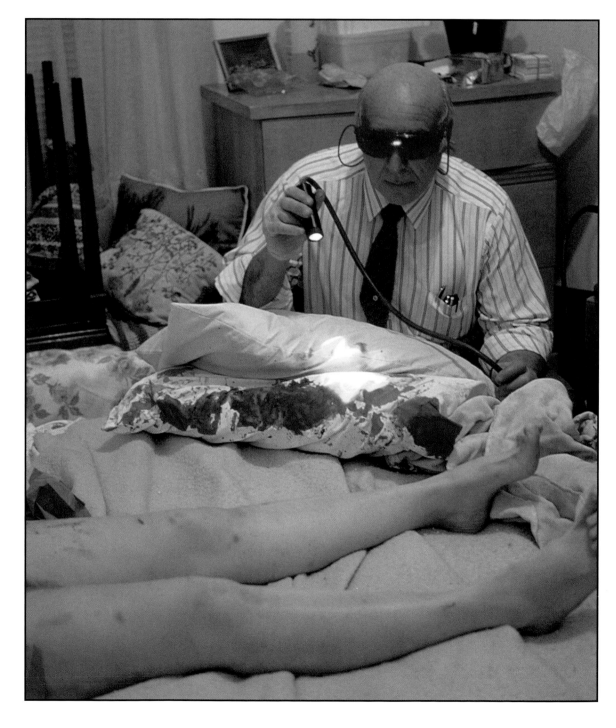

Right A forensic investigator at work at the scene of a rape-homicide in New York City. The bloodstains are evident, but he is using a laser-type light source to search for traces of semen, which will glow in the light after being sprayed with a marker chemical. They can then be analyzed to determine the blood type of the perpetrator.

One of America's most prominent forensic scientists, Dr. Herbert MacDonnell (the inventor of the Magna-Brush™ for fingerprints), set up the Institute on the Physical Significance of Human Bloodstain Evidence, in Corning, New York. He regularly takes a select class of law enforcement officers and demonstrates by practical example the many different types of bloodstains that may be found, and how they are produced.

Other body fluids that may be found at a crime scene include saliva, sweat, semen, and urine. (In some cases of psychopathic murders, feces may also be discovered.) A very important discovery about ABO typing was made in 1925: Some 80 percent of humans are "secretors"— their body fluids contain the same distinctive agglutinating substances as their blood does. Particularly in cases of rape, and also in some psychopathic killings, the determination of the perpetrator's blood type from such evidence can prove of great value. Apart from traces on the victim's body—saliva in a bite mark, for example— something like a discarded cigarette butt or a tissue can yield sufficient saliva or sweat for typing. Furthermore, DNA analysis is nowadays the most powerful identity indicator of all.

TRACE EVIDENCE

The case of Adrienne Piraino (see page 79) dramatically illuminates the importance of trace evidence, and the crime scene investigator and his or her search team must look for the tiniest particles: "foreign" soil and plant fragments; shards of glass and paint that may have resulted from impact with a car; scraps of paper, card, and fabric; hairs and fibers of all kinds. Similarly, in the case of a fire or an explosion, the fire officer will test the scene for traces of materials that may have been used as accelerants.

In the open, the search for traces is long and hard; indoors, the investigator may use a small, handheld type of vacuum cleaner to gather up dust and other evidence, which can be subsequently examined in detail.

Trace material cannot be submitted as evidence until it has been identified and shown to be connected with the crime. Forensic laboratories maintain constantly updated databanks of the physical characteristics and manufacturing processes of paint, glass, paper, fabrics, and other materials, together with actual samples that can be used for comparison. In the United States, for example, the National Automotive Paint File contains samples of many thousands of paint finishes. The majority of

these cases involve chips from car paintwork: Eight or more layers of finish are usually applied during manufacture, and examination under the microscope can often reveal the successive undercoats along the edge of the paint chip. The color and type of the various layers can frequently make it possible to identify a particular model of car, the plant from which it came, and even the period of time during which

CASE STUDY
HIT AND RUN

About 3 a.m. on February 22, 1987, a young girl was crossing a well-lit street in Tottenham, northeast London, when a rapidly moving car struck her, throwing her on to the windshield and then to the ground. The car then swerved to the other side of the street and drove off, leaving the girl dead.

An experienced accident investigator arrived two hours later, and he collected fragments of glass, a broken piece of black plastic that appeared to have come from a fog light, and a sliver of paint with a pale-green metallic topcoat. Witnesses were unable to provide a license plate number, and, while two people described a white Volkswagen Golf, another said that the car was a Ford Fiesta.

At the Metropolitan Police laboratory, Dr. Brian Gibbins began to assemble the fragments of glass; he found enough to determine that they came from a car's headlight cover and that the manufacturer's code markings were visible. Consulting his databank, Gibbins learned that the light had been made by the Carello company and had been fitted to Italian Fiat Uno cars sold in the United Kingdom since 1983. The black plastic bore the letters "oni," and it was identified by a Fiat concessionaire as part of a door-mounted mirror made by the Vitaloni company, and a standard fixture on the Fiat Uno.

Both the jacket and jeans of the victim were covered with glass particles. Those on the jeans had a refractive index identical to that of the headlight glass, while those on the jacket had a greenish tinge, and had obviously come from a broken windshield.

Examining the flake of paint, Gibbins found that the topcoat matched a color that Fiat called aquamarine, a pale metallic green. Its surface was in excellent condition, suggesting that it was recently applied, but a search of reports of stolen Fiats revealed nothing helpful.

The inquiry nevertheless was narrowed to northeast London and the surrounding suburbs, and the names and addresses of ninety-five registered owners of aquamarine Fiat Unos were obtained and given to local police forces. A call at the home of Robert Henry Dale established that his car was currently being repaired at a local garage. Just twelve days after the fatal incident, Gibbins was able to examine Dale's car. He found that the left-hand headlight was new, as was the windshield. The left-hand door mirror was missing, and a new unit was still in its box on the car seat. Another box contained the broken headlight, and seven pieces of glass that had been picked up from the roadway fitted exactly into the damaged remains.

it was painted, as well as the dealers to which it was delivered.

The investigation of small pieces of glass at a crime scene will usually follow one or both of two routes: (1) the identification of the type of glass, such as that from a car's headlight cover following a hit-and-run incident; and (2) the matching of fragments from, for example, a window (smashed during a break-in or by a gunshot) with traces that may be found on the clothing of a suspect.

The first step in identifying glass is to determine its refractive index; that is, to put it simply, the degree to which the glass will "bend" a ray of light passing through it. A vacuum—and, effectively, air—has a refractive index of 1; most glass has a refractive index between 1.5 and 1.7. This characteristic of glass can be measured in a sample particle no thicker than a hair. The specimen is placed on a slide on the stage of a microscope specially fitted with a heating element and is then covered with a drop of silicone oil (or one of a range of kerosene-related liquids known as Cargill fluids). Visual observation is often sufficient, but nowadays the microscope is usually also fitted with a video camera connected to a computer screen, so the image is further enlarged and the data can be stored for later evaluation.

The refractive index of any of these Cargill fluids, at room temperature, is considerably higher than that of any known type of glass, but it decreases steadily, and in a known relationship, as the temperature is raised. At first, the glass specimen is visible as a halo, known as the Becke line. At a critical temperature, when the refractive index of the glass is the same as that of the liquid, the Becke line vanishes.

Another determinable characteristic of glass is its physical density—or the weight in grams of one cubic centimeter. The glass does not have to be weighed; if it neither sinks nor floats but remains suspended in a liquid of known density, its density is the same as that of the liquid.

Glass can also be identified by spectroscopy—although this presents forensic problems because the evidence is destroyed in the process. The glass sample is burned using a carbon arc or laser beam, and each element in the glass contributes light of specific wavelengths to the flame. Analysis of these individual wavelengths identifies the elements present. This, although a destructive technique, is especially valuable in the analysis of colored glass.

Most recently, neutron activation—which does not destroy the sample—has been employed

CASE STUDY
STEPHEN BRADLEY

On July 7, 1960, eight-year-old Graeme Thorne was abducted on his way to school in a suburb of Sydney, Australia. Shortly afterward, a man with a marked foreign accent telephoned his parents, demanding Aus$25,000 (U.S.$17,000) for the boy's return unharmed. Although the police found some of the boy's belongings dumped in various distant parts of the city, there was no further development until his body was discovered on August 16, some 10 mi. (16 km) from his home.

Graeme had been asphyxiated and beaten to death, and his body was wrapped in a rug—with one tassel missing. His clothes bore traces of a crusty, pink material, and fungus had begun to grow on his shoes and socks. Examination of hairs found on the rug established that they were from three different people and a dog, which Dr. Cameron Cramp of the State Medical Office reported was probably a Pekinese. A botanist, Professor Neville White, calculated that the fungus (four different species) had been growing for some five weeks, which meant that Graeme had been killed soon after his abduction. And the pink substance was a type of mortar used as facing for houses.

A number of leaves, twigs, and seeds were found among the boy's clothes; they were identified, and one seed proved to be from a rare species of cypress that was not growing in the area where his body was discovered. The police broadcast an appeal

for anyone who knew of a pink-mortared house with this species of tree growing near it, and a mailman reported that he knew such a house.

The house was found to be deserted. The former occupant, Stephen Bradley—a Hungarian immigrant whose real name was Istvan Baranyay—had left with his family on the day of the kidnapping, and was now aboard a ship sailing for England, while neighbors confirmed that the family had owned a Pekinese dog. The family had also taken temporary accommodation in a nearby apartment. A search of this apartment produced a discarded roll of film, which, on development, revealed a photograph of Bradley and his family at a picnic, seated on the rug in which Graeme's body had been wrapped—and the missing tassel was also discovered.

Police inquiries established that Bradley had sold his car shortly before the ship sailed; it was found, and in the trunk were pink fragments that matched those on the house and on Graeme's body.

Learning that the ship was due to call at Colombo, Sri Lanka, detectives flew there, and arrested Bradley after the ship docked. He was found guilty at trial, and was sentenced to life imprisonment. The case is a shining example of the Locard principle that every contact leaves a trace.

in the analysis not only of glass, but also of tiny fragments of metal, paint, fibers, and other materials. Bombardment of the specimen with neutrons causes the individual elements to become radioactive and to emit gamma rays, each of which has a characteristic energy level, which can be measured. As many as seventy constituent elements can be identified in a speck of material no larger than a period (.).

The positive identification of tiny specks of glass can be very important in establishing that a suspect was present at a crime scene. When a criminal smashes a pane of glass in a window or door, as much as 30 percent of the fragments travel not in the direction of the blow but toward him, many lodging in his clothes. The same is true of glass shattered by gunshot. Tiny particles are likely to travel as far as 18 ft. (5.5 m) toward the person firing the gun. Even dry-cleaning will not remove the smallest fragments, which can still be detected by the forensic examiner.

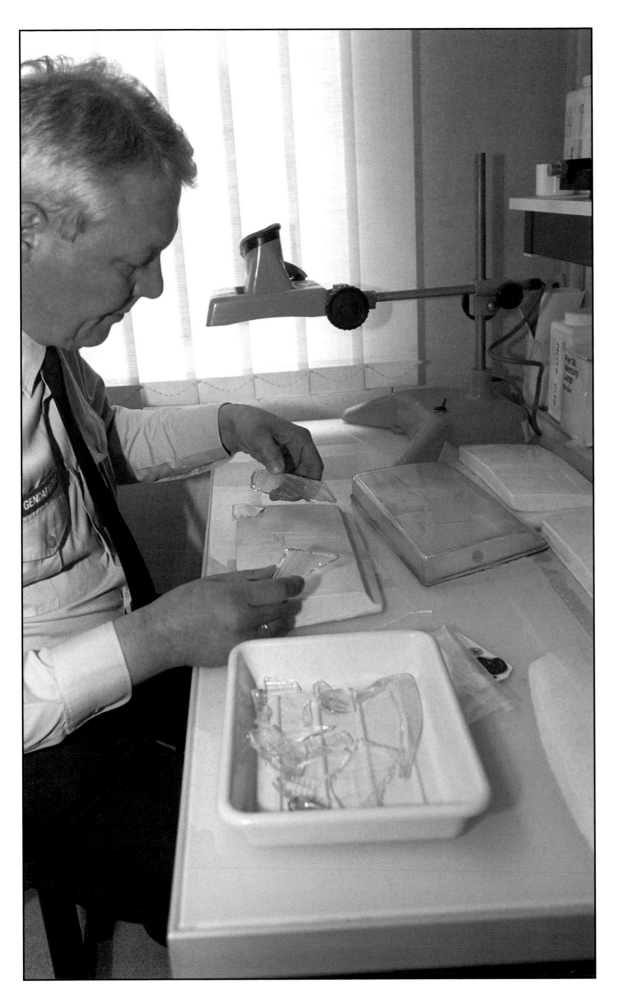

LEFT A FRENCH POLICEMAN
METICULOUSLY FITS TOGETHER
FRAGMENTS OF GLASS FROM
A CAR INCIDENT. IF THE
FRAGMENTS ARE FROM
A HEADLIGHT COVER, THE
COMPLETED ASSEMBLY
FREQUENTLY REVEALS THE
NAME OF THE COMPANY
THAT MANUFACTURED IT,
LEADING TO IDENTIFICATION
OF THE MAKE AND MODEL OF
THE VEHICLE INVOLVED.

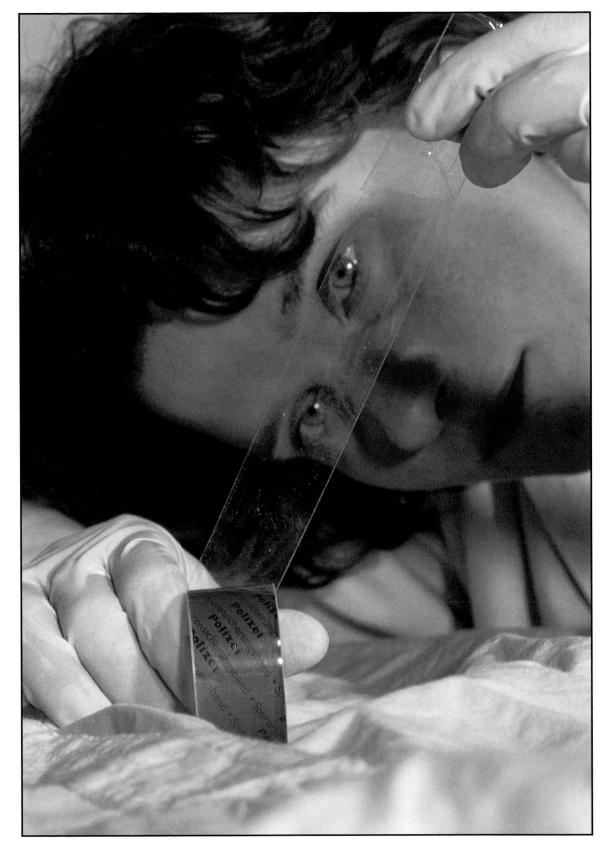

FACING PAGE THE SAMPLE TRAY OF THE LATEST TYPE OF MASS SPECTROMETER. THE SURFACE OF THE SAMPLE IS BOMBARDED WITH IONS: AT LOW INTENSITY, ONLY THE SMALLER MOLECULES ARE IONIZED, LEAVING THE LARGE MOLECULES, SUCH AS PLASTIC POLYMERS, UNAFFECTED. THE RELEASED IONS ARE THEN ACCELERATED TOWARD A DETECTOR; THE TIME THEY TAKE TO REACH THE DETECTOR IS A MEASURE OF THEIR MASS. THIS PROVIDES AN ACCURATE ANALYSIS OF THE CHEMICAL COMPOSITION OF THE SURFACE OF THE SAMPLE.

LEFT HAIRS AND FOREIGN FIBERS CAN BE LIFTED FROM THE SURFACE OF CLOTHING AND OTHER FABRICS BY THE USE OF STICKY TAPE. EACH CAN THEN BE INDIVIDUALLY MOUNTED ON GLASS SLIDES FOR EXAMINATION AND IDENTIFICATION UNDER THE MICROSCOPE, BEFORE BEING SUBMITTED, IF NECESSARY, TO FURTHER ANALYSIS.

In cases such as hit-and-run incidents, larger pieces of glass, usually from headlight covers, are likely to be found. These must be painstakingly reassembled, with the intention that their shape, and therefore the make of car from which they came, be ascertained. Although it appears solid, glass is in fact a supercooled liquid, held between two highly stressed "skins." When the glass fragments are examined under the microscope, they can be seen to have scooped-out (conchoidal) fractures on the side opposite to that on which the breaking force was exerted. This can be of great assistance in fitting the broken flakes together.

FACING PAGE A FORENSIC EXAMINER AT THE SCENE OF AN APARTMENT FIRE. ALTHOUGH CARBONIZED, CORPSES ARE NEVER FULLY CONSUMED IN FIRES OF THIS KIND, AND IT IS POSSIBLE TO DETERMINE WHETHER OR NOT THE VICTIM WAS DEAD BEFORE THE FIRE STARTED. THE EXAMINER WILL COLLECT SAMPLES OF ALL SURROUNDING MATERIAL, PARTICULARLY TO DISCOVER WHETHER THE FIRE WAS ACCIDENTAL OR DELIBERATELY STARTED WITH THE USE OF ACCELERANTS.

BELOW THE SCENE OF THE TERRORIST BOMBING OF THE SARI NIGHTCLUB AT KUTA BEACH, ON THE INDONESIAN ISLAND OF BALI, IN OCTOBER 2002. THE EXPLOSION SET OFF AN INTENSE FIRE, WHICH QUICKLY SPREAD TO A NEIGHBORING NIGHTCLUB. SOME 180 PEOPLE, MANY OF THEM AUSTRALIANS, WERE KILLED, AND 274 WERE INJURED.

FIRE AND EXPLOSION

The investigation of scenes of fires or explosions, whether or not fatalities have occurred, is somewhat different from normal crime scene investigation because much of the trace evidence will have been destroyed. Specialist experts are needed, particularly to determine whether the event was accidental or criminal.

Arson is the deliberate setting of fire to another person's—or one's own—property. In principle, there are three possible motives: insurance fraud, revenge, or the concealment of another crime, such as embezzlement, theft, or murder. The possibility of suicide must also be considered when a body is found at the scene.

The first essential for the fire investigation team is to secure the site, making sure that the building—usually a home, apartment block, office, or factory—will not collapse further. This, unfortunately, may mean that some important clues will be destroyed or obscured.

Once the site is declared relatively safe, the next step is to discover the "seat" of the fire—its point of origin. Flames burn away from where they begin, usually upward, and the seat of the fire is generally found at the lowest point. In addition, wood floors and beams are likely to carbonize in a checkerboard pattern, and the checks are found to be smaller nearest the seat of the fire. It is equally important to determine whether there is more than one seat—a sure indication that the fire was started deliberately.

Around the seat of the fire, the debris must be sifted for any trace of a timing device. A heavy concentration of debris and ash can reveal where flammable material, such as paper and card, had been piled together before the fire was started.

Accelerants—gasoline, kerosene, or other flammable liquids—may have been used to start the fire. Traces of liquid will be absorbed into charred wood or will seep into cracks in the flooring, where they fail to burn away completely because of the lack of oxygen. Often, the arsonist will leave a trail of accelerant, or even paper or fabric, in order to give himself time to escape before the fire takes hold.

(leucocytes) migrate to the injury; they produce a characteristic inflammation—hyperemia—and blistering, and these blisters can be tested in the laboratory for a positive protein reaction. Burns sustained after death are generally hard and yellow in color, with little blistering, and any liquid present will not give a protein reaction.

Fire may follow an explosion, or the explosion may follow from the fire; there are also many cases in which the explosion is the result of an accident or criminal action, and is not accompanied by fire. Whatever the circumstances, the result is that the debris will be scattered over a wide area—and any evidential traces with it.

As with a fire, the first task (after the site has been made safe) is to establish the center of the explosion by examining the way its shock wave had traveled outward. Lengthy metal objects, such as piping, railings, window frames, and even long nails or bolts, will be bent away from the origin of the blast. Sheet metal (doors, domestic equipment, empty containers) will be "dished" inward. At explosives research labs, similar objects can be tested to determine how much pressure produced the damage, providing some indication of the type of explosive employed, as well as its quantity.

Explosions can be caused by the accidental ignition of escaping domestic gas or of leaking flammable liquids. In criminal events, however, the explosive needs a detonator of some kind, and the search for its fragments (wires, crimping caps, timing devices) is of the greatest importance. Every forensic explosives laboratory holds a collection of commercial products, and it is frequently possible to identify the manufacturer, and even the source, of the explosive and the detonator. The clothing of any dead bodies or injured persons must also be examined for fragments and chemical traces of the explosive.

Nearly all explosives leave some solid residue, so the entire debris-covered area must be explored and any suspicious surfaces swabbed with solvent to obtain minute traces for analysis. Snifters should also be used, to detect traces of vaporized material. When suspects are detained, their hands, clothing, and personal possessions must be examined in a similar way. The hands are particularly important, because even if gloves had been used in handling the explosive, traces are likely to penetrate through to the skin.

In a hugely destructive explosion, victims' bodies are likely to be dismembered. The sorting of the remains, and the identification of the individual victims, requires the skills of the forensic anthropologist.

When gasoline or kerosene has been used, an experienced fire officer can often detect a residual scent. This, however, is not possible if alcohols or odorless liquids, such as paint thinners, have been employed as accelerants. In any event, it is preferable to use a portable instrument popularly known as a snifter. Originally developed to detect flammable gases in industrial plants, this instrument is capable of registering volatile residues as low as ten parts per million. Other equipment is used to take air samples, which then can be analyzed in a crime laboratory using gas chromatography.

When a body is located among the debris of a fire, it is frequently found with the fists clenched and the arms raised in front of the body, and with the knees drawn up. Intense heat has caused the muscles to contract and stiffen, to produce what is known as the pugilist posture. Even a fierce and continuous fire, however, is unlikely to consume the body, despite the intention of a murderer to conceal all traces of his crime. In a crematorium, for example, the furnace will attain temperatures as high as 2,732°F (1,500°C)—far higher than that of the typical fire—and even so reduction of the body to ashes will take two to three hours.

It is also possible to discover whether injuries from a fire were sustained before death, despite extensive burns to the body. When a living person is burned, the white blood cells

THE LOCKERBIE DISASTER

On December 21, 1988, PanAm Flight 103A, a 747 en route from London's Heathrow Airport to New York, exploded high in the sky over the town of Lockerbie in Scotland. Much of the wreckage fell on the town: One engine created a crater 15 ft. (4.5 m) deep in the middle of a street; one wing demolished two houses and threw up 1,524 tons (1,500 tonnes) of earth and rock; and the fuel tanks, still filled with 200,000 lbs. (91,000 kg) of gasoline, erupted in a huge fireball. Upper winds at the time were blowing eastward at 115 knots, and smaller debris was found scattered over an area of 845 square miles (1,200 square kilometers) in southern Scotland. All 259 persons aboard the aircraft perished; eleven inhabitants of Lockerbie were also killed, and a further five were injured. As in the aircraft disaster at O'Hare airport,

ABOVE SOME OF THE DEBRIS THAT FELL ON THE TOWN OF LOCKERBIE ON DECEMBER 21, 1988. EVERY SCRAP OF EVIDENCE HAD TO BE COLLECTED BY ACCIDENT EXAMINERS OVER A HUGE AREA OF SOUTHERN SCOTLAND. SOME PIECES, CARRIED BY A STRONG WESTERLY WIND, WERE FOUND AS MUCH AS 45 MILES (70 KM) AWAY FROM THE SCENE OF THE DISASTER.

investigators were faced with the daunting task of confirming the identity of those who had died; a matter of equal concern was the cause of the explosion. Some 4 million pieces of debris were gradually recovered and were then painstakingly laid out at the Army Central Ammunition Depot, located 20 mi. (12 km) from Lockerbie. Piecing them together revealed that the explosion had occurred in the forward cargo bay, on the lower left side of the fuselage. Further examination showed that two adjacent containers, one of metal and one of fiberglass, were damaged most by the explosion, and that it had occurred in the metal container. Trapped in its metal skin, a tiny piece of printed-circuit board was found by an accidents inspector; this

was eventually identified as part of a Toshiba Model 8016 radio-cassette player, which, it was calculated, had been packed with between 12 and 14 oz. (340 and 397 g) of Semtex explosive.

Further investigation was carried out by scientists at the Royal Armament Research & Development Establishment (RARDE) at Fort Halsted in Kent, England. Weeks of probing through the debris revealed additional fragments of the Toshiba player, and final confirmation came when a partially burned Toshiba manual, in English and Arabic, was found. Other evidence indicated that the bomb had been packed inside a brown Samsonite suitcase.

Detailed examination of the check-in manifest and interviews with airport employees suggested that the suitcase had not originated at Heathrow, but had been loaded off a connecting flight from Frankfurt, and had probably arrived there aboard Air Malta Flight KM180 from Valletta. After many weeks, the RARDE scientists announced that they were able to identify many of the pieces of clothing that had been packed in the suitcase, particularly pieces of a blue Babygro romper suit, labeled "Malta Trading Company," and a pair of patterned trousers.

In September 1989, Detective Chief Inspector Harry Bell of the Scottish police flew

BELOW THE FORWARD SECTION OF THE PANAM BOEING 747 "CLIPPER MAID OF THE SEAS," WHICH FELL—FORTUNATELY— IN OPEN COUNTRYSIDE, CLOSE TO A FARMHOUSE ON THE OUTSKIRTS OF LOCKERBIE. THE EXPLOSION HAD OCCURRED IN THE FORWARD CARGO BAY, AFT OF THE FLIGHT DECK.

FACING PAGE THE REMAINS OF THE METAL LUGGAGE CONTAINER, PARTIALLY REASSEMBLED IN A SUPPORTING FRAME, IN WHICH THE BOMB EXPLODED ABOARD PANAM FLIGHT 103A. EXAMINERS WERE ABLE TO DISCOVER FRAGMENTS OF A BROWN SAMSONITE SUITCASE THAT HAD CONTAINED THE BOMB.

BELOW THE TWO LIBYANS—KHALIFA FHIMAH (LEFT) AND ABDEL BASSET ALI AL-MEGRAHI (RIGHT)—WHO WERE ACCUSED OF PLACING THE BOMB ABOARD THE PANAM AIRCRAFT. ALTHOUGH AL-MEGRAHI WAS FOUND GUILTY, DOUBTS HAVE SINCE BEEN RAISED ABOUT HIS RESPONSIBILITY FOR THE BOMBING, AND APPEALS HAVE BEEN LODGED AGAINST HIS CONVICTION.

to Malta. The director of the Malta Trading Company confirmed the manufacture of the romper suit and patterned trousers, and his records showed that they had been sold to retailer Tony Gauci. Remarkably, Gauci remembered the man who had bought the trousers, together with a large amount of other clothing, about a month before the bombing. His sales record matched the items identified at RARDE—including the Babygro romper. Gauci described the purchaser as probably Libyan, aged about fifty, and clean-shaven and well-dressed. It had been raining at the time, and the man had also bought an umbrella.

The remains of five umbrellas had been recovered from the debris, with one showing signs of explosive damage. At RARDE, fibers from the Babygro were found embedded in the umbrella's fabric, implying that it had been in the same case that had contained the bomb. Meanwhile, U.S. investigators had found another fragment of circuit board. This was identified as part of an electronic digital timer manufactured by Meister & Bollier in Zurich. Only twenty of the devices had been made, for a special order from the Libyan government, in 1985. Ten had been seized from two Libyans in Senegal in February 1988; another was recovered from the wreckage of a French UTA DC-10 that had exploded over Niger in September 1989. The finger of suspicion pointed firmly at Libya as the instigator of the Lockerbie incident.

In November 1991, U.S. and Scottish authorities named two Libyans as responsible for the bombing: Khalifa Fhimah, an Arab Airlines representative in Malta, and Abdel Basset Ali Al-Megrahi, an intelligence agent. The two men were eventually surrendered to the Netherlands in 1999, on the condition that their trial would not take place in the United States or United Kingdom. In order that the two could be prosecuted, Camp Zeist, a former U.S. camp in the Netherlands, was designated Scottish territory for the purposes of the trial, which opened in May 2000. On January 31, 2001, Al-Megrahi was found guilty, but Fhimah was acquitted. In August 2003, the Libyan leader, Colonel Mu'ammar Gadhafi, announced that U.S. $2.7 billion (£1.67 billion) would be paid in compensation to the relatives of victims of the Lockerbie disaster.

PART 2

THE VICTIM'S REMAINS

Officer John Burton was standing by the burial site near the tree, scanning the surrounding area and muttering into his handheld tape recorder. Deputy Coroner Dr. Alvin Hackenbacker stood impatiently beside him, awaiting CSI officer Tamara Gregory's arrival, while the search team formed a respectful circle at a distance. Arriving on the scene, Gregory recorded all their names, particularly noting those who had found the bones, and then dismissed them. Deputies O'Malley and Rodriguez fetched shovels, and under the eye of the video camera they slowly and carefully began to dig the earth—samples of which were also put into evidence bags—to uncover what lay below.

Within minutes they had revealed a rolled carpet, from which the single bone protruded. Anatomist Ivan Vrba moved forward and watched as the carpet was gently drawn apart. Inside was a nearly complete skeleton, missing only one leg and both feet. There was, however, no trace of clothing.

Hackenbacker coughed gently. "I declare this an unnatural death, almost certainly homicide," he said. He glanced at Dr. Jane Kurosawa, who nodded in agreement.

While he oversaw the taking of photographs, Ivan Vrba also made his own sketches of the skeletal remains, numbering each piece. The bones and skull were then gathered up as Gregory turned her attention to the carpet. Calling Burton over as a supporting witness, she used forceps to pick up a number of hairs adhering to the pile, half a dozen unusual-looking plant seeds, and finally some empty insect pupal cases. These were put into individual plastic boxes, labeled, dated, and initialed. "Extensive dark stains as well," she announced. "Could be blood. We'd better send the whole carpet to the technicians." She glanced over at the sightseers. "And we should keep the scene sealed, right, Sheriff? At least until the lab results come in."

Back at the morgue, Vrba laid out the victim's skeleton on a measuring board. Gregory, Kurosawa, and Verdian gathered round. Within a few minutes, Vrba and Kurosawa had agreed that the pelvis and skull clearly indicated that the victim was female, between 5 feet, 3 inches and 5 feet, 7 inches (1.6–1.7 m) in height. Sutures on the skull that were only partially closed suggested that the victim was somewhere between twenty and thirty years old. And adhering to the skull were two or three remaining strands of long, black hair. Vrba also pointed out faint scarring to the inside of the pelvis, suggesting that the victim had borne a child.

The stage of fusion of the epiphyses supported the estimate of the age, and faint signs of the development of arthritis were visible. "Now, this is very interesting," said Dr. Kurosawa, as she pointed to the leg bones. "Typical, I would say, of a hit-and-run injury—except that, in this case, the driver of the vehicle didn't run. Look here—a compound fracture of both tibia and fibula in the left leg, characteristic of the victim's being struck by one of the car's fenders. There is also this hairline fracture of the pelvis, no doubt due to the headlight or hood. The force of impact was considerable; the victim was flung onto the hood, and her head possibly struck the frame of the windshield before she was thrown clear into the road. Either of those events could account for this impression in the skull."

"And that was how she died?" asked Verdian.

Kurosawa sighed, looking grave. "Probably not at that time," she said.

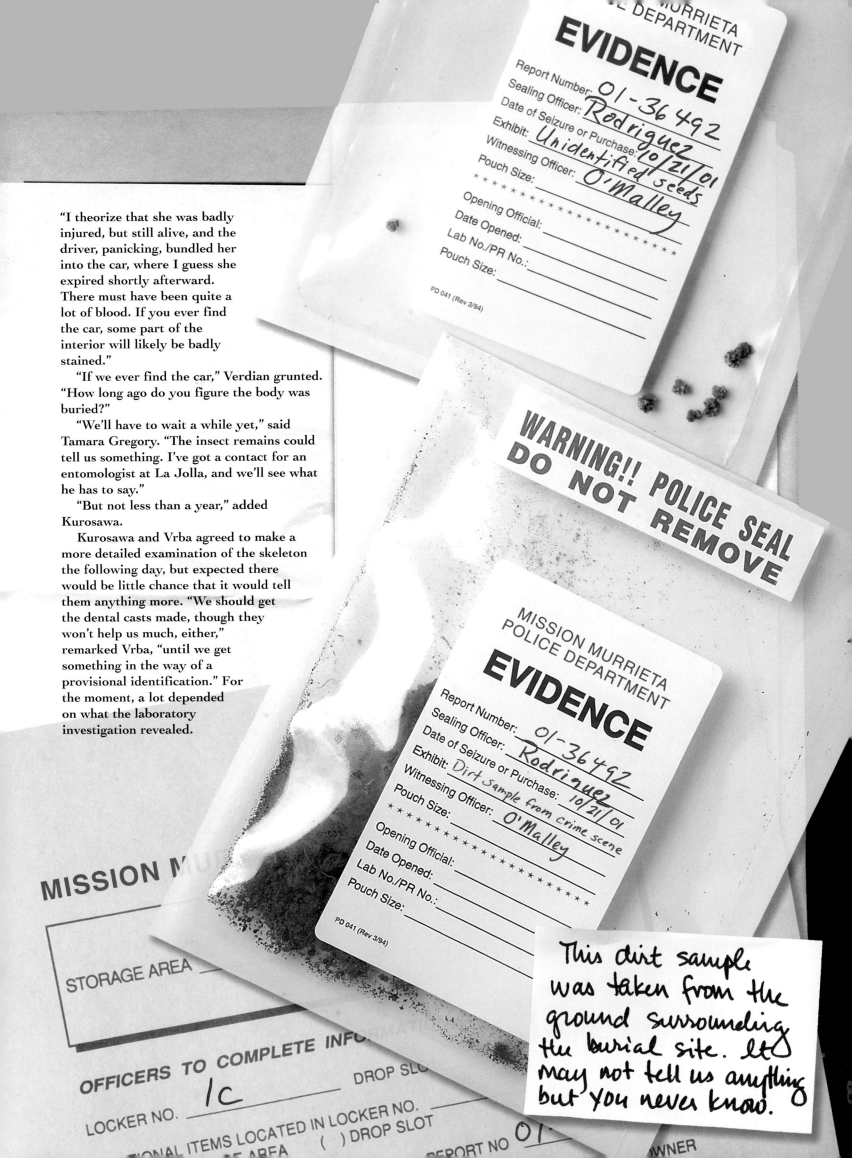

"I theorize that she was badly injured, but still alive, and the driver, panicking, bundled her into the car, where I guess she expired shortly afterward. There must have been quite a lot of blood. If you ever find the car, some part of the interior will likely be badly stained."

"If we ever find the car," Verdian grunted. "How long ago do you figure the body was buried?"

"We'll have to wait a while yet," said Tamara Gregory. "The insect remains could tell us something. I've got a contact for an entomologist at La Jolla, and we'll see what he has to say."

"But not less than a year," added Kurosawa.

Kurosawa and Vrba agreed to make a more detailed examination of the skeleton the following day, but expected there would be little chance that it would tell them anything more. "We should get the dental casts made, though they won't help us much, either," remarked Vrba, "until we get something in the way of a provisional identification." For the moment, a lot depended on what the laboratory investigation revealed.

MISSION MURRIETA POLICE DEPARTMENT

EVIDENCE

Report Number: 01-36492
Sealing Officer: Rodriguez
Date of Seizure or Purchase: 10/21/01
Exhibit: Unidentified seeds
Witnessing Officer: O'Malley
Pouch Size:
* * * * * * * * * * * * * * * * * *
Opening Official:
Date Opened:
Lab No./PR No.:
Pouch Size:

PD 041 (Rev 3/94)

WARNING!! POLICE SEAL DO NOT REMOVE

MISSION MURRIETA POLICE DEPARTMENT

EVIDENCE

Report Number: 01-36492
Sealing Officer: Rodriguez
Date of Seizure or Purchase: 10/21/01
Exhibit: Dirt sample from crime scene
Witnessing Officer: O'Malley
Pouch Size:
* * * * * * * * * * * * * * * * * *
Opening Official:
Date Opened:
Lab No./PR No.:
Pouch Size:

PD 041 (Rev 3/94)

This dirt sample was taken from the ground surrounding the burial site. It may not tell us anything but you never know.

MISSION MUR

STORAGE AREA

OFFICERS TO COMPLETE INFO
LOCKER NO. 1c   DROP SLO
...ONAL ITEMS LOCATED IN LOCKER NO.
( ) DROP SLOT
...REPORT NO 01   WNER

TIME OF DEATH

Estimating the time at which a person died can be of the utmost importance, even if there is no question of a crime having been committed. In the case of an unidentified body, a measure of the time at which death probably occurred can prove of great help in identification. This will be of particular value if it can later be related to what witnesses may have to say about the possible earlier movements of the as-yet-unidentified deceased. In addition, there may well be questions of inheritance if another heir has died at about the same time—possibly even within hours or minutes—as well as problems with life-insurance claims. And, when the death is a homicide, establishing the time frame is vital in eliminating possible suspects from the inquiry.

> *"There will be time to murder and create,*
> *And time for all the works and days of hands ..."*
> —T.S. Eliot,
> *The Love Song of J. Alfred Prufrock*

THE BODY TEMPERATURE

The corpse may be newly dead; it may have lain in the open air or in water for several days, or be wholly or partially buried; it may be in an advanced stage of decomposition; it is possible that it has become mummified; or it may have been reduced to skeletal remains. Many different techniques have been proposed to determine how much time has elapsed since death occurred. Most are only approximate, but others have proven remarkably effective.

All readers of classic crime fiction are familiar with the time-honored estimation of the time of death of a fresh corpse: The medical examiner takes the temperature of the body, and announces confidently: "Death took place between 6:30 and 8 p.m. yesterday evening. I can give you a more accurate time after the autopsy." Unfortunately, despite extensive research over nearly two centuries, this is indeed only fiction. It is impossible to determine time of death with anything like such accuracy. As the eminent English pathologist Francis Camps frequently remarked, "The only way to tell the time of death is to be there when it happens." Very occasionally, it must be said, it is possible—though this is still truer in fiction than it is in real life—to postulate a nearly exact time of death if, for example, a clock has been stopped by a stray bullet, or the victim's wristwatch has been shattered.

It is true that the body after death gradually loses its natural temperature of 98.6°F (37°C), but circumstances can radically affect the rate at which this occurs. In temperate regions, a clothed body of average build shows a fall in temperature of about 3.24°F (1.8°C) over the first six to eight hours, but after this the rate of cooling steadily decreases. Unclothed bodies cool more rapidly, while fat bodies cool more slowly. Children, whose skin area is greater in relation to their body mass than adults', generally lose heat more rapidly. The rate of temperature loss is also related to ambient temperature: Bodies in the tropics, or lying near a fire, may actually become warmer after death.

Many other factors can complicate matters. If the person has died from hypothermia, for example, their temperature at death will be below 98.6°F (37°C); someone who dies from a brain hemorrhage or sepsis following abortion, or even asphyxia, will likely have a higher than normal temperature. Violent physical activity—perhaps due to a struggle with the assailant—can also raise the body temperature before death. The position in which the corpse is lying; dehydration or edema; wet clothing; air movement and humidity—all these can affect the rate of heat loss. And, finally, the activities of bacteria, which begin the process of decomposition almost immediately after death occurs, or a mass of maggots feeding on the remains, can generate heat.

In the past, it was customary for the medical examiner to take the corpse's temperature on the spot, using a thermometer placed in the rectum.

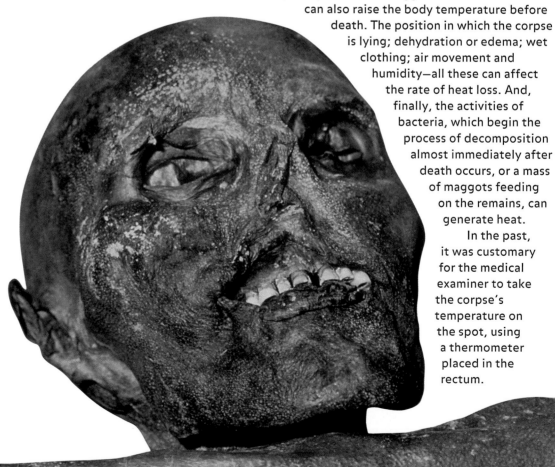

RIGHT A DEAD BODY, IN THE RIGHT CONDITIONS, WILL NOT UNDERGO DECOMPOSITION. IN AN EXTREMELY DRY SITUATION, FOR EXAMPLE, THE TISSUES WILL NOT DECAY, AND THE BODY BECOMES MUMMIFIED. FREEZING COLD CAN LIKEWISE RESULT IN MUMMIFICATION. THIS BODY OF A PREHISTORIC HUNTER, WHO HAD APPARENTLY FALLEN INTO A CREVASSE IN A GLACIER SEVERAL THOUSAND YEARS AGO, WAS DISCOVERED IN 1990 IN THE AUSTRIAN TYROL. THE PHYSICAL CONDITION OF A MUMMIFIED BODY MAKES IT IMPOSSIBLE, OF COURSE, TO DETERMINE THE TIME OF DEATH; ONLY ASSOCIATED MATERIALS CAN PROVIDE A CLUE.

ABOVE FORENSIC EXPERTS FROM THE *INSTITUT DE RECHERCHE CRIMINELLE* IN PARIS, EXAMINING A CADAVER DISCOVERED IN A FORESTED AREA. THE BODY SHOULD BE PHOTOGRAPHED *IN SITU* BEFORE IT IS TOUCHED, AND REMOVED TO THE MORGUE FOR DETAILED EXAMINATION.

This is not recommended modern practice, however, as it may well interfere with other forensic evidence—particularly in cases that include rape—and body temperature measurement is best left to the autopsy room. Nevertheless, the crime scene investigator will generally record the atmospheric temperature at the time the body is found, as an aid to the pathologist.

At present, the favored calculation is that of two German researchers, Claus Henssge and Burkhard Madea, who have developed a computer program along with a complicated chart on which rectal temperature, ambient temperature, and body weight are plotted, together with modifications for clothing, wetness, and air or water movement. The greatest accuracy for time of death that this method can claim, however, is within a time bracket of something over five hours. But this is only 95 percent indicative, and the remaining 5 percent of cases fall outside these limits.

French pathologists favor taking the temperature within the ear canal, but, while this may give a more accurate reading, it in no way allows for all the variables that have been described above. In a different approach to the problem some researchers, particularly those in Germany, have examined the way muscles can be made

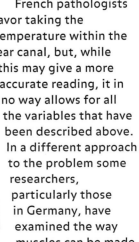

LEFT DR. FRANCIS CAMPS, PROFESSOR OF FORENSIC MEDICINE AT THE UNIVERSITY OF LONDON, WAS AMONG THE LEADING CRIMINAL PATHOLOGISTS IN BRITAIN FROM THE 1940S TO THE 1970S. HE WAS FREQUENTLY IN CONFLICT WITH FELLOW PATHOLOGISTS—NOTABLY SIR BERNARD SPILSBURY— OVER THE ESTIMATION OF TIME OF DEATH.

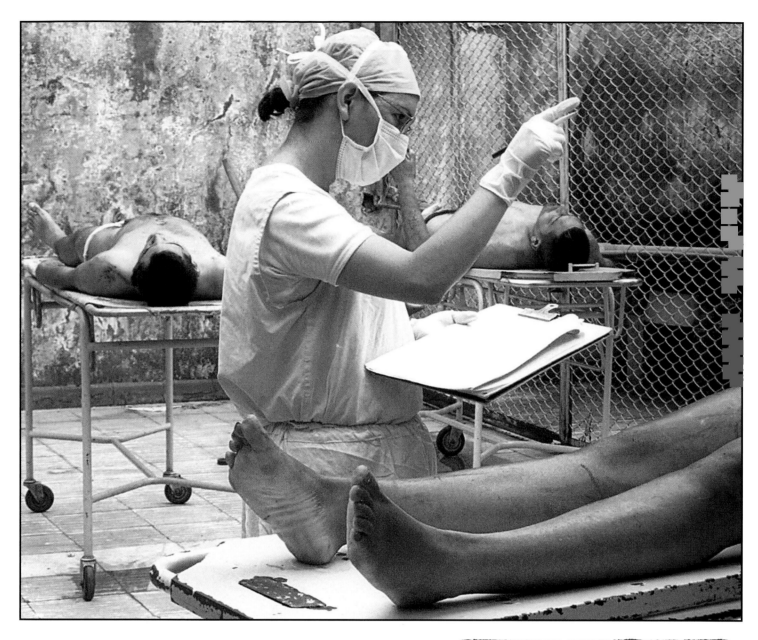

ABOVE BEFORE INTERNAL EXAMINATION OF A CORPSE, ALL RELEVANT EXTERNAL FEATURES—IN PARTICULAR WOUNDS, BUT ALSO ANY PHYSICAL PECULIARITIES THAT MAY BE OF ASSISTANCE IN IDENTIFICATION—MUST BE CAREFULLY RECORDED BY THE EXAMINER. THESE BODIES WERE AMONG THOSE KILLED IN A GANGLAND-STYLE SHOOTING IN A BAR IN SOUTHERN COLOMBIA ON NOVEMBER 24, 2000. THE BODY IN THE BACKGROUND (RIGHT) REVEALS RIGOR MORTIS PERSISTING IN THE LEFT ARM.

to contract by electrical stimulation for several hours after death. The iris of the eye will also contract or expand under the influence of various drugs—but all such reactions are equally affected by environmental and climatic variations.

At autopsy, samples will be taken of several body fluids, including the blood, urine, and cerebro-spinal fluid. It was hoped that a biochemical assay of changes in the cerebro-spinal fluid could provide a more accurate measure of the time elapsed since death, but these, like the body temperature, are subject to many external variables. Another experimental technique is based on an apparent increase in the concentration of potassium in the vitreous humor of the eye, which rises fairly steadily over four or five days. Because the initial potassium content of a dead person's eye can be only approximated, however, this method is little more reliable than any other.

RIGOR MORTIS

The facial muscles of a dead body usually begin to stiffen, due to chemical changes, within one to four hours of death, the limbs in four to six hours. After some twelve hours the whole body is rigid; it then gradually relaxes as tissue decomposition sets in. The onset and progress of this condition (rigor mortis), however, is as dependent as any other is on temperature. In fact, two bodies of persons who died or were killed at the same time in the same environment can show significant differences in their stage of rigor.

Electrocution may result in an unusually rapid onset of rigor, and there is also the condition known as cadaveric spasm. Although many pathologists believe reports of its occurrence to be nothing but myth, it has been claimed that, in circumstances of extreme

IS THIS DEATH?

One of the responsibilities of a certifying physician or medical examiner is to confirm that death has occurred. Medical history provides many cases in which a declared corpse has shown signs of life in the morgue, or even on the autopsy table. Moreover, poisoning (usually by drug overdose) or electrocution can result in a condition of "suspended animation," in which there is no discernible heartbeat or respiration. Even the electrical activity of the brain may be undetectable, yet the victim can be revived successfully in an intensive care unit.

A typical case is that of a young woman of twenty-three who was found, apparently dead, on a beach near Liverpool, England, in October 1969. A local doctor, after examining the body for a quarter of an hour, pronounced her dead, and this diagnosis was confirmed by the police pathologist, who arrived soon afterward. The body was removed to the morgue, and, just as the autopsy was about to begin, someone fortunately noticed a flickering of the right eyelid, and a tear beginning to form. The woman was immediately transferred to intensive care, where she remained critically ill for several hours. When her condition improved she was moved to a mental hospital, as it transpired that she had taken a barbiturate overdose. After a week, she discharged herself from the hospital, apparently none the worse for her brush with death.

Because the standard criteria—lack of detectable respiration, heartbeat, and brain activity—cannot be relied on, the medical profession has attempted, in recent years, to reach a legally sound definition of death. What is now generally accepted is the condition known as brain death: The patient is unable to breathe without a ventilator, there are no reflex responses from the brain stem or spine, and no electrical activity in the brain can be detected by electroencephalography, all over a period of twenty-four hours.

BELOW THE BODY OF IRENE RICHARDSON, ONE OF THE VICTIMS OF PETER SUTCLIFFE, THE "YORKSHIRE RIPPER," MURDERED IN FEBRUARY 1977. THE POLICE TAPE CORDONING OFF THE CRIME SCENE CAN BE SEEN, AND DUCKBOARDS HAVE BEEN LAID OVER THE GRASS, SO THAT FOOTPRINTS OF THE INVESTIGATING TEAM CANNOT BE CONFUSED WITH ANY LEFT BY THE KILLER AND IMPORTANT TRACE EVIDENCE IS NOT TRAMPLED INTO THE GRASS. RICHARDSON'S BODY WAS FOUND EARLY IN THE MORNING AFTER HER MURDER, AND IT WAS POSSIBLE TO PLACE THE TIME OF DEATH WITHIN AN HOUR OR TWO.

HYPOSTASIS

When the heart stops beating at the moment of death, the circulation of the blood ceases, while the effect of gravity causes it gradually to sink, via the blood vessels, to the lowest parts of the body. This is called hypostasis, or postmortem lividity. The red cells settle quickest, forming purplish-blue patches that are visible one to three hours after death. These patches gradually join up as purple-red areas in six to eight hours. These generalized time figures are not reliable, however; in anemic old people, for example, hypostasis may not occur at all.

The red patches will not form where the weight of the body presses against a hard surface, preventing the accumulation of blood. If the body is lying on its back, for example, patches will be found only on the back of the neck, the small of the back, and the thighs; in a hanged body, hypostasis will develop in the hands and legs.

Although, therefore, the state of hypostasis cannot be used to estimate accurately the time of death, even within a few hours, it can sometimes provide an indication that the body has been moved some hours after death—if the lividity is found not to be in the lowest areas.

ABOVE THE HAND OF AN EMBALMED CORPSE. THIS TECHNIQUE OF PRESERVING DEAD BODIES ORIGINATED WITH THE ANCIENT EGYPTIANS, BUT WAS BROUGHT TO THE UNITED STATES DURING THE CIVIL WAR. SEVERAL GALLONS OF PRESERVATIVE FLUID CONTAINING FORMALDEHYDE ARE INJECTED INTO AN ARTERY, EMPTYING THE BODY OF BLOOD THROUGH AN OPENED VEIN.

emotion or violence, complete rigor can occur immediately after death. Among the tales told is that of a soldier killed during the battle of Balaclava, Crimea, in 1854, who remained mounted stiffly on his horse. And, during the defense of Sedan, in the Franco-Prussian war of 1870, the body of a soldier, decapitated by a shell, is said to have remained upright, his hand still holding firmly his cup of wine.

CASE STUDY
HASH BROWNS WITH ONIONS

On October 22, 1993, the body of hardware store owner Gerry Boggs was found at his home in Steamboat Springs, Colorado. He had been electrically stunned, beaten with a shovel, and shot many times in the chest. Suspicion fell on his ex-wife Jill, a former fashion model. She was now married to a man named Carroll; it was her ninth marriage, her third husband had also been shot under suspicious circumstances, and she had been involved in a series of bitter disputes with Boggs.

The county medical examiners recovered a pint of gastric contents from Boggs's stomach, which they described as having the consistency of noodles. Boggs had last been seen alive at lunchtime on October 21, and his employees reported that he never ate lunch, but took his breakfast every day at a neighboring diner, where he always ordered eggs, toast, and hash browns.

"Jill Coit," as she now called herself, had no alibi for the afternoon of October 21, but witnesses could corroborate that she had spent the evening with a boyfriend, 160 miles (257 kilometers) away in Thornton. And her defense argued that the presence of noodles in Boggs's stomach established that he had eaten an evening meal.

Professor David Norris of the University of Colorado School of Medicine was asked to examine the "noodles." He quickly identified the characteristic cell fragments of potato and onion, and confidently announced, "Hash browns with onions."

There was one problem. The cooks at the diner insisted that they never added onions to their hash browns. So one of the detectives from the Steamboat Springs PD visited the diner, ordered a breakfast identical to that regularly eaten by Boggs, and discovered that everything cooked on the griddle became contaminated with—fragments of fried onions. Jill Coit, her alibi destroyed, was found guilty, and sentenced to life imprisonment without possibility of parole.

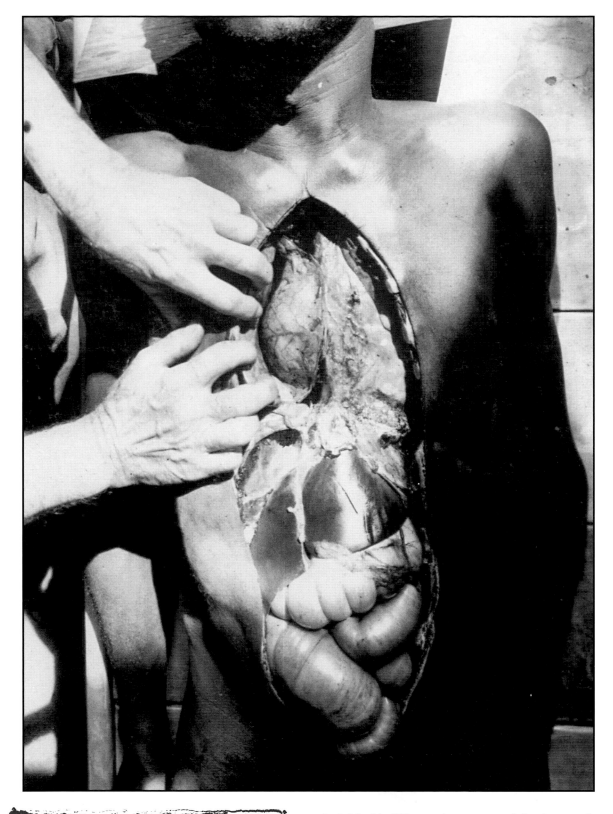

STOMACH CONTENTS

It has been suggested that the food found in a victim's stomach, as well as the state of its digestion, can provide an estimate of time of death within two to three hours. Every individual is different, however, and the degree of digestion can depend not only on their personal characteristics, but also on the nature of the food ingested. In addition, any severe physical or emotional event can affect, or even halt, digestion.

If the stomach contents can be identified as that of a particular meal, and that meal can be timed, then, of course, it can be determined that death must have occurred at a later hour—but that is all that can be determined.

OVERLEAF, PAGE 116:
FOLLLOWING A THOROUGH
AUTOPSY, A MORTUARY
TECHNICIAN REASSEMBLES
THE BODY OF A YOUNG MAN
SHOT ON THE STREETS OF
WASHINGTON, D.C., AT THE
CITY MORGUE OF D.C.
GENERAL HOSPITAL,
MARCH, 1996.

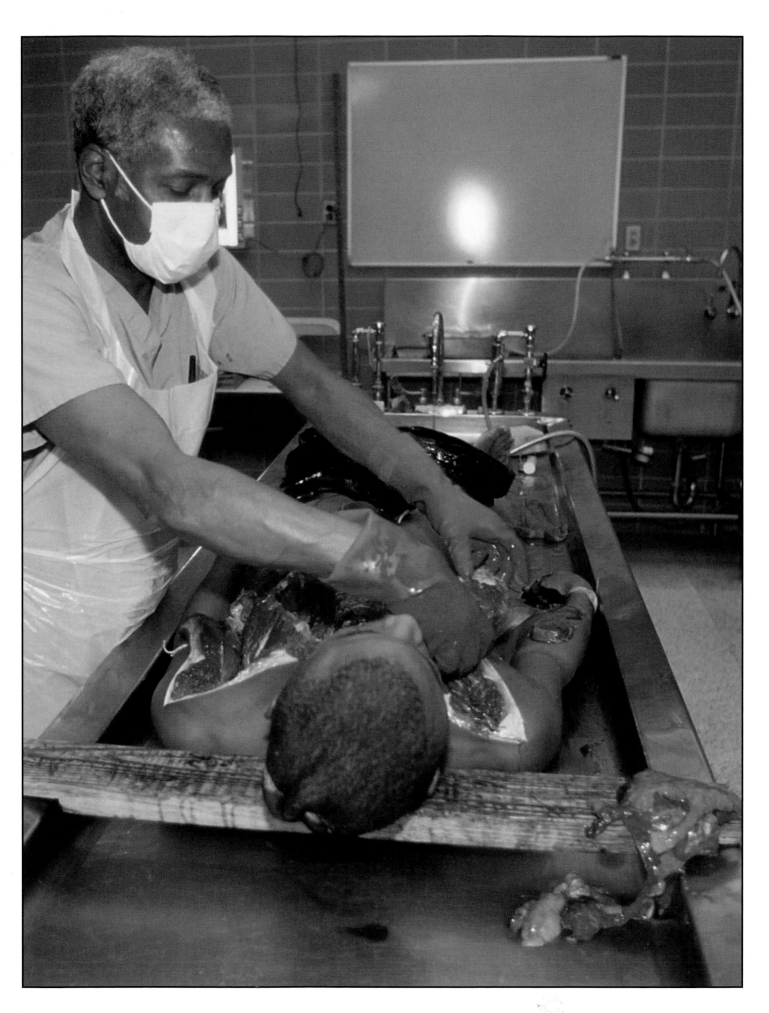

A famous case in which the stomach contents provided a rough estimate of time of death, and led to the conviction of a murderer, occurred in Scotland in 1913.

One afternoon in the summer of that year, two men noticed a dark bundle floating in the waters of a flooded quarry in West Lothian; drawing it to the bank, they were horrified to find that it was actually two small bodies tied together with cord.

Examination by forensic pathologist Sydney (later Sir Sydney) Smith soon established that they were the bodies of two young boys, aged about seven and four. What remained of their clothing was similar, suggesting they were brothers, and one of their shirts bore a faint laundry mark from a poorhouse in Dysart, Fife.

Because the two had been immersed in water very shortly after death, their body fat had been converted into adipocere (see below). This had inhibited further decomposition, leaving the stomachs intact, with their contents nearly unchanged. Smith reported:

"In each stomach were several ounces of undigested vegetable matter—whole green peas, barley, potatoes, turnips and leeks; in fact the traditional ingredients of Scotch broth."

And, from the development of the adipocere, Smith calculated that the two boys had been in the water between eighteen months and two years; that is, they had taken their last meal in the summer or autumn of 1911.

Two local boys of the right ages, who had previously spent some time in the poorhouse at Dysart, had disappeared in November 1911. Their father, a laborer named Patrick Higgins, had told an acquaintance at the time, "The kids are alright now. They're on their way to Canada."

The police found a local woman who remembered giving two young boys a meal of broth on a night in November 1911. This was sufficient confirmation of Smith's findings. Patrick Higgins was soon found and arrested for the murder of his sons. He was found guilty at his trial in Edinburgh, and hanged.

LEFT SIR SYDNEY SMITH, THE RENOWNED SCOTTISH PATHOLOGIST. SOME OF HIS MOST IMPORTANT WORK WAS IN THE FIELD OF BALLISTICS.

ADIPOCERE

The formation of adipocere—a grayish, waxy material similar to soap, produced by chemical action on the body's fat—usually takes place if a corpse has been immersed in water for a considerable time or has been buried in wet surroundings. Normally, its development suggests that death took place several months previously, but it can develop more rapidly if the temperature of the body remains high. The heat produced by active maggot infestation, for example, has been known to raise a dead body's temperature to as high as 78°F (26°C), and, in such circumstances—or in similar temperature-raising conditions—adipocere formation can occur in as few as three weeks.

From all that has been detailed here, therefore, it is obvious that it is practically impossible to state exactly when a death took place. At best, and only if the corpse is newly dead, the estimate can lie within a time bracket of some five hours. Nevertheless, in many cases of homicide, such as that outlined on page 114, this estimation can often prove sufficient to destroy—or support—an alibi established by one or more of the suspects.

There is a particular area of related research, however, that has achieved dramatic results in recent years and can sometimes pinpoint the time of death to within an hour or so, certainly within days. Forensic entomology, in fact, has helped to cast doubt on alibis in a number of murder cases—or to establish a suspect's innocence.

BELOW THE FORMATION OF ADIPOCERE BY CHEMICAL ACTION ON THE BODY'S FAT—PARTICULARLY IN WET SURROUNDINGS—WILL PRESERVE MANY OF THE BODY'S FEATURES. IT CAN EVEN HALT THE ACTIVITY OF BACTERIA IN CAUSING THE DECOMPOSITION OF THE INTERNAL ORGANS, LEAVING THE STOMACH CONTENTS, FOR EXAMPLE, UNCHANGED.

FORENSIC ENTOMOLOGY

Very soon after death, and sometimes even before the heart has stopped beating, flies begin to arrive at the scene, attracted by the first very faint odors of decay. They are followed by wave upon wave of other insects—beetles, parasitic wasps, mites, woodlice, and even moths—at defined intervals according to their tastes. This successive infestation follows a somewhat predictable timescale that can provide a relatively accurate indication of time of death. In the earliest stages of decay, the day, and often the time of day, can be determined; or, even after several years, it is possible to estimate how long the body has remained undiscovered.

The first recorded application of this knowledge in a forensic investigation occurred in 1850. While repairing a fireplace in a house in Arbois, France, a workman discovered a mummified baby's body in the chimney behind it. By good fortune, the physician summoned to the scene, Dr. Marcel Bergeret, was also an amateur naturalist. He was able to establish that the corpse was that of an aborted or prematurely born child, but the most important question still to be answered was how long it had been in the chimney. Four different groups of tenants had lived in the house during the past three years, and it was necessary to determine which had lived there at the critical time.

Dr. Bergeret turned his attention to the various insect traces that he discovered with the body. He wrote:

"The eggs of the larvae we found on the corpse in March 1850 must have been deposited there in the middle [summer] of 1849.... Next to the many living larvae there were numerous pupae present, and they must have come from eggs that had been laid earlier, i.e., in 1848.... The fly that emerges from the pupae is *Sarcophaga carnaria* [a flesh fly] that lays its eggs before the flesh dries out. The larvae were of little night moths that attack bodies that are already dried out.... In conclusion, two generations of insects were found on the corpse, representing two years post mortem: on the fresh corpse, the flesh fly deposited its eggs in 1848; on the dried-out corpse, the moths laid their eggs in 1849."

Dr. Bergeret's evidence was sufficient in persuading the French magistrates to issue arrest warrants for the couple who had lived in the apartment in 1848.

Unfortunately, however, his reasoning was incorrect. The insects he examined do not have a life cycle of one year, as he had assumed; in warm summer weather (a point he rightly observed), they can mature in a matter of days or weeks. Nevertheless, this remains a classic example of what has come to be known as forensic entomology.

THE FAUNA OF CADAVERS

There is no record of Dr. Bergeret's pioneering work being advanced for more than twenty-five years. Then, in 1878, the half-mummified body of a newborn infant, found at an abandoned site

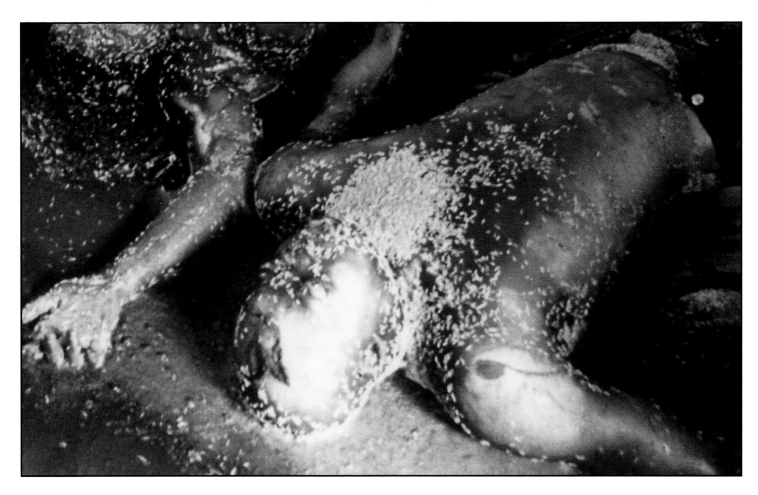

in Paris, was brought to forensic pathologist Paul-Camille Brouardel. Immediately reminded of the Arbois case, he noticed swarms of tiny mites in a brown powder that covered the corpse, and approached Jean-Pierre Mégnin, a respected researcher in entomology at the Museum of Natural History in Paris.

At the city morgue, Mégnin quickly identified the brown powder as the excrement of beetles that had fed on the dried remains, and the mites as a species that infested dried meat and animal hides. Mégnin was able to offer only an approximate estimate of the time of death—somewhere between six and twelve months earlier—but the case fascinated him. He became a regular visitor to the morgue, and in 1894 he published his *La Faune des Cadavres,* a detailed study of the insects that infest dead bodies. Mégnin wrote:

"We have been struck by the fact that we have been the first to observe that the insects of cadavers, the workers of death, only arrive at their table successively, and always in the same order."

He noted that the first arrivals, the blowflies, could be dated to the day the death occurred or even to within a very narrow range of hours—and, in some cases, to within minutes of the time of death.

These flies lay their eggs in wounds, on the eyes and lips, and in orifices such as the mouth or vagina within hours—or, depending on the time of day and climatic conditions, within moments—of death. Between eight and fourteen hours later, according to the ambient temperature, the eggs hatch, and the first tiny maggots emerge. Their first stage of development (the first instar) lasts a further eight to fourteen hours, after which they shed their skins. The second instar lasts two to three days. In the third instar the maggots are large and creamy-white in color, and feed voraciously for some six days. As the Swedish naturalist Linnaeus wrote in 1767: "The progeny of three flies can consume a dead horse quicker than a lion." Because maggots are particularly attracted to wounds, their feeding in these areas can often lead to the wounds becoming apparent only at autopsy, or even being completely obliterated.

When they have finished feeding, the maggots usually migrate a short distance from the cadaver, burrowing into the ground and pupating for some twelve days before emerging as newly formed flies. In a murder investigation in the open, therefore, it is

ABOVE THE BODIES OF CIVILIANS DISCOVERED AFTER A MASSACRE IN FREETOWN, SEIRRA LEONE, LIE EXPOSED, FOLLOWING FIERCE FIGHTING BETWEEN RIVAL GROUPS IN 1998. BLOWFLY MAGGOTS BEGIN TO INFEST AND FEED UPON A CORPSE WITHIN HOURS OF DEATH. EACH FLY WILL LAY THOUSANDS OF EGGS, PARTICULARLY IN THE BODY ORIFICES, SUCH AS THE MOUTH, EYES, AND IN ANY OPEN WOUNDS. THE MAGGOTS GROW THROUGH THREE STAGES OF DEVELOPMENT OVER TEN TO TWELVE DAYS BEFORE LEAVING THE CORPSE TO PUPATE. THEY ARE FOLLOWED BY FURTHER INSECT INFESTATION.

important to excavate the soil for some distance around the body; if the crime scene is indoors, it is important to search under every carpet or piece of low-lying furniture in the room—as these flies prefer fresh flesh, they are unlikely to return to the corpse.

Meanwhile, on the second or third day, as decomposition progresses, the houseflies arrive. They do not usually lay their eggs on cadavers, preferring sites such as manure, but they will feed busily on the decaying matter. Then come beetles, to feed on both the rotting tissues and the maggots themselves, while parasitic wasps will lay their eggs in the pupae. Other tiny flies and maggots—scuttle flies and cheese skippers—feed on the broken-down proteins at a later stage; scuttle flies after two to three weeks, and cheese skippers at about two months.

When the last liquid matter has gone and the remains are dry, after six to twelve months, mites will swarm over the corpse, followed in the second year by hide-eating beetles. Finally, clothes moths and spider beetles scavenge any organic material that is left. Mégnin wrote:

RIGHT A SCANNING ELECTRON MICROGRAPH (SEM) OF TWO-HOUR OLD MAGGOTS OF THE GREENBOTTLE, OR GREEN BLOWFLY, *LUCILIA CAESAR*. THE GREENBOTTLE LAYS EGGS IN PLACES OF ABUNDANT FOOD FOR THE FUTURE MAGGOTS, SUCH AS ROTTING VEGETATION, DUNG PILES, AND CORPSES. BLOWFLY MAGGOTS BEGIN TO INFEST, AND FEED UPON, A CORPSE WITHIN HOURS OF DEATH. THE MOUTH END OF THE MAGGOT TAPERS INTO A THIN WEDGE WITH TWO HOOKS THAT ENABLE IT TO ATTACH TO THE FLESH.

On a cold night in September 1956, the stabbed body of a mail carrier was found behind some pilings near a ferry dock in Hungary. The captain of one of the ferryboats, who had arrived for work about 6 p.m., was accused, found guilty, and sentenced to a long term of imprisonment, though he stoutly protested his innocence.

Eight years later, the captain succeeded in having his case reexamined, and Ferenc Mihalyi, curator of entomology at the National History Museum in Budapest, gave evidence in his defense. The coroner's report on the autopsy of the murdered man, carried out in the afternoon of the following day, had mentioned masses of yellowish fly eggs, as well as a few tiny larvae that were 0.04–0.08 in. (1–2 mm) in length. Mihalyi testified that his personal experiments with three typical species of fly showed that their eggs took from ten to sixteen hours to hatch in the warm conditions of his laboratory, and would have taken even longer in the climatic conditions in which the body was found.

The eggs could not have been laid in the cold morgue, as they would not have begun to hatch, and Mihalyi therefore concluded that they had been laid—in daylight—on the previous day, at a time for which the captain was able to establish an alibi. He was freed, and the police subsequently found the real culprit.

"In the end, nothing rests next to the white bones but a sort of brown earth.... Thus is accomplished this parable of the scripture: For dust thou art, and unto dust shalt thou return."

Mégnin's principal findings related to bodies that had lain in the open, but he also investigated insect infestation of bodies buried in caskets. In temperate summer conditions, unless strict precautions are taken, or if the corpse is effectively buried immediately after death, blowflies will have already laid eggs, and these may develop into six or more generations inside the casket before finally dying off. Bodies buried in winter are unlikely to be so infested. Other species of insect will be unable to follow the blowflies into the casket—with the exception of the so-called coffin flies, scuttle flies whose larvae burrow into the ground and can find their way even into closed caskets.

Despite the renown that his book brought him, Mégnin urged caution on those investigators who might regard his research as definitive. He was well aware that insect species can vary from one region to another, and he

LEFT AN ASSORTMENT OF FLIES AND BEETLES COLLECTED BY A FORENSIC ENTOMOLOGIST. EACH HAS BEEN LABELED ACCORDING TO ITS SPECIES, EXAMPLES OF THE MANY INSECTS THAT INFEST A CORPSE OVER TIME.

BELOW IDENTIFYING EACH SPECIES OF INSECT IS OF VITAL IMPORTANCE IN ESTIMATING THE TIME THAT HAS ELAPSED SINCE DEATH. HERE, A FORENSIC ENTOMOLOGIST AT THE *INSTITUT DE RECHERCHE CRIMINELLE*, PARIS, USES A MICROSCOPE LINKED TO A VIDEO SCREEN TO EXAMINE A ROVE BEETLE. SPECIMENS OF OTHER INSECTS COLLECTED FROM THE DEATH SCENE ARE IN THE TEST TUBES (LEFT).

even questioned whether his findings would be equally valid beyond Paris. Only gradually have entomologists been able to identify more than a small proportion of the thousands of insect species that exist. Nevertheless, there were occasional cases during the first half of the twentieth century in which knowledge of entomology provided vital evidence.

In the trial of Buck Ruxton for the murder of his wife and maid (see page 67), for example, the accused was able to provide alibis for the days (September 18–20) on which the pathologist roughly estimated that the deaths had occurred. However, in what was probably the first occasion on which a professional entomologist gave evidence in court, Alexander Mearns of Glasgow University testified that maggots found with the remains, on October 1, were at the conclusion of their third instar. As the weather had been cool to chilly, he concluded that their eggs had been laid at least thirteen days before; that is, prior to September 18.

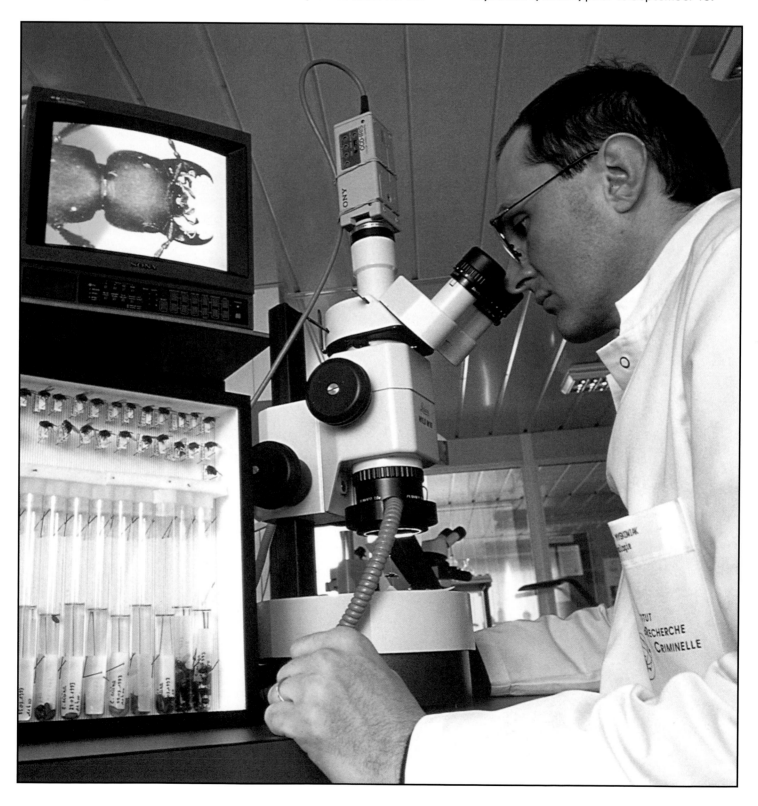

FACT FILE

DR. ZAK

Dr. Zakaria Erzinçlioglu (1951–2002), known to police and forensic scientists throughout the world as Dr. Zak, or the "maggotologist," was the leading British forensic entomologist of his era, aged just fifty at his untimely death. Born in Turkey but brought up partly in England, he graduated in applied zoology in 1975. He worked for some years for the Zoological Society of London, later for Cambridge University, and in 1995 was director of the Forensic Science Research Center at Durham University. His interest in blowflies and other insect species led to an increasing demand for his expertise in murder investigations, and he was involved in more than five hundred cases. In the case of "Little Miss Nobody" (see page 65), for example, it was Dr. Zak who was able to provide the police with an estimate of how long the body had been buried. Calculating the time it would have taken succeeding generations of coffin flies to consume the soft tissues in such enclosed conditions—the corpse was rolled in a carpet inside firmly tied plastic bags—he concluded that at least three years had elapsed since the insects' arrival.

Following this, a colony of several generations of woodlice had established itself inside the carpet, and Dr. Zak estimated that this represented at least an additional two years—setting the time of the body's burial in 1984, or even earlier. The victim, Karen Price, had disappeared in 1981.

In his later years, Dr. Zak became very concerned with miscarriages of justice, and he campaigned tirelessly to raise standards in forensic science. He reported that he had refused, on a number of occasions, to doctor his findings in order to provide evidence for the prosecution, and in 1997 he announced that he would carry out forensic casework only if paid by the judiciary—not by the police. Shortly before his death, Dr. Zak had plans to establish the Solon Institute, devoted to forensic research, whose casework would be undertaken free of charge. His widow has said that she will endeavor to fulfill this ambition.

Dr. Zak's book, *Maggots, Murder, and Men: Memories and Reflections of a Forensic Entomologist,* was shortlisted for the Macallan Gold Dagger for Non-Fiction Award in 2001.

BELOW THE FAMOUS FORENSIC ENTOMOLOGIST KNOWN AS DR. ZAK EXAMINES THE PARTIALLY MUMMIFIED REMAINS OF A BODY FOUND COVERED WITH SACKING. THE SUCCEEDING GENERATIONS OF INSECTS THAT HAVE VISITED THE CORPSE—REVEALED BY FRAGMENTS OF PUPAL CASES AND DEAD ADULTS—WILL PROVIDE A MEASURE OF HOW LONG IT HAS BEEN LYING THERE.

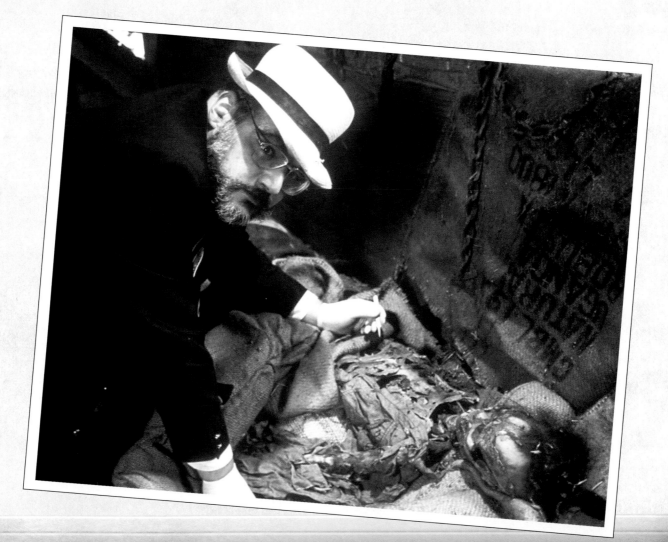

On May 28, 1980, eighteen-year-old Faith Hathaway was reported as missing, in Mandeville, Louisiana. Two days later, another teenager, covered with blood, staggered into the sheriff's office in neighboring Madisonville. She hysterically told her story: Two men had abducted her and her boyfriend at gunpoint and had driven around for two days, repeatedly raping her. They then stabbed and shot the boyfriend and had left his body tied to a tree, before dumping her at the roadside.

Robert Lee Willie and Joseph Vaccaro were soon arrested for the abduction and rape; remarkably, the boyfriend had survived, and Willie and Vaccaro confessed, but they denied any responsibility for the earlier disappearance of Faith Hathaway. Four day's after Hathaway's disappearance, her purse and blouse were found in a ravine by a party of picnickers; on June 4, deputy investigator Michael Varnado discovered the missing girl's body, swarming with maggots in their third instar. From this, forensic entomologist Lamar Meek calculated that the first blowflies had laid eggs on the body seven days previously—that is, during daylight hours on May 29. Faced with this evidence, Willie and Vaccaro confessed to kidnapping Hathaway, but each accused the other of killing her. Lamar Meek testified in the separate trials of both men. Vaccaro was sentenced to life imprisonment, but Willie received the death sentence. He gained fame posthumously when his story was made into the movie *Dead Man Walking*.

BELOW ROBERT LEE WILLIE, LED INTO COURT FOR HIS TRIAL FOR THE MURDER OF FAITH HATHAWAY. IN THE MOVIE BASED ON THIS CASE, THE ROLE OF THE CONVICTED KILLER WAS PLAYED BY SEAN PENN.

ENTOMOLOGY IN THE UNITED STATES

In the United States, the National Museum of Natural History in Washington, D.C., was the institution at which the most important classification of flies (*Diptera* in biological description) was carried out over the first half of the twentieth century. It was not far from FBI headquarters, and agents occasionally brought in maggots, asking whether the museum's staff could provide an indication of the time of the host's death. In 1949, Curtis Sabrosky was appointed curator of Diptera, and he made strenuous efforts to convince the FBI of the importance of collecting as many maggots as possible from bodies found dead. It was not until 1966, however, that Sabrosky was able to prove his point.

A burned-out car had been found below a cliff in southwest Virginia, and inside were the charred remains of a young woman, shot through the head. Fifty feet (15 m) away lay the gun. The young woman's boyfriend confessed to having had a passionate argument with her, shooting her, and dropping the gun as he scrambled away in a state of shock—which meant that he would be convicted only of second-degree murder. The prosecution, however, suspected that he had returned to the scene of the crime a number of days later, and had then set fire to the car in an attempt to render the body unrecognizable.

Sabrosky received two items of evidence: the gun, with a single blowfly pupa in the barrel, and an envelope containing many more of the same pupae that had been found beneath the floor mat of the car. At trial, he gave a brief résumé of the life cycle of the blowfly, then answered questions from the prosecuting attorney. Sabrosky said that the gun had been inside the car when the larvae had finished their feeding, and that they had then migrated in search of a dark place—under the mat or in the gun's barrel—to pupate. It was unlikely that a maggot could have migrated 50 ft. away; leaving the car, it would have burrowed into the soil within only 2 to 3 ft. (60 to 90 cm) of the vehicle. Therefore, the gun had to have been retrieved some days later, and discarded as part of an attempt to cover up the crime. The boyfriend was found guilty of murder in the first degree.

During the past half a century, a growing amount of controlled research has been carried out into the times at which the various insect species arrive at a cadaver. Much of this was done with the easily obtainable bodies of laboratory mice, rats, and rabbits, but in more recent years university researchers in the United States and Canada have gone rather further.

In the summer of 1962, Jerry Payne at Clemson College, South Carolina, began to obtain a number of stillborn and newly dead young piglets from local farmers, and to expose them, both in the open and in insect-proof cages. Pigs' general physical and tissue characteristics—and particularly their nearly hairless bodies—most closely approximate those of human beings. Payne's initial findings replicated those of homicide investigators: The bodies in the cages gradually dried out and became mummified, until finally coming under attack by fungi; those in the open were rapidly reduced to skeleton and dried skin by insect action.

Payne collected altogether 382 different invertebrate species from his corpses, 301 of them insects, most of the others being crustaceans. He described six stages of decomposition, each characterized by the arrival of different waves of insects: fresh, bloated, active decay, advanced decay, dry decay, and remains. In particular, Payne recognized that it was the release of different gases during decomposition that attracted the insects. Instrumentation for the detection of these gases has recently been developed at Oak Ridge National Laboratory, Tennessee, by Arpad Vass, who began analyzing the chemical composition of the liquids produced during the stages of decay (see pages 130–31).

Because the piglets were relatively small, their decomposition took place more rapidly than that of humans, and so Payne's findings showed the waves of insects arriving much closer together than they had in Mégnin's research. The dead piglets had in addition been immediately deep-frozen by the farmers, but Payne observed a few flesh flies depositing larvae in body apertures even before thawing was complete. Later in the same day, blowflies and greenbottles arrived on the scene, together with wasps, and ants came to feed on the pig

BELOW PROFESSOR BERNARD GREENBERG (LEFT) JOINS POLICE AT THE SITE OF A BODY THAT HAS BEEN COMPLETELY SKELETONIZED. TRACES OF INSECT PUPAL CASES AMONG THE BONES, OR IN THE SURROUNDING SOIL, CAN STILL PROVIDE AN ESTIMATE OF HOW LONG THE REMAINS HAVE BEEN LYING IN THIS POSITION.

CRIME SCENE — DO NOT ENTER

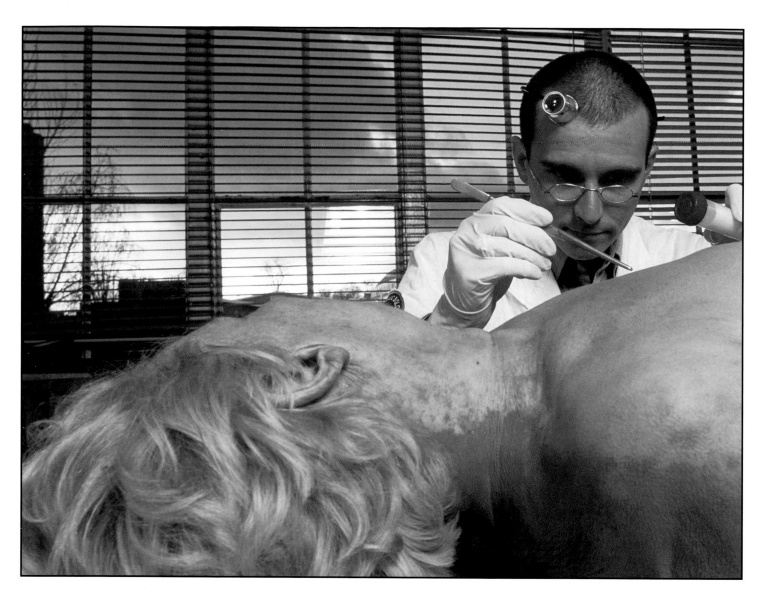

flesh and fly eggs. As decay fluids began to drip from the bodies, houseflies appeared.

On the second day, the piglets' bodies became bloated as bacteria multiplying in their guts began to produce methane, sulfur dioxide, and other gases. The smell attracted swarms of flesh and blowflies, fruit and vinegar flies, and even some cheese skippers.

By the third morning, blowflies and flesh flies had abandoned the bodies, as their maggots hatched and fed. Within hours the maggots had eaten through to the guts, thereby releasing the bloating gases. The decay liquids, dripping into the soil, attracted beetles, which in turn fed on the maggots; this was the stage of active decay, as the bloated bodies rapidly deflated. Butterflies, moths, and bees were also drawn to the scene by the scent of decomposition.

By the sixth day, most of the soft tissue had been consumed, and the odor of decay had faded. Third-instar maggots began to leave the bodies, and as they disappeared the first wave of beetles also departed. The next two days represented the stage of dry decay, with many

of the piglets no more than a mass of bones, cartilage, and skin. Skin and hide beetles, as well as mites, arrived, together with various species of gnats, which Payne suspected had come to feed on the fungi that had begun to cover the remains. For a month or more, this process continued, until nothing consumable remained.

Jerry Payne continued his research for a year or two, but then took up a post to study crop pests, and, unfortunately, he did not pursue this particular line of inquiry. It was more than ten years later, in the mid-1970s, that Lamar Meek, newly appointed as a professor of entomology at Louisiana State University, was given the responsibility of liaising with the local homicide investigators who occasionally brought in maggots.

Reading through the sparse literature on the subject, he came across the report of Payne's experiments. But, even before he could begin to repeat these tests—with the bodies of full-grown pigs—Meek encountered his first forensic case, that of Robert Lee Willie (see page 124).

NOT WHAT IT SEEMED

Sometimes the activities of flies, when feeding on a decomposing corpse, can lead to deceptive evidence. During a Texas heat wave, the body of a man was found hanging in his home. It had been there three or four days, and the walls and ceiling looked to be spattered with drops of blood, as if the man had been savagely beaten. When an FBI expert examined photographs of the scene, however, he quickly realized that the spots were not blood, but fly excrement. "One of the things that made that obvious," he said, "was a photograph showing a light bulb that had been left on. There wasn't a spot on it. The flies hadn't gone near it because it was too hot for them."

THE DIRTY DOZEN

Over the next few years, a number of anthropologists and entomologists were able to obtain funding for the study of dead bodies: Paul Catts at Washington State University; Wayne Lord of the FBI; Rob Hall at Missouri State University; Lee Goff at the University of Hawaii; William Bass and William Rodriguez, at the University of Tennessee, who were granted permission to work with human cadavers on what became known as the Body Farm; Gail Anderson of Simon Fraser University, British Columbia; and Bernard Greenberg at the University of Illinois at Chicago. It was during the November 1984 annual meeting of the Entomological Society in San Antonio, Texas, that these researchers first gained the name "the Dirty Dozen"—even though they were, as yet, a little short of that number.

The paper read by Bernard Greenberg at that meeting described his first attempt to attain a more accurate estimate of the time taken by maggots to reach their stages of development under different climatic conditions.

Agriculturists had known for many years that they could predict an insect's development and maturation from the calculation of its growth per unit of ambient temperature, known as accumulated degree-hours. For example: If a particular species takes 100 hours at 50°F (10°C) to reach its second instar, it will take some 50 hours at 68°F (20°C), or 40 hours at 77°F (25°C). This simple formula had allowed government advisers to inform farmers of when was best to

spray their fields, but Greenberg realized that it should also be possible to backtrack the calculation—from the observed growth stage of a maggot and a knowledge of the ambient temperatures at which it had developed—to when the flies' eggs had been laid. He had an opportunity to validate his theory in June 1984, in the case of Vernita Wheat (see page 131).

Greenberg convened the first Forensic Symposium at the 18th International Congress of Entomology, in Vancouver in 1988, where he shared his expertise with the rest of the so-called Dirty Dozen. It was consequently decided that forensic investigators needed detailed instruction on the collection and presentation of insect evidence, and the outcome was the publication, two years later, of *Entomology & Death: A Procedural Guide,* dedicated to the "luckless victims of homicides whose plight has made this endeavor necessary." Continuing study of the life cycle of flies and other insects offers hope that estimation of time of death can be made ever more accurate. As another entomological consultant, Neal Haskell, often says, "Time's fun when you're having flies."

BELOW PROFESSOR BERNARD GREENBERG IN HIS LABORATORY AT THE UNIVERSITY OF ILLINOIS AT CHICAGO. WITH COLLEAGUE PROFESSOR J.C. KUNICH, HE IS THE AUTHOR OF THE LEADING WORK ON FORENSIC ENTOMOLOGY, *FLIES AS FORENSIC INDICATORS— ENTOMOLOGY AND THE LAW.*

FACT FILE

THE BODY FARM

Officially known as the University of Tennessee's Anthropological Research Facility, the "Body Farm" was given its nickname by workers at the site, but gained international fame as the title of Patricia Cornwell's 1994 crime novel, so named after she had made a visit to the facility. The director of the site, Dr. Bill Bass, studied as an academic anthropologist, but, after he had been consulted in a number of forensic investigations, he realized that much more needed to be known about the stages of decay undergone by a dead body over time.

At any point, some twenty cadavers of people who have donated their bodies to medical research are on-site. Some are exposed in the open; others are buried in shallow graves or under slabs of concrete, submerged in tanks of water, or locked in the trunks of cars. Every day, researchers make their rounds, recording the stages of decomposition, noting the arrival of different insect species, and taking tissue and soil samples for analysis.

The climate of Tennessee is generally warm and humid, and the decay of a human body there tends to be relatively rapid. These photographs show the changes that occurred to the naked body of a middle-aged male, exposed in the open, over a period of thirty days.

DAY 1 BLOWFLIES ARRIVE VERY SOON AFTER THE BODY IS PLACED IN POSITION. THE EGGS THEY LAY CLOSE TO THE MOUTH AND NOSTRILS CAN BE SEEN IN THE MOUSTACHE.

DAY 3 MAGGOTS IN THEIR FIRST AND SECOND INSTAR HAVE BEGUN TO PROLIFERATE AROUND THE OPEN ORIFICES. THE SKIN HAS BEGUN TO BLISTER, AND MAGGOTS ARE FEEDING BELOW THE SKIN.

DAY 5 SOME MAGGOTS ARE ALREADY INTO THEIR THIRD INSTAR. THE CONCENTRATION IN THE MOUTH IS SO GREAT THAT THE CORPSE'S DENTURES HAVE BEEN FORCED OUT.

DAY 6 THE SOFT TISSUES OF THE FACE AND HEAD ARE RAPIDLY CONSUMED BY THE SWARMING MAGGOTS. DECAY FLUID IS BEGINNING TO LEACH INTO THE SOIL BESIDE THE HEAD.

DAY 7 AFTER A WEEK, THE MAGGOTS HAVE CONSUMED NEARLY ALL THE SOFT TISSUE OF THE HEAD, AND ARE BEGINNING TO MOVE EN MASSE DOWN INTO THE TORSO. DECOMPOSITION GASES PRODUCE THE FOAMING THAT CAN BE SEEN NEAR THE HEAD AND LEFT SHOULDER.

DAY 10 SO MUCH FLESH HAS BEEN CONSUMED BY THE MAGGOTS THAT THE SKULL AND UPPER THORAX ARE ALREADY NEARLY SKELETONIZED, AND THE MAGGOT MASS IS MOVING DOWN INTO THE ABDOMEN. TRACES OF SKIN THAT HAVE NOT BEEN EATEN ARE BEGINNING TO DARKEN AND DRY OUT.

DAY 12 FULLY GROWN, THE MAGGOTS BEGIN TO LEAVE THE CORPSE, TO BURROW INTO THE GROUND, AND PUPATE. THE SOFT TISSUE AND SKIN THAT HAS NOT BEEN CONSUMED WILL CONTINUE TO DRY OUT AND MUMMIFY.

DAY 22 AFTER TWO WEEKS THE LAST OF THE BLOWFLY MAGGOTS QUIT THE BODY. OTHER INSECT SPECIES, ONES THAT FEED ON DRY TISSUE, BEGIN TO COLONIZE THE REMAINS.

DAY 30 IN THE WEEKS THAT FOLLOW, THERE IS LITTLE PROGRESSIVE CHANGE IN THE PHYSICAL APPEARANCE OF THE CORPSE; THE TISSUES ARE DRIED OUT, AND IT MAY BE MANY MONTHS BEFORE THE SKELETON IS FINALLY REDUCED TO BARE BONES.

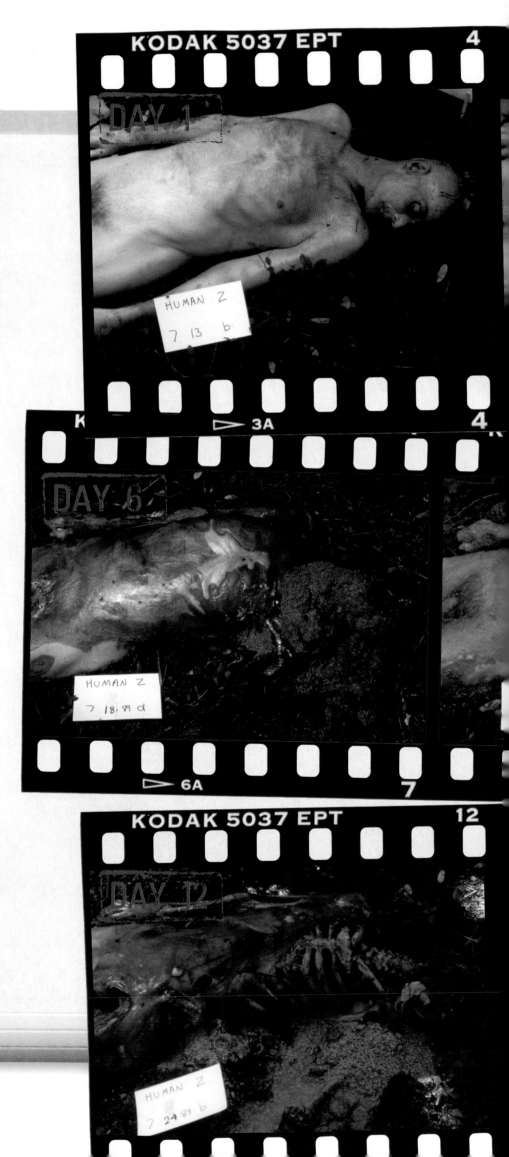

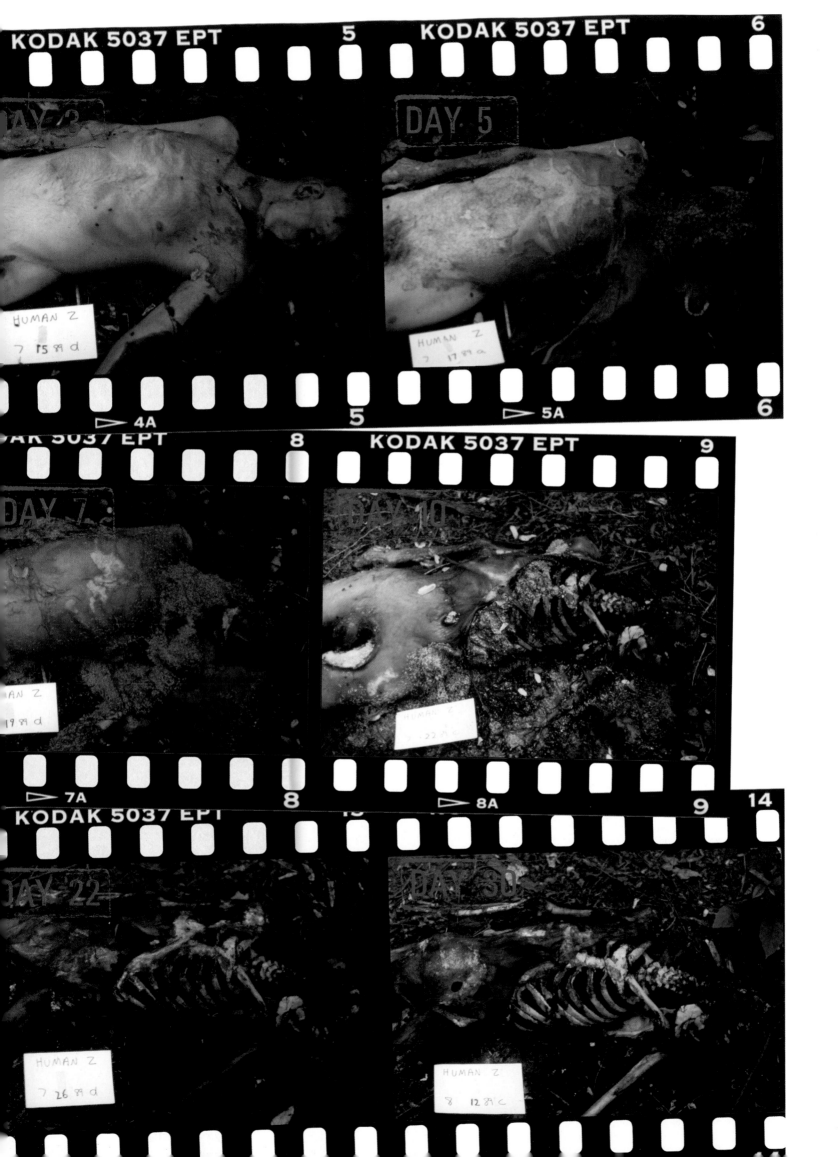

DECAY PRODUCTS

As bacteria initiate their decomposition of a dead body, liquid by-products begin to soak into the surroundings. At the University of Tennessee, beginning his work at William Bass's Body Farm in 1988, Arpad Vass studied the succession of relatively simple chemical compounds that are produced during the course of this process.

The soil on which the farm's bodies lay proved an ideal absorbent, and Vass found that it was usually sufficient to take a 3-in. (75-mm) plug as a sample, which could then be analyzed for its constituents using standard laboratory gas chromatography. As markers for the decay of the soft tissue, he chose the primary fatty acids, which do not occur naturally in the environment. Following the advice of entomologist Neal Haskell, Vass plotted the concentration of each fatty acid. The result was a set of figures that, as with maggot development, could be backtracked to the time at which decomposition began. From the proportion and concentration of the various fatty acids, plotted against recorded daily temperatures, it was possible to calculate the probable number of days since death.

For more extended decay times, after soft-tissue decomposition was completed, Vass chose inorganic ions, such as calcium, magnesium, potassium, sodium, ammonium, chloride, and sulfate. These too can be readily assayed using standard laboratory methods.

As an example, Vass's first forensic case featured the skeletonized remains of a teenaged boy; he had been identified, but it was important to know when he had died. The soft-tissue decay products had long dispersed, but the analysis of the inorganic ions present, with allowance made for the boy's known weight, indicated a time range of 2,250 to 3,000 accumulated degree-hours since decomposition had begun. Calculated against daily temperature records, this established that the boy had been dead between 168 and 183 days—a period of some two weeks after he had first disappeared—which was considerably more accurate than forensic anthropologists were able to calculate.

Arpad Vass continued his research at Oak Ridge National Laboratory, Tennessee, and, with two graduate assistants, he pursued two different approaches. One is the experimental development of an electronic "nose" that can identify thirty-two different chemical components in the aroma of a decaying body—much as female flies detect them naturally. Vass has proposed that a portable instrument could be used by police officers in the field to locate bodies, and that eventually it may be possible for it to enable a close estimate of time of death. The second research program is directed to analysis of the ratio of different amino acids that are produced by the progressive breakdown of proteins in various organs in the dead body, and relating this analysis to time.

There seems little probability that time of death will ever be pinpointed with the accuracy imagined by popular science-fiction and crime writers. There is no doubt, however, that the research carried out by entomologists, anthropologists, and chemists over the past quarter of a century has made it possible to backtrack—even after several years have passed—to within a time bracket of no more than a few days since death, rather than weeks or months.

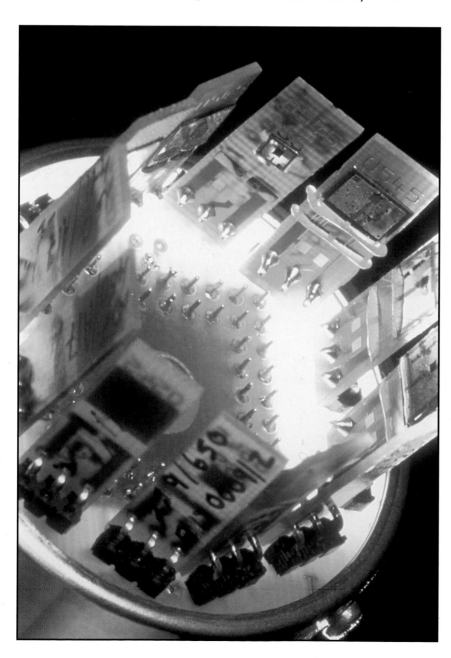

BELOW The essential head of the electronic "nose" (Neotronics Olfactory Sensing Equipment) first developed by Arpad Vass. The various chemical components of vapors—whether arising from a buried body or in many other applications—change the conductivity of the array of sensors, and the result is displayed as a "fingerprint" of the sample.

VERNITA WHEAT

On May 29, 1984, nine-year-old Vernita Wheat disappeared in Kenosha, Wisconsin; on June 19 her decomposed remains were discovered in the bathroom of a boarded-up building in nearby Waukegan, Illinois. She had been strangled with a TV cable, and around her body was a litter of dead flies, newly emerged ones, maggots in their third instar, pupae, and empty pupa cases.

Bernard Greenberg identified the flies as black blowflies and greenbottle flies, which have a life cycle of fourteen to seventeen days. If Vernita had been killed on May 29, he reasoned, the maggots were of the second generation. Everything depended, however, on the remaining pupae, which he collected to hatch in his laboratory. On June 30, the first pupae began to open, releasing bluebottles. Greenberg knew that the greenbottle has a development time, from newly laid egg to adult fly, of thirty-three days at 59°F (15°C), for a total of 11,880 accumulated degree-hours. With a set of hourly temperature readings that he had obtained from an airport

weather station near Waukegan, he began subtracting each hour's figure from the time the first greenbottle had emerged. The final time reached was about midnight on May 30–31.

Because at the time it was thought that greenbottles were inactive after dark, Greenberg reasoned that the first eggs must have been laid either late in the day on May 30 or at dawn on May 31, and he favored the latter. The principal suspects in the case—Alton Coleman and his girlfriend Debra Brown, who were later found guilty of additional similar murders—had no alibi for the times in question. Nevertheless, Greenberg realized that, impressive as this result was, ambient temperatures alone were insufficient for his calculations. So he performed experiments on the heat generated by swarms of feeding maggots, the difference in temperature between bodies lying in the sun and those in the shade, and the effects of naturally fluctuating ambient temperature on fly development, contrasted with the constant temperature of the laboratory.

BELOW ALTON COLEMAN AND DEBRA BROWN, BROUGHT TO COURT FOR THE KILLING OF VERNITA WHEAT AND OTHER SIMILAR MURDERS. BERNARD GREENBERG'S CALCULATION OF ACCUMULATED DEGREE-HOURS PINPOINTED THE TIME AT WHICH VERNITA MET HER DEATH.

PART 3

A CLOSER EXAMINATION

The county crime laboratory was well equipped, but small. The criminologist in charge, Dr. Anita Jones, was renowned for her caution and meticulous attention to detail.

"Fortunately, our caseload's unusually light right now," she told Gregory the next morning. "So we can give you have a preliminary report very soon." She also explained that the condition of the remains meant that mitochondrial DNA would have to be looked for and typed, but this was not something that could be done in the county lab. "And then we'll need to find the victim's mother, or a close maternal relative, to confirm identification."

Examination of the trace evidence and the stained carpet, however, was already well under way.

"One thing I can tell you," said Dr. Jones, "the hairs you picked off the carpet aren't the victim's. They're almost certainly dog hairs, and at a guess I'd say from a German shepherd; I'll get a more expert opinion in a couple of days. On the other hand, those few strands of hair from the skull have something significant to tell us. They're long and straight, and—most indicative of all—under the microscope I found that the medulla was almost continuous. If you're looking at Missing Persons, you might concentrate on young women from Southeast Asia, and particularly Malaysians."

"Thanks," Tamara Gregory sighed. "Do you know how many missing persons are listed for the state of California? Thirty-five thousand, some fourteen thousand of them women—and over one thousand in this county alone. What about the blood on the carpet?"

"I sympathize," said Dr. Jones. "As for the stain on the carpet, a preliminary phenolphthalein test had confirmed it was blood. Swab samples had been taken, but, after twelve months or more, the material was seriously degraded, and typing would be at best difficult and—most likely—nonspecific. However," she went on, "there may be some traces of usable DNA, so I'll run a PCR this afternoon."

"And there's something you didn't spot—but, then, they are rather tiny, and hidden deep in the pile of the carpet." Dr. Jones brought out a glass microscope slide with specks of material on it, some translucent and some dark red. "Dr. Kurosawa suggested an automobile rundown, and these are fragments from the car that did it, glass and paint. The glass is probably from one of the headlights. As for the paint, with a little help from our friends at Paint File, I should be able to tell you the make of car and the year, if not more. You don't have any of the victim's clothing?"

"Zilch," said Gregory. "But she was probably dressed when she got hit. Kurosawa thinks the perp picked her up off the road and put her in the car before she died. There could have been a lot of fragments like those

We can't be sure until the analysis comes back from the lab, but Jones is convinced that these are dog hairs.

EVIDENCE

MISSION MURRIETA POLICE DEPARTMENT

Report Number: 01-36492
Sealing Officer: Rodriguez
Date of Seizure or Purchase: 10/21/01
Exhibit: Unknown hair
Witnessing Officer: O'Malley
Pouch Size: _____
★ ★ ★ ★ ★ ★ ★ ★ ★ ★ ★ ★
Opening Official: _____
Date Opened: _____
Lab No./PR No.: _____
Pouch Size: _____
Pouch:

POLICE SEAL REMOVE

on her clothes, and that's probably how these few got into the carpet."

Their conversation was interrupted by a lab technician, who was clearly excited. "Hey, those seeds," he said. "I'm a bit of an amateur botanist, you know? I'll have to wait until one or two of them germinate to confirm, but I'm almost certain that they're skunk cabbage."

"So?" said Gregory, despondently. "Plenty of that grows around these parts."

"No," replied the tech. "Not our local species—that's *Symplocarpus foetidus*. This is *Lysichiton americanus*. It's mostly native up along the northern West Coast, from Oregon to Alaska. And here and there east of the Rockies, like in parts of Montana," he added.

Tamara Gregory hastily excused herself, and hurried to Sheriff Verdian's office to tell him. "Well," she said, "looks like we've maybe got ourselves a case of abduction here. The victim was likely carried from one state to another—or even over the border from British Columbia. I think we have to bring in the FBI."

Verdian looked put out. "Hell," he said, "I never did get along with those smart-asses from San Diego, but I guess you're right. And we may have a fine little facility here for Dr. Jones, but the Feds have truly amazing labs. You should see what it's like out at Quantico! Anyway, I better make the call right away. They're only an hour's drive away, but what do you bet it's two, three days before they decide to get over here?"

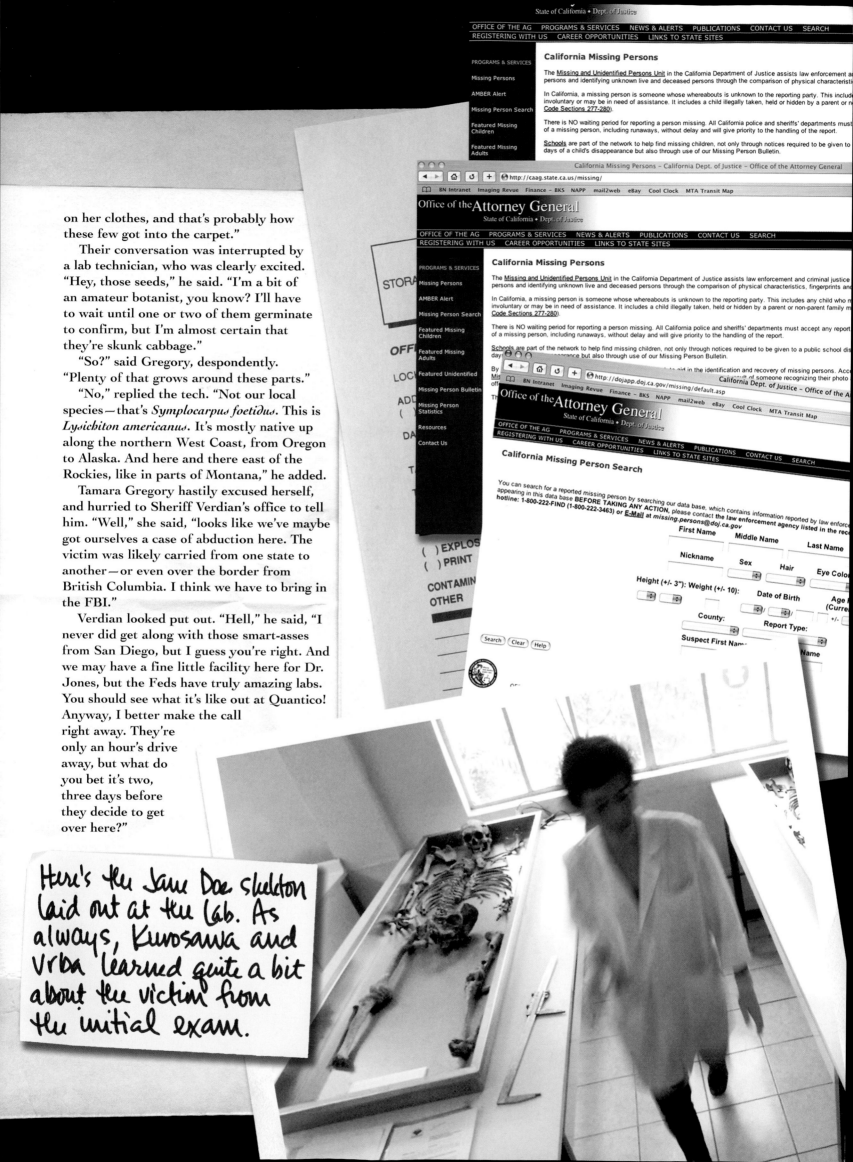

Here's the Jane Doe skeleton laid out at the lab. As always, Kurosawa and Vrba learned quite a bit about the victim from the initial exam.

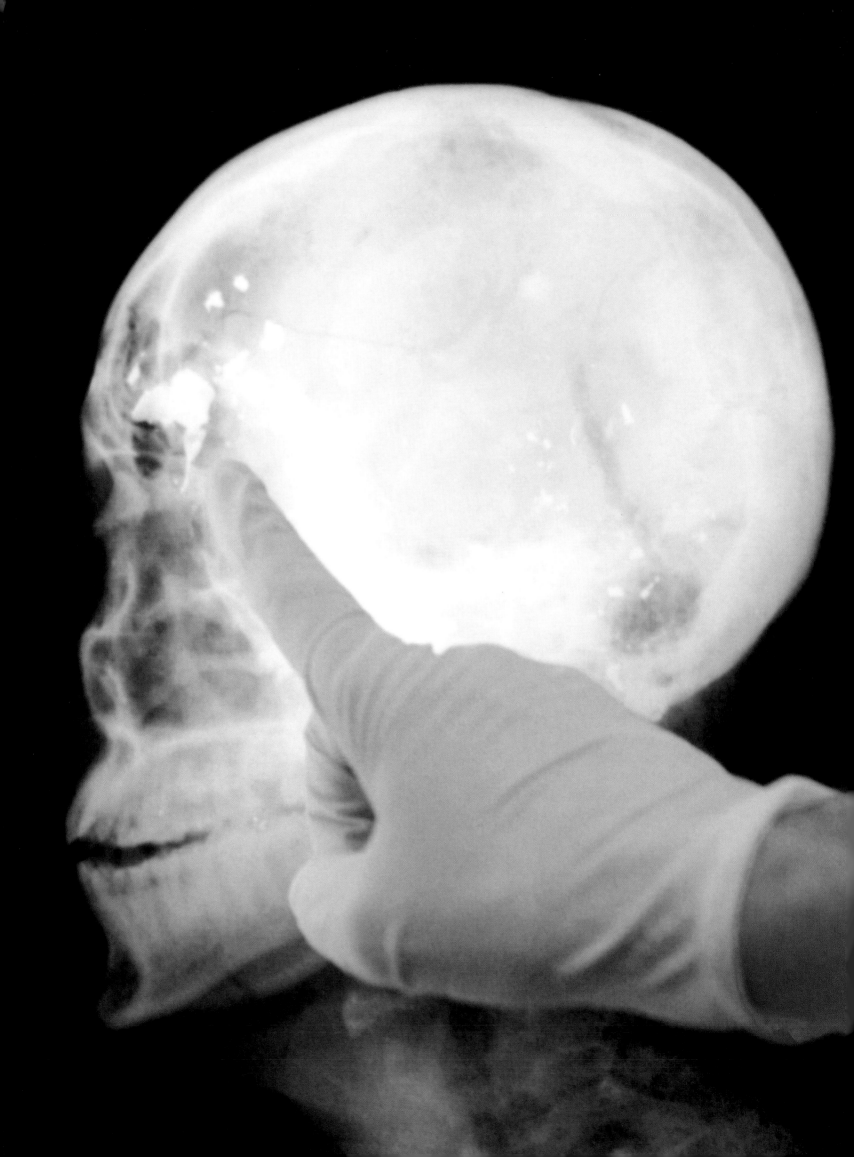

CHAPTER FIVE

CAUSE OF DEATH

The word *autopsy* means "seeing for oneself," and what the medical examiner or pathologist hopes to discover is what has brought about the death of the body on the mortuary table. In many cases of homicide, the likely cause will be immediately apparent: a ligature of some kind around the throat; evidence of extensive beating with a blunt instrument; loss of blood from stabbing or slashing; one or more gunshot wounds—or it may be a more questionable case of death by water or fire. Other causes (manual strangulation, suffocation, or poisoning, for example) may become evident on closer examination before the autopsy is begun, while suspicious deaths may need extensive investigation.

> "... continual fear and danger of violent death; and the life of man, solitary, poor, nasty, brutish, and short."
>
> —THOMAS HOBBES, *LEVIATHAN*

FACING PAGE A MEMBER OF THE AUTOPSY TEAM POINTS OUT CLEAR EVIDENCE OF THE CAUSE OF DEATH—FATAL DAMAGE BY GUNSHOT—IN THIS X-RAY OF THE SKULL OF A HOMICIDE VICTIM IN HOUSTON, TEXAS.

THE INITIAL EXAMINATION

What seems to be the cause of death, however, is not always so; there have been, for example, cases in which the victim has suffered heart failure or a brain hemorrhage in the first moments of being attacked—a circumstance that can seriously affect any charge to be brought against the assailant. In other cases, the examiner will have to express an opinion on whether the death is from natural causes, accident, or suicide. And the only way to reach this decision is by a thorough examination of the body, both externally and internally.

The first stage of an autopsy is documenting a detailed description of the appearance of the body. The medical examiner will dictate every stage into a tape recorder; photographs will also be taken, and possibly a video recording. After the clothing has been carefully cut away and placed in evidence bags, and fingerprints, footprints, and dental casts have been taken—when considered necessary—the naked body is carefully examined: Open wounds and contusions of any kind are described, and a search is made for marks of any injections. Swab specimens are taken from the mouth, breasts, sexual organs, and rectum, and also from any visible bite marks.

In a case of sexual assault, the pubic hair is combed, so that any "foreign" hair can be detected and analyzed. Scrapings will also be taken from beneath the fingernails; if the victim has struggled sufficiently to scratch his or her assailant, there will be traces of flesh and blood that can be typed.

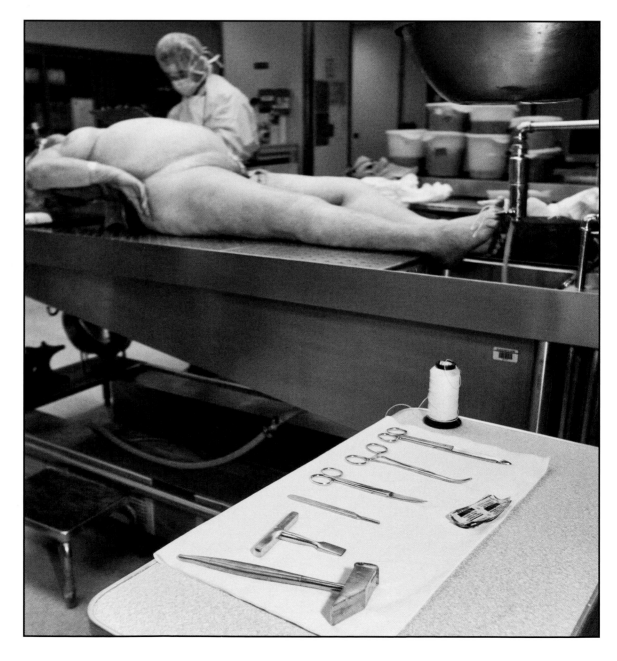

RIGHT RESIDENT PATHOLOGIST XIN MIN ZANG PREPARES TO CARRY OUT AN AUTOPSY ON A CORPSE AT THE NEW YORK CITY MEDICAL EXAMINER'S OFFICE, EARLY 2004. SOME OF THE TOOLS NEEDED FOR THE EXAMINATION ARE LAID OUT ON A TABLE IN THE FOREGROUND.

On July 23, 1976, Catherine Fried reported that she had found the body of her sixty-one-year-old husband, Paul, a leading Philadelphia gynecologist, lying face down on his bedroom floor. His nose had bled, and a bloodstained pillow lay over his head. The couple had been married only a year, but they were living apart, though they visited each other regularly. Catherine said that her husband was addicted to alcohol and barbiturates; concerned that Paul had not answered her phone calls, she had gone to his home and discovered him dead.

A scrawled note found on the bedside table appeared to be evidence of suicide, and the assistant medical examiner shortly signed the death certificate, "drug overdose." Arrangements were made for the body to be cremated, but Paul Fried's daughters by a previous marriage refused to accept that their father had killed himself, and they halted the cremation, demanding an autopsy.

This was carried out by the retired former New York City chief medical examiner Dr. Milton Helpern. He reported that there were no pathological signs of imminent fatal disease; he also noted pinpoint petechiae (tiny ruptured blood vessels) in Fried's eyes, as well as minor contusions on his neck, but nevertheless declared the death to be by natural causes. After these findings, Paul Fried's cremation took place accordingly.

ABOVE CATHERINE FRIED, WHO WAS FOUND GUILTY OF SUFFOCATING HER HUSBAND, GYNECOLOGIST PAUL FRIED, IN 1976. SHE APPEALED, BUT THE VERDICT WAS UPHELD AT A SECOND HEARING.

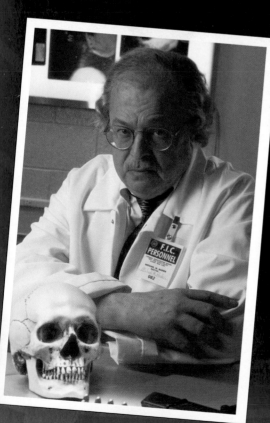

It was some time later that a man named Jerald Sklar approached the FBI, reporting that he and another man had been offered money by Catherine Fried to murder her husband. When he refused, she had herself suffocated Paul Fried with the pillow, according to Sklar.

Doubtful of prosecuting on this evidence alone, the Philadelphia DA asked Dr. Helpern's successor, Dr. Michael Baden, to review the file. Baden was first of all struck by Helpern's observation of the petechiae and minor contusions. Then he discovered the report from the toxicology laboratory, which had been filed only after permission for cremation had been given. It revealed the presence in Fried's body of only a small quantity of barbiturates, and no alcohol.

At Catherine Fried's trial, Dr. Baden testified that the cause of her husband's death was "consistent with suffocation," and she was found guilty. She appealed on the grounds of insufficient evidence, but was again found guilty in a second hearing.

LEFT DR. MICHAEL BADEN, FORMER CHIEF MEDICAL EXAMINER OF NEW YORK CITY. HIS REVIEW OF THE EVIDENCE IN THE FRIED CASE, AND HIS TESTIMONY AT THE TRIAL, ESTABLISHED THAT PAUL FRIED HAD DIED BY SUFFOCATION.

STAGES OF AN AUTOPSY

WHETHER AN AUTOPSY IS PERFORMED FOR MEDICAL OR FOR LEGAL REASONS, THE PROCEDURE FOLLOWED IS SUBSTANTIALLY THE SAME. IN THIS SERIES OF PHOTOGRAPHS, THE AUTOPSY IS BEING CARRIED OUT IN A HOSPITAL BY THE RESIDENT PATHOLOGIST, XIN MIN ZANG, AT THE NEW YORK CITY MEDICAL EXAMINER'S OFFICE, FOLLOWING THE DEATH OF A PATIENT. IN SUCH AN EVENT, PERMISSION MUST BE OBTAINED FROM NEXT OF KIN, IF KNOWN, AND CARE IS TAKEN TO PRESERVE THE APPEARANCE OF THE FACE AND UPPER TORSO, FOR LATER VIEWING IN THE CASKET. FOR THAT REASON, IF THE DECEASED IS A WOMAN (AS HERE), THE INITIAL INCISION IS U-SHAPED. IT SHOULD ALSO BE NOTED THAT THE WHITE IDENTIFICATION TAG, WHICH IS NORMALLY ATTACHED TO ONE OF THE TOES, IS HERE TIED TO A FINGER.

1. WHEN THE FLESH OF THE TORSO HAS BEEN LAID OVER THE HEAD OF THE CORPSE, THE ABDOMEN CAN BE OPENED, AND THE INTESTINES REMOVED. THEY ARE KEPT SEPARATE FROM OTHER ORGANS, SO THAT THEY DO NOT CONTAMINATE THEM WITH FECAL MATTER. THE BONE SAW IS USED TO CUT THROUGH THE RIBS AND REMOVE THE BREASTBONE, TO REVEAL THE HEART, LUNGS, TRACHEA, AND BRONCHI. AFTER THESE HAVE BEEN LIFTED OUT AS A BLOCK, THEY ARE FOLLOWED BY THE SPLEEN, LIVER, PANCREAS, AND STOMACH; THEN BY THE KIDNEYS, BLADDER, AND SEX ORGANS.

2. ALL THE ORGANS ARE WEIGHED, AND WASHED, BEFORE THEY ARE EXAMINED— AND IF NECESSARY DISSECTED—BY THE PATHOLOGIST OR HIS ASSISTANT. THE SPINAL CORD IS ALSO REMOVED AND PRESERVED. TO MAINTAIN CONTROL OF EVERY STAGE OF THE AUTOPSY, A DETAILED CHECKLIST OF THE ORGANS IS KEPT.

3. A SECOND INCISION IS MADE FROM EAR TO EAR BEHIND THE CROWN OF THE HEAD, SO THAT THE SKIN OF THE SCALP CAN BE PEELED FORWARD TO EXPOSE THE SKULL. USING A ROTARY ELECTRIC BONE SAW, THE PATHOLOGIST CUTS AWAY THE TOP OF THE SKULL, SO THAT THE BRAIN CAN BE LIFTED FREE; TO ACHIEVE THIS HE SEVERS THE ARTERIES, OPTIC NERVES, AND CERVICAL CORD. SOME PATHOLOGISTS PREFER TO EXTRACT THE BRAIN BEFORE ANY OF THE INTERNAL ORGANS. THE BRAIN IS ALSO WEIGHED, AND THEN PRESERVED IN FORMALIN FOR LATER EXAMINATION.

4. AS IN THE CASE PHOTOGRAPHED HERE, ONCE THE PATHOLOGIST IS SATISFIED THAT ALL NECESSARY PARTS OF THE BODY HAVE BEEN OBTAINED, AND THAT THE CAUSE OF DEATH IS EVIDENT, THE CORPSE MUST BE PREPARED FOR TRANSPORT TO THE FUNERAL PARLOR. THERE, THE FUNERAL DIRECTOR WILL SUPERINTEND ITS COSMETIC TREATMENT, EMBALMING (IF REQUIRED), AND CLOTHING. AS A TEMPORARY MEASURE, ABSORBENT MATERIAL IS STUFFED INTO THE ABDOMINAL CAVITY, TO FILL IT AND ABSORB LIQUIDS, AND IT IS THEN SEWN UP WITH SURGICAL THREAD. AFTER THE BODY HAS BEEN CLOSED, IT IS TRANSFERRED FROM THE DISSECTION TABLE TO A BODY BAG ON A GURNEY, AND WHEELED AWAY TO THE HOSPITAL MORGUE.

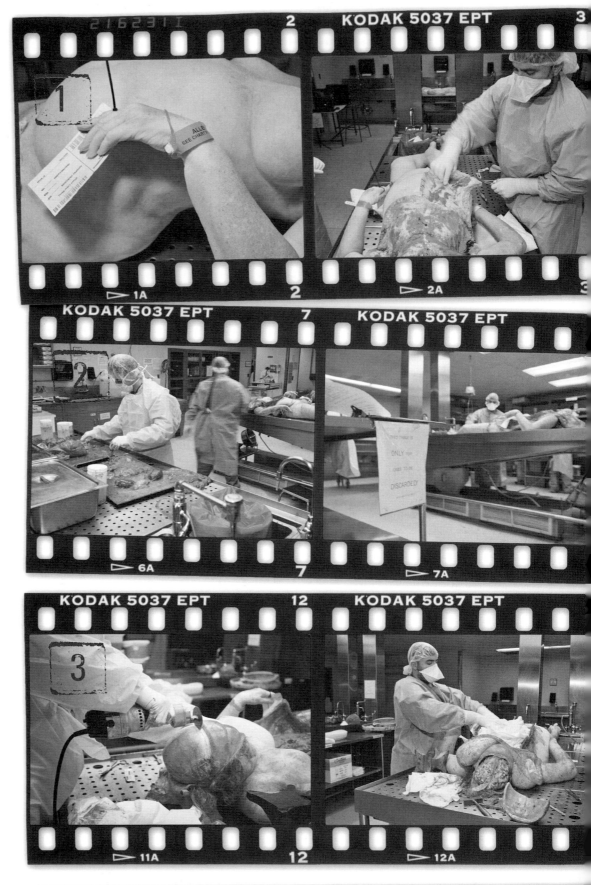

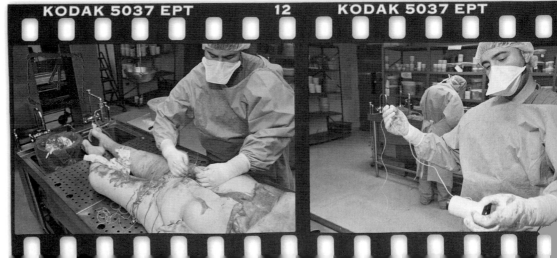

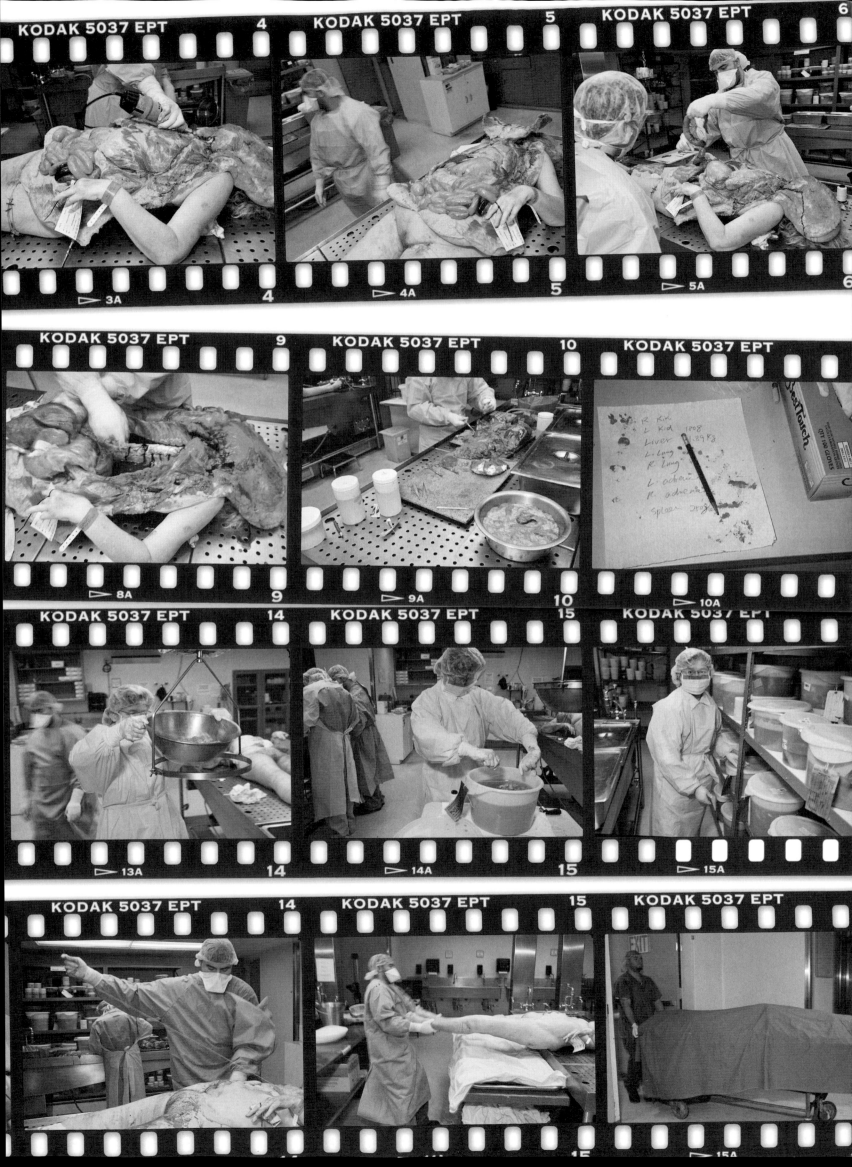

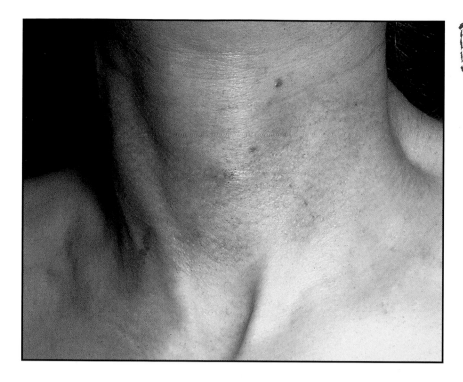

ASPHYXIATION

Before opening up the body, the examiner will look particularly for signs of asphyxiation. Deprived of oxygen, the body will quickly die; the muscles of the lungs and heart cease operation, and the brain is denied oxygenated blood. This is the condition known medically as asphyxia, a word derived from the Greek, meaning "no pulse." The brain can remain alive for some ten minutes after the heart has stopped beating, but there is an inevitable neurological deterioration during this time.

Asphyxiation occurs when the lungs are unable to take in air, and it can happen in a number of ways. Intense compression of the thorax, preventing the movement of the lungs, is often the cause of death in crowd disasters, or when an excavation collapses. Blockage of the windpipe can occur after the overly rapid

ABOVE IN CASES OF MANUAL STRANGULATION, THE NECK OF THE VICTIM WILL SHOW BRUISE MARKS FROM THE FINGERS OF THE ATTACKER. IF THE GRIP IS SHIFTED DURING THE ATTACK, THE BRUISING WILL BE LARGE AND IRREGULAR.

RIGHT MASS SUICIDE IS RARE, BUT SEVERAL CASES HAVE OCCURRED IN RECENT YEARS. IN 1977, "REVEREND" JAMES WARREN (JIM) JONES ESTABLISHED THE COLONY OF JONESTOWN IN THE RAIN FOREST OF GUYANA, WEST AFRICA. IN NOVEMBER OF THE FOLLOWING YEAR, HE ORDERED HIS CO-RELIGIONISTS TO COMMIT "REVOLUTIONARY SUICIDE." AFTER THE CHILDREN HAD BEEN INJECTED WITH CYANIDE, THE ADULTS LINED UP TO DRINK PURPLE KOOL-AID, LACED WITH CYANIDE, IN PAPER CUPS. WHEN U.S. AIR FORCE PERSONNEL ARRIVED, THEY FOUND THE BODIES OF 913 VICTIMS.

swallowing of food, for example, or in cases of drowning. Suffocation or strangling can produce a similar blockage.

Strangulation, either manually or with a ligature (anything that can be tightened around the throat), can result in death in other—but related—ways. Pressure on the windpipe can directly cut off the supply of blood to the brain; or it may overstimulate the vagus nerve. This cranial nerve detects variations in the pressure in the carotid artery; the brain responds by stopping the beating of the heart.

In the preliminary examination of a corpse, signs of asphyxia will often be immediately apparent. The face will have swelled because of raised pressure in the veins, and it will be visibly blue from the venous blood, a condition known as cyanosis. Very small ruptured blood vessels, known as petechiae, will be seen, particularly in the whites of the eyes, on the eyelids, the lips, and behind the ears.

When homicidal strangulation is manually committed one or both hands may be used, from either in front or behind the victim. The external signs are contusions and abrasions on the neck, with the fingers producing disc-shaped bruises, frequently a little smaller than the fingertips' actual size, while the thumb leaves a slightly larger mark. If death takes place within a few seconds, due to cardiac arrest, and the strangler immediately releases his hold, congestion and petechiae in the victim's face do not usually occur. If the pressure is kept up for more than fifteen seconds, however, they will appear.

Manual strangulation generally indicates that the assailant is bigger and stronger than the victim; usually, manual strangulation is carried out by a man against a woman, often during, or following, a rape.

A ligature used for strangulation can be anything capable of constricting the windpipe: cord, wire, electrical or telephone cable, a strip of cloth, a scarf, a necktie—even pantyhose or a bra. Inevitably, it will leave a distinct mark on the flesh. If the assailant does not leave it in place, this mark alone can frequently provide evidence of the nature of the ligature and its approximate width. When it is left around the throat it may be knotted, and the nature of the knot can sometimes offer a clue, particularly if it is recognized as the "signature" of a serial killer. Congestion and petechiae will develop, as in manual strangulation, if pressure is maintained for more than fifteen seconds.

Suffocation—whether with a pillow or similar soft material, inside a plastic bag, or even just by hand—leaves few traces for the examiner. The development of cyanosis and petechiae is unusual, unless there has been a struggle; because most victims of suffocation are old people or infants, this is unlikely.

Cases of drowning can take two different forms. In what is known as dry drowning, because little or no water enters the lungs, death occurs within seconds. The shock of entering the water can cause instant cardiac arrest, particularly if the water is very cold. Alternatively, water entering the nose can produce a spasm in the larynx, which reacts by tightening up to prevent water from entering the lungs; deprived of oxygen, the person rapidly becomes unconscious, and death soon follows. Dry drowning occurs in some 15 percent of cases.

Wet drowning is the inhalation of liquid into the lungs. The liquid can be anything: It can come from a puddle of water only a few centimeters deep, into which the victim has fallen face downward. Wet drowning can result from falling into a vat in a brewery or factory—or even from the victim's choking on their own vomit. If the drowning occurs in freshwater, large quantities will be absorbed from the lungs into the victim's bloodstream, the volume of which can increase as much as 50 percent within only a minute. This places such a strain on the heart that it fails. Seawater, on the other hand, has a higher salt concentration than human blood. This causes liquid from the tissues to move into the blood vessels of the lungs, resulting in pulmonary edema. As this places no immediate strain on the heart, it is possibly the reason those who drown in

BELOW THE FORMATION OF PETECHIAE—TINY RUPTURED BLOOD VESSELS—ON THE EYELIDS AND FACIAL SKIN IS A COMMON SIGN OF ASPHYXIATION.

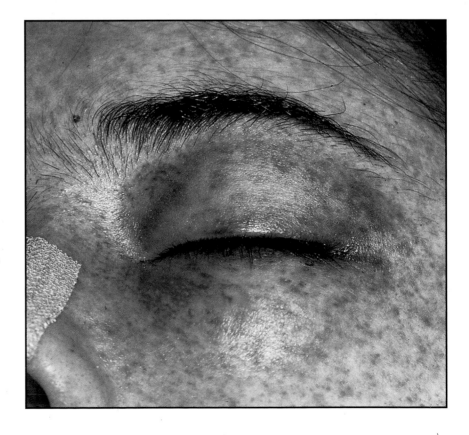

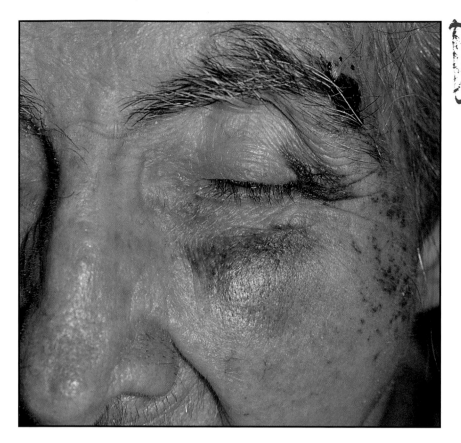

ABOVE A "BLACK EYE." AS THE SKIN SURROUNDING THE EYE IS PARTICULARLY THIN, BRUISING IN THIS AREA APPEARS DARKER THAN IN OTHER PARTS OF THE BODY. A SIMILAR CONTUSION CAN SOMETIMES RESULT FROM A BLOW TO THE SCALP.

CONTUSIONS AND OTHER INJURIES

A contusion, or bruise, is the result of a blow, either from a "blunt instrument" or from collision with a solid object. This causes the rupture of some of the smaller blood vessels, and this blood spreads into the surrounding tissue. It can be concluded that such injuries, therefore, must have been inflicted while the victim was still alive, as blood does not flow after death. The frenzied beating of a corpse can result in marks that resemble bruising, but these will be relatively small in relation to the force applied.

It is a common belief that a contusion will indicate the point of injury, the force of the blow, and even the shape of the object causing the injury, but this is a fallacy. The intense local pressure between the object and the underlying bone ruptures the blood vessels, and the blood diffuses along the fascial planes (the layers of tissue under the skin or between the muscles). For this reason, the shape of the contusion seldom reproduces the shape of the object that caused it. An exception is intradermal bruising, which occurs only in the uppermost layer of tissue. This can be seen when the skin has been squeezed into grooves, as by the tread of a car's tire, or has been struck with something like a plaited whip or belt.

Most contusions, however, are rounded in shape, as the blood diffuses fairly evenly into the surrounding tissue, with a diameter as wide as several inches across. They tend to be raised slightly above the surrounding skin, due to the accumulation of blood, and this is the first distinction from apparent contusions inflicted after death. The longer the victim remains alive after the first attack, the larger the visible contusion is likely to be; it must be remembered that bruising is not in itself a cause of death, but only an indication of what occurred before. If the blow releases sufficient blood, it can continue to diffuse through the tissue—even after death—either toward the surface of the skin or through lower tissues. A blow on the thigh, for example, may subsequently appear as a contusion on the knee, and a blow high on the scalp can result in a black eye.

Because it is the underlying bone that resists the force of a blow, deep bruising can occur in any intervening organ, and may not be visible at the surface. The English pathologist Sir Bernard Spilsbury wrote that this was true of up to 50 percent of severe abdominal injuries,

seawater can struggle for much longer than they could have in freshwater. When water enters the lungs, it results in the production of a frothy mixture of water, mucus, and air, which can appear in the nostrils and mouth.

Oxygen deprivation of the tissues is also produced by two deadly poisons: carbon monoxide and cyanide. Carbon monoxide is a major constituent of coal gas, and also of inefficiently burned natural gas (butane or propane), and of much car exhaust. It is highly toxic because it has an "affinity" for the hemoglobin in the blood some 300 times greater than that of oxygen; as it replaces the blood's oxygen, asphyxia rapidly ensues. A sure sign of carbon monoxide poisoning is a cherry-pink coloration of the skin, lips, and internal organs; this is particularly noticeable in hypostasis (see page 114).

Cyanide—whether in the form of the gas hydrogen cyanide, in its aqueous solution (prussic acid), or in a wide range of industrial compounds—also kills by preventing oxygen from reaching the bodily tissues. The mechanism is different from that produced by carbon monoxide, however: Cyanide inhibits the enzyme involved in the uptake of oxygen from the tissues, an effect that is almost immediate. The resulting coloration of the blood can be mistaken for that due to carbon monoxide poisoning, but it is usually a little darker. Certain drugs can also produce a similar but browner coloration.

wherein the blow caused the rupture of a vital internal organ without rupturing the blood vessels at the point of impact.

Contusions are most readily visible on prominent parts of the body, but the examiner must give attention to all parts. Bruising of the scalp is the most easily overlooked because the hair conceals it. If the shoulder blades are bruised, this is evidence that the victim was held down forcibly against a hard surface. Bruising of the arms reveals that the victim was seized brutally. Female rape victims usually suffer bruising of the inner thighs and vulva; bruising of the arms and face as the result of a struggle is also likely.

In time, the color of a contusion will change because of the breakdown of the blood hemoglobin; from red it changes rapidly to blue-black, then progressively to brown, green, and yellow, before finally fading. It is impossible, however, to date a contusion by its color; even two bruises sustained by the same individual at the same time may change color at different rates. Nevertheless, the examination of contusions is particularly important in cases of alleged child abuse: If multiple bruises are seen to be distinctly different in color, they can indicate a history of blows.

As for the force of the blow, it is possible that a heavy blow could produce a larger contusion than a light one would. However, large, superficial contusions on the eyelids and genitals, for example, can be produced with relatively light force, while only blows of considerable force will bruise the scalp. And the very young, the elderly, the obese, and those in poor physical condition generally bruise more easily than the fit.

Abrasions are superficial injuries, involving only the outer layers of the skin, but for the examiner they can be significant, as they may be the only indication of severe internal damage that will be discovered later. Moreover, unlike contusions, they mark the exact point at which the injury occurred. Fingernail scratches, whether on the body of the victim or that of a suspect, are obviously of importance, as are bite marks. Abrasions may also be produced if the victim has been tied around the wrists or ankles, or they can occur in the course of strangulation. However, visible abrasion can result from moving the corpse, particularly if it has been recovered by a rescue team from a location difficult to access, or from the water.

When a heavy blow splits the skin, the injury is called a laceration. The tissues edging the injury will be abraded and bruised, and the split irregular in shape, with strands of nerve tissue and minor blood vessels stretched across

it. The shape and location of the laceration is not directly related to the nature and site of the blow. A single blow with a metal rod, for example, will often result in a Y-shaped laceration; a blow to the side of the head can result in laceration of the lower jaw, the ear, and the front of the brow; and a blow to the lower part of the body may not lacerate the skin, but can result in extensive laceration of the underlying tissues.

SHARP INSTRUMENTS

Wounds from a sharp instrument are immediately visible. They can be of two general types: incised wounds, produced by slashing, whether from a weapon, such as a razor or knife, or by a jagged piece of metal or glass; and punctured wounds, from the point of a knife or similar long, narrow instrument. There usually is a considerable loss of blood from such wounds, but there have also been cases in which the killer has slashed or stabbed the body only after

BELOW A SEVERE LACERATION TO A WOMAN'S SCALP, IN THIS CASE CAUSED BY A FALL, NOT A HOMICIDAL ATTACK. LESSER WOUNDS TO THE SCALP ARE FREQUENTLY COVERED BY THE HAIR, AND ARE ONLY REVEALED AT THE AUTOPSY.

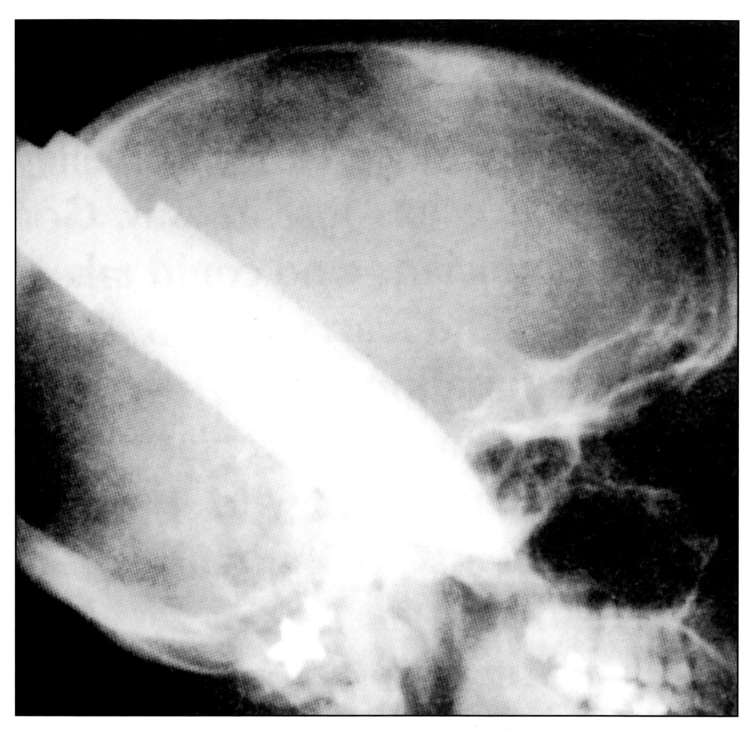

death, resulting in little blood loss, as the heart had already stopped.

Although incised wounds are usually straight, they may be curved if the direction of the blade is changed. Because they generally gape, it is not possible to assess the breadth of the edge that produced them. And, in a deep wound, not only are blood vessels and nerves severed, but muscles and tendons may also be cut through. As a result, the wound will gape even wider.

With punctured wounds, similarly, their external appearance is no firm indication of the shape and dimensions of the weapon that caused them. The pressure of the point on the

skin at the moment before entry can stretch it, so that the subsequent size of the puncture may appear smaller than the actual breadth of the blade that produced it. Moreover, if the knife is twisted as it is withdrawn, the wound will be larger and possibly X-shaped in appearance. Even after conducting an internal examination of the victim, a pathologist will be very cautious in speculating on the size and shape of any weapon suspected in the death.

Finally, the examiner will note characteristic defense wounds on the victim's hands and forearms. These typically result from an attack with a knife or similar weapon, as the person attempts to seize it or ward off blows.

GUNSHOT WOUNDS

When a gun is fired at a person at close range, burned—and sometimes unburned—particles of the propulsive powder will produce a distinctive "tattooing" of the skin around the wound, or a related pattern will appear on the clothing. However, if the gun has been held against, or very close to, the skin, these particles will be driven into the wound, without any characteristic tattooing. The pattern is usually absent, also, if the gun is fired from a distance of more than 9 or 10 ft. (3 m). But if tattooing is present, the size and shape of the pattern can provide a guide to the distance from which the shot was fired, as well as its direction. Analysis of the particles may further provide identification of the powder, which may subsequently prove traceable to a specific bullet manufacturer.

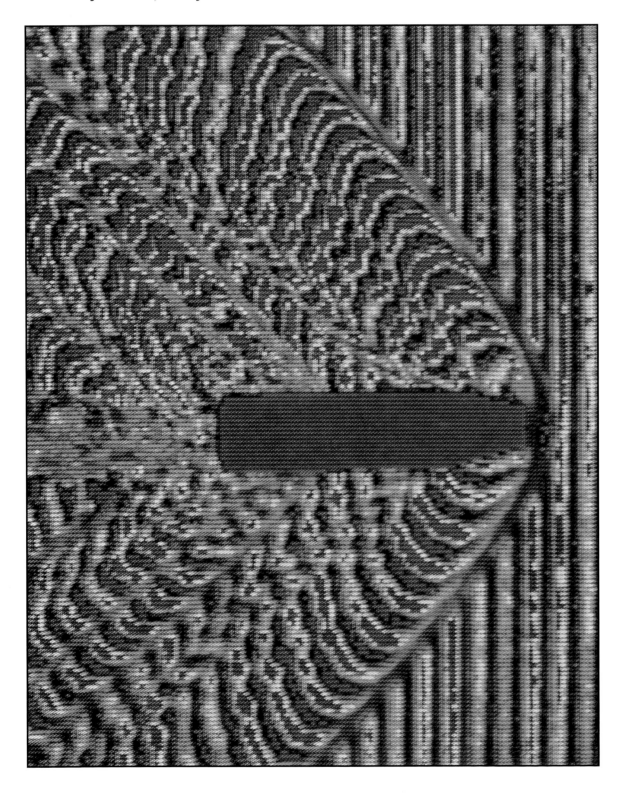

LEFT A DRAMATIC PHOTOGRAPH OF A .20 CALIBER (5MM) BULLET IN FLIGHT, REVEALING THE SHOCK WAVE THAT ACCOMPANIES IT AT 500 METERS PER SECOND. THE PHOTOGRAPH WAS TAKEN AT THE FRANCO-GERMAN RESEARCH INSTITUTE, ST. LOUIS, FRANCE, A SPECIALIZED CENTER FOR BALLISTICS INVESTIGATION. IT WAS OBTAINED USING POLARIZED LIGHT FROM A PULSED LASER, AND THE EXPOSURE TIME WAS 20 NANOSECONDS.

Small traces of the bullet's metal will be found around the wound or a hole in the clothing. A bullet, after its passage through the barrel of a gun, is also very hot, and it can cause synthetic fibers in clothing to melt. Both of these factors can give an additional indication of the distance from which the gun was fired.

All this can prove of great importance in determining whether the death was a suicide, as the victim usually will not have held the gun at a greater distance from their body than the length of their arm—although, in one or two rare cases, it was claimed that they had pressed the trigger with their big toe! In the same way, the distance from which the gun was fired can also be vital evidence when the killer claims that it was triggered accidentally during a struggle.

When a bullet leaves a rifled gun barrel it is spinning, and traveling at some 1,650 ft. (500 m) per second. It then begins to develop "tail wag," or a wobbling in its flight. At close range, it will produce a small, clean hole, approximately the size of its own caliber, together with a characteristic "abrasion collar" caused by frictional heat as it penetrates the skin; at greater distances the tail wag will result in a large, lacerated wound.

Inside the body, the bullet produces cavitation as it causes the tissues to expand, then collapse upon themselves, leaving a clearly

CASE STUDY
KENNEDY ASSASSINATION

RIGHT THIS PHOTOGRAPH SHOWS THE BLOOD-STAINED REAR SEAT OF THE PRESIDENTIAL LIMOUSINE. ONE OF THE TWO BULLETS WAS LATER FOUND ON THE FLOOR OF THE VEHICLE.

RIGHT, CENTER THE WARREN COMMISSION PUBLISHED TWENTY-SIX VOLUMES OF EVIDENCE PRESENTED BEFORE IT, BUT DID NOT CONSULT A SINGLE FORENSIC PATHOLOGIST.

BELOW A PHOTOGRAPH OF THE ASSASSINATED PRESIDENT, TAKEN DURING THE AUTOPSY OF HIS BODY. TWO SEPARATE EXAMINATIONS WERE PERFORMED: THE FIRST AT PARKLAND HOSPITAL, DALLAS, AND THE SECOND AT BETHESDA NAVAL HOSPITAL, IN WASHINGTON, D.C.

After the killing of President John F. Kennedy and the wounding of Governor John Connally by Lee Harvey Oswald in Dallas, Texas, on November 22, 1963, there were bitter arguments concerning the number of shots that had been fired. None of the pathologists who examined the president's body at the time were experienced in gunshot wounds; and the Warren Commission, which was set up in 1964 to examine the evidence, failed to interview or consult a single forensic expert.

It was not until 1977 that the Congress Select Committee on Assassinations empanelled a group of forensic pathologists, headed by Dr. Michael Baden, the New York City medical examiner, to review the evidence.

The panel learned that a tracheotomy had been performed on the president's throat, in an attempt to allow him to breathe, and that this had completely obscured the exit wound of the bullet that had struck him in the back. This bullet, it was decided, had then hit Governor Connally's back sideways on—leaving an entry wound 2 in. (5.08 cm) long—exited below his right nipple, entered his right wrist, and finally passed through part of his left thigh. The bullet had, in fact, been found lying on the stretcher that carried Connally to the hospital.

Enhanced prints of existing X-rays revealed that a second bullet had struck the president in the head, exiting above his right ear. It then struck the windscreen pillar of the car, and was later found on the floor. Dr. Baden and his colleagues concluded that there had been only two shots, and that both had come from behind.

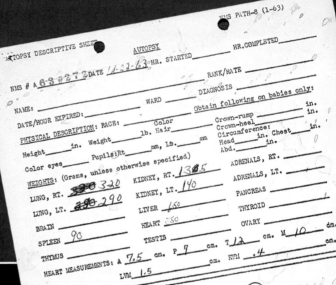

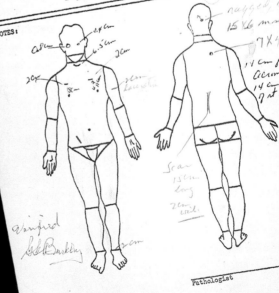

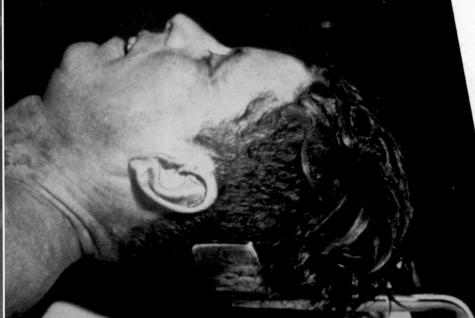

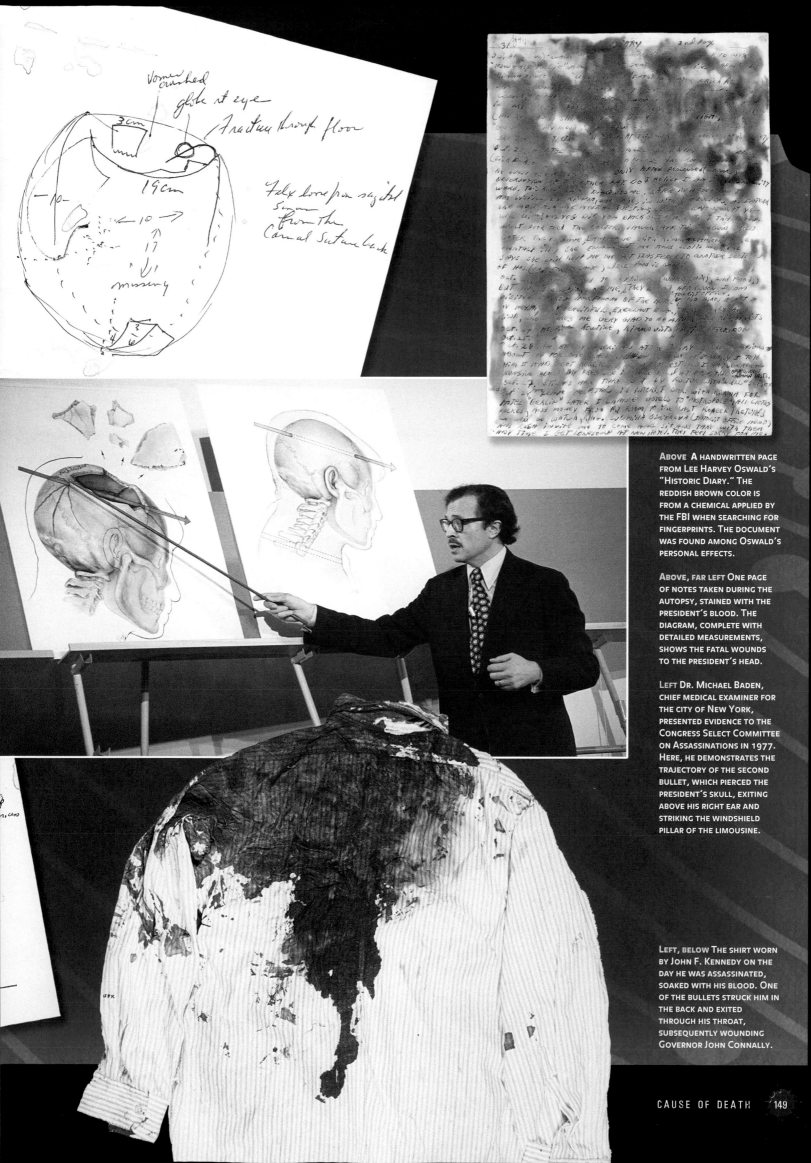

Above A handwritten page from Lee Harvey Oswald's "Historic Diary." The reddish brown color is from a chemical applied by the FBI when searching for fingerprints. The document was found among Oswald's personal effects.

Above, far left One page of notes taken during the autopsy, stained with the president's blood. The diagram, complete with detailed measurements, shows the fatal wounds to the president's head.

Left Dr. Michael Baden, chief medical examiner for the city of New York, presented evidence to the Congress Select Committee on Assassinations in 1977. Here, he demonstrates the trajectory of the second bullet, which pierced the president's skull, exiting above his right ear and striking the windshield pillar of the limousine.

Left, below The shirt worn by John F. Kennedy on the day he was assassinated, soaked with his blood. One of the bullets struck him in the back and exited through his throat, subsequently wounding Governor John Connally.

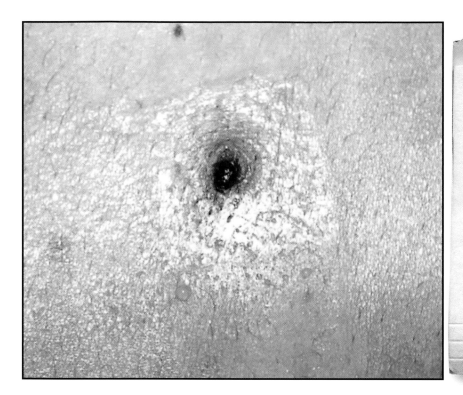

ABOVE A TYPICAL ENTRY WOUND FROM A BULLET, FIRED FROM A DISTANCE OF MORE THAN 9 FT. (3 M). THE HOLE IS APPROXIMATELY THE SAME SIZE AS THE CALIBER OF THE BULLET, AND THE CHARACTERISTIC ABRASION COLLAR AROUND THE WOUND—CAUSED BY THE HEAT OF THE BULLET—CAN BE SEEN.

defined track that is easily detected by dissection. The exit wound is usually larger than the entry wound, bursting the skin outward in a star shape. If the skin was tightly restricted (by a belt, for example, or if the victim was against a wall), however, the exit wound may be no bigger than the entry wound.

A bullet can be deflected from its path by bone or tissue, so that any exit wound will be much larger than the entry wound, and roughly torn. The bullet may also disintegrate, leaving some fragments in the tissues and producing a similarly torn exit hole. In some cases, a bullet has been found to have traveled inside the body in strange ways. Sufficiently deflected, it can pass up a limb, or even from one part of the body to another.

Two cases from the FBI archives provide particularly striking examples of this. In one, a small-caliber bullet entered the wrist of the victim, traveled up a vein to his heart, and killed him. In the second, a bank robber attempted to kill a woman teller with a shot to her head from a .357 Magnum. The bullet traveled round inside her skull without damaging her brain; although she fell unconscious, apparently dead, she recovered and was able to testify in court.

RIGHT A BULLET'S EXIT WOUND IS USUALLY LARGER THAN THE ENTRY WOUND, BURSTING AND PULLING AWAY THE SKIN. EXIT WOUNDS VARY CONSIDERABLY IN SIZE AND SHAPE BECAUSE THE BULLET CAN BE DEFORMED IN ITS TRANSIT THROUGH THE BODY. IF THE BULLET STRIKES BONE IT MAY DISINTEGRATE, TEARING A LARGE HOLE. BY CONTRAST, THERE MAY BE NO EXIT WOUND AT ALL IF THE BULLET'S ENERGY IS ABSORBED BY THE TISSUES. SOME BULLETS ARE DESIGNED TO DEFORM SO THAT ALL THEIR ENERGY IS CONVERTED TO TISSUE DAMAGE, AND THEY DO NOT EXIT THE BODY.

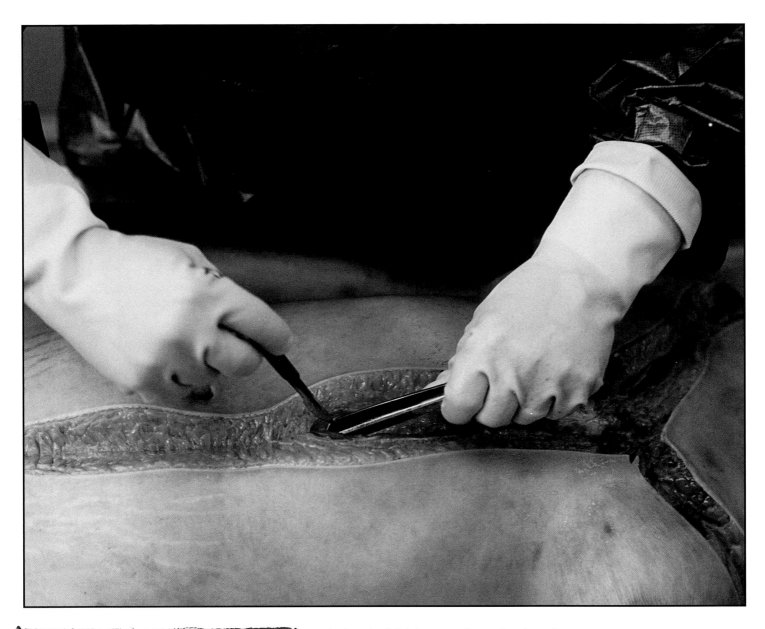

INTERNAL EXAMINATION

Once the examiner has completed the description of the external appearance of the body, the internal examination can begin.

Using a very sharp knife—considerably larger than those used by surgeons—the pathologist makes an incision straight down the front of the body, from the larynx to the pubis. Alternatively, particularly in cases of young children, a Y-shaped cut is made from behind each ear and down the sternum as far as the groin. The pathologist is then able, with the aid of the knife, to peel back the skin and muscles of the chest to reveal the ribs. This exposes the neck and chest, the bones, muscles, and internal organs; it may also reveal bruising to the trunk that was not apparent during the initial external examination. A second incision is made from behind each ear, meeting behind the crown of the head.

Any wounds and contusions must be carefully explored and described, and tissue samples are usually taken at this stage. In firearm fatalities, the track of the bullet or bullets is traced, and all fragments, as well as any whole bullets, are recovered. The examiner will also make a note of any broken bones.

Next, the cartilage joining the ribs is cut through, together with the abdomen, to enable the removal of the heart, lungs, liver, and other organs, including the stomach and intestines. Each of the organs is weighed and set aside for later examination.

The incisions on the back of the head make it possible to peel away the skin of the scalp and expose the skull, which is examined for depressions and fractures. A circular saw is used to cut round the skull, and the top is prized off. Some examiners prefer to do this first of all;

ABOVE IN FORENSIC EXAMINATIONS THE INCISION IS USUALLY Y-SHAPED, AS SHOWN HERE. IN HOSPITAL AUTOPSIES, FOLLOWING THE DEATH OF A PATIENT, THE INCISION IS NORMALLY A WIDE U. THIS PRESERVES THE APPEARANCE OF THE UPPER TORSO FOR SUBSEQUENT PRESENTATION IN A FUNERAL CASKET.

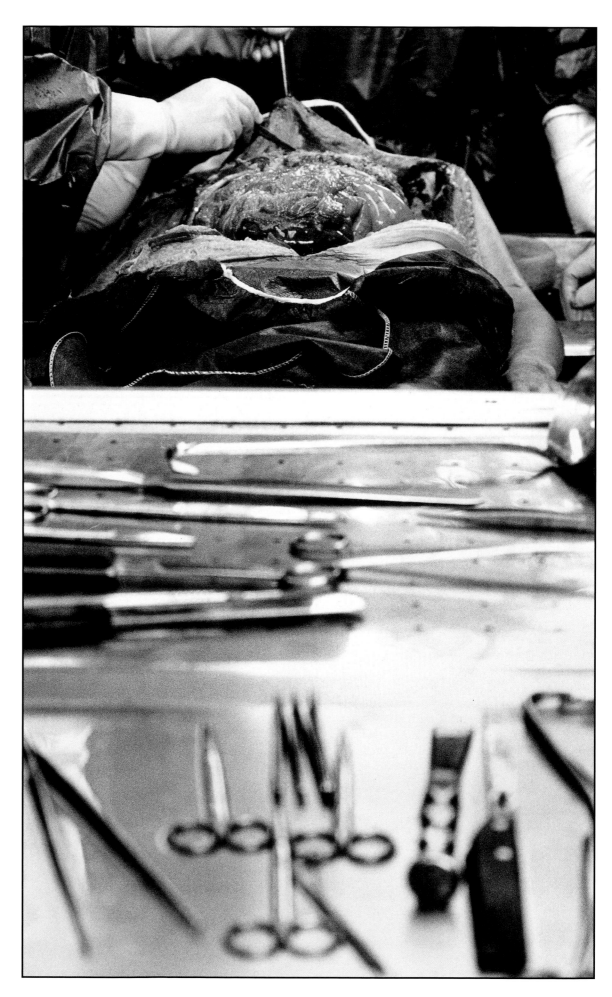

RIGHT A TYPICAL SCENE IN
THE MORTUARY DURING AN
AUTOPSY. THE EXAMINER'S
RANGE OF STERILIZED SURGICAL
INSTRUMENTS, INCLUDING THE
LARGE, SHARP KNIVES USED
FOR OPENING UP THE CORPSE,
ARE LAID OUT ON THE TABLE
IN THE FOREGROUND. EVERY
STAGE OF THE OPERATION
IS DICTATED INTO A TAPE
RECORDER.

An unusual case of homicide, in which the murderer claimed the death to be an accident, occurred during the 1970s. One day, Iris Seagar plunged to her death, landing on the sidewalk some 197 ft. (60 m) below the balcony of the penthouse apartment she shared with her husband in Baltimore, Maryland. When neighbors described how she had suffered the brutality of her drunken husband, the police were prepared to accept her death as suicide.

Mr. Seagar, however, insisted that her death was an accident. "She was fiddling with a faulty air conditioner," he said, "and tipped over the guardrail." Then the police learned that he was the beneficiary of his wife's $100,000 insurance policy, which would have been invalid in the case of suicide, and they initiated further inquiries. A forensic expert built several dummies of the same weight and height as Mrs. Seagar's, and a video recording was made as they were tipped, pushed, and thrown over the rail of the balcony. The recording clearly showed that, if the fall had been accidental, the body would have struck the ground no more than 10.4 ft. (3.2 m) away from the wall of the building. If Mrs. Seagar had jumped, the distance would have been, at most, 14.1 ft. (4.3 m). But the body had in fact landed 16.4 ft. (5 m) away from the wall. Confronted with this evidence, Seagar admitted that he had thrown his wife from the balcony in a drunken rage.

in certain cases of poisoning there is a distinctive smell to the brain, which might be masked by other odors if the abdomen is opened as the initial stage of dissection.

The pathologist examines the brain and the inside of the skull very closely for any signs of injury, new or old; traces of past injuries can give a clue to the victim's lifestyle and identity. The brain is then removed and weighed.

All the extracted organs are washed in a stream of water to remove blood, and each is dissected separately. The recommended order of examination is: tongue, carotid arteries, esophagus, larynx, trachea, thyroid, lungs, the great blood vessels and the heart, stomach, intestines, adrenals, kidneys, spleen, pancreas, liver, bladder, uterus and ovaries, and testes, with the brain left for last.

If it appears that the victim was strangled, the examiner will pay particular attention to the smaller, fragile structures of the neck. In such a case, the larynx may be found to be damaged, with the upper horns of the thyroid cartilage fractured on one or both sides. The horns of the small hyoid bone below the jaw may also be broken, with hemorrhaging found in the muscles of the neck. If possible, an X-ray of the area is taken before dissection.

In the case of a corpse recovered from a fire, or apparently drowned, the pathologist will search all the air passages and the lungs for traces of soot or water. If little or no traces are found, the victim was probably dead before the fire was started, or before the body entered the water. (Although, as described previously, water may be absent in some cases of drowning.) If water is present, the lungs will be waterlogged and soggy to the touch. As much liquid as possible will be collected for later analysis. In a case of fire, the victim's blood will also be sent to the laboratory; if carbon monoxide is found, it is a sure sign that he or she was still breathing when the fire began.

Examination of the heart and its major vessels is essential in order to discover evidence of heart disease. The condition of the liver may reveal cirrhosis or hepatitis, although many drugs (particularly an overdose of acetaminophen, otherwise known as paracetamol, a widely available analgesic) can produce a similar appearance. Inflammation of the kidneys can be caused by toxic metallic salts such as those of mercury, or from chronic lead poisoning.

The stomach is opened to inspect its contents, which may provide evidence of the last meal taken before death, and possibly some indication of the time that has elapsed since then (see page 115). A keen sense of smell is important at this stage, in order to detect chemicals such as ammonia or phenol (carbolic acid), or the characteristic odor of cyanide. One eminent English pathologist was able to detect the bitter-almond smell of cyanide only if he smoked while carrying out his dissection of the stomach.

After examination of the remaining organs, the pathologist's work is effectively completed. Tissue samples and body fluids will now go to the laboratory for analysis by serologists, toxicologists, and other specialists. In certain cases, such as extensive body injury or gunshot wounds, examination of the limbs—including X-radiography and, possibly, dissection—may also be necessary. In hit-and-run fatalities, for example, fractures of the large bones can indicate the succession of impacts with the body of the car, and perhaps even the angle at which they occurred. If the victim is unidentified, a note of any old repaired fractures will be made, to compare with relevant medical records.

BIZARRE SUICIDES

Medicolegal literature provides many examples of cases of suicide that could be mistaken for homicide. In *Mostly Murder* (1959), the eminent Scottish pathologist Sir Sydney Smith described how "a maid in a hospital hacked the front of her head, inflicting twenty cuts; then, finding this ineffective, she filled a bath with warm water and drowned herself." He commented: "I wonder how many of us doctors, finding a number of hatchet wounds in the skull, would think of suicide."

The English pathologist Dr. Keith Simpson described, in *Forty Years of Murder* (1978), an equally unusual case to which he was called. A man was found drowned, his body trussed with rope, and the circumstances convinced the police that it was murder. Simpson disagreed. The man had died, he announced, "by his own hands and teeth." He demonstrated how the suicide had tied a noose around his legs, then, pulling the rope upward and tightening a succession of knots, had

succeeded in tying off the end with his teeth. And, to prove his point, he shone a torch into the man's mouth, and showed a strand of the rope caught between his teeth.

In concluding the lectures he gave to medical students, Sir Sydney Smith would frequently describe a case—though not one of his own—of an extraordinary suicide attempt. A man decided to hang himself from a branch of a tree standing on the edge of a cliff, jutting out over the sea below. He first took a large dose of opium, then, to make sure of his death, decided to shoot himself as well. "The noose adjusted, the poison taken, and the revolver cocked, he stepped over the cliff, and as he did so he fired. The jerk of the rope altered his aim, and the bullet missed his head but cut partly through the rope. This broke with the jerk of the body, and he fell fifty feet into the sea below. There he swallowed a quantity of sea water, vomited up the poison, and swam ashore a better and wiser man."

THE NATURE OF THE DEATH

Finally, the examiner is required to express an opinion as to whether the death is due to natural and progressive physical causes, accident, suicide, or was at the hand of another person.

In the case of natural death, the examination at autopsy, and any subsequent laboratory investigation, will almost invariably provide confirmation of the fact. There are cases, however, in which a suicide or an accident can appear to be the result of homicide, and conversely. As Professor Cyril Polson put it in his *Essentials of Forensic Medicine,* "The cunning suicide ... may plan his death in a manner which suggests homicide. More often, attempts are made by a murderer to present the result of his crime as suicide."

In an article in *The Criminologist* magazine, Professor Polson further exemplified how misleading the apparent cause of death can be. He listed twelve cases that appeared to the police, at first sight, to be homicide. All were subsequently shown to be due to accident or suicide. For example, an "ax murder" proved to be a shotgun suicide; an apparent strangling was shown to be death by heart attack; the "sea of blood" that was at first assumed to be the result of a violent assault was due to a burst varicose vein; and a victim who appeared to have been "kicked to death" had suffered an accidental fall.

Innumerable suicides have been committed by slashing the wrists or the carotid artery in the neck. In many cases, it is essential to be certain that the death is not homicide. Almost always, a genuine suicide is preceded by two or three experimental cuts, which are not deep enough to cause the massive flow of blood that results in death. A single deep slash, therefore, will arouse suspicions of homicide, particularly if it is in the neck.

There are other signs to look for. When a right-handed person cuts his or her own throat, for example, the deepest part of the slash usually begins high up on the left, ending lower on the right. The opposite is true, of course, for a left-handed suicide. Only another person standing behind the victim could inflict a similar wound, and it would probably be deeper on the right, lower on the neck, and more horizontal. A slash made by a murderer standing in front of the victim can be distinguished relatively easily.

A suicidal neck wound is usually cleanly cut because the person has thrown back his or her head to stretch the skin of the throat. A murder victim, taken unawares, has the skin relaxed, and it creases under the pressure of the blade, resulting in an uneven edge to the slash. Sometimes, however, the murderer will seize the victim's hair to pull the head back. If there is a struggle, some hair may be pulled out, and signs of this can be detected in the initial examination of the body. Moreover, a murderer will often have to use a degree of force in restraining the victim, and contusions may be found on one or both of the body's arms.

Murder by hanging is often made to look like suicide. In such cases, the crime scene investigator will be the first to look for signs of a struggle, or marks on the floor where the body has been dragged. If the noose is tightened around the victim's neck, then passed over a convenient hook or beam, loose fibers of the rope are likely to be detached as the body is hauled up, and the rope itself may also be affected.

In other cases, the murderer leaves the body on the ground, cuts the rope in two, knots the free half over the hook or beam, then claims to have found the body hanging and cut it down. Laboratory examination of the rope will reveal, however, that it was not cut under tension; there is also unlikely to be any grooving of the beam that would be caused by the weight of a hanging body. A classic case of murder, claimed to be suicide by hanging, is the killing of Elsie Cameron by Norman Thorne, in England in 1924, which is described on page 239.

Homicidal poisoning too can often be mistaken for suicide, particularly if the murderer leaves the poison near the body—and, sometimes, even forges a farewell note. Signs of some poisons can be detected in the external appearance of the body, or in the report of symptoms exhibited by the victim before death, while others may be detected during autopsy. Confirmation, however, must rely on the analyses performed by a toxicologist in the laboratory.

An odd, and inexplicable, fact noted in many cases is that a person committing suicide usually removes his or her spectacles before taking poison. If the body is found still wearing glasses, therefore, it can be a good reason for suspecting murder and warrants further investigation.

LABORATORY EXAMINATION

A wide range of analytical tests is available in the crime laboratory. Principal among these are the investigation of blood, semen, sweat, and saliva as detailed in Chapter 2 (for DNA typing see Chapter 6); if there is any suspicion that the victim was poisoned, priority is also given to the search for the toxic agent, more particularly in the stomach and other relevant organs, as well as in the blood, urine, and brain. Analysis of tissue samples may also prove necessary.

It is a fact, though few people would believe it, that any substance can act as a poison, if taken in sufficient quantity. There are even cases in which people have died from consuming too much water, a condition known as hyponatremia that is frequently associated with long-ditance running and cycling events. As the flamboyant physician and alchemist Theophrastus Bombastus (only too appropriate a name) von Hohenheim—who named himself Paracelsus, or "second to none"—wrote as long ago as the sixteenth century, "All substances are poisons: there is none that is not a poison. The right dose differentiates a poison and a remedy." The term *poison*, however, is by common consent applicable to those substances that can bring about death rapidly, when administered once or twice in relatively small quantities, or slowly, when taken cumulatively over an extended period.

In many cases in the recent past, the analyses to be carried out by the toxicologist were relatively straightforward, as the cause of death was already suspected. The physiological effects of poisoning by arsenic (see Chapter 1) or

CASE STUDY
HAROLD SHIPMAN

Right Dr. Harold Shipman, the English physician and serial killer, convicted of fifteen murders of his patients. Although he had served a term of imprisonment for drug abuse, he was allowed to continue practicing. In January 2004 he was discovered hanging in his prison cell.

Below Police exhuming the body of one of Dr. Harold Shipman's victims for toxicological analysis. He is now credited with more than two hundred killings, but unofficial estimates set the figure at more than six hundred.

Although the nineteenth and early twentieth century saw a number of cases of serial poisoning, usually by the use of arsenic or strychnine, none can match the recent activities of the English physician Dr. Harold Shipman, who was a respected local doctor in Hyde, a suburb of the city of Manchester. Most of his patients were relatively elderly women, and for several years it caused little surprise that many expired soon after he had visited them, or had even died on his premises.

Nevertheless, suspicions were eventually aroused, and Shipman was arrested in 1998. An analysis of his computer data (which he mistakenly believed he had deleted), as well as a comparison with pharmacists' records, revealed that he had purchased large quantities of diamorphine (heroin) that were not accounted for. He was charged with, and found guilty of, murdering fifteen of his patients. Following his imprisonment for life, further inquiries have suggested that he may have been responsible for as many as six hundred deaths. He is suspected of committing an average of three or four murders a month at the height of his activities, including seven in February 1998 and six the following month. After his arrest, and throughout his trial, Shipman maintained a confident—even arrogant—attitude, and denied his guilt. In prison before his death, he consistently refused to reveal his motive; it seems it was nothing but the obsessive desire to kill, and kill again.

In 1957, Kenneth Barlow, a male nurse in Bradford, England, killed his wife with several massive injections of insulin. He claimed to have found her drowned in the bath, but the abnormally high level of blood sugar found in her heart strengthened suspicions that had already been aroused by the circumstances in which she had been found. It transpired that Barlow had once remarked to another nurse that insulin would be his choice for the perfect murder because it would rapidly induce coma and could not be traced.

There was, in fact, no known analytical test for insulin at that time. Moreover, the drug is designed specifically to *reduce* blood sugar levels in sufferers from diabetes. A panel of experts, headed by toxicologist Dr. Alan Curry, was assembled

to consider the problem. Eventually they uncovered reports that, in cases of sudden death, the liver often flooded the bloodstream with sugar in the last moments.

The question now was to determine whether, and how much, insulin had been injected. A painstaking examination of Mrs. Barlow's body had revealed the minute marks of four injections in her buttocks, and tissue samples were taken. Extracts from these were injected into laboratory mice, and various amounts of insulin were injected into a control group. All became comatose, then died. It was possible to calculate that Barlow had, indeed, injected his wife with massive doses of the drug. He was found guilty of murder, and sentenced to life imprisonment.

strychnine, for example, are likely to have been reported by the victim's physician; confirmation is easily obtained by laboratory tests.

The symptoms of strychnine poisoning are dramatic; the muscles go into spasm, so that breathing becomes very difficult, and the back arches, so that only the head and heels touch the surface on which the victim's body lies. The

face becomes darkly suffused with blood, and spasms of the mouth muscles result in a characteristic grimace that is known as *risus sardonicus*. Nevertheless, physicians occasionally fail to observe these symptoms. When Arthur Major died unexpectedly in Lincolnshire, England, in May 1934, his doctor certified the cause of death as "status

LEFT BECAUSE CONTEMPORARY POISONING CASES ARE RELATIVELY RARE, AMERICAN-BORN DR. HAWLEY HARVEY CRIPPEN, WHO KILLED HIS WIFE IN LONDON WITH HYOSCINE, HAS REMAINED ONE OF THE FAMOUS MURDERERS OF THE TWENTIETH CENTURY. HE WAS IDENTIFIED ABOARD A SHIP BOUND FOR CANADA, HIS DESCRIPTION HAVING BEEN SENT BY RADIO—THE FIRST TIME IT WAS USED IN A MURDER HUNT—AND APPREHENDED WHEN THE SHIP ARRIVED AT ITS DESTINATION.

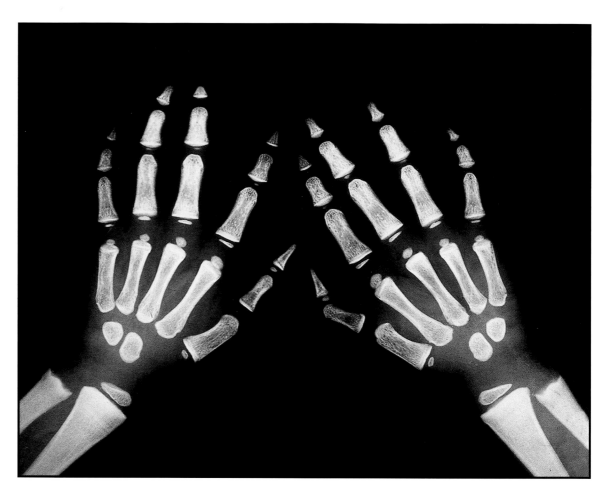

epilecticus." It was only after an anonymous letter reported that a neighbor's dog had died similarly, after eating scraps fed to it by Major's wife, Ethel, that the police obtained an exhumation order, and analysis revealed that Major had been poisoned with strychnine.

As described before, the effects of poisoning by carbon monoxide or cyanide will be apparent at autopsy, and can be confirmed by analysis. Physical examination of the internal organs, particularly the liver, spleen, and kidneys, will have indicated the cumulative effects of poisonous metallic salts, or overdoses of drugs such as phenacetin or paracetamol, leading the pathologist to request further tests. All these organs, including the brain, lungs, and stomach, must be subjected to analysis. Whatever the pathologist may have suspected, confirmation depends on the skills of the toxicologist. His or her task is not only to identify any poison, but also to provide an estimate of the quantity involved.

The principal problem facing the modern toxicologist, however, may well be what to look for. Even seventy years ago, Dr. John Glaister, in his invaluable *Medical Jurisprudence and Toxicology* (8th edition, 1945), listed several hundreds of poisonous substances, from abortifacients to war gases (and the 1995 use of the nerve gas sarin, by the Aum

Shinrikyo sect in Japan, reminds us that the employment of such gases is not restricted to warfare). Nowadays, when so many people consume an increasing variety of pharmaceutical drugs—both prescribed and bought over the counter—the average home medicine cabinet is likely to contain enough poisons to commit several murders.

In 1984, one toxicologist wrote, "There are more than five million chemical compounds in the world, of which approximately 80,000 ... are used daily in the industrial, domestic, pharmaceutical and agricultural sectors of society. It is estimated that these numbers grow by as much as 1,000 compounds per annum, either by synthetic preparations or by isolation from naturally occurring plant or animal life." Twenty years later, how many more compounds might there be? Fortunately for the toxicologist, however, it is estimated that 80 percent of all poisoning cases involve only some forty to fifty known substances.

Given the range of potentially lethal substances available, it is surprising that so few contemporary cases of murder by poison are known, compared to other methods of killing. As Professor Keith Simpson put it in his *Forty Years of Murder* (1978): "Homicide by poison is rare. The Maybricks, Seddons, Crippens and Merrifields are famous only because they are of

LEFT VICTIMS OF THE ATTACK
WITH SARIN, A NERVE GAS, IN
THE TOKYO SUBWAY ON
MARCH 19, 1995. THE GAS
WAS RELEASED BY MEMBERS
OF THE AUM SHINRIKYO SECT;
TWELVE PEOPLE WERE KILLED,
AND MORE THAN FIVE
THOUSAND SUFFERED ILL
EFFECTS.

Origins of Chromatography

Chromatography derives its name from its first development by the Russian botanist Mikhail Tsvett in 1903, who used it to separate plant pigments, although it no longer implies the identification of colored substances. Tsvett placed a mixture of pigments, dissolved in alcohol, at the top of a glass tube containing a column of aluminum oxide granules. As more alcohol was added, the mixture moved down the tube, and the pigments were separated according to the "affinity" by which they were absorbed on the surface of the granules. Further washing with alcohol caused the individual pigments to emerge as separate fractions from the bottom of the tube.

A rather similar principle is employed in some water-softening equipment, and can also be employed in the laboratory to remove interfering substances, such as metallic salts, prior to chromatography. This is termed ion exchange. A water softener, for example, is a cylinder packed with a special resin that exchanges the calcium ions in the water for sodium ions that will not cause "scaling" in pipes or washing machines. At intervals, the resin is reactivated by washing with a strong salt (sodium chloride) solution, which replaces the calcium once more with sodium.

Tsvett's technique remained largely ignored for some thirty years, but it has since seen a variety of important laboratory developments.

ABOVE THE RUSSIAN BOTANIST MIKHAIL TSVETT. HIS ORIGINAL METHOD HAS NOW BEEN DEVELOPED INTO A FULLY-AUTOMATED LABORATORY PROCEDURE, WHICH CAN BE USED FOR THE SEPARATION AND ANALYSIS OF A WIDE RANGE OF COLORLESS MIXTURES.

rare interest." A report in 1989, for instance, stated that, out of 18,954 registered homicides in the United States, only twenty-eight were caused by poison. This number does not, of course, include cases in which poisoning was neither suspected nor detected. Nobody will ever know how many doctors, or caring relatives, have hastened an invalid's death to avoid unnecessary suffering—or the threatened rewriting of a will!

The readiness with which lethal drugs can be obtained by physicians, or by those involved in hospital care, has produced a number of cases of medical murderers. Among a host of modern pharmaceutical drugs are insulin and succinylcholine chloride (synthetic curare), both of which have been used in homicide, and both have proved particularly difficult to identify by analysis.

Insulin was the alleged poison of choice in the trial of Claus von Bulow for the murder of his wife, "Sunny," in New York in 1980—a charge of which he was eventually acquitted. In 1991, English nurse Beverley Allitt was found guilty of four murders and three charges of attempted murder of children in her charge, all with injections of insulin.

A very similar case, some eight years earlier, was that of Genene Jones, a children's nurse in Texas. The poison she used was succinylcholine chloride, which was available at her hospital, and it was established that she had tampered with vials of the drug. It was eventually diagnosed that she suffered from Munchausen's syndrome by proxy: She obtained such a thrill from the resuscitation of babies who had suffered sudden cardiac arrest that she began to inject them with the drug in order to experience the pleasure of nursing them. She has been considered responsible for the death of more than thirty youngsters. Genene Jone was found guilty of murder in February 1984, and was sentenced to at least twenty-five years' imprisonment before she will be eligible for parole.

In small doses, succinylcholine chloride, or synthetic curare, is used during surgery to relax the skeletal muscles, so that lesser amounts of anesthetic are necessary. As a lethal drug, it has a horrifying effect: It produces extensive and painful muscular paralysis, but the victim remains conscious, "except"—as the British handbook *Martindale's Extra Pharmacopoeia* somewhat unfeelingly puts it, regarding a similar drug— "for faintness and a feeling of impending disaster." Death occurs within half an hour, and it is impossible to imagine the emotions of the unhappy victim.

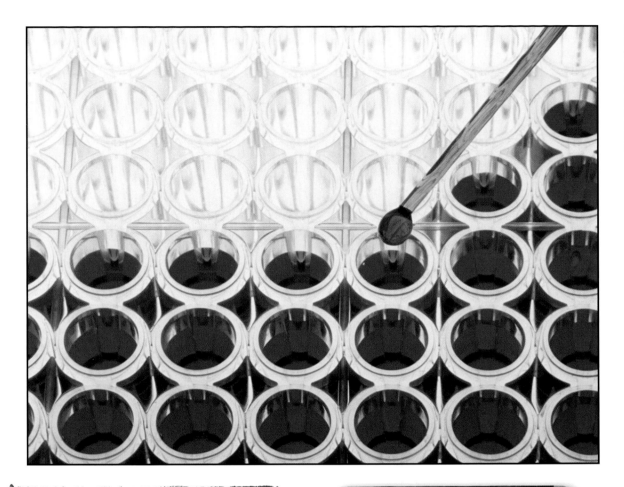

TOXICOLOGY SCREENING

The equipment currently available in toxicology laboratories is, in spite of certain exceptions, capable of analyzing—and so detecting—most poisonous substances in the body fluids or organs. The principal techniques available comprise: simple chemical "spot tests" or related procedures; various types of chromatography; mass spectrometry; and immunoassay.

Chemical tests are exemplified by the Marsh test for arsenic (see Chapter 1). Other toxic inorganic substances, such as compounds of mercury, lead, or thallium, can be detected in similar ways, but confirmation by spectroscopy is usually required. There are also tests for a considerable number of substances found in blood and urine.

The basic principle of chromatography is easily explained. It involves two "phases": a stationary phase, a material that will absorb the components of a mixture; and a mobile phase, in which all the components are soluble. With each component, there is competition between the stationary phase, to which the molecules are attracted, and the mobile phase,

CASE STUDY
CARL COPPOLINO

In August 1965, Carl Coppolino, a retired anesthesiologist, reported that he had found his wife, Carmela, a local physician, dead of a heart attack in their Florida home. Carmela's body was buried, but later, after suspicions had been aroused, it was exhumed and examined by the eminent Dr. Milton Helpern, then the chief medical examiner of New York. He found no evidence of heart failure, and no trace of poison could be discovered.

Nevertheless, Helpern wondered whether succinylcholine chloride—a drug to which an anesthesiologist would have access—could have been the cause of death. He enlisted the help of his chief toxicologist, who injected rabbits with the drug, then buried the carcasses for six months. Following their exhumation, large amounts of succinic acid were found in the rabbits' brains, while excessive quantities were also discovered in Carmela's. Coppolino was convicted of her murder, and also of that of Colonel William Farber, whom he was shown to have killed by suffocation in 1963.

ABOVE CARL COPPOLINO, AS HE APPEARED OUTSIDE THE COURTROOM DURING HIS TRIAL.

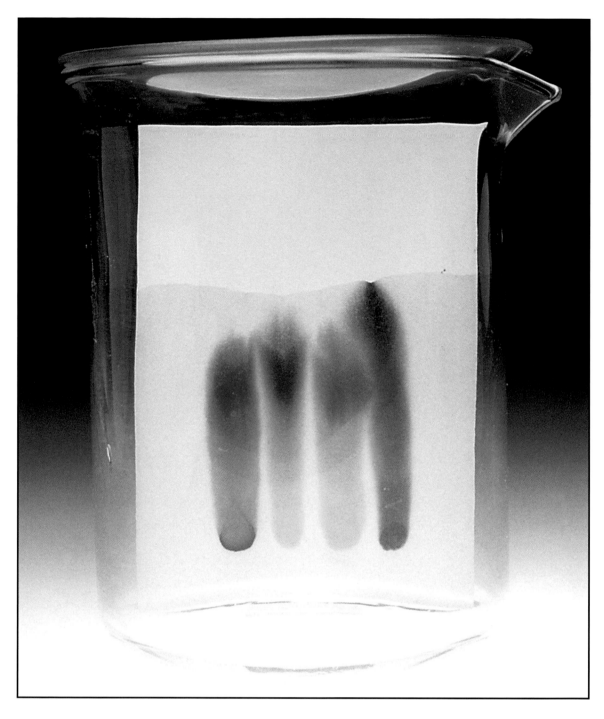

in which they are dissolved. As the mobile phase moves through the stationary phase, the components are absorbed at different rates, and so become separated.

The first refinement of Tsvett's original technique was the development of paper chromatography, which was soon followed by thin-layer chromatography. Both transform Tsvett's absorption column into a wide, effectively two-dimensional, surface. The great advantage is that both techniques employ quite small quantities of the mixture under investigation, and that samples of single specific control substances that are being searched for can be placed alongside, across the width of the surface, for comparison.

Paper chromatography employs a sheet of damp filter paper as the stationary phase, while in thin-layer chromatography the stationary phase is a thin film of aluminum oxide or silica gel, held between two glass or plastic plates. The lower end of the stationary phase is dipped into a suitable solvent, which moves upward at a constant rate by capillary action. When the solvent reaches the top, the paper or film is dried, and the separated substances are detected by spraying with appropriate reagents, or by illumination with ultraviolet light. If a spot from a component of the mixture being investigated has moved the same distance as one of the control samples, this is the first step in its identification.

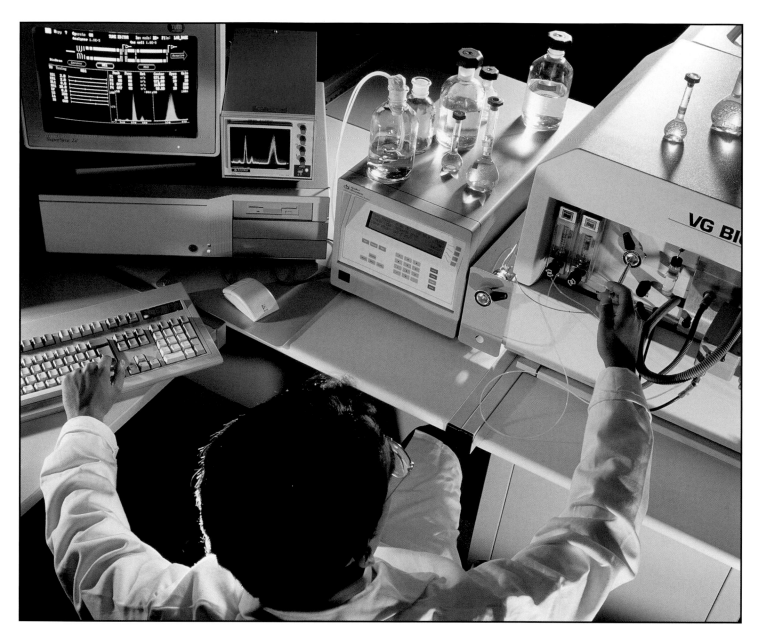

A not dissimilar technique, but making use of an electric current rather than a liquid mobile phase, is employed in DNA analysis.

A further development in liquid chromatography is in many respects a return to Tsvett's original method: high-performance liquid chromatography (HPLG). In this procedure, the liquid is forced downward through the absorbent column by a pump, and the emergent fractions are detected using an optical monitor—usually employing ultraviolet light—and recorded as a series of peaks, either as a pen trace on a moving band of paper or on a computer. The rate at which the various fractions emerge can then be compared with control samples.

Gas-liquid chromatography, or gas chromatography, as it is commonly called, is used for the separation of both liquids and gases (although more recently HPLG has been favored for many investigations of liquid solutions). In

this instance, the stationary phase is coated on clay or glass beads packed into a steel tube, and the mobile phase is the mixture to be analyzed, which is blown through the tube using an inert gas such as nitrogen. Liquid mixtures must be heated to above their boiling point, and in this case the tube also must be heated. The emergent fractions are discovered using various types of detector. Gas chromatography is used, for example, to confirm the presence of carbon monoxide in the blood.

If liquid chromatography, followed by gas chromatography, has failed to identify the toxic agent, the gas chromatograph must then be linked to a mass spectrometer. This instrument will analyze an organic compound in terms of the constituent parts of its molecular structure, and, if the components of a mixture obtained by gas chromatography are too small in quantity to be identified by chemical means, its use is invaluable.

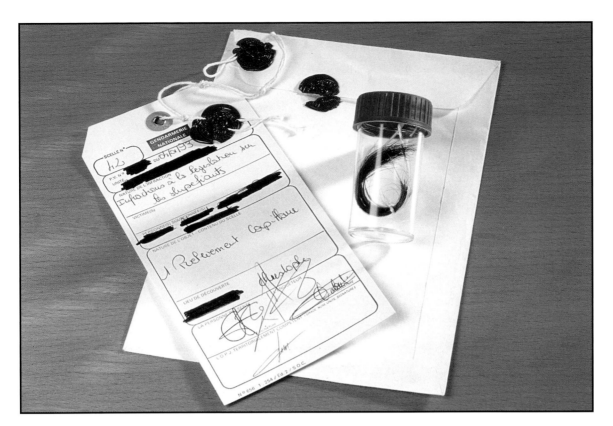

The material to be analyzed is bombarded with electrons emitted from a heated wire cathode. This breaks up the molecules in the sample into fragments, each of which is electrically charged. These pass through an electrical field, which accelerates them, then through a magnetic field, which deflects their straight path into a circular one. The radius of this path is dependent on the mass of the fragment: the heavier the fragment, the greater the radius.

The body of the mass spectrometer is curved, with a narrow slit at the far end. The strength of the deflecting magnetic field can be gradually increased, so that at first only the lightest fragments will be deflected sufficiently to pass through the slit, followed in succession by heavier fragments. A detector moves slowly across on the far side of the slit; linked to a computer, it records the arrival of each fragment as a series of peaks in a spectrum. The position of each fragment in the spectrum is thus a measure of its mass, and the height of the peak measures its relative proportion in the sample. A knowledge of molecular structure will make it easy to identify the compound concerned.

Toxicological screening can also make use of immunoassay, although this is the slowest and most expensive of the techniques available. The method is, in effect, a logical development of the discoveries of Jules Bordet and Paul Uhlenhuth. Antibodies specific to individual drugs are isolated from the serum of injected animals, then added to the victim's serum to discover whether a precipitate is formed. A simple form of this reaction is used in tests for pregnancy.

In laboratory practice, radioimmunoassay is usually employed. A known quantity of antibody is mixed with a known quantity of the drug (the antigen), which has been "labeled" with a radioactive element and then added to the sample being analyzed. Formation of a precipitate identifies the drug, and a measurement of its radioactivity provides an estimate of its quantity.

A recent development of immunoassay makes use of one of several specific enzymes, which is attached to the antigen. An enzyme is a catalyst; that is, it will initiate and facilitate a reaction without itself being changed. When the antigen-enzyme complex binds to an antibody, the enzyme's catalytic property is inhibited. However, any antigen in the sample

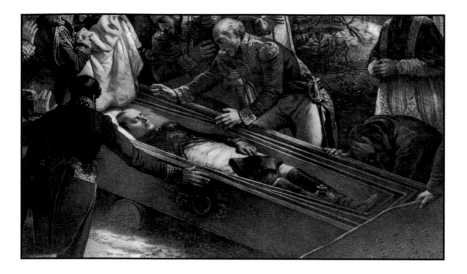

ABOVE THE CORPSE OF NAPOLEON BONAPARTE, AFTER IT WAS BROUGHT BACK FROM HIS IMPRISONMENT ON THE ISLAND OF ST. HELENA. IT WAS SUBSEQUENTLY PLACED IN A MAGNIFICENT TOMB IN LES INVALIDES, PARIS. RUMORS THAT NAPOLEON HAD BEEN POISONED WITH ARSENIC BY HIS BRITISH JAILERS PERSISTED FOR MORE THAN A CENTURY. A MODERN ANALYSIS REVEALED AN UNUSUALLY HIGH ARSENIC CONTENT IN THE BODY, BUT THE SOURCE OF THE POISON WAS NOT ESTABLISHED.

being assayed will compete with the complex for binding with the antibody, and the enzyme's activity will be freed. This results in a chemical reaction that forms a colored product, and the amount produced is a measure of the drug in the sample. The technique is as accurate as radioimmunoassay, but the test is much easier to perform, and it produces results more rapidly.

Finally, one point must be stressed. Even though there are, perhaps, a few cases in which analysis has failed to reveal it, there is no such thing as an undetectable poison. There may well be a few natural poisons, known only to the natives of the deepest Amazonian jungle, for example, which so far remain unidentified; however, once known, and its physiological effects recorded, it is only a matter of time before an analytical technique for the drug will be developed. Indeed, the modern laboratory combination of gas chromatography and mass spectrometry could even lead to the provisional identification of a hitherto unknown compound.

ANALYSIS OF MATERIALS

The physical examination of paint flakes and glass fragments has been described in Chapter 3. Further analysis of these and other materials will make use of spectroscopy or, in a relatively small number of specialized establishments, neutron activation.

Spectroscopy is of two types: emission and absorption. Both rely on the fact that, when elements are heated to a high temperature, they will emit light of characteristic wavelengths.

Emission spectroscopy is of particular value in the analysis of glass, paint, and metals. A sample is heated by carbon arc, laser beam, or

FACING PAGE EMISSION SPECTROSCOPY WILL PROVIDE DETAILED INFORMATION ON THE COMPOSITION OF THE SUBSTANCE BEING ANALYZED. HERE, A SAMPLE IS VAPORIZED BY ELECTRIC ARC IN THE PATH OF A BEAM OF INFRARED LIGHT. THE CHARACTERISTIC WAVELENGTHS OF COMPONENTS OF THE COMPOUND RESULT IN A SPECTRUM THAT ENABLES THEIR IDENTIFICATION.

by electronic bombardment—as in the mass spectrometer—and the emitted light is focused through a prism or diffraction grating to produce a spectrum of individual lines, each of a specific wavelength. These lines may be colored or in the ultraviolet range, and are detected and recorded by a suitable instrument. A mixture of a considerable number of elements can therefore be analyzed in a single operation.

Absorption spectroscopy makes use of the opposite principle. A colored object possesses that color because it has absorbed light of other wavelengths; a piece of glass appears blue, for example, because it has absorbed light of the red wavelengths. The sample to be analyzed is vaporized in a flame, and white, infrared,or ultraviolet light shone through it will have only specific wavelengths absorbed. This light is then passed through a diffraction grating, which reveals the wavelengths absorbed as dark lines in an otherwise continuous spectrum.

Neutron activation analysis has been briefly described in Chapter 3. A striking example of its use occurred in 1968. For nearly a century, there was doubt about the circumstances in which American explorer Charles Hall had died, on November 7, 1871, during his quest for the North Pole. It was suggested that the scientist aboard his exploration vessel, Dr. Emil Bessels, had poisoned him.

Hall had been buried on the shore of Thank God Harbor, some 500 mi. (800 km) from the pole, and in August 1968 two scientists flew there to exhume the body. It was found to have been remarkably well preserved in the frozen soil, and samples were taken. A fingernail was analyzed by neutron activation at Toronto's Center of Forensic Sciences. At its tip, the arsenic content was 24.6 parts per million (ppm), but at the base it was 76.7 ppm. It has long been known that arsenic will migrate from the body's internal organs to the hair and fingernails, and, although the soil surrounding Hall's body contained 22 ppm, it seemed unlikely that it could have been absorbed so unevenly. The analyst therefore concluded, "Arsenic poisoning is a fair diagnosis."

In a similar case, hair from the French emperor Napoleon Bonaparte, who died of unexplained causes on the island of St. Helena in 1821, was analyzed some 140 years later. It was reported that the arsenic content was fifteen times that normally found in human tissue, and the distribution along the hair suggested that Napoleon had received a series of strong doses over the four months before his death. But whether he had been poisoned by his English jailers, by a member of his staff, or by medicines that he himself had taken can no longer be determined.

RIGHT A PHOTOMICROGRAPH
OF BONE MARROW TISSUE.
BONE MARROW PRODUCES THE
RED AND WHITE BLOOD CELLS,
WHICH ARE ESSENTIAL TO THE
CIRCULATORY AND IMMUNE
SYSTEMS.

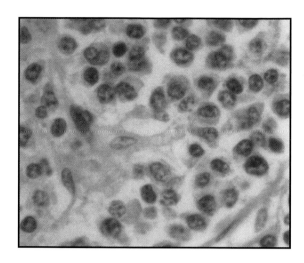

FOUND DROWNED

When a body is apparently drowned, determining whether or not the victim was alive at the time of entering the water, and inhaled some, is obviously of great importance. In cases of wet drowning (see page 141), several methods have been proposed for the chemical examination of the blood in two of the four chambers of the heart—the left ventricle being more affected than the right—but none has so far proved reliable. In the laboratory, what is probably the

most indicative approach is the search for diatoms. These are minute organisms that live both in seawater and unpolluted freshwater; there are at least 25,000 different species, many of which can be distinguished by the characteristic shape of their acid-resistant silica shells.

While a drowning person remains alive and the heart continues to beat, the diatoms, entering the lungs, are absorbed into the bloodstream, and so are distributed to organs such as the kidneys, the brain, and even the bone marrow. But if the body is lifeless when it enters the water, diatoms may be found in the lungs, but they cannot enter the bloodstream.

It has not been established conclusively, however, that diatoms cannot enter the bloodstream in everyday life. The "diatomic war" between pathologists, as to whether or not this is possible, has not yet been concluded. Nevertheless, the occurrence of diatoms in the bone marrow is usually taken as evidence that the victim was alive, and had subsequently drowned in the water.

For example, in one dramatic case, by identifying particular species of diatom biologists were able to establish that a body that had washed up on the coast of Belgium had actually entered the water from a yacht off the Isle of Wight in the English Channel.

RIGHT SOME OF THE MANY
BEAUTIFUL FORMS IN WHICH
DIATOMS—MINUTE ORGANISMS
LIVING IN WATER—CAN BE
FOUND. THEY CAN ENTER THE
BLOODSTREAM OF A DROWNING
PERSON, PROVING THAT THE
VICTIM WAS STILL ALIVE ON
ENTERING THE WATER.

Before dawn on November 5, 1991, publishing tycoon Robert Maxwell disappeared from his yacht in the sea surrounding the Canary Islands. Late in the afternoon, a search plane spotted his naked body, floating face up; it was gathered into a net, winched aboard a helicopter, and taken to Las Palmas, the capital of the islands. Maxwell's death resulted in the uncovering of an unprecedented program of crime and corruption that he had practiced over many years; it also generated a host of wild rumors concerning how he had died—rumors that have never been wholly put to rest.

As with any other unexpected death, suspicions were aroused, and the question to be answered was, Is this an accident, suicide, or murder? Maxwell had not been in good health recently; many people had already begun to realize that his vast business empire was, financially, in bad shape; and he had won many bitter enemies over the years.

Within hours, an autopsy was carried out at the Las Palmas Institute of Forensic Medicine; the doctors reported that there were no signs of violence on Maxwell's body, and that he had died of a heart attack. His family, however, ordered an investigation into the backgrounds of the yacht crew, in case someone had been planted aboard to murder him; one of his daughters even suggested that her father had died of an embolism, caused by his being injected with an air bubble. Possibly the wildest theory involved the Israeli secret service, Mossad. A recently published book had named Maxwell as a Mossad agent, and claims were made that he had been murdered to prevent his revealing their secrets.

The Las Palmas pathologist Dr. Carlos Lopez Lamela admitted that he did not have the facilities or equipment to carry out a detailed examination. He twice asked for British forensic experts to be sent out to the islands, but the Maxwell family insisted that the body had to be released for burial in Jerusalem before the end of the week. The local magistrate, however, arranged for samples of Maxwell's organs to be sent to Madrid for toxicological analysis, together with scrapings from his fingernails to determine whether he had been involved in a struggle.

Maxwell's insurers required an independent opinion on the cause of death, and asked Dr. Iain West, a leading pathologist at Guy's Hospital, London, to oversee a postmortem examination at the Institute of Forensic Medicine, Tel Aviv, to be performed by a group of Israeli pathologists. They were hampered by the fact that the body had been hastily embalmed, and a considerable amount of tissues and organs were missing—in particular, most of Maxwell's heart. There were a great number of bruises and abrasions, but most could be immediately attributed either to the way in which the body was recovered from the water or to the first autopsy.

However, this second examination nevertheless revealed something that had been missed previously. The muscles of Maxwell's left shoulder and side were badly torn, as if he had hung from something by his left hand. The implication seemed to be that he had held on to one of the boat's rails for some moments, then—being a large and overweight man—had been forced by extreme pain to let go.

Samples of Maxwell's bone marrow were taken to London and examined for the presence of diatoms, in the hope that this would establish whether he had drowned or was already dead when his body entered the water. No trace of diatoms could be found—but 5.3 pints (3 liters) of Atlantic water, taken from the area where the body was found, contained only very few. There was also little water in Maxwell's lungs, but this would not be surprising if the shock of falling into the sea had been sufficient to cause instant cardiac arrest.

The final Spanish ruling was that Maxwell had suffered a heart attack, and had fallen overboard by accident. Dr. West summed up his personal opinion: "There is no evidence for homicide, but it remains a possibility because I am in no position to exclude it. I don't think he died of a heart attack. Without the background of a man who was in financial trouble, and who knew it, I would probably say accident. As it is, there are probably only a few percentage points between the two main options, but I favor suicide."

BELOW THE CORPSE OF DROWNED TYCOON ROBERT MAXWELL BEING BROUGHT ASHORE BY SPANISH POLICE, AFTER HIS BODY HAD BEEN FOUND FLOATING IN THE SEA NEAR THE CANARY ISLANDS.

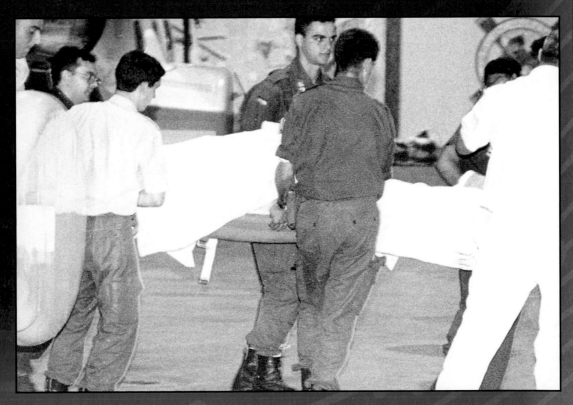

THE CASE OF JANE DOE

PART 4

THE EVIDENCE BUILDS

Despite Sheriff Verdian's skepticism regarding the FBI, their response was immediate. Special Agent Allen Pedersen arrived that same day in time to eat lunch with Tamara Gregory at a local diner. Over ham sandwiches and hash browns she detailed the case so far: an unidentified skeleton, female, aged twenty to thirty, possibly Southeast Asian; victim of a hit-and-run, likely some twelve months previously; body apparently transported from a northwestern state.

"After I took your call," said Pedersen, "I did a quick computer search on missing female Asians up and down the West Coast. I'm afraid it's not going to be much help. There's more than a thousand in your age bracket alone. We'll get your DNA typing done every which way, but, as you've pointed out, that'll only become significant when we find a record of a suspected victim. However, what we could do is to create a computer reconstruction of the facial features, if you're willing to release the skull. May take a few days, but then we can distribute photos of the reconstruction up the coast here. Hopefully, someone will recognize her." Gregory said she thought it was worth a shot.

After lunch, Gregory and Pedersen went to the morgue, where Dr. Kurosawa confessed that there was nothing further to be deduced from the skeletal remains. The unknown's skull was packed in a cardboard box that had once held cans of soft drinks, sealed with tape, logged, and signed for.

With the box in the car, Gregory drove the FBI agent to meet Dr. Jones at the laboratory. The criminologist told them: "I've swabbed some of the bigger stains from the carpet, and I'm running a PCR right now, but I'll be happy for the Bureau to take some of the samples for more sophisticated analysis."

"You appreciate, of course," said Pedersen, "that that will take some time."

"Yes," replied Dr. Jones, "But we won't be able to make use of the results until we've got a provisional identification for the victim, so the time involved may not be a significant factor."

"Alright, then," Petersen said. "I think I can help in other ways, too. If you could cut me an unstained portion of the carpet, we'll see whether we can trace the manufacturer. Also, Officer Gregory tells me you have some traces from the vehicle believed to be involved? I'd be happy to take a look at those, too, if you'll let me have some."

Disappointment showed on Gregory's face, as she realized that much of the investigation was being taken away from her. At that moment, however, the lab telephone shrilled, and the call was for her. After taking the call, she was smiling once again.

"That was my entomologist at La Jolla," she said. "He canceled his classes because the case intrigued him so much, and got right down to examining the insect remains. He says he'll need until the day after tomorrow to verify his identifications, but, judging by the evidence of successive waves of insect infestation, he reckons the body had lain in that location for twelve to sixteen months. It was buried, most likely, he says, around August of last year."

"We might be able to get a bit closer than that," said Pedersen. "You took soil samples? I'll request that Quantico send 'em off to Oak Ridge, see if they can give us a reading on the decomposition products."

A slight figure in a white lab coat had been hovering hesitantly near the group, holding some still-damp photographic prints. Now he coughed, and Jones, looking over her shoulder, saw him and waved him forward, introducing him as Denis Lo, latent fingerprint expert.

"That wallet?" Lo said. "No chance of finding any prints on the outside—the surface was pretty much destroyed. But inside—well, I ran the vac in there first, got a little dust and fluff that might be of interest to you. Then I gave it a quick laser scan, found a number of identical prints, rather smudged—but also a single very different print, clear enough. So I did the trick with the superglue vapor and got these prints for you." He held them out. Gregory took the photos and spread them out on a nearby countertop. She looked them over triumphantly: "Now, at last, we've got a positive lead. You'll want to e-mail a set to your head office, but meantime we'll run them through the local databanks, look for a known violent sex offender."

Lo went off to run another set of photographs, and, while they stood around with their Styrofoam cups, Gregory ran through a quick recap of what was known to date. A female victim, height and age within fairly narrow brackets, was murdered and buried, possibly last August. Initial inquiries would be directed to a young woman of Malaysian or similar origin, from the Northwest, who had borne a child. The perp had taken great pains to conceal her identity, removing clothing and all personal possessions, but they were holding out hope that DNA typing and facial reconstruction could lead to confirmation. And they had the perp's prints, as well as trace evidence from his vehicle.

"We're on our way," Gregory said, looking around the countertop at her colleagues.

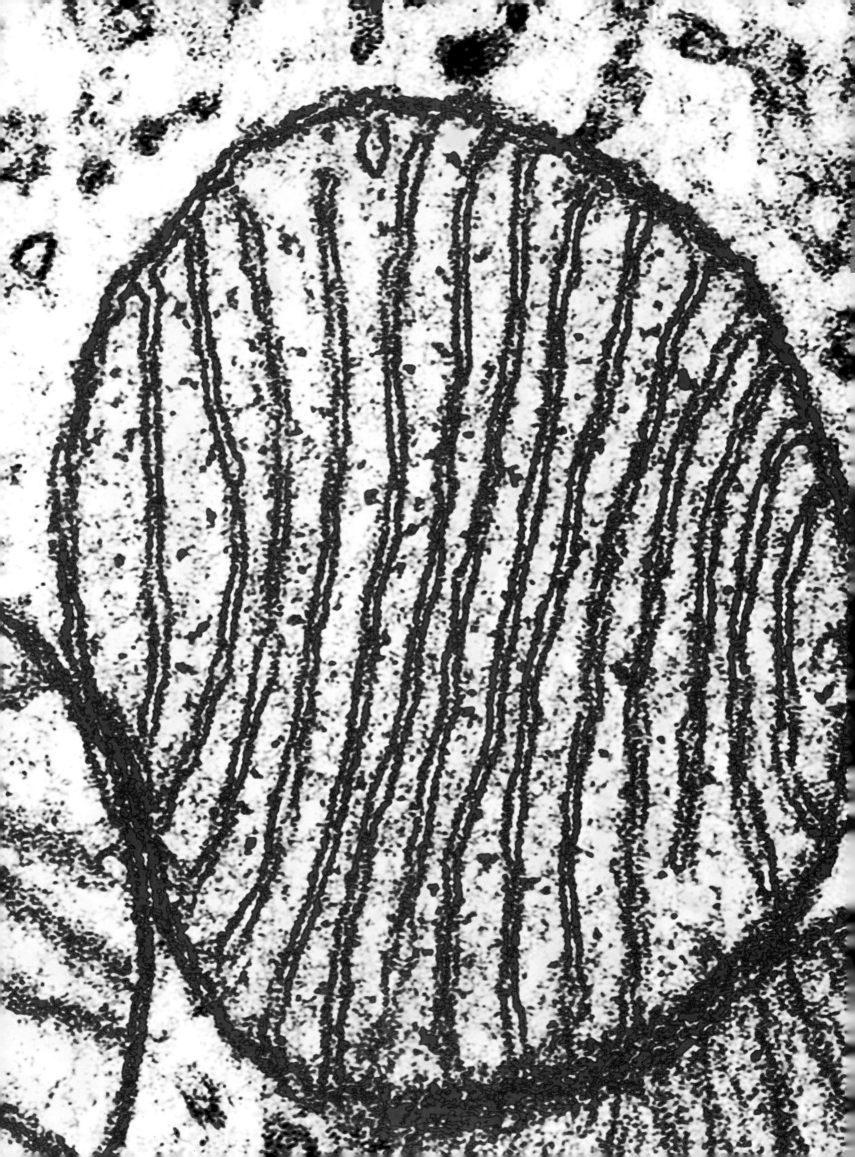

THE GUILTY PARTY

As soon as the medical examiner has confirmed that a death was not

natural, accidental, or suicidal—as well as in cases of rape,

abduction, or violent

physical assault—the hunt is on for

the perpetrator of the crime. All trace

evidence collected at the crime scene

must be submitted to intense scrutiny

and analysis. Similarly, the specimens taken

during the examination of a dead body, or of one

still alive, will be assayed for serological evidence. At the same time,

behavioral analysts will endeavour to put together a psychological profile

of the offender. With all this information at their disposal, as well as the

accumulated experience of years in the field, the crime team can hope

to trace the guilty party—and bring him or her to justice.

> *"Crime leaves a trail like a water-beetle, Like a snail it leaves its shine."*
>
> *MALAY PROVERB*

FACING PAGE AN ELECTRON MICROGRAPH OF A MITOCHONDRION, MAGNIFIED 80,000 TIMES. MOST CELLS CONTAIN A NUMBER OF "ORGANELLES"— MITOCHONDRIA AND OTHER BODIES—WHICH CONTAIN ENZYMES VITAL TO THE METABOLISM OF THE CELL. THE MITOCHONDRIA ARE OF PARTICULAR IMPORTANCE IN FORENSIC WORK BECAUSE IT HAS BEEN DISCOVERED THAT THEY, AS WELL AS THE NUCLEUS, CONTAIN DNA. GENETICALLY, THIS IS DERIVED ONLY FROM THE MOTHER.

EYEWITNESS ACCOUNTS

Photographs, of both the crime scene and of bodily injuries, are of the utmost value in an investigation, and they can be subjected to computer enhancement to clarify particulars that were not apparent to the eye. They may also reveal significant, tiny details that had escaped the attention of the crime scene officer or the medical examiner.

There may be eyewitnesses, or people who have caught sight of someone behaving in a suspicious manner: hurrying from the vicinity of the crime; cruising a back road in a car or parked near the scene of the murder, abduction, or assault; carrying a large bundle, perhaps stuffing it into a car or van; or even wearing clothing splashed with blood or mud. Alternatively, it may just be a person who is not known to them and who they believe does not belong to the local community. And, of course, there is also the traumatized victim of a rape or other criminal assault. These witnesses can give a description of the suspect or attend an identification parade, or lineup, but their recollections must be treated with great caution. An outstanding example of this was related by Dr. Donald Thomson, a lecturer in psychology at Monash University, Australia. An outspoken critic of

the value of lining up suspects for witness identification, he appeared on a television program in which he commented scathingly on the procedures of the New South Wales police. A few days later, he was brought in off the street to stand in just such a lineup.

A local woman had been violently assaulted in her home. After a quick glance at the row of men at the police station, she unhesitatingly identified Dr. Thomson as the assailant. "My first thought," said Thomson, "was that the police were trying to scare me," following his criticisms of their procedures. Fortunately, his live appearance on television at the same time of the attack provided him with an unshakable alibi. Further inquiries made it clear that the television in the woman's home had been switched on to the program, and, in the stress of the attack on her, the image of Thomson's face was somehow superimposed, in her memory, onto that of her attacker.

Prejudice—whether it is racial or concerns something like a style of dress that is associated with criminal activity—can equally affect an identification. Some years ago, in a recruiting campaign, the Metropolitan Police in London employed large posters featuring photographs of a typical street scene, with the words, "What would you do?" One showed an Afro-Caribbean male in a short, blouson jacket and open-necked shirt, running out of one side of the picture. Behind him, pictured running equally fast, came a uniformed constable. The implication seemed

FACT FILE

WHAT DO WE SEE?

It has been reported that the first facial features registered by a witness are the hair, mouth, and eyes, followed by the shape and length of the hair, the shape and attitude of the mouth, and the shape and color of the eyes. Sunglasses, for example, can so alter the appearance of even a familiar face that it can be unrecognizable at first glance. After the eyes comes the overall form of the face. Only when a witness has had sufficient time to concentrate on the details is it possible to identify a face completely, compare it with what is stored in the memory, and recognize it. Working with rhesus monkeys in the Department of Experimental Psychology at Oxford University, England, Dr. Edmund Rolls identified a set of cells, in a side portion of the brain, that respond only to faces. They are not the only cells that respond to faces; the amygdala, an adjacent part of the brain, also plays its part.

But how do we distinguish one individual from another? At one time it was suggested that single brain cells could be imprinted with information that would recognize any one

object—so that, for example, there would be a "grandmother cell" that enabled one to recognize one's own grandmother. However, as Professor Whitman Richards, a researcher in artificial intelligence at the Massachusetts Institute of Technology, pointed out: "If you have grandmother cells, or cells to react to every possible animal or thing you might see, you're going to run out of cells pretty quickly…. You cannot build a visual system out of grandmother cells."

One of Richards's colleagues, Englishman David Marr, put forward a theory that differs from that of the above. Marr suggested that the eye first feeds the brain with a swift overall impression, in the form of signals from cells in the eye that detect the contrast between light and dark—much in the same way that an optical character reader attached to a computer scans a printed page. Marr proposed that the brain, after first identifying an object from so crude a sketch, gradually focuses closer on the essential features to build up a detailed image that is then stored in the memory.

ABOVE THE DEVELOPMENT OF THE SATELLITE GLOBAL POSITIONING SYSTEM (GPS), WHICH CAN ESTABLISH A POSITION ANYWHERE ON EARTH TO WITHIN ONLY A FEW METERS, CAN BE OF GREAT VALUE IN CRIME INVESTIGATION. HERE, BRITISH POLICE MAKE USE OF GPS EQUIPMENT IN THE SEARCH FOR A MISSING WOMAN IN 2002.

clear: A criminal was being pursued by a policeman. But the accompanying text revealed that this was in fact a photograph of a plainclothes detective chasing a suspect, backed up by the uniformed officer.

Highlighting the danger that prejudice can play in identification is now part of police instruction. At Hendon Police Training College in north London, recruits were shown a short video of a man with short, spiky hair, wearing a leather jacket, snatching a bag from a middle-aged woman. They were then asked the age of the snatcher. Nearly always, the confident reply came that the man was in his twenties—yet he was, in fact, more than fifty years of age. The audience had assumed, from their everyday experiences, that all spiky-haired wearers of leather jackets were young.

SYSTEMS OF IDENTIFICATION

When there is no immediate suspect to be detained, the police will try to develop a possible likeness from the description—usually only partial and frequently mistaken—provided by a witness. One of the earliest systems of identification was the *portrait parlé* introduced by Alphonse Bertillon. This was designed as a means of describing a known criminal, in order to be able to identify him or her at a later date, but the principle was further developed nearly half a century later into the first graphic identification system, known as Identikit.

In the administrative confusion following the end of World War II, black marketeers and con men flourished, particularly in the defeated countries. Toward the end of the 1940s, Hugh McDonald, chief of the civilian division of the Los Angeles Police Department, was sent to Europe in an attempt to help track down these very active criminals in the U.S.-administered zones. He soon discovered that descriptions given by victims and witnesses were often incomplete and frequently contradictory.

RIGHT EVEN AFTER THE WIDESPREAD ADOPTION OF IDENTIFICATION USING FINGERPRINTS, MANY POLICE FORCES CONTINUED FOR SOME TIME TO EMPLOY THE BERTILLON ANTHROPOMETRIC SYSTEM AS AN ADDITIONAL MEANS OF CLASSIFYING CRIMINALS. HERE, A NEW YORK OFFICER TAKES THE MEASUREMENT OF A SUSPECT'S EAR, DURING THE 1920S.

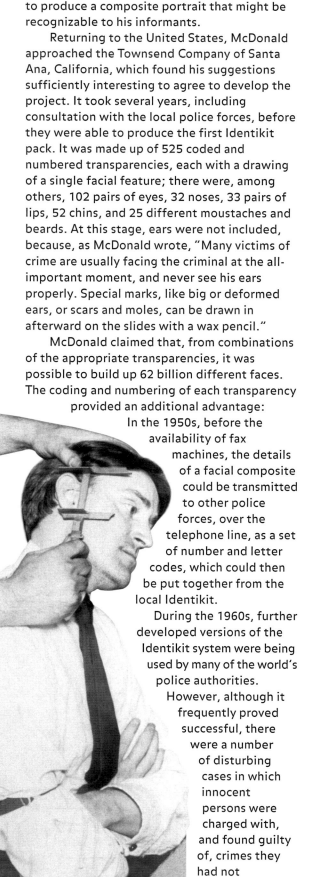

He therefore began to make rough sketches of different types of facial shapes, eyes, noses, and other characteristics on transparent sheets, which could then be overlaid, one with another, to produce a composite portrait that might be recognizable to his informants.

Returning to the United States, McDonald approached the Townsend Company of Santa Ana, California, which found his suggestions sufficiently interesting to agree to develop the project. It took several years, including consultation with the local police forces, before they were able to produce the first Identikit pack. It was made up of 525 coded and numbered transparencies, each with a drawing of a single facial feature; there were, among others, 102 pairs of eyes, 32 noses, 33 pairs of lips, 52 chins, and 25 different moustaches and beards. At this stage, ears were not included, because, as McDonald wrote, "Many victims of crime are usually facing the criminal at the all-important moment, and never see his ears properly. Special marks, like big or deformed ears, or scars and moles, can be drawn in afterward on the slides with a wax pencil."

McDonald claimed that, from combinations of the appropriate transparencies, it was possible to build up 62 billion different faces. The coding and numbering of each transparency provided an additional advantage: In the 1950s, before the availability of fax machines, the details of a facial composite could be transmitted to other police forces, over the telephone line, as a set of number and letter codes, which could then be put together from the local Identikit.

During the 1960s, further developed versions of the Identikit system were being used by many of the world's police authorities.

However, although it frequently proved successful, there were a number of disturbing cases in which innocent persons were charged with, and found guilty of, crimes they had not committed.

On August 22, 1961, Michael Gregsten and his lover Valerie Storie were sitting in a parked car near Slough, southern England. Suddenly, a man climbed into the backseat of the car with a gun in his hand, and ordered Gregsten to drive. Eventually, the man told Gregsten to stop in a turnout at a spot named—ominously—Deadman's Hill, where he fired the gun twice, killing Gregsten instantly. He then raped and shot Storie, and drove the car away. She survived, but remained permanently paralyzed. A loaded revolver, identified by ballistics experts as the murder weapon, was later found on a London bus.

Storie was able to provide a description of the gunman, from which an Identikit portrait was made. It differed in many details from another Identikit picture prepared from descriptions given by three witnesses who said they had seen a man driving Gregsten's car. The only common characteristic was the "deep-set brown eyes" that Storie positively recalled.

The police had detained two suspects. They were James Hanratty, in whose hotel room detectives had found shells from the murder weapon, and Peter Alphon, who had taken the room the following night. Hanratty did not resemble the Identikit pictures; in particular, his eyes were not brown, but blue. Alphon, however, did resemble Storie's description.

At this point, Valerie Storie changed her mind; she stated that her attacker had "icy-blue eyes" that were "saucer-shaped." At a lineup she failed to identify Alphon, but, three weeks later, she picked out Hanratty during a second lineup. He was at once charged, found guilty at trial, and hanged in April 1962—one of the last people to be executed before the abolition of capital punishment in the United Kingdom.

All along, Hanratty had maintained that he was 200 mi. (320 km) away, in Rhyl, north Wales, on the night of the murder; later, witnesses came forward with some support for this alibi. Furthermore, Peter Alphon, free from fear of prosecution, made several statements alleging that he had been hired by "an interested party" to break up the affair between Michael Gregsten (who was a married man) and Valerie Storie. These statements cast doubt on the validity of the Identikit system of identification, and the controversy continued for nearly forty years.

In October 2000, Hanratty's family appealed for his conviction to be set aside and a posthumous pardon granted. The DNA samples they provided, however, revealed a probable match with traces found on Storie's underwear and on a handkerchief that had been wrapped around the murder weapon. In March 2001, Hanratty's remains were exhumed and a DNA analysis was performed, the result of which matched with two samples from the crime scene. In May 2002, on the basis of this evidence, the Court of Criminal Appeal ruled that James Hanratty's conviction was sound.

LEFT JAMES HANRATTY, FOUND GUILTY OF THE MURDER OF MICHAEL GREGSTEN AND THE VIOLENT RAPE AND DISABLEMENT OF VALERIE STORIE, IN ENGLAND IN 1961. DESPITE CONTINUED DOUBTS OVER HIS IDENTIFICATION, HIS DNA WAS JUDGED CONFIRMATORY EVIDENCE IN 2002.

BELOW THE SPOT ON DEADMAN'S HILL WHERE VALERIE STORIE WAS FOUND TERRIBLY INJURED, CLOSE BY THE BODY OF MICHAEL GREGSTEN, WHO HAD BEEN SHOT THROUGH THE HEAD. THE WHITE CANVAS SCREEN MARKS THE PLACE WHERE GREGSTEN'S CORPSE WAS DISCOVERED.

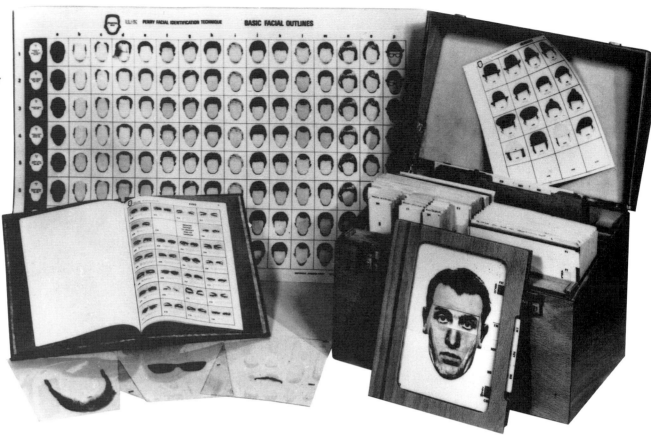

PHOTOFIT AND VIDEO-FIT

A considerable improvement to Identikit was the introduction, in 1971, of the Penry Facial Identification Kit, which became known as PhotoFIT. Its developer, photographer Jacques Penry, claimed that he had not been influenced by the availability—or the shortcomings—of Identikit. The concept, he said, had first occurred to him in 1938, when he was selecting photographs to illustrate his book, *Character from the Face.* Nevertheless, it was not until thirty years later that he first approached the British Home Office Police Research and Development Branch, and was given a contract to develop PhotoFIT.

Basically similar to Identikit, PhotoFIT makes use of photographic images rather than drawn elements. First produced in 1969, Penry's "Front-view Basic Caucasian Kit" comprised 204 foreheads and hairstyles, 96 pairs of eyes, 89 noses, 101 mouths, 74 chin and cheek sections, as well as a wide range of "accessories," such as headwear, moustaches and beards, spectacles, age lines, and ears. In all, it was capable of composing 5 billion different faces. Other kits followed, including the "Afro-Asian Supplement," in 1970, which added the

possibility of a further 500 million composites, and the "Female Supplement," in 1974.

More recently, with the ready availability of desktop computers, both Identikit and PhotoFIT have been largely replaced by "Video-Fit." A computer program can easily store a vast number of photographic elements, and these

CASE STUDY
JOHN LIST

In 1971, accountant John List murdered his wife, mother, and three children in New Jersey, then disappeared. No sightings of him were reported, and, although the case remained open, the police and FBI eventually gave up all hope of finding him.

Then, in 1989, the unsolved crime was featured on the popular TV program *America's Most Wanted.* The producers of the program called on the specialist skills of artist Frank Bender, who, working from an old photograph of List, sculpted a bust of how he might look, aged by eighteen years.

The television station received hundreds of telephone calls, many of them identifying a man named Robert Clark, who was living quietly in Richmond, Virginia. The FBI called on Clark, who protested his innocence.

However, although he could change his name and his home, he could not change his fingerprints. John List, alias Robert Clark, was returned to New Jersey, where he was found guilty on five counts of murder.

RECENT DEVELOPMENTS

Two Russian-born identical twins, Michael and Alex Bronstein, graduate students at the Technion Institute in Haifa, Israel, have claimed the development of a computerized surveillance system that successfully distinguished one twin from the other. A person's face is scanned three-dimensionally, and the computer measures the distances between various points on the surface of the head. These measurements are then converted into an abstract three-dimensional "signature."

Changing light conditions or facial expressions do not affect the recognition of this signature. However, the system cannot be employed with existing two-dimensional photographs of wanted persons or suspects, so considerable time will most

likely elapse, therefore, before sufficient three-dimensional images can be obtained to make it operable.

In the United States, the company Visage Inc., among others, has patented a similar system, originally developed at the Massachusetts Institute of Technology, known as principal component analysis (PCA).

The company's software converts facial characteristics into a unique digital set, which Visage calls an eigenface, from the German *eigen*, meaning "singular." Visage also plans to include other characteristics, such as the color of the iris of the eye, voice recognition, and fingerprints, in a comprehensive security system.

can be modified in any desired way. The relative dimensions of each element can be changed at will, the composite can be rotated or tilted to provide a three-dimensional image, and coloring and texture can be added. An experienced operator can also modify a photograph of a wanted person to indicate their probable appearance as they have aged.

The principal drawback to both the PhotoFIT and Video-Fit systems is the huge number of elements that must be explored by the investigator who tries to produce an image that will be recognized by a witness, and the time that this takes. While facial identification

or recognition is now increasingly used in computerized security systems, the computer is required only to confirm facial characteristics already stored in its memory. Further development along these lines has seen the use of surveillance cameras that can scan a crowd and pick out a known criminal or suspect.

In 2001, the British Metropolitan Police introduced an experimental scheme designed to scan crowds in the street and pick out known criminals; patrolling officers could then be alerted. However, a similar system, installed by the police in Tampa, Florida, was discontinued in 2002 after only two months' trial.

BELOW AFTER THE DISMEMBERED REMAINS OF AN UNIDENTIFIED MURDER VICTIM WERE FOUND ON THE SHORE OF THE RIVER THAMES IN LONDON, POLICE ISSUED THIS SET OF COMPUTER RECONSTRUCTIONS OF THE HEAD. DIFFERENT ASPECTS OF FACIAL AND HEAD HAIR WERE ADDED TO AID IDENTIFICATION.

EVERY CONTACT LEAVES A TRACE

The identification of fingerprints, palm and footprints, as well as tire impressions, and the typing of blood have been described previously. The discovery of hair, particularly pubic hair, that does not belong to the victim, or of "foreign" fibers, has also proved the essential clue in a number of cases.

In the twenty-two months between July 1979 and May 1981, more than twenty young African-American males—many of them children—were found asphyxiated or otherwise murdered on the outskirts of Atlanta, Georgia. Forensic investigators at the Georgia State Crime Laboratory found identical fibers on the clothing of a number of the victims, which turned out to be of two types: a yellowish-green nylon, apparently from a carpet, and a violet-colored acetate.

Unfortunately, news of this finding was published, and the serial killer immediately changed his tactics, stripping his victims of most of their clothing and dumping their bodies in rivers. When another such victim was discovered, however, there was a single strand of rayon found on his shorts.

During a police watch on a bridge over the Chattahoochee River in May 1981, twenty-three-year-old Wayne Williams, who described himself as a music-biz talent scout, was questioned about a large splash that had been heard. He claimed that he had just thrown some garbage in the river, and was permitted to leave after showing identification. Two days later, another body was dragged from the river, and a yellowish-green carpet fiber was found in its hair. Police obtained a warrant to search the home that Williams shared with his parents, and it was found to be carpeted throughout with matching yellowish-green nylon.

This evidence, in itself, was insufficient to connect Williams to the killings, and the fibers were submitted to the FBI laboratory. Analysis revealed that the nylon was manufactured by a Boston company, and sold to a number of carpetmakers between 1967 and 1974. The dye was tracked to the West Point Pepperell Corporation of Dalton, Georgia, which had used the particular nylon only between 1970 and

1971, and had sold carpets throughout just ten southeastern states.

The FBI then made a series of statistical calculations. Beginning with the assumption that there had been a fairly equal distribution of the carpet throughout the ten states, and knowing the total area over which West Point Pepperell had made sales and the number of homes in the Atlanta area, they calculated that the probability that the fibers had not come from the Williams home was 1 in 7,792.

A search of Williams's car further revealed that fibers from its carpet matched the rayon found on the shorts of the latest victim. A second calculation put the probability that this was by chance at 1 in 3,828. A combination of these two figures put the overall odds at nearly 24 million to 1. To clinch the matter, violet acetate fibers were also found in the car, and they matched both a blanket found in Williams's bedroom and fibers from earlier

victims' clothing. Hairs matching that of Williams's German shepherd were also found on the clothing of one victim.

In spite of the difficulty of explaining these calculations to the jury (the prosecution prepared forty charts and 350 photographs), Williams was found guilty on two charges of the most recent murders. He appealed, but the Georgia Supreme Court upheld the verdict—and there were no further similar murders in Atlanta in the months following his arrest.

The analysis of glass and paint chips in criminal cases has also been described previously. But above all, as has already been pointed out, probably the most powerful tool in the hands of the forensic scientist today is the analysis of DNA, which occurs in every cell of the human body—with the exception of the red blood cells—and can therefore be obtained from skin, hair, blood serum, sweat, semen, and even bones.

ABOVE FLANKED BY POLICE CHIEF GEORGE NAPPER (LEFT), ATLANTA PUBLIC SAFETY COMMISSIONER LEE P. BROWN (CENTER) ANNOUNCES THE ARREST OF WAYNE WILLIAMS OUTSIDE THE FULTON COUNTY JAIL ON JUNE 21, 1981. AT THE TIME, WILLIAMS WAS SUSPECTED OF CARRYING OUT TWENTY-EIGHT MURDERS IN THE ATLANTA AREA.

BELOW CAPTAIN JEFFREY MACDONALD OF THE U.S. ARMY, FOUND GUILTY OF THE MURDER OF HIS WIFE AND TWO YOUNG DAUGHTERS IN 1974.

A notorious case in which hairs proved, in the end, to be unconnected with the murder was that of U.S. Army doctor Captain Jeffrey MacDonald. On the night of February 17, 1970, military police at Fort Bragg, North Carolina, responded to an emergency call from MacDonald's home. They arrived to find his wife lying dead, stabbed twenty-one times, and his two young daughters stabbed and beaten to death in an adjoining bedroom. MacDonald himself was covered with bleeding wounds, although still conscious, and on the couple's headboard the word PIG had been daubed in blood. He claimed that he had woken to find four "hippies" standing over him, led by a woman in a long blonde wig, who chanted "acid is groovy … kill the pigs," and slashed him with a knife and an ice pick. When he recovered, he discovered the carnage in the bedrooms.

On May 1, MacDonald was charged with murder, but the investigation by the military police had been bungled, and many items of trace evidence were missing; in October the charges against him were dropped. He resigned from the army, but his subsequent actions aroused the suspicions of the FBI, and, after a grand jury hearing, he was tried and found guilty of all three murders in July 1974.

Sentenced to three terms of life imprisonment, MacDonald persistently appealed, and the renowned Harvard lawyer Alan Dershowitz applied for a retrial in 1992. The appeal centered on the fact that blonde wig hairs found on MacDonald's wife's hairbrush had not been entered as evidence in his trial, and supported his claim to have been attacked by a woman in a blonde wig.

The FBI reexamined the evidence and found two types of wig hair, one of which was used for Barbie dolls. Other fibers and hairs came from a hairpiece owned by Mrs. MacDonald and from her clothing, and one proved to belong to MacDonald herself. Although it could not be established that the two murdered girls had ever owned Barbie dolls, the appeal was disallowed.

DNA: A BRIEF HISTORY

In 1858, German pathologist Rudolf Virchow made an important and, at the time, revolutionary pronouncement: "Every cell is derived from a preexisting cell." This statement represented the first true realization that the growth and development of every living organism derives from cell division, and it became the foundation of the science of genetics.

At the same time, biologists were studying the interior structure of cells, and in 1879 it was discovered that cell nuclei contained threadlike structures that would readily absorb colored dyes, and for this reason they were named chromosomes. The cells of the human body contain forty-six chromosomes, in twenty-three pairs. It was not long before it was known that one of each pair derives from the mother, and the other from the father; twenty-two of the pairs determine hereditary characteristics, while the last pair determines sex.

Meanwhile, Friedrich Miescher (1844–95) was looking into the chemical composition of the cell nucleus. He had studied under Felix Hoppe-Seyler (1825–95), who had previously been Virchow's assistant. Miescher isolated a substance, which he called nuclein, and in which he discovered a considerable amount of phosphorus was contained. He later found that the structure of the molecule contained several acidic groups, and one of his students renamed it nucleic acid.

Within a few years of Miescher's death, the building blocks of nucleic acid had been identified. One was ribose, a sugar; another was a molecule containing phosphorus. Also involved were a group of molecules known as purine bases: guanine, adenine, cytosine, thymine, and uracil—now always referred to as G, A, C, T, and U. The ribose gave the complete molecule its new name, ribonucleic acid (RNA). It was later discovered that one base was attached to each ribose molecule, sticking out from the side. Then, in the 1920s, another nucleic acid was discovered; it contained less oxygen than RNA did, and so was named deoxyribonucleic acid (DNA). And, while RNA contains G, A, C, and U, DNA contains G, A, C, and T.

American biologist Thomas Hunt Morgan (1866–1945) had already observed separate groups along the thread of chromosomes, called genes, and postulated that these were the individual determinants of hereditary characteristics. Beginning in the 1930s and continuing to 1944, American microbiologist Oswald Avery (1877–1955) and his team, in a long series of careful experiments, found that the properties of a growing colony of bacteria could be changed by dead bacteria of a similar type, and that the substance being transferred to them was DNA.

It became obvious that DNA was the agent of genetic inheritance, but because genes varied from individual to individual, DNA therefore had to have many different internal structures, even though the overall chemical content remained the same. Austrian-born Erwin Chargaff (1905–2002), working at Columbia University, established a set of "Chargaff rules," which he published in 1950. These state that the total quantity of G+A in any sample of DNA is equal to the total quantity of C+T; the amount of A is the same as that of T; and the amount of G is the same as that of C. With this knowledge to work from, the search began for an understanding of the structure of the DNA molecule.

The first break came when Linus Pauling (1901–94), at Caltech in the United States, and Lawrence Bragg (1890–1971), at the Cavendish Laboratory in Cambridge, England, published their studies on proteins from 1950 to 1951. Proteins were shown to have a coiled helical

structure, and it seemed probable that DNA's structure was similar.

Two new recruits to the Cavendish Laboratory were American James Watson (b. 1928), who joined in 1951, and Englishman Francis Crick (b. 1916), who had already been there for some two years. Although the two men were not part of the team working on DNA, they spent much of their time discussing the problem of its structure, and studying X-ray crystallography photographs produced by Rosalind Franklin (1920–58), who was herself part of a team working at King's College, London. Crick and Watson began to build models of a molecule composed of two helical coils, joined together by bridges of A–T and C–G, and, when this structure was confirmed by one of Franklin's photographs, they were able to announce in 1953 that they had discovered the molecular structure of DNA.

Crick and Watson received the Nobel Prize for Physiology in 1962, but, unhappily, Rosalind Franklin had died four years previously, and she was therefore not named in the citation.

ABOVE THOMAS HUNT MORGAN, THE AMERICAN BIOLOGIST WHO FIRST OBSERVED THE SEPARATE GROUPS ALONG THE THREAD OF CHROMOSOMES THAT ARE IDENTIFIED AS GENES. HE WAS AMONG THE FIRST TO PROPOSE THAT THESE WERE WHAT DETERMINED HEREDITARY CHARACTERISTICS.

LEFT FRANCIS CRICK (LEFT) WAS BORN IN NORTHAMPTON, ENGLAND, IN 1916. HE BEGAN RESEARCH ON MOLECULAR BIOLOGY AT THE CAVENDISH LABORATORY IN 1949. JAMES DEWEY WATSON (FAR LEFT) WAS BORN IN CHICAGO, ILLINOIS, IN 1928. AFTER A PROFESSORSHIP AT HARVARD, HE WAS APPOINTED DIRECTOR OF COLD SPRING HARBOR LABORATORY, LONG ISLAND, N.Y., IN 1968.

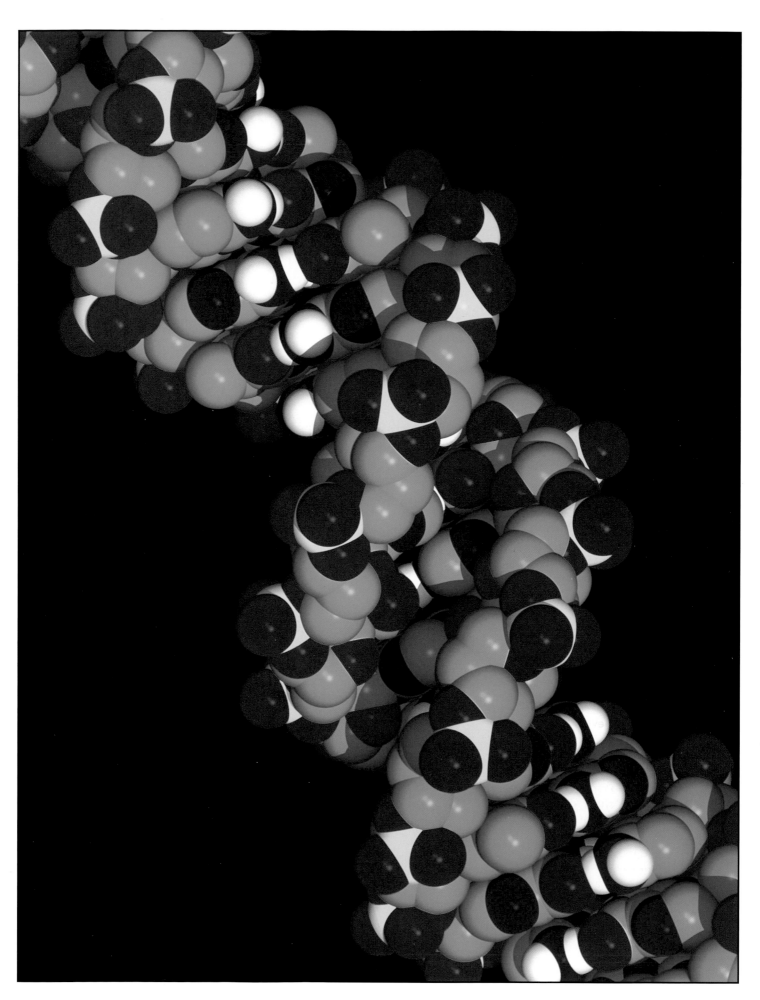

FRAGMENTING DNA

The molecular structure of DNA can be visualized as a long, twisted ladder. The sides of the ladder are made up of alternating groups of the sugar deoxyribose (S) and phosphate (P). The rungs of the ladder are made up of two of the four "bases," linked at each side to an S molecule. A will link only to T, and C to G, so a single rung can consist of S–A–T–S, S–T–A–S, S–G–C–S, or S–C–G–S. There are more than 3 billion of these rungs in human DNA, and it is possible for them to occur in any order along the ladder.

When a cell divides during the growth or replacement of tissue, the two halves of the ladder separate, and each half then acts as a model for the formation of a new DNA molecule. Each half is made up of a long succession of units comprising S, P, and one base; these units are called nucleotides. A gene is made up of a number of nucleotides, and provides a code for the manufacture of amino acids and enzymes in the cell, each of which governs a particular aspect of the body's metabolism, and determines the hereditary characteristics. No two people—with the exception of identical twins developed from a single egg—are completely physically alike, so a considerable number of their genes will be different. Nevertheless, some genes, of course, will be identical; genes that determine that a human body will have two arms, two legs, two eyes, etc., are common to most who are born naturally—and, indeed, it has been found that human beings and chimpanzees are different by only a very few genes.

The completed Human Genome Project, to which researchers all over the world have contributed, has been devoted to the identification of every one of these genes. One of the project's discoveries is that certain gene groups appear—so far—to have no hereditary function. In fact, DNA typing, although it can successfully identify an individual by a succession of nucleotides, does not appear to be directly related to gene structure. However, there seems to be a connection between certain DNA fragments and the X/Y sex chromosomes.

Certain enzymes are particularly useful because, as they operate as catalysts, they can be used to cut a strand of DNA into sections. These are called restriction enzymes (first discovered by American scientist Hamilton Smith in 1970), and they are produced by

BELOW THIS COLORED-LIGHT MICROGRAPH SHOWS THE WAY IN WHICH THE FORTY-SIX CHROMOSOMES OF THE HUMAN CELL ARE PAIRED. IN SOME MALES, HOWEVER, THE SEX CHROMOSOME IS TRIPLE IN STRUCTURE.

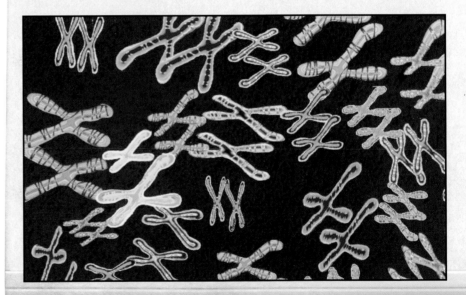

bacteria to attack foreign DNA, and so protect themselves from viruses. More than four hundred restriction enzymes have been identified so far, each of which will cut a DNA strand at a different place.

Because the sides of the DNA ladder are made up solely of alternating S and P groups, a fragment of DNA can be described in terms of its rungs alone. For example, consider the following sequence of rungs:

FACING PAGE A MODEL OF A SHORT PORTION OF THE DNA MOLECULE, SHOWING THE TYPICAL TWISTED HELICAL STRUCTURE.

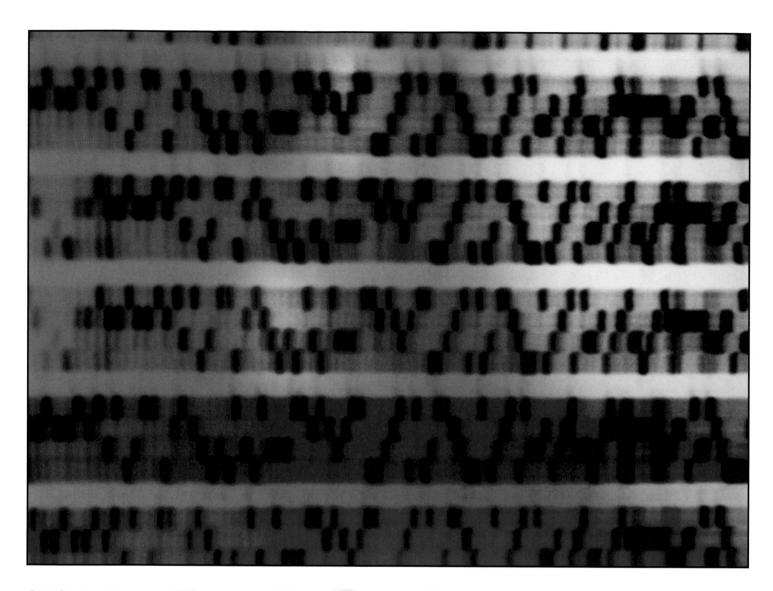

```
-AT *GGCCCCT †AGGCA *GGCCT †AGGCATA-
 ||  |||||||  |||||  |||||  |||||||
-TC *CCGGGGA †TCCGT *CCGGA †TCCGTAT-
```

Restriction enzymes will cut the strand only at the site of a specific sequence of base pairs. An enzyme known as Hae III—obtained from the bacterium *Haemophilus aegyptius*—will cut the DNA strand only where it finds this sequence:

```
-GGCC-
 ||||
-CCGG-
```

Two of these sequences are marked above with an asterisk (*); the fragment released will be:

```
CCTAGGCA
||||||||
GGATCCGT
```

Another enzyme, Hae I, will cut the strand only where it finds this sequence:

```
-AGGCA-
 |||||
-TCCGT-
```

Two other sequences are marked above left with a dagger (†), and result in the fragment:

```
GGCCT
|||||
CCGGA
```

Because all such fragments are related to the overall genetic structure, one or more of them can be shown to be specific to an individual person. A combination of a sufficient number of these fragments is very unlikely to occur in any other person's DNA—the chances are astronomical.

RFLP AND VNTR TYPING

The analysis of DNA fragments is known, by analogy with that of blood groups, as DNA typing. Each of these fragments will vary in length according to the genetic structure of the individual's DNA; that is, their molecular sizes will differ. If there is sufficient DNA available in a sample, it can be submitted to restriction fragment length polymorphism (RFLP) analysis.

A well-established analytical method for the separation of different-size molecules is electrophoresis, which employs a relatively simple piece of equipment, not unlike that used in chromatography. A glass or plastic plate is coated with a thin layer of gel, along which a low-voltage direct current is applied. DNA fragment samples are spotted at the negative end of the plate, and travel along it at different speeds depending on their molecular size, the largest being the slowest. Because the molecules travel in a straight line from negative to positive, a number of samples can be placed side by side for comparison. After some sixteen hours, the various fragments will have separated along the plate.

The position of the separate DNA fragments is detected by means of a method developed by Scottish scientist Edward Southern in 1975, known as the Southern blot. The gel is soaked in a solution that will separate the double-stranded fragments into single strands, while it is also being pressed against a plastic membrane, to which the strands are transferred. The nucleotide bases—A, T, C, G—are thus exposed along the length of the two fragment halves, and are "labeled" with one or more "probes": a short length of a single-strand DNA or RNA fragment labeled with a radioactive atom. The bases in the probe find their complementary bases in the fragment halves, and attach themselves (hybridize) to them.

The membrane is then washed and placed in contact with a sheet of X-ray film, and the radioactivity of the probe produces an image on the film. The result is an autoradiograph (or autorad) of short, dark bands across the film—not unlike the bar codes used in stores—and each band represents a specific fragment. Bands that are level with one another indicate that the fragments are of the same molecular size.

In a related type of RFLP analysis, probes that will locate only one pattern of bases (a locus) are used, because the results are more easily interpreted. The specificity of the identification is not, however, unique.

Another method of RFLP analysis will detect the occurrence of a number of identical base sequences (such as C–G–G–A–T–C–G–G–A–T–C–G–G–A–T) along the DNA strand. These are called variable number tandem repeats (VNTR), because

CASE STUDY
THE GREEN RIVER KILLER

On November 5, 2003, Gary Leon Ridgway confessed, in a Seattle, Washington, courtroom, to being the "Green River killer" of forty-eight young women. He had been charged with seven murders after his arrest two years earlier, but investigators were anxious to establish the final fate of many more victims whose bodies had been found, or who had disappeared, since July 1982. At one point, serial killer Ted Bundy, awaiting execution in Florida, had offered his "expert advice" to the puzzled investigators. In exchange for a plea bargain to avoid the death penalty, Ridgway agreed to confess, and led them to the remains of several of his victims. "I hate most prostitutes," said Ridgway in his statement, "and I did not want to pay them for sex." He confessed: "I killed so many women, I have a hard time keeping them straight." He had been a suspect since 1983, but successfully passed an earlier polygraph test. Semen samples from three of his earliest victims had been taken, but original DNA typing was not sufficiently advanced at that time. It was not until a PCR (polymerase chain reaction, see page 192) analysis was carried out in November 2001 that a match was obtained with Ridgway's saliva. He is still suspected of more than sixty killings, the last as late as 2000.

LEFT THE GREEN RIVER KILLER, GARY LEON RIDGWAY, WHO CONFESSED TO FORTY-EIGHT HOMICIDES IN NOVEMBER 2003. HE WAS SENTENCED TO LIFE IMPRISONMENT WITHOUT PAROLE, BRINGING TO A CLOSE A CASE THAT HAD HAUNTED WASHINGTON STATE FOR MORE THAN TWENTY YEARS.

BELOW AN ELECTROPHORESIS
PLATE. ELECTROPHORESIS
INVOLVES TAKING A GLASS
PLATE COATED WITH GEL AND
APPLYING A LOW-VOLTAGE
ELECTRICAL CURRENT DIRECTLY
ACROSS IT. A NUMBER OF
SAMPLES FOR ANALYSIS CAN BE
SPOTTED AT ONE END OF THE
PLATE, AND THEIR RATES OF
TRAVEL ACROSS THE PLATE
COMPARED.

the number of repeated sequences can vary from locus to locus. The procedure is more complex than standard RFLP typing, and it takes longer. An exploitation of this VNTR analysis was named DNA fingerprinting, after its development by the English scientist Alec Jeffreys (now Sir Alec) in 1984. It is much more discriminating than single-locus methods, claiming to be able to identify a single individual among 1,000 trillion trillion trillion—far greater than the present population of the world. More recently, the use of autorads has been superseded in part by another technique:

Specific fluorescent chemicals are used to color the fragments, and the individual bands, as they emerge from electrophoresis, are scanned by laser. Its output is fed into a computer, which produces a printout of profile peaks.

The first criminal case in England to make use of the Jeffreys technique—and so establish the precedent for DNA evidence—was heard in November 1987. A burglar had broken into a house near Bristol in June, raped a forty-five-year-old disabled woman, and made off with her jewelry. Later, a man was arrested for another burglary in the vicinity, and the rape

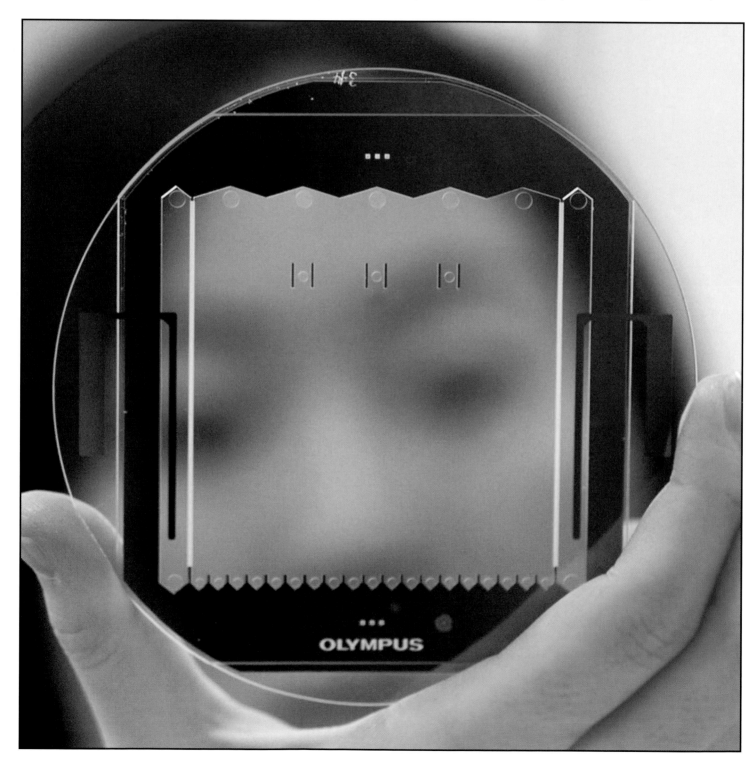

OLYMPUS

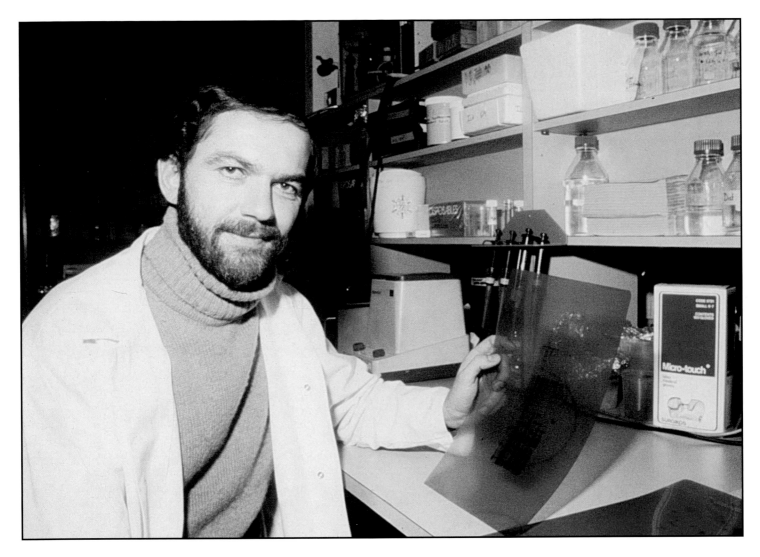

victim was asked to attend a lineup, at which she identified the man as her assailant. The "bar code" of the DNA from semen on the woman's underclothes matched that of the burglar. He was tried and found guilty of rape and robbery, and sentenced to eighteen years' imprisonment.

Jeffreys' VNTR technique has not been seriously challenged in British courts, but in the United States RFLP typing suffered a temporary setback during the trial of Joseph Castro in New York State. Castro was accused of stabbing Vilma Ponce and her two-year-old daughter to death, and the evidence submitted for DNA typing was a spot of blood, alleged to be Vilma Ponce's, that was found on Castro's wristwatch. The analysis was carried out by a private

ABOVE SIR ALEC JEFFREYS, THE DEVELOPER OF VNTR DNA FINGERPRINTING IN 1984, HOLDING A TYPICAL AUTORADIOGRAPH. THE FIRST TIME DNA FINGERPRINTING WAS USED IN A BRITISH MURDER CASE WAS IN 1987, WHEN A TEENAGER, WHO HAD CONFESSED TO THE KILLING, WAS SHOWN BY DNA ANALYSIS TO BE INNOCENT.

CASE STUDY
TOMMY LEE ANDREWS

In the same month that the first DNA evidence was established in a British court, November 1987, the trial of Tommy Lee Andrews was heard in Florida. Between May and December 1986, twenty-three rapes at knifepoint occurred in Orlando, and continued into 1987. In March 1987, Andrews was arrested, and later identified from his fingerprints and the partial descriptions of his victims. His blood type also matched with semen samples. However, in respect of the first rape—for which he had been positively identified by his victim, Nancy Hodge—he offered an apparently unshakable alibi. The assistant state attorney therefore requested an RFLP typing, which also matched samples from victims.

After a pretrial hearing the judge agreed that the evidence was admissible; however, the prosecutor—who was ill prepared in regard to the significance of the results—made such exaggerated claims concerning the probability of positive identification that the defense challenged the figures he quoted, and the trial resulted in a hung jury.

Nevertheless, the retrial of Andrews resulted in a conviction—with a sentence of twenty-eight years, together with twenty-two years for another rape, twenty-two for robbery, and fifteen for burglary—and both the judge's ruling and the conviction were upheld in the appellate court.

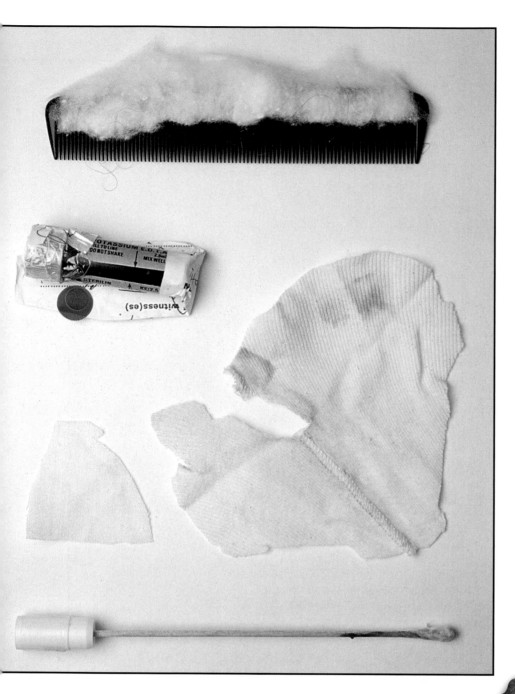

the probability that a DNA sample taken from a crime scene will match that of a suspect must be based on knowledge of the frequency with which each fragment can occur in the population at large. For example, suppose that four fragments have been identified, with calculated frequencies of, respectively, 42 x 32 x 2 x 1 in 100.

The probability that all four will appear in a single sample is 42 x 32 x 2 x 1 = 2,688 in 100 million; that is, approximately 1 in 37,000. Such population statistics are only gradually compiled, however, and the calculations can be complicated by the fact that most crimes occur within local communities, often of very similar ethnic backgrounds. In the Bonds case, for example, the defense argued that considerations of this kind made the prosecution's claim of positive identification completely invalid.

This problem provoked a great deal of controversy in the United States during the 1990s concerning the statistical claims of individuality that were made by prosecution counsel in trials. In 1992, the National Research Council (NRC) established a committee to consider the problem. Only two of the fourteen members were working forensic scientists; the others, although experts in DNA technology, had no forensic experience. They were able to make valuable recommendations concerning the standards to be exercised by analytical laboratories, but found it hard to reach an agreement on the assessment of population statistics. As a result, a second NCR committee was convened in 1994, and made a series of proposals that have now been generally adopted.

ABOVE FORENSIC EVIDENCE IN A CASE OF RAPE, FROM WHICH A DNA MATCH WILL BE SOUGHT. FROM THE TOP: PUBIC HAIR TRAPPED IN A COMB WITH COTTON WOOL; A SAMPLE OF A SUSPECT'S BLOOD; BLOOD AND SEMEN STAINS ON A TORN PAIR OF PANTIES; A STAINED PIECE OF CLOTH; AND A VAGINAL SWAB FROM THE VICTIM.

FACING PAGE A SCIENTIST AT WORK IN THE SEROLOGICAL LABORATORY OF THE FBI IN WASHINGTON, D.C. SHE IS TAKING SAMPLES OF BLOOD FROM A HANDGUN, WHICH COULD BE FROM EITHER THE VICTIM OR THE PERPETRATOR OF THE CRIME.

company that had only recently taken up forensic work, and the autorads they produced were of doubtful quality. The judge ruled the evidence inadmissible, and—in an unprecedented consensus—four of the expert witnesses, from both the prosecution and the defense, drew up a statement on its inadequacy. Castro was convicted on other evidence, however, and later confessed. The judge remarked that only two people in the courtroom knew whether or not the blood was truly Vilma Ponce's: Castro himself, and the analyst.

This case resulted in the improvement of methods and standardization in DNA laboratories, but it was not until 1990 that the FBI accepted evidence from RFLP analysis, in the case of John Ray Bonds. In RFLP typing,

CASE STUDY
JOHN RAY BONDS

In February 1988, the body of David Hartlaub was found outside the night depository of a bank in Perkins Township, Ohio. He had been shot six times, in or near his van, allegedly by gunmen. It later transpired that the crime was a murder for hire, and that Hartlaub had been mistaken for the intended victim. There were no witnesses, but a group of Hell's Angels was suspected, and DNA from blood inside the van was matched by the FBI with that of one of them, a man who had driven it away from the scene, John Ray Bonds.

When Bonds and others stood trial for homocide in 1990, the defence mounted an attack on the admissibility of DNA evidence in principle, and in particular the statistical calculation of its individuality. The judge, however, ruled in favor of DNA analysis. In a later case the same year, a federal appellate court upheld the admissibility of RFLP DNA typing.

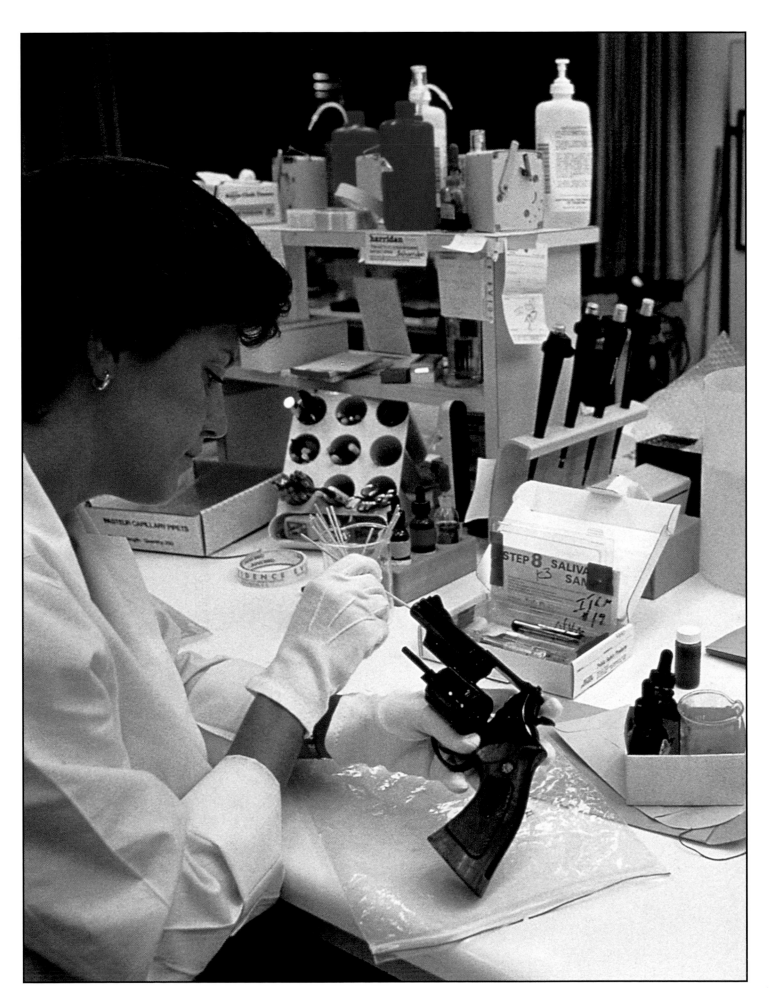

In May 1992, the body of a woman, Denise Johnson, was discovered at the foot of a paloverde tree in Phoenix, Arizona. In addition to signs that a car had been at the site a pager was discovered, which led the sheriff's deputies to Mark Bogen, who admitted picking up the woman but denied killing her. A search of his truck, however, revealed paloverde seedpods.

DNA analysis of these pods, and of others from the tree itself, produced an exact match. The pods, rather than the seeds, had to be analyzed because they derived solely from the maternal tissue of the tree, whereas the seeds would be the result of cross-pollination with another tree. Before the DNA results could be admitted at trial, a Frye hearing (see page 236) had to be held, following which the judge ruled, for the first time in Arizona, that plant-DNA profiles could be allowed as evidence. These profiles, together with a wealth of other physical evidence, secured Bogen's conviction.

While the ruling was upheld by the Arizona State Court of Appeals, a minority opinion maintained that the DNA evidence should not have been admitted—though it was nevertheless agreed that it had resulted only in "harmless error."

PCR ANALYSIS

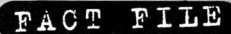

The principal drawback to the analysis of DNA by the methods described before is that it requires a sufficiently large sample, and much of the DNA may already have become degraded, due to exposure to light, contamination by microorganisms, temperature changes, or the effects of various chemical substances.

A technique that is claimed to be able to recover the DNA from a single cell is known as the polymerase chain reaction, or PCR, which was developed by American Kary Mullis in 1983. PCR makes use of an enzyme that will copy the DNA strand; the two strands are copied again, making four, and so on in a chain reaction that can result in a million or more copies in the course of only a few hours. For this reason, PCR analysis is often referred to as molecular photocopying. Mullis won a Nobel Prize for his technique in 1993.

The major problem with PCR is that it will copy any strand of DNA, including that of

RIGHT DR. KARY MULLIS, WHO DEVELOPED THE POLYMERASE CHAIN REACTION (PCR) FOR THE MULTIPLICATION OF SINGLE DNA STRANDS. AFTER POSTDOCTORAL WORK AT THE UNIVERSITY OF KANSAS MEDICAL SCHOOL, HE JOINED CALIFORNIA'S CETUS CORPORATION AS A RESEARCH SCIENTIST IN 1979. MULLIS MADE HIS DISCOVERY WHILE WORKING AT CETUS IN 1983.

FACT FILE

MITOCHONDRIAL DNA

Mitochondria are molecules made up of DNA that are found in the cells of nucleated living organisms, and are responsible for the generation of energy. They are smaller than the DNA strands of the nucleus, generally circular in form, and, interestingly, they derive only from the mother. Following the development of RFLP and VNTR typing, research into mitochondrial DNA temporarily took a backseat, but recently its analysis has proved valuable, as in the identification of the bones of the Russian Tsarina Alexandra by comparison with a blood sample provided by her grandnephew, the Duke of Edinburgh.

contaminants. In cases of gang rape, for example, identification can prove extremely difficult, and in the laboratory great care must be taken to ensure that the initial sample is not contaminated during handling. On the other hand, the versatility of PCR is valuable in that it is usually employed to copy DNA fragments. This forms the basis of typing by short tandem repeats (STRs). STRs are similar to VNTR fragments, but the repeat-sequence units consist of only two to five base pairs.

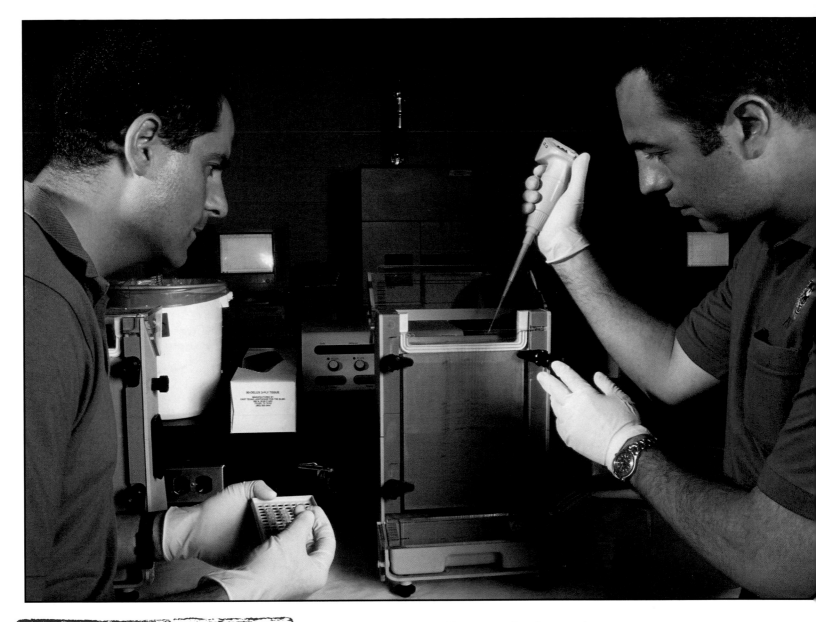

DNA DATABANKS

Since the passing of the federal DNA Identification Act of 1994, a large number of local, state, and federal databanks have been set up in the United States, which function very much like fingerprint records. The Act limits the use of the databanks to include only convicted criminals; all record the DNA of sex offenders, but individual states vary in whether they collect samples from other criminals, such as murderers, burglars, and those who commit crimes against children. In New York State, for example, all felons are included in the databank, whereas California allows only those committing one of nine specific offenses to be included.

By September 2001, 116 laboratories in thirty-seven U.S. states participated in the National DNA Information System (NDIS). More than 500,000 offender samples and 25,000 casework samples had been typed and entered. More than 1,600 cases had been solved by this means. DNA samples for analysis and recording in databanks are usually obtained by taking swabs from the epithelial cells of the inside of the mouth, which are constantly being detached. Alternatively, blood samples may also be taken.

In Britain, it is now customary for a blood sample to be taken upon the arrest of anyone suspected of a violent crime. Canada, South Africa, and Australia also maintain databanks, under the control of their respective national police forces, and the practice is spreading rapidly throughout the world.

The widespread use of DNA typing has resulted in the conviction of many offenders, but recently, particularly in the United States, doubt has been cast on the validity of some of the evidence. Investigation of closed cases has revealed carelessness and confusion in the handling of samples, and incidents of contamination.

ABOVE THE FBI ACADEMY AT QUANTICO, VIRGINIA, PROVIDES TRAINING IN DNA ANALYSIS TO INVESTIGATORS FROM AROUND THE WORLD. HERE, TWO SPANISH DELEGATES ARE SEEN LOADING A SAMPLE, FROM DANDRUFF TRACES OBTAINED IN A CRIMINAL INVESTIGATION, INTO THE ANALYTICAL EQUIPMENT.

THE INNOCENCE PROJECT

Lawyer Barry Scheck, who was a member of the defense counsel in the case of Joseph Castro, together with his colleague Peter Neufeld, set up a DNA task force, with the approval of the National Association of Criminal Defense

Lawyers, in the early 1990s. They were inspired by the case of Gary Dotson, who was exonerated by DNA typing in 1988 after spending nearly twelve years in prison for a rape that he had not committed.

While a professor in the Cardozo School of Law at Yeshiva University, New York City, Scheck invited lawyers to contact him with cases of what they believed to be wrongful convictions; Scheck and Neufeld offered their services free when DNA typing could be

CASE STUDY
A QUESTION OF INNOCENCE

RIGHT THE PASSPORT PHOTOGRAPH OF MURDERER COLIN PITCHFORK. HE WAS ONE OF THE FIRST PEOPLE IN BRITAIN TO BE CONVICTED ON THE BASIS OF DNA EVIDENCE.

One of the first cases of rape and murder in which DNA typing was used, in England, established the innocence of the man who had confessed to the crime, and revealed the true perpetrator.

During the evening of November 21, 1983, fifteen-year-old Lynda Mann was raped and killed on a footpath close by a local psychiatric hospital near the village of Narborough, Leicestershire. Semen samples established that the killer's blood type was the same as that possessed by some 10 percent of the British male population, but the high sperm content suggested a young man. The police therefore decided to narrow their inquiries to males between the ages of thirteen and thirty-four. No suspect was identified, however, and the investigation was stalled after nine months.

More than two years later, on July 31, 1986, another fifteen-year-old, Dawn Ashworth, was similarly assaulted and killed not far from the same hospital, and the police were convinced that the same man was responsible for both crimes. At the time of the first murder, they had questioned fourteen-year-old Richard Buckland as a suspect, but had eventually eliminated him from their investigation. Later, aged sixteen, he was working as a

RIGHT FIFTEEN-YEAR-OLD LYNDA MANN, THE FIRST OF PITCHFORK'S VICTIMS, WHOSE BODY WAS DISCOVERED ON NOVEMBER 22, 1983.

porter in the psychiatric hospital, and he was again taken in for questioning. After two days of incoherent rambling, Buckland signed a confession and was charged with Dawn Ashworth's murder—but he denied responsibility for the murder of Lynda Mann. The police asked Alec Jeffreys to carry out his newly developed DNA typing on a sample of Buckland's blood, together with semen samples from the bodies of the two murdered girls. At that time, the VNTR technique took several weeks to complete, and it was close to the date set for Buckland's trial when Jeffreys finally announced that both murders had been committed by the same man—and it was certainly not Buckland.

Baffled, the police decided to institute a voluntary mass sampling of more than 5,000 local males. Any samples of the appropriate blood type were then sent to the Home Office Forensic Laboratory for DNA typing. Not a single positive identification was found—but the case was broken by a remarkable accident. Idly chatting in a pub, a man happened to mention that one of his coworkers, twenty-seven-year-old Colin Pitchfork, had paid him to give a blood sample in his name. Pitchfork himself was revealed as a convicted "flasher," as well as a former outpatient at the psychiatric hospital. His DNA matched the semen samples, and he was convicted in a trial that lasted only a day.

employed to reverse a conviction. At first, the applications were few; then, in 1992, appearing on TV's *Phil Donahue Show*, Scheck appealed for anyone who believed that they, or a member of their family, had been wrongfully convicted to contact the Innocence Project at Cardozo.

A flood of letters ensued, with most of the cases dating to a time before DNA typing was available. Scheck charged his students with the task of sorting them out; cases that did not involve physical evidence had to be set aside, as did those in which the evidence was no longer available. Jane Siegel Greene, who was executive director of the Innocence Project for many years, has said: "DNA is not the magic bullet. It is not going to fix the criminal justice system, but what it does do is open this window on what is wrong with the system. It allows us to show with complete certainty that these people are truly innocent."

By April 2002, the Innocence Project had successfully demonstrated that 104 people had spent an average of ten years in prison for crimes they had not committed.

THE FATAL BULLET

The earliest use of ballistics examination, of both bullets and guns, has been described earlier, but forensic ballistics as an exact science owes its establishment to the pioneering work of Charles Waite (1865–1926), who was an assistant in the office of the New York State prosecutor when he first took an interest in the subject.

After serving in the U.S. Army during World War I, Waite spent two years traveling, both in the United States and Europe, to assemble data from a large number of firearms manufacturers. Within a few years, Waite, together with Major (later Colonel) Calvin Goddard, Philip Gravelle, and John Fisher, was able to establish the Bureau of Forensic Ballistics in New York City, the first of its kind in the world. When Waite

died in 1926, he was succeeded as head of the bureau by Goddard.

While Goddard became the leading American expert on firearm identification, the other founding members of the bureau were responsible for the development of two instruments that were to prove invaluable in the examination of bullets and guns. Gravelle produced the comparison microscope, essentially an instrument with two objectives and a single eyepiece, so that the striations on two bullets, placed side by side, could be compared exactly; and Fisher adapted a cystoscope, a medical device for the internal examination of the bladder, into the helixometer, which could explore the interior of a rifled gun barrel.

Meanwhile, research into the identification of bullets, and the guns from which they had been fired, had continued in many other countries. Egypt, the country to which Scottish pathologist Dr. Sydney (later Sir Sydney) Smith was appointed Principal Medico-Legal Expert in 1917, proved an exceptional

BELOW A FRENCH BALLISTICS EXPERT IN THE MIDST OF HIS COLLECTION OF GUNS FROM AROUND THE WORLD. THESE WEAPONS CAN BE TEST-FIRED, TO REVEAL CHARACTERISTIC FIRING-PIN AND RIFLING MARKS, WHICH WILL HELP TO IDENTIFY A WEAPON USED IN A CRIMINAL ASSAULT.

NICOLA SACCO AND BARTOLOMEO VANZETTI

On April 15, 1920, two men shot two security guards outside a shoe factory in South Braintree, Massachusetts, and made off with the company's payroll. Around the guards' bodies lay a number of .32 shell cases, which were identified as being from bullets manufactured by three separate companies: Peters, Winchester, and Remington.

Soon afterward, two suspects were arrested in nearby Bridgewater; they were Nicola Sacco and Bartolomeo Vanzetti, two Italian immigrants. Sacco was carrying a loaded .32 Colt revolver, and in his pockets were twenty-three bullets, variously manufactured by Peters, Winchester, and Remington. Vanzetti was carrying a .32 Harrington and Richardson revolver, together with four shotgun cartridges, identical to a cartridge found at the scene of a failed payroll robbery some months previously.

The trial of the two gunmen acquired a political dimension; it was suggested that their actions were a form of protest against the poor working conditions of immigrants, and left-wing organizations around the world supported a fund for their

defense. However, the most damning evidence against them consisted of the twenty-three bullets—shown to be of obsolete manufacture and no longer obtainable—found in Sacco's pocket. Both were found guilty, and condemned to death. But, when international protest continued, a stay of execution was granted.

At the trial, two experts called by the defense, James Burns and August Gill, had disagreed entirely with the evidence brought forward by the prosecution. It was not until 1927 that Colonel Calvin Goddard offered himself as an unbiased expert. In the presence of Gill, he fired a test bullet into cotton wool, then placed it beside one of the fatal bullets under his comparison microscope. "Well, what do you know about that!" exclaimed Gill, as he was forced to agree to the match. Sacco and Vanzetti were sent to the electric chair two months later.

LEFT A MASSIVE DEMONSTRATION IN UNION SQUARE, NEW YORK CITY, 1924, TO PROTEST AGAINST THE CONVICTION OF NICOLA SACCO AND BARTOLOMEO VANZETTI. LEFT-WING ORGANIZATIONS AROUND THE WORLD RAISED A FUND FOR THE DEFENSE, AND SECURED A TEMPORARY STAY OF EXECUTION.

"I examined the car, reconstructed the crime, and considered the material evidence. This consisted of nine cartridge cases, found at the scene of the crime, and six bullets that had been extracted from the bodies of the victims. The cartridge cases were all .32 automatic pistol ammunition. The marks on them showed that three different types of automatic had been used, and three of the cases bore extractor and ejector marks characteristic of a Colt.... The bullets had been fired from three different types of weapon: a pistol of the Mauser type, with four right-handed rifling grooves; a pistol of the Browning or Sureté type, with six right-handed grooves; and a pistol of the Colt type, with six left-handed grooves.

The bullet that had killed the Sirdar bore the marks characteristic of a Colt. The pistol was evidently in a bad state, with the lands worn ... but on the bullet there was a clearly marked scratched groove, lying between two normal grooves and broader than them, which betrayed a fault in the muzzle end of the barrel.

I had seen this scratched groove before. I had seen it many times—and when I compared the bullet microscopically with other crime bullets in my collection I was sure that the Colt .32 that had killed the Sirdar was the same weapon that had been used repeatedly in previous political murders...."

"laboratory," due to the prevalence of political assassination. As Smith later wrote, "The steady and copious supply of shooting enabled us to test, correct, and increase our knowledge without intermission."

The climax of Smith's work came in 1924, when Sir Lee Stack Pasha, the sirdar (commander in chief) of the Egyptian Army and governor of Sudan, was shot while driving through the streets of Cairo. His driver and aide-de-camp were also killed. In *Mostly Murder* (1959), Smith wrote:

The serious political nature of the assassinations provoked a massive investigation. Two suspects, brothers named Enayat, were arrested, and their weapons examined by Smith; these included both the Colt and the Sureté pistols. The Enayats named their collaborators, and eventually eight men were found guilty, principally on Smith's evidence.

As Smith pointed out, the shell cases ejected from an automatic or semiautomatic weapon can also provide vital evidence. The bullet, before firing, lies against a breechblock of hardened steel. When the gun is fired, the trigger drives the firing pin through a small aperture in the breechblock to strike the detonator cap of the cartridge, and the intense pressure generated by the explosion of the bullet's charge drives the case against the breechblock. The softer metal of the cap therefore becomes imprinted with any manufacturing imperfection in the steel. The firing pin also leaves its own impression on the cap, and the ejector mechanism will most

CASE STUDY
CARL STIELOW

In 1915, an illiterate German immigrant farmer named Carl F. Stielow was found guilty of shooting his employer, Charles Phelps, and Phelps's housekeeper. A self-proclaimed firearms examiner pronounced that a revolver found in Stielow's possession was the murder weapon, and Stielow was committed to Sing Sing prison in upstate New York to await execution. His attorneys obtained a stay of execution in July 1916, and shortly afterward two vagrants confessed to the crime, and the state governor ordered a reexamination of the case. Ballistics expert Charles Waite undertook a thorough investigation and, assisted by microscopy expert Dr. Max Poser and Captain John Jones of the New York City homicide squad, established that the murder weapon could not have been Stielow's. The prisoner was given a free pardon.

likely produce characteristic marks on the shell case as well.

In Britain, the development of Philip Gravelle's comparison microscope attracted the attention of Robert Churchill, a London gunmaker who had appeared as an expert witness in firearms cases since 1912. In collaboration with Major Hugh Pollard, Churchill had been experimenting since 1919 with a similar—but relatively crude—apparatus used by Sydney Smith, and in 1927 he traveled to the United States to consult with Colonel Calvin Goddard. Upon his return, Churchill had a comparison microscope made to his specification, and was soon to have a historic success (see sidebar, left).

Some months previously, Churchill had given evidence, not concerning bullets, but regarding the pattern of wounds produced by shotgun pellets. During the night of

BELOW A HIGH-SPEED PHOTOGRAPH OF THE CHARGE OF PELLETS LEAVING THE MUZZLE OF A 12-GAUGE SHOTGUN, FOUR MILLISECONDS AFTER DISCHARGE. MOST SMOOTH-BORE SHOTGUN BARRELS ARE "CHOKED," TO PREVENT THE PELLETS' SCATTERING TOO WIDELY.

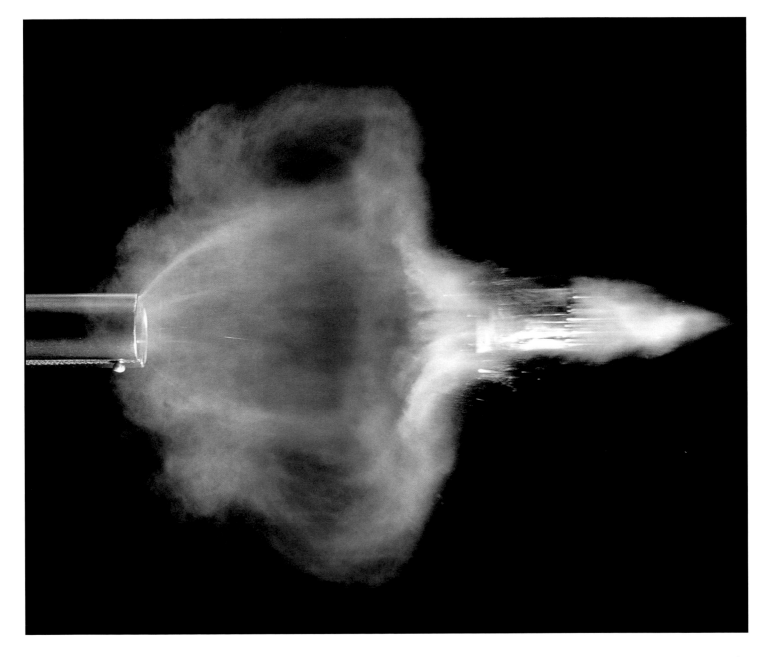

RIGHT USING A LASER BEAM
ALIGNED ON THE POINT OF
IMPACT OF A BULLET,
INVESTIGATORS CAN
ACCURATELY DETERMINE
THE DIRECTION FROM WHICH
IT CAME AND CALCULATE
THE POINT FROM WHICH
IT WAS FIRED.

BELOW AN AGENT AT THE FBI
BALLISTICS LABORATORY IN
QUANTICO, VIRGINIA, USING
A COMPARISON MICROSCOPE
TO COMPARE THE STRIATIONS
ON TWO BULLETS, ONE FROM
THE SCENE OF CRIME AND THE
OTHER FROM A SUSPECT'S
WEAPON.

October 10, 1927, a head gamekeeper was shot dead on the estate of Lord Temple, near Bath, western England. The assailant, a well-known poacher named Enoch Dix, was identified by the gamekeeper's assistant, who had taken a shot at Dix as he fled. When Dix's cottage was searched, the police found a gun, and discovered that the poacher's back was peppered with pellet wounds. Dix claimed that the assistant gamekeeper had fired at him first, and that his own gun had gone off accidentally as a result.

Churchill was asked to advise on which gun had been fired first, and at what range. With both the guns in question at hand, he loaded them with the appropriate cartridges, and test-fired each gun at a succession of whitewashed steel plates. At 15 yards (13.7 m), he found the spread of shot to be between 27 and 30 inches (68–76 cm); at 20 yards (18.2 m), it was between 36 and 38 inches (91–96 cm). From the wounds on Dix's back, as well as accompanying pellets that had hit a tree, Churchill calculated that Dix must have been at least 15 yards (13.7 m) off when the assistant gamekeeper fired.

If Dix's gun had then gone off, the head gamekeeper would have been similarly peppered. But his fatal wound was only 4 to 5 inches (10–12 cm) across, indicating that he had been shot at point-blank range. Despite the judge's direction to the jury, however, Dix was found guilty only of manslaughter. Nevertheless, the study of shotgun wounds is now an important part of ballistics investigation.

In 1929, Colonel Goddard, using the comparison microscope, was able to identify the two Thompson submachine guns used in the bloody "St. Valentine's Day massacre" in Chicago in 1928, and to confirm that no police guns were responsible. Following this success, he was invited to establish the Scientific Crime Detection Laboratory (SCDL) at Northwestern University, Evanston, Illinois.

In 1932, J. Edgar Hoover, director of the Federal Bureau of Investigation, set up an FBI ballistics laboratory in Washington, D.C. Goddard retired from the SCDL in 1934, to take up private practice, and in 1938 the laboratory

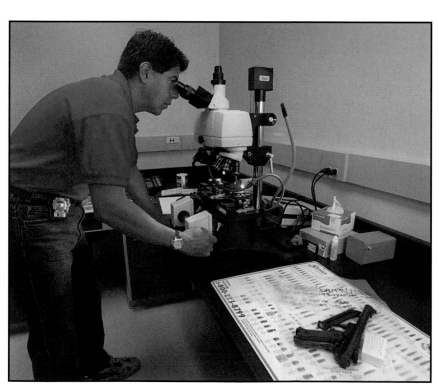

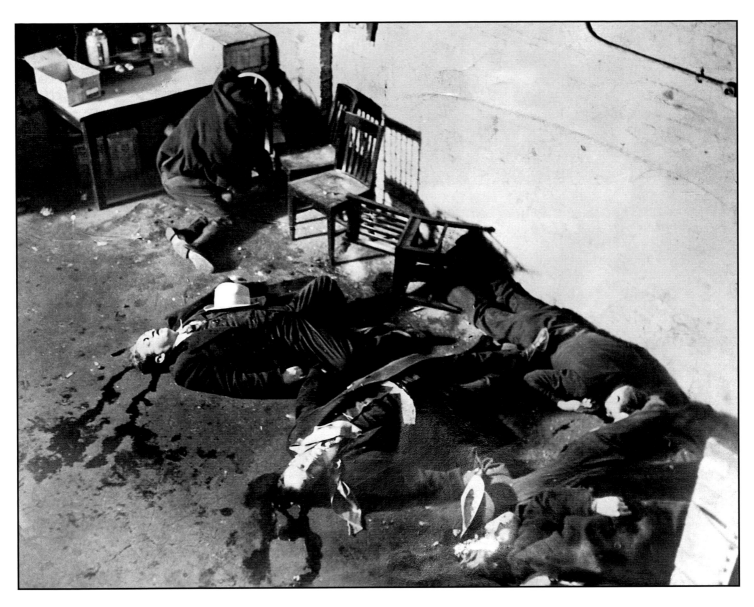

was transferred to the Chicago Police Department. About the same time, individual firearms laboratories were established in a number of American states, as well as in Canada, Britain, France, Germany, Norway, and the Soviet Union, among other countries.

Meanwhile, controversy over the Sacco-Vanzetti case (see page 197) continued for many years after their execution. More than thirty years later, in 1961, Frances Russell, a Boston author, made arrangements for the ballistics evidence to be reexamined by Frank Jury, formerly head of the New Jersey State Police Laboratory, and Jack Weller of the West Point Museum. They concluded that the fatal bullet had indeed been fired from Sacco's revolver. And in 1983, another team of investigators, funded by a Boston television station, finally confirmed Goddard's original findings.

The comparison microscope is still a vital tool in the hands of ballistics examiners, although optical-fiber lighting is now generally used to improve definition. Many instruments today are also equipped with video units, which allow not only for direct viewing but also digital storage of images on a computer. Software systems such as IBIS and the FBI's Drugfire make it possible for the examiner to compare stored data from his or her laboratory with that of other laboratories.

Another important technical development is the use of the scanning electron microscope (SEM), which provides magnification many times greater than a conventional microscope. In 1997, the attorneys for the late James Earl Ray, found guilty of assassinating Dr. Martin Luther King Jr. in April 1968, petitioned for the case to be reexamined, on the grounds that "new groundbreaking technology"—optical-fiber lighting and SEM—had not been available during previous examinations carried out in 1968 and 1977. However, it was established that the SEM had been in use as early as 1972, while optical-fiber lighting had been employed in 1977 by the examiners for the Congress Select Committee on Assassinations. The petition was denied.

ABOVE THE SCENE OF CARNAGE AT THE 1928 ST. VALENTINE'S DAY MASSACRE IN CHICAGO, WHEN MEMBERS OF AL CAPONE'S GANG, DISGUISED AS POLICE OFFICERS, SLAUGHTERED RIVAL GEORGE "BUGS" MORAN AND SIX OF HIS FELLOW GANGSTERS. RUMORS THAT GENUINE POLICE WERE INVOLVED WERE SCOTCHED BY COLONEL CALVIN GODDARD'S EXAMINATION OF THE BULLETS USED IN THE KILLINGS.

FACING PAGE A RESEARCHER
USING A COMPUTER TO
ANALYSE THE CHARACTERISTICS
OF A VOICEPRINT. THE 2.5-
SECOND BURST OF SOUND
BEING EXAMINED IS THE
SPOKEN WORD "BABY."

VOICEPRINTS

A witness's testimony concerning the recognition of a person's voice has sometimes been admitted as evidence in court, although more often it is allowed only as grounds for the issue of a warrant. The problem is that identification by ear is subjective—the hearer may easily be mistaken—and evidence should be presented in material form, preferably, to persuade a jury. Even a tape recording can be challenged by the defense. Great care has to be taken, therefore, when a recorded interrogation is entered as evidence, to establish that the tape has not been selectively edited.

Accordingly, forensic investigators cautiously welcomed a new technique of voice identification in 1967, when the use of "voiceprints" first became admissible in a United States jurisdiction. It had taken some twenty years to develop a satisfactory apparatus; experiments had begun during World War II, when scientists and engineers at Bell Telephone Laboratories, in New Jersey, were asked whether they could develop a method of distinguishing different speakers in German military radio communications.

One of these researchers was Lawrence Kersta, who continued his experiments after the war, and in 1963 finally developed a reliable means of electronically recording the pitch,

volume, and resonance of the human voice, in what he called a spectrogram. The sound of an individual's voice depends on a number of personal characteristics—including the articulation of the lips, tongue, and teeth that produces the particular sounds of speech, as well as the resonance of the cavity of the mouth, the larynx, and the thorax—and Kersta pointed out that no two persons were likely to be physically identical in this respect.

To prove his point, Kersta made 50,000 recordings of individual voices; although many sounded superficially quite similar, his apparatus revealed distinct—and characteristic—differences. He also made use of professional mimics, successfully demonstrating that, although what they said was indistinguishable from the voice of the person they were imitating, the mimics' voiceprints were nevertheless noticeably different.

The most commonly used words in English speech are *a, and, I, is, it, on, the, to, we, you.* The Kersta apparatus records a short 2.5-second burst of the voice on a high-speed magnetic tape, which is then scanned electronically and recorded either on a cathode-ray display or by stylus on a rotating drum. Two types of voiceprint can be obtained. One, which is of the type usually presented as evidence, is a bar print: The horizontal scale represents the time taken in recording, and the vertical scale measures the sound frequency. Volume is represented by the density of the individual bars. The other type of print, which is most suitable for storing and comparing on a computer, displays the more complex characteristics of a voice, resulting in a complete representation of the unique frequencies and volume of the subject's speech.

The first admission of voiceprints at trial occurred in California. During the rioting in the Watts district of Los Angeles in 1965, a young man was interviewed by a CBS television reporter. Keeping his back to the camera, he boasted of setting fires. Some time later the police arrested Edward Lee King on suspicion that he was the interviewed person in question; Kersta was asked to make a comparison of his voice, taped during interrogation, with that on the TV recording. At King's trial, Kersta testified that the voiceprints were identical, and the young man was convicted of arson.

King appealed, on the grounds that providing a sample of his own voice amounted to self-incrimination, but the U.S. Supreme Court, after due deliberation, ruled that the right of privilege did not apply in this case.

Since then, voiceprint evidence has been admitted on occasion in American courts, but it is still regarded with marked skepticism in Europe.

BELOW A COMPUTER
RECONSTRUCTION OF THE
COMPLEX PATTERN OF
WAVEFORM GENERATED BY
A SINGLE SPOKEN SOUND.
THE VOLUME OF SOUND
INCREASES TO A MAXIMUM,
THEN DIES AWAY.

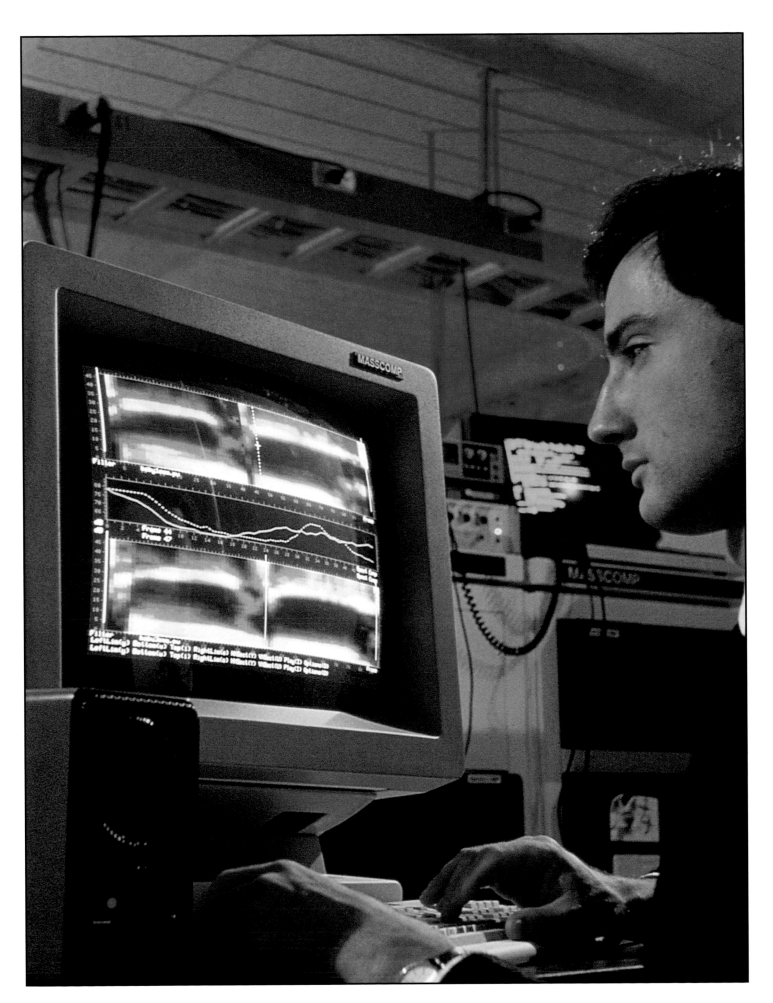

The Jepsons and Razaks during happier times →

PART 5

A POSITIVE IDENTIFICATION

CSI Tamara Gregory waited several days before preliminary reports came back from the FBI, and they were disappointing. The fingerprints matched no known criminal, neither in the state files nor in the national databank, and nothing was to be learned at VICAP from the MO.

"Well, at least," said Sheriff Verdian, when informed of the results, "we know that we don't have a serial killer on our hands." As for the DNA, it matched only that of the victim. The best positive lead came from analysis of the vehicle trace fragments: They were identified as coming, not from a car, but from a Chevy van, painted burgundy.

A few days later, Agent Pedersen produced the photographs—full-face, three-quarter view, and profile—that had been extrapolated from the skull through the use of digital reconstruction. They showed a young, good-looking woman, of

There were a few hairs found with the Jane Doe skull. They provided the DNA we compared with the DNA from the Razak blood sample. →

MURRIETA PO...

STORAGE AREA

PROPERTY U...

OFFICERS TO COMPLETE INFORM...

LOCKER NO. 1c

ADDITIONAL ITEMS LOCATED IN LOC...
( ) BULK STORAGE AREA

DATE 10/21/01

TAKEN FRO...

TYPE OF...
( ) SAF...

WARNING!! POLICE SEAL
DO NOT REMOVE

MISSION MURRIETA
POLICE DEPARTMENT

EVIDENCE

Report Number: 01-36492
Sealing Officer: Rodriguez
Date of Seizure or Purchase: 10/21/01
Exhibit: Unidentified hair
Witnessing Officer: O'Mall...
Pouch Size:
Opening Official:
Date Open...
Lab...

Southeast Asian descent, with long, straight black hair. The computer expert had even given her a faint, shy smile. "Poor girl," sighed Gregory. "Let's hope someone recognizes her."

"Well, they're already on the wire to newspapers and TV stations all up the coast to Seattle," replied Pedersen. "If the photos actually look like anyone, we should hear about it soon."

By great good luck, calls began to come in within hours. More than a quarter of them identified the photographs as depicting a Mrs. Anna Jepson, wife of Carl Jepson, deceased, and daughter of Mr. and Mrs. Ahmad Razak of Longview, Washington. In particular, Ahmad Razak himself reported in a tearful voice that the photographs closely resembled his daughter, missing since August the previous year. Razak said that he and his wife had been looking after their three-year-old grandson ever since.

The following day, after further calls identifying the photographs, two agents from the FBI's Seattle field office visited the Razak home, on the outskirts of Longview. The Razaks confirmed that the photographs looked very much like their missing daughter, and produced family portraits for comparison. Anna, they said, had been living with them since the death of her husband in late 1999. She had left early on the evening of August 14, 2000, to see a movie at a neighborhood theater, leaving her young son in their care, but had not returned. Mrs. Razak agreed immediately to provide both blood and saliva samples for mitochondrial DNA comparison, which were quickly taken by the police pathologist and rushed to the state crime laboratory. By the next morning, a PCR analysis had established provisional identification. Local police files also confirmed that Anna had been reported missing by the Razaks on the morning of August 15.

Back in California, the county investigation team was greatly heartened by the news. "But," said Verdian, "though we've gotten an ID on the victim, are we any nearer to finding our UNSUB?"

Tamara Gregory shook her head. "What have we got?" she said. "The Feds have confirmed that the Razaks don't own a German shepherd, so most likely it's the killer's, but that's the only lead we have so far. And how many people do you think own that type of dog? Thousands in this county alone, I would guess. Right now we're stymied, unless the Feds can give us a pointer. I'm going to go home, take a long shower, and switch off my brain. Maybe I'll subconsciously spot something I've missed."

The next morning, Gregory breezed into Sheriff Verdian's office looking refreshed and positively chipper. "There's one item of evidence that we haven't considered so far," she said. "That square of carpet we sent off to Washington, D.C. I wonder, have they gotten a lead on that? Let's see if the San Diego field office people have finished their breakfast yet." She picked up the phone.

On the other end, Pedersen sounded equally chipper. "A couple of faxes just came in," he said. "Looks like we've got something to work with. Yes, there's a lot of stuff on the carpet that you'll be anxious to see. And there's also a preliminary profile of our UNSUB. Seems one of our behavioral science mavens, like your bug man at La Jolla, got real interested in the case, set all other work aside and worked late on it. The fax was sent at 1:30 a.m. East Coast time — must have been burning the midnight oil. Anyway, I'd better bring these faxes over, so we can go through them together. Be there within the hour."

It was a long hour, and Tamara Gregory had drunk several more cups of coffee than she was allowing herself these days before Pedersen's car turned into the parking lot. Gregory met him at the door. He was smiling.

"It may still be a long haul," Pederson said, "but this could be enough to crack the case. Which do you want first? The good news or the good news?"

RAZAK, C.   10/28/01

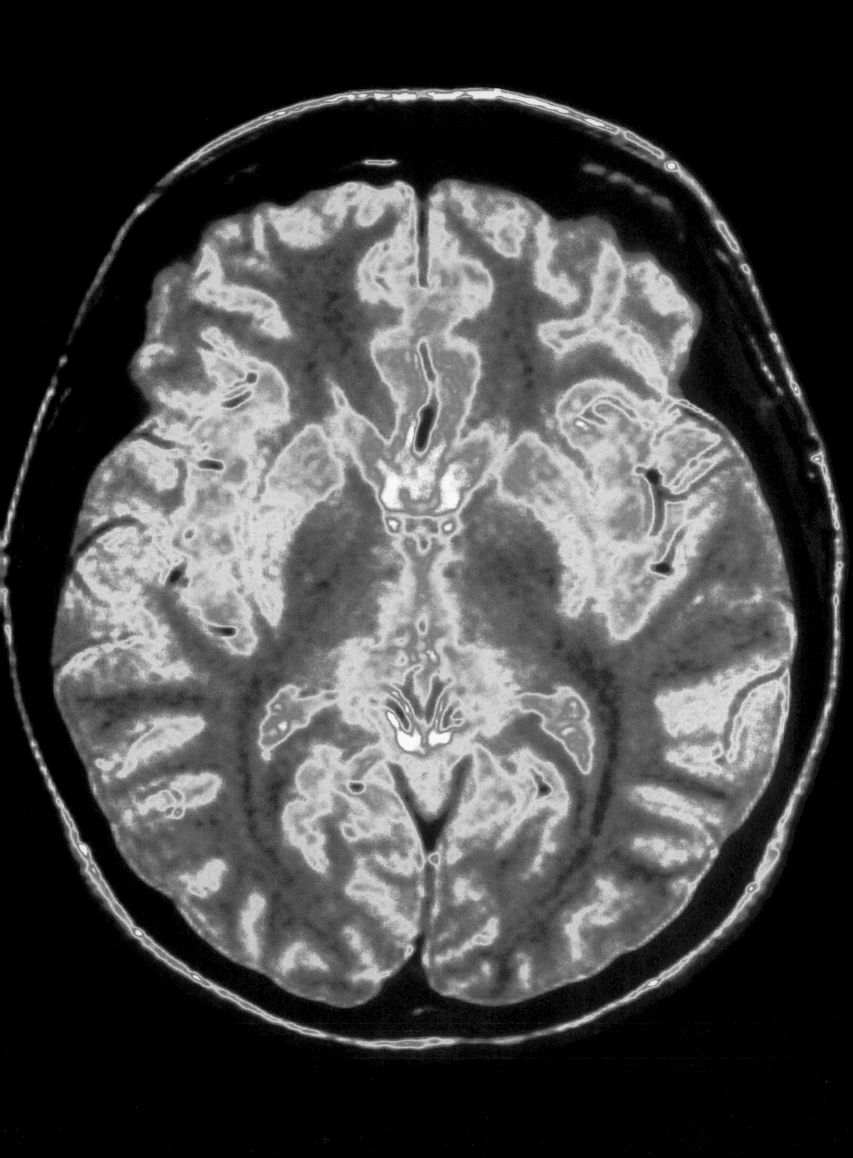

THE MIND OF THE CRIMINAL

All the investigative methods detailed so far depend on an unpredictable factor: the availability of a suspect. Admittedly, fingerprints or video surveillance—even, sometimes, blood or DNA typing—can lead to the identification of a previously recorded criminal, but in most cases it is necessary to be able to compare data from the crime scene, such as visual descriptions, serological evidence, or physical material, with the characteristics of a person detained on suspicion of the crime, or objects in his or her possession. If there is no immediate suspect, the investigating team can call upon the skills of a variety of experts capable of using the evidence to guide the investigators to indentifying the unknown perpetrator.

"O, the mind, mind has mountains; cliffs of fall Frightful, sheer, no-man-fathomed ..."

—GERARD MANLEY HOPKINS, *NO WORST, THERE IS NONE*

FACING PAGE NEUROSCIENTISTS, EMPLOYING MAGNETIC RESONANCE IMAGING (MRI), BELIEVE THAT THEY ARE WELL ON THE WAY TO IDENTIFYING AREAS OF THE BRAIN THAT REVEAL SPECIFIC EMOTIONS AND MOTIVATIONS. RECENTLY, FOR EXAMPLE, IT HAS BEEN CLAIMED THAT BRAIN ACTIVITY ASSOCIATED WITH RACIAL PREJUDICE HAS BEEN DETECTED.

With no likely suspects, of course, the trail is harder to follow. In some cases, criminals must obtain specific materials for the execution of their crime, and trace evidence—ammunition, detonators and explosives, accelerants used to initiate fires, poisons, even plastic bags or rope used to bind a victim—can lead to a specific supply source, which may be able to provide a description, or even name, of the person to which they were sold. The most important recent development in the identification of a perpetrator, however, is what is known as profiling. Based on the existing evidence, experts in this field can frequently provide a description of the probable perpetrator and his or her behavior, and pinpoint their center of operation.

THE ANALYTICAL APPROACH

Sherlock Holmes is renowned for the predictions he could make about an unknown criminal. He may be a fictional character, but his creator, Sir Arthur Conan Doyle, based Holmes on a real person: Dr. Joseph Bell, consulting surgeon at Edinburgh Royal Infirmary, Scotland, who was Doyle's instructor when he was a medical student. In developing a protagonist for his first Holmes story, Conan Doyle wrote, "I thought of my old teacher Joe Bell, of his eagle face, of his curious ways, of his eerie trick of spotting details. If he were a detective, he would surely reduce this fascinating but unorganized business to something nearer to an exact science."

Dr. Bell delighted, without consulting a patient's case notes, in deducing the occupation and previous history of whomever came before him. In a story that he liked to tell

against himself with amusement, Bell took a quick glance at an apparently civilian patient, and confidently announced that he had been in the army, in the Royal Scots regiment, and was not long discharged. He had also seen service for a considerable time in the East, and was likely a bandsman, playing a large brass instrument.

Bell then explained to his astonished students how he had reached these conclusions. As the man entered the examining room, he had stood at attention—something that a discharged soldier would only eventually learn not to do—and his belt buckle bore the Royal Scots badge. The deep tanning of his face and neck suggested that he had served in a hot and sunny climate, while a tattoo suggested that it was Eastern. He was not tall enough for the regular infantry, and therefore was most likely to have been in the band. "Now, if you look at his chest and observe the way he breathes, you will note all the signs of emphysema, which may well be due to the playing of a large wind instrument."

RIGHT DR. JOSEPH BELL, THE SURGEON AT THE EDINBURGH ROYAL INFIRMARY, SCOTLAND, WHO TAUGHT YOUNG ARTHUR CONAN DOYLE, AND BECAME THE MODEL FOR THE FICTIONAL SHERLOCK HOLMES. BELL COULD TELL PATIENTS THEIR HABITS, THEIR OCCUPATIONS, NATIONALITY, AND OFTEN THEIR NAMES, AND RARELY MADE A MISTAKE. "IN TEACHING THE TREATMENT OF DISEASE AND ACCIDENT," DR. BELL STATED, "ALL CAREFUL TEACHERS HAVE FIRST TO SHOW THE STUDENT HOW TO RECOGNIZE ACCURATELY THE CASE. THE RECOGNITION DEPENDS IN GREAT MEASURE ON THE ACCURATE AND RAPID APPRECIATION OF SMALL POINTS IN WHICH THE DISEASED DIFFERS FROM THE HEALTHY STATE."

Bell turned to the patient, who confirmed his previous career. "And we can take it that you played the euphonium or a similar instrument?"

"No, sir, the big drum."

Some years after the Holmes stories began to appear in *Strand* magazine at the end of the nineteenth century, Dr. Bell himself confirmed his methods in a letter to that publication:

"Physiognomy helps you to detect nationality, accent to district, and, to an educated ear, almost to county. Nearly every handicraft writes its sign manual on the hands. The scars of the miner differ from those of the quarryman. The carpenter's callosities are not those of the mason. The shoemaker and the tailor are quite different. The soldier and the sailor differ in gait—though last month I had to tell a man who said he was a soldier that he had been a sailor in his youth. The subject is endless: the tattoo marks on hand or arm will tell their own tale as to voyages; the ornaments on the watch-chain of the successful settler will tell you where he made his money...."

Dr. Bell, of course, made his deductions only from the subject before him; Conan Doyle ingeniously adapted Bell's methods, giving Holmes the ability to *forecast* the characteristics and behavior of the criminal who was being sought. Dr. Edmond Locard, the French criminologist, was a great admirer of the Sherlock Holmes stories, and recommended them to his colleagues.

During the first half of the twentieth century, psychologists and psychiatrists devoted their time to studies of the criminal personality, but seldom applied them to forensic questions. The first reported face-to-face psychological interview with a convicted killer was conducted, in 1930, by German psychiatrist Professor Karl Berg. He closely questioned Peter Kürten, the "Vampire of Düsseldorf," in prison before his execution.

THE MAD BOMBER OF NEW YORK

The first important attempt to apply psychological analysis to predict the future behavior of an individual was made during World War II. In 1943, the U.S. Office of Strategic Services (or OSS, the forerunner of

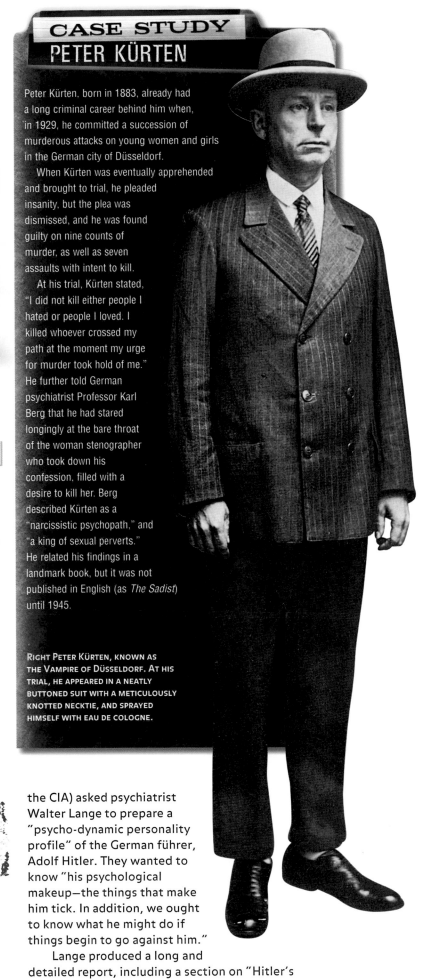

CASE STUDY
PETER KÜRTEN

Peter Kürten, born in 1883, already had a long criminal career behind him when, in 1929, he committed a succession of murderous attacks on young women and girls in the German city of Düsseldorf.

When Kürten was eventually apprehended and brought to trial, he pleaded insanity, but the plea was dismissed, and he was found guilty on nine counts of murder, as well as seven assaults with intent to kill.

At his trial, Kürten stated, "I did not kill either people I hated or people I loved. I killed whoever crossed my path at the moment my urge for murder took hold of me." He further told German psychiatrist Professor Karl Berg that he had stared longingly at the bare throat of the woman stenographer who took down his confession, filled with a desire to kill her. Berg described Kürten as a "narcissistic psychopath," and "a king of sexual perverts." He related his findings in a landmark book, but it was not published in English (as *The Sadist*) until 1945.

RIGHT PETER KÜRTEN, KNOWN AS THE VAMPIRE OF DÜSSELDORF. AT HIS TRIAL, HE APPEARED IN A NEATLY BUTTONED SUIT WITH A METICULOUSLY KNOTTED NECKTIE, AND SPRAYED HIMSELF WITH EAU DE COLOGNE.

the CIA) asked psychiatrist Walter Lange to prepare a "psycho-dynamic personality profile" of the German führer, Adolf Hitler. They wanted to know "his psychological makeup—the things that make him tick. In addition, we ought to know what he might do if things begin to go against him."

Lange produced a long and detailed report, including a section on "Hitler's

probable behavior in the future."
After considering all the possibilities
of Hitler's fate after Allied victory was
sealed, Lange predicted that the führer
would commit suicide when defeat
became inevitable. And so it proved.

A case that attracted the attention
of crime fighters throughout the United
States, and in other parts of the world,
was the first recorded success in the
identification of an unknown criminal.
Indeed, the case of the "Mad Bomber of
New York" has acquired an almost mythic
dimension in the annals of psychological
profiling. The man responsible, Dr. James
Brussel, described it in his *Casebook of a
Crime Psychiatrist* (1968).

In November 1940, an unexploded
homemade pipe bomb was found on a
windowsill on the premises of the
Consolidated Edison electricity company
in New York City. With it was a neatly
lettered note: "CON EDISON CROOKS, THIS
IS FOR YOU!" A second similar bomb was
discovered ten months later. But, when the
United States entered World War II, New
York City police received a letter, mailed in
nearby Westchester County:

"I WILL MAKE NO MORE BOMB UNITS
FOR THE DURATION OF THE WAR—MY
PATRIOTIC FEELINGS HAVE MADE ME DECIDE
THIS—I WILL BRING CON EDISON TO JUSTICE
LATER—THEY WILL PAY FOR THEIR
DASTARDLY DEEDS. F.P."

After several years had passed without
further incidents, the New York police began to
hope that the bomber had given up his
campaign, or perhaps had died. Then, on March
25, 1950, another unexploded bomb was
discovered in Grand Central Station. It seemed
possible that the "Mad Bomber" did not intend
his devices to detonate; however, the next
bomb, left in the New York Public Library, did
explode—luckily, without injuring anyone.
Twelve more bombs exploded, from 1951
through 1954, but no one was hurt until the last
bomb of 1954 went off, hidden in a seat in a
movie theater, slightly injuring four people.

Six bombs were planted in 1955, of which
two failed to detonate. They were more
destructive, however, and it was clear that the
Mad Bomber's frustration was growing. He sent
letters to newspapers, and even made
telephone calls; however, his voice was quietly
anonymous and completely unidentifiable. In a
letter to the *Herald Tribune* he announced that,
so far, fifty-four bombs had been planted. The
first serious injuries occurred when one of his
devices exploded in the Paramount Theater,

THE BOSTON STRANGLER

In his *Casebook*, Dr. James Brussel described how, in 1964—eight years after the "Mad Bomber of New York" case—he was invited to be a member of a panel of psychiatrists who were attempting to draw up a profile of the "Boston Strangler." From June 1962 through January 1964, thirteen women, mostly elderly and all single, were sexually assaulted, beaten, or stabbed, and their naked bodies laid out as if for a pornographic photograph. Each had been strangled, usually with an item of her own clothing, and the murderer had left his "signature" in the form of a neat bow tied under the victim's chin. The majority opinion of the panel was that two different persons, both unmarried, were the perpetrators: one a schoolteacher, the other a man living alone. And both, their report concluded, had a weak and distant father. Dr. Brussel was the sole dissident. His "psychofit" was of a strongly built thirty-year-old man, of average height, clean-shaven and dark-haired, probably of Spanish or Italian origin.

In October 1964, the Strangler struck again, but this time—unaccountably—he left his victim alive. Her description matched that of a man already in police files, but he was listed as a burglar rather than a sexual deviant. Local handyman Albert DeSalvo, who closely resembled Brussel's psychofit, was arrested and charged—but only for breaking and entering. He was committed to the mental institution in Bridgewater, Massachusetts, where he allegedly confessed to a fellow inmate that he was, in fact, the Boston Strangler.

The police, however, were unable to develop sufficient evidence to prosecute him. In December 2001, DNA analysis of semen stains from the underwear of one of the Strangler's victims raised doubts about the killer's identity, but there is no question that further similar killings did not occur following DeSalvo's confinement. Commented one pathologist, "Not finding someone's DNA at a crime scene doesn't mean they weren't there."

ABOVE ALBERT DESALVO, THE LOCAL HANDYMAN SUSPECTED OF BEING THE BOSTON STRANGLER IN 1964. HE DID NOT STAND TRIAL, AND WAS CONFINED IN A MENTAL INSTITUTION, BUT HE CLOSELY RESEMBLED THE "PSYCHOFIT" PUT FORWARD BY DR. JAMES BRUSSEL.

LEFT SOME OF THE THIRTEEN FEMALE VICTIMS ATTRIBUTED TO THE BOSTON STRANGLER, WHO WERE SEXUALLY ASSAULTED AND MURDERED BETWEEN JUNE 1962 AND JANUARY 1964. ALTHOUGH MOST WERE MIDDLE-AGED OR ELDERLY, SEVERAL WERE IN THEIR TWENTIES.

Brooklyn, on December 2, 1956, and the police became apprehensive that the bomber's campaign was accelerating.

The editor of the *Journal-American* published an open letter, begging the Mad Bomber to give himself up, and promising full publicity for his grievances. A letter in reply announced that twelve bombs had been set during 1956—a number of which had never been discovered. A second letter provided the first clues to the bomber's identity; it stated that he had been injured while working for Consolidated Edison, was permanently disabled, and had received no compensation. It seemed improbable that company records

would have been kept for a period of some sixteen years, so Inspector Howard E. Finney of the New York City police made the decision—at that time revolutionary—to consult Dr. Brussel, who had many years of experience with the criminally insane.

From the content and style of the letters, Brussel first deduced that the writer was not of American parentage, and was of an older generation. He diagnosed the perpetrator as a paranoiac (someone who suffers from delusions of persecution), and, because he believed that paranoia developed in persons in their thirties, he set the present age of the bomber, most likely male, as being about fifty. Brussel was

LEFT GEORGE METESKY SMILES CHEERFULLY AFTER HIS ARREST IN WATERBURY, CONNECTICUT, IN 1957. HE READILY CONFESSED TO BEING THE "MAD BOMBER OF NEW YORK," BUT WAS JUDGED INSANE AND UNFIT TO STAND TRIAL.

particularly struck by the shape of the capital *W*s, which were made up of two *U*s. He thought that these looked like female breasts, and suggested that the wanted man had a fixation on his own mother.

Much of Brussel's final "psychofit" could be deduced from the content of the letters, and some of his conclusions were later found to be incorrect, but he also made some remarkably accurate predictions. He informed the police that the bomber was well built and clean-shaven; he was unmarried, and was probably living with an older female relative; and he wore double-breasted suits, buttoned up.

While Inspector Finney was mulling over this report, the *Journal-American* received another letter, neatly typed, which contained the following essential information: "I was injured on the job at the Con Edison plant—September 5, 1931." By great good fortune, a search of the company's records turned up a report that George Metesky, the son of a Polish immigrant, born in 1904, had been injured in a boiler explosion in 1931. He had received the paltry sum of $180 in compensation, and would now be fifty-two or fifty-three years old.

Metesky lived in Waterbury, near Bridgeport, Connecticut—and Westchester County, from which the letters had been mailed, lay between Bridgeport and New York City. Detectives armed with a warrant called at Metesky's home, which they discovered he shared with two elderly half sisters. It was past midnight when a mild-faced, heavily built, middle-aged man opened the door, wearing a robe over pajamas. The detectives told him to get dressed, and when Metesky returned he was wearing a shirt and tie beneath a double-breasted suit—neatly buttoned up. A search of his garage quickly revealed a lathe and a length of the piping used to manufacture the bombs. In Metesky's bedroom was the typewriter he had used to write his last letters, and he willingly confessed to being the Mad Bomber. He was judged unfit to stand trial, and was committed to a hospital for the criminally insane, where he died shortly afterward of tuberculosis.

THE FBI TAKES UP PROFILING

Although Dr. Brussel's analysis had proved relatively accurate, it was Metesky's final letter that had led to his identification, and it was to be nearly twenty years before the publication of Brussel's book led to a wider investigation of psychological profiling. In 1970, FBI agent Howard Teten began to lecture in "Psych-crim" at the bureau's National Academy in Washington, D.C.

He was soon joined by Pat Mullany, from the FBI's New York office, and, when the expanded academy was opened at Quantico, Virginia, in 1972, the two men established a Behavioral Science Unit (BSU) there. Teten also consulted with Dr. Brussel, concluding, "We reasoned that his method was more capable of providing detailed information, while my approach was less subject to error."

The new—and tiny—BSU began to study the similarities between one violent crime and another, in particular the modus operandi (MO),

CASE STUDY
PETER STOUT

The first successful psychological profiling of a killer in Britain occurred in 1974. Early on the morning of September 22 of that year, a young woman was stabbed on her way to Rochester cathedral, in southeast England, where she was a bell-ringer and chorister. The murder was linked to two attacks in the previous year, but the police had little positive evidence. Professor J.M. Cameron, who had performed the autopsy, consulted his colleague, forensic psychiatrist Dr. Patrick Tooley, who drew up a psychological assessment.

Dr. Tooley reported that the assailant was a man, aged between twenty and thirty-five, possibly with previous convictions. He was most likely a manual worker, either unemployed or frequently changing jobs; his father was absent, and his mother was restrictive, yet spoiled him. Although the killer therefore had a hate complex toward women, he still desired them, but could not approach them in a normal manner. He walked alone; he might be a "peeper," as well, but seldom resorted to indecent exposure.

After interviewing more than six thousand men, the police focused their inquiry on one man in particular, a dock laborer named Peter Stout. He was nineteen, single, with four siblings; their father, a drunkard, was dead, but they all reportedly loved their mother. At age fourteen, Stout had been convicted of indecently assaulting a woman.

After a prolonged interrogation, Stout wrote and signed his confession. It ended: "All I can say is the Devil has got at me—and when he thinks I have my funny turns, he does some extra poking and things like that, and I give in to him."

or the characteristic way in which a crime is carried out, as well as a killer's "signature," and what these could tell them overall about the behavior and mind-set of a criminal. They soon found an opportunity to put their theories into practice, in the case of the abduction of a young girl in Montana (see facing page).

Far from Quantico, a Los Angeles homicide lieutenant named Pierce Brooks had been pursuing his own research for some time. While the search was on for the killer, or killers, of three models in 1957 and 1958 (the killer was later identified as amateur photographer Harvey Glatman), Brooks spent many hours searching through newspaper and police files for murders with the same MO.

He realized independently that a study of criminal behavior could be the key to the identification of a suspect—and, when Harvey Glatman was arrested, Brooks interviewed him extensively, and he was able to write one of the first full documents about a serial killer's mind-set since Karl Berg's groundbreaking

DAVID MEIERHOFER

In June 1973, seven-year-old Susan Jaeger from Michigan disappeared from the tent in which her family was camping, near Bozeman, Montana. Preparing a profile of the likely perpetrator, two FBI agents from Quantico, Howard Teten and Pat Mullany, outlined a young white male from the vicinity, who had unpremeditatedly come upon the tent while out for an night-time walk. And—despite her family's desperate hopes—they concluded that Susan was already dead.

Peter Dunbar, the local FBI agent, already had a suspect in his sights: a twenty-three-year-old Vietnam veteran named David Meierhofer, but there was no material evidence to go on.

In January 1974, a young woman also disappeared in the Bozeman area, and Meierhofer was once again a suspect. He volunteered to take a polygraph lie-detector test, and passed it; however, the Quantico team reasoned that psychopaths were frequently able to dissociate the out-of-control part of their personalities under just such conditions. They suggested that the killer was also of the type who would later telephone his victim's relatives, if possible, in order to experience once more the excitement of the crime, and Dunbar advised the Jaegers to keep a tape recorder by their home telephone.

On the anniversary of Susan Jaeger's abduction, a man telephoned. He said that Susan was still alive, and he sounded "very smug and taunting," said Mrs. Jaeger, who recorded the conversation. Although an FBI voice analyst concluded that the voice on the tape was Meierhofer's, this was judged to be insufficient evidence in Montana. Mullany arranged for Mrs. Jaeger to confront Meierhofer in his attorney's office, where the suspect appeared fully in command of his feelings. Shortly after she had returned home to Michigan, however, she received a collect call from a "Mr. Travis in Salt Lake City." Before the man had spoken many words, Mrs. Jaeger said to him, "Well, hello, David."

On this evidence, Dunbar obtained a warrant to search Meierhofer's home. Remains of the missing girl and young woman were found there, and Meierhofer further confessed to the unsolved murder of a local boy. He was arrested and jailed, but hanged himself in his cell the next day.

study of Peter Kürten. In 1982, Brooks, retired from the LAPD as a commander after thirty-five years of service and now established as a consultant, was one of those instrumental in setting up the Violent Criminal Apprehension Program (VICAP, see page 219).

Gradually, to cope with the agents' burdensome dual task of teaching while dealing with profiling cases, the bureau's BSU was expanded. Among the new instructors was Robert Ressler, who later was joined by John Douglas, as his assistant, and Roy Hazelwood. The remit of the FBI did not cover murder, rape, child molestation, or similar instances of violent behavior because these were not violations of federal law, and instead were dealt with by the city, county, or state in which they occurred. Ressler, however, decided to lecture principally on cases in which the facts were publicly available, for example in newspaper articles and books, such as that of Harvey Glatman.

"At last," Ressler later wrote, "I came to the point where I wanted very much to talk to the people about whom I'd been lecturing, the killers themselves." He nevertheless realized that there was danger in this—not so much physical as psychological. It was essential to maintain an impartial stance, and to avoid the trap of identifying—and even sympathizing—with the criminal's thought processes. He came across a cautionary quotation from the German philosopher Friedrich Nietzsche, in his book *Beyond Good and Evil* (1886): "Whoever fights

LEFT MILD-MANNERED DENNIS NILSEN, WHO ADMITTED IN 1983 TO KILLING AND DISMEMBERING FIFTEEN YOUNG MEN IN LONDON AND KEEPING HIS VICTIMS' BODIES IN HIS APARTMENT FOR SEVERAL DAYS. ONE COMMENTATOR WROTE: "MOST PEOPLE LIKE SOMEONE TO COME HOME TO, AND SO DID DENNIS NILSEN. HE JUST PREFERRED THEM TO BE DEAD."

monsters should see to it that in the process he does not become a monster. And when you look into the abyss, the abyss also looks into you." From this he took the title of his first book, *Whoever Fights Monsters* (1992).

Independently (in fact, he later had to face a disciplinary inquiry for his initiative), Ressler, often accompanied by John Douglas, began to visit a number of penitentiaries and interview a succession of convicted killers. At the BSU, they built up extensive files on these conversations, and what these conversations revealed of the criminals' motivations. Exonerated for his unofficial activities, Ressler was given FBI approval to set up a Criminal Personality Research Project, and he and his colleagues set about convincing police departments that profiles of unknown criminals were a valuable part of violent crime investigation. They soon scored a success in a case that had baffled the police in New York City (see sidebar, facing page).

THE FBI'S CLASSIFICATION SYSTEM

Following the successful conviction of Carmine Calabro (see facing page), police departments all over the United States began to send details of their unusual cases to the FBI. The BSU had by now assembled data on a large number of cases of repetitive violent behavior, and it was obvious that some sort of classification system should be developed, but free of confusing psychiatric terms. At that time, the only relevant publication was the *Diagnostic and Statistical Manual of Mental Disorders* (DSM), so the FBI decided to begin putting together their own *Crime Classification Manual* (CCM), which

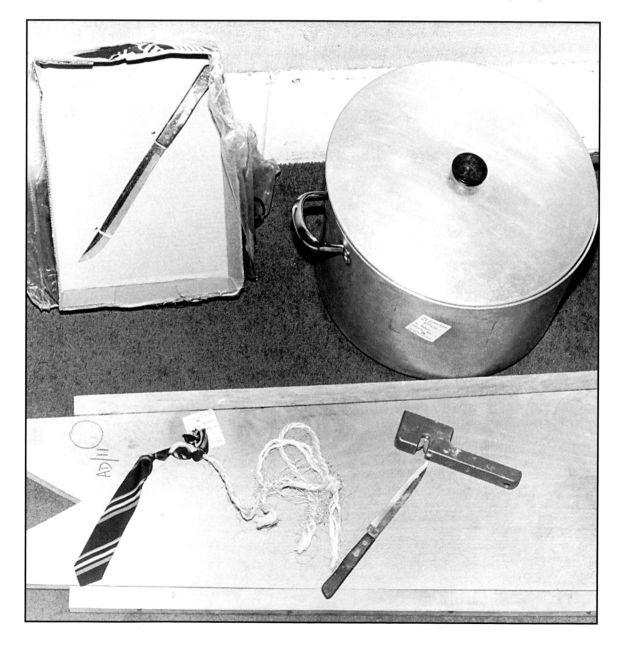

RIGHT SOME OF THE EQUIPMENT USED BY DENNIS NILSEN TO DISMEMBER HIS VICTIMS IN HIS NORTH LONDON HOME. IT INCLUDES THE PAN IN WHICH HE BOILED SOME OF THEIR HEADS, A NECKTIE WITH WHICH HE THROTTLED SEVERAL OF HIS VICTIMS, AND—PERHAPS MOST GRISLY OF ALL—THE BOARD ON WHICH HE CUT THEM UP.

was eventually published in 1992. Wrote John Douglas: "With CCM we set about to organize and classify serious crimes by their behavioral characteristics and explain them in a way that a strictly psychological approach such as DSM has never been able to do. For example, you won't find the type of murder scenario of which O. J. Simpson was accused in DSM. You will find it in CCM."

The first stage of the FBI classification was to divide criminals, both serial murderers and violent rapists, into "organized" and "disorganized" personalities. The organized criminal plans his crime, and the planning is an element in his fantasies. The victim is most likely a stranger, of a particular type, and part of the planning lies in finding ways to approach the victim and win their confidence. The disorganized criminal, on the other hand, does not pick his victims logically; he has no interest in their identity or characteristics. Furthermore, also unlike the organized criminal, he is probably of below-average intelligence.

Profilers—and psychiatrists—have discovered that the underlying motive behind serial murder is usually sexual. From his first crime, the killer derives a perverted sexual satisfaction; for some time after, he can dwell on the memory of the excitement that it provoked. In due course, however, the memory is insufficient, and he feels the need to kill again. With each killing, the excitement wanes quicker, and the interval between murders decreases. The same is true of perpetrators of rape and other violent sexual assaults.

The organized offender learns from crime to crime, refining his technique as he progresses. FBI agents advise police that, if a series of murders reveals a similar MO, for

CASE STUDY
CARMINE CALABRO

One afternoon in October 1979, the naked body of Francine Elverson was found on the roof of an apartment building in the Bronx, where she had lived with her mother and father. It appeared that she had been beaten unconscious on the stairway, then carried to the roof, where she was strangled and brutally mutilated. After questioning two thousand persons and assembling a list of twenty-two suspects, the police declared the investigation stalled, and all the relevant files and crime scene photographs were submitted to Quantico.

A team of four behavioral experts examined the evidence. They concluded that this was a "crime of opportunity," not previously planned. They described the killer as a white male, aged twenty-five to thirty-five, who lived in the building—or close by—with a relative, and knew the victim by sight. He would be untidy in appearance, though not a drug or alcohol abuser, and was either unemployed or worked at night. He was mentally ill, had probably been released from a mental-care institution in the past year, and was still taking medication. And he was most likely a school dropout, who got his ideas about women from a large collection of pornography.

This FBI profile persuaded the police to turn their attention from the primary suspects, and to concentrate instead on thirty-year-old Carmine Calabro. An unemployed stagehand (that is, a night worker), he lived in an apartment he shared with his father. However, the father maintained that his son had been in a secure mental institution at the time of the murder.

Looking more closely into Calabro's alibi, the police discovered that, although he had been in the institution more than a year, it was possible for him to leave and return without his absence being noticed. Moreover, his room at home was full of pornographic literature; finally, bite marks on the victim's body were conclusively matched to his dentition. After Calabro had been found guilty, Lieutenant Joseph D'Amico of the NYPD commented, "They had him so right that I asked the FBI why they hadn't given us his phone number, too."

LEFT MANY "ORGANIZED" MURDERERS AND VIOLENT RAPISTS ARE FOUND TO EQUIP THEMSELVES WITH A DISTINCTIVE "RAPE KIT" FOR RESTRAINING THEIR VICTIMS. THESE "NOVELTY" HANDCUFFS, OF A TYPE THAT CAN BE PURCHASED OPENLY, WERE FOUND BY THE FBI IN THE POSSESSION OF A RAPE SUSPECT. THEY HAD BEEN MODIFIED BY THE ADDITION OF EXTRA-STRONG WIRE.

example, they should pay particular attention to the first, as it will probably have occurred closest to where the criminal lives or works, with later crimes committed farther and farther away, as he extends his area of operation in search of new victims.

Other evidence of planning often consists of the "rape kit" that the killer carries with him, generally in the trunk of his car: rope, handcuffs, or other materials for restraining his victim. He takes his weapon with him as well (whereas the disorganized killer often picks up a "weapon of opportunity"), and carries it away afterward. He will probably wipe away any fingerprints, and even clean up blood at the site of the murder.

Furthermore, he may carry off the body and conceal it some distance away, while the disorganized criminal often leaves his victims in full view. Attempts may also be made by the organized criminal to delay identification of the victim, often by removing clothing and all personal belongings.

An important aspect of serial murderers, organized or not, is that both types of criminal like to retain "trophies," which can be gloated over to renew their fantasies. However, while the organized serial killer will carry off wallets, jewelry, or articles of victims' clothing, the disorganized serial killer is more likely to cut off a random part of the body, or perhaps something like a lock of hair.

Another point that must be considered in the analysis of crime is "staging:" making changes to the crime scene in an attempt to mislead investigators.

After more than fifteen years of profiling, Robert Ressler retired from the FBI, and he then set himself up as an independent consultant. Ressler's expertise was to prove invaluable in a case involving an insurance claim (see below), which he described in his book *Whoever Fights Monsters*.

CASE STUDY
ATTEMPTED INSURANCE FRAUD

In 1991, retired FBI agent Robert Ressler advised an insurance company regarding a claim for $270,000 worth of damage to a home, which was allegedly the work of teenage vandals. Examining photographs of the scene, Ressler noted that the damage was spread through most rooms of the house. Walls, furniture, paintings, clothing, vases, carvings, and other items had been broken or defaced. Spray-painted graffiti, mostly of single-word obscenities, was also visible.

The overall pattern of destruction, however, appeared selective. Paintings that did not look particularly valuable were seriously damaged, but their ornate frames were left intact, and one large oil of a little girl was untouched. Vases and statuettes lay on the floor, but were unbroken; curtains had been taken down and laid unharmed on the floor. As for the graffiti, Ressler opined that it was not typical of teenage vandals. He concluded that the damage had been committed by a lone white female,

between forty and fifty years old. The mother of an only daughter, she had suffered several divorces, and experienced severe stress in the days before the event, and the graffiti reflected her fantasies of male hostility. He suggested that the woman's rage was directed at a close family member; that she was seeking attention; and that the staged destruction was carried out in the hope that she could obtain compensation, to pay for improvements to her home that she could not otherwise afford.

A psychologist employed by the insurance company confirmed that this description closely matched that of the claimant. As Ressler wrote, "White and in her 40s, she had broken up with her boyfriend, had money problems, had a daughter who lived with her former husband … Compared to the profiles of unknown, vicious, antisocial criminals that I had struggled to compile and make accurate over the past 17 years in the FBI, this attempt at puzzle solving was kid stuff."

THE ESTABLISHMENT OF VICAP

Through the 1950s and 1960s, an average of ten thousand homicides were committed each year in the United States. Most were attributable to someone close to the victim—a spouse, a relative, a neighbor, or a coworker—and were solved within twelve months. The number of "stranger murders," however, accelerated rapidly throughout the 1970s, and in 1980 alone some twenty-three thousand persons were killed, with many of the cases remaining unsolved at the time. Elected president that same year, Ronald Reagan promised additional powers for law enforcement agencies, and a Task Force on Violent Crime was set up.

In October 1983, the FBI announced that an estimated five thousand persons had been killed by "strangers" during the previous year; Roger Depue, who had been appointed head of the BSU, additionally figured that there were as many as thirty-five serial killers at large in the United States. The problem lay in their detection; their crimes might be spread over

ABOVE TEXAN OFFICERS SURVEY A SITE NEAR STONEBURG, WHERE THEY BELIEVED HENRY LEE LUCAS HAD PREVIOUSLY BURIED THE BODY OF EIGHTY-YEAR-OLD MRS. KATE RICH. LUCAS LATER LED THEM TO A STOVE NEAR HIS HOME, WHERE HER BURNT BONES WERE DISCOVERED.

LEFT HENRY LEE LUCAS BEING LED AWAY BY TEXAS RANGERS. HE ORIGINALLY CONFESSED TO MORE THAN ONE HUNDRED HOMICIDES, SPANNING THE LENGTH AND BREADTH OF THE UNITED STATES, BUT LATER ADMITTED TO "PERHAPS FIVE." THE FALSITY OF HIS CONFESSION WAS ESTABLISHED BY AN INVESTIGATION CARRIED OUT, AFTER HIS CONVICTION, BY TWO JOURNALISTS.

a wide area, and there was no existing way of connecting their activities.

Partly as a result of pressure exerted by Pierce Brooks, a federal task force was provided with limited funds to consider the establishing of a Violent Criminal Apprehension Program (VICAP). It was during one of its sessions, at Sam Houston State University in Texas, that one of the members, arriving late, burst into the room. He announced that a man named Henry Lee Lucas had just confessed to well over one hundred murders, committed in nearly every state in the Union—and surely this was sufficient justification for the establishment of VICAP?

Lucas was convicted and sentenced to death, but subsequent investigation (much of it carried out by two journalists from the *Dallas Times Herald*) revealed that most of his confession was untrue. Interviewed later by Robert Ressler, Lucas admitted that he had "killed a few, perhaps five." He had lied dramatically "to have fun," and to spotlight the "stupidity" of the police. As Ressler wrote, "If we had had VICAP up and running at the time Lucas made his startling admission, it would have been easy to see what was truth and what was falsehood in his confession."

In July 1983, at about the same time that Lucas was making his "confession," Pierce Brooks and Roger Depue testified before a Senate subcommittee considering the VICAP proposal. It was suggested that the program be run by the BSU at Quantico, and a few months later President Reagan approved its establishment as part of the National Center for the Analysis of Violent Crime (NCAVC).

Hitherto, FBI experts had relied largely on photographs of the scene in assessing a crime. Now they introduced a VICAP Crime Analysis Report form—comprising 189 crucial questions that had to be answered—which was distributed to all fifty-nine FBI field divisions. For the first time, the FBI was able to make full use of recent computer developments, and, in May 1985, Pierce Brooks was present at Quantico to witness the fulfillment of his ambitions, as the first data from the VICAP forms was logged.

Since that time, the advantages that a computer presents have become ever more valuable. Vast databases can be scanned in less than a minute, and comparative information brought up onscreen within seconds. The FBI's "Big Floyd" program now carries many thousands of files; in Britain a computer system

PROFILING IN BRITAIN

In Britain, the earliest successes of psychological profiling relied, more often that not, on the intuitive approach, and came some ten years after the FBI's first application of its own methods. One of the best-known British profilers of this kind is Dr. Paul Britton, a clinical psychologist in Leicestershire, whose first book, *The Jigsaw Man*, was published in 1997.

Britton's initial involvement in a murder investigation came in 1984, when he was asked by police to give his professional advice regarding the unsolved killing of a woman in the previous year. Her hands and feet had been bound with twine, and she had been stabbed seven times. More than fifteen thousand persons had already

LEFT THE PSYCHOPATHIC MARRIED COUPLE, FRED AND ROSEMARY WEST, WHO MURDERED AT LEAST TEN GIRLS—INCLUDING FRED'S ELDEST DAUGHTER—IN THEIR HOME IN GLOUCESTER, ENGLAND. SOME BODIES WERE BURIED IN THE BASEMENT OF THE HOUSE, OTHERS IN THE BACKYARD. CLINICAL PSYCHOLOGIST DR. PAUL BRITTON (BELOW) TOLD THE POLICE: "THEY USED THE GARDEN BECAUSE THE HOUSE IS FULL."

BELOW CLINICAL PSYCHOLOGIST DR. PAUL BRITTON. HIS PROFILING SUCCESSES HAVE BROUGHT HIM REQUESTS FOR HELP FROM MANY POLICE FORCES IN ENGLAND, BUT HIS ADVICE IN THE CASE OF THE MURDER OF RACHEL NICKELL (SEE PAGE 223) RESULTED IN HIS BEING CALLED BEFORE A DISCIPLINARY COMMITTEE OF THE BRITISH PSYCHOLOGICAL SOCIETY.

named—deliberately—HOLMES (Home Office Large Major Enquiry System) maintains, for the first time, communication between the forty-three separate police authorities in England and Wales, together with those of Scotland and Northern Ireland.

Despite the great advances that have been made in the computerization of VICAP and similar data, however, it must be pointed out that the success of profiling still depends on the experience of the operator. Links between crimes committed throughout the United States, and even abroad, can be rapidly established by the FBI, but, in preparing a behavioral assessment, the expert will inevitably make a number of intuitive decisions, based on his or her knowledge of previously solved cases.

In Canada, a system similar to VICAP, the Violent Crime Linkage Analysis System (ViCLAS), was instituted by the Royal Canadian Mounted Police (RCMP) in 1990. Dr. David Cavanaugh of Harvard University, who was one of the consultants on the FBI system, has commented that the Canadians "have done to automated case linkage what the Japanese did to assembly-line auto production. They have taken a good idea and transformed it into the best in the world."

been interviewed, and eighty men arrested on suspicion before being released.

After studying photographs of the crime scene, Britton concluded that the random nature of the stabbings indicated a young man, aged some five years either side of twenty. He was lonely and immature, without the necessary social skills to keep a girlfriend; he probably lived with his parents not far from the crime scene, and knew his victim by sight. "His violent sexual fantasies will be fed by pornographic magazines," wrote Britton. "When you find him ... I expect you'll find ample evidence of this, as well as his strong interest in knives."

Fourteen months after the original murder, another woman was killed in the vicinity; although the victim had not been tied this time, the random nature of the knife wounds was similar, and Britton agreed with police that the crime had been committed by the same man. However, he said that the attack had not been premeditated and that it was very unlikely that the killer knew the woman. He suggested that

BELOW BRITISH PSYCHOLOGIST PROFESSOR DAVID CANTER. HIS WORK ON CRIMINAL PROFILING HAS CONCENTRATED ON THE WAY IN WHICH MAPPING CAN BE INVALUABLE IN LOCATING THE "CENTER OF OPERATIONS" OF A VIOLENT CRIMINAL.

something about her had attracted him at the moment he was most sexually aroused.

Suspicion fell on Paul Bostock, a nineteen-year-old meat processor. A search of his bedroom at the home he shared with his parents revealed a collection of knives, martial arts weapons, and pornographic literature, as well as crude sketches of women being tortured. When Bostock finally confessed, he was asked why he had chosen his second victim. "Because she wore red shoes," he said.

After this, Britton was consulted in an increasing number of rape and murder cases. However, his advice in 1992, although it was approved by lawyers of the Crown Prosecution Service, resulted in an abandoned trial (see facing page), and Britton was subsequently called before a disciplinary hearing of the British Psychological Society.

Equally well known in Britain is another psychologist, Professor David Canter, whom the police first consulted in early 1986. In his book *Criminal Shadows* (1994), he wrote, "At that time I had never heard of 'profiling,' but the whole idea of reading a criminal's life from the details of how he carries out his crime was enormously appealing." In his first case (see page 224) Canter discovered, almost by accident, that the use of maps could provide an indication of the home area of an offender.

His important contribution to the "Railway Rapist" case brought Canter considerable publicity, and he became involved in a number of subsequent cases. Realizing that those cases submitted to him by the police were atypical (they were the ones the police found difficult to solve, and many of their significant details were not known until the offenders were apprehended), Canter and his colleagues turned their attention to already-solved cases: first of all rape, then murder, sexual abuse, fraud, and extortion.

Studying the behavioral analyses of rape cases, they evolved a computer program that plotted particular types of behavior as a "map," on which the more similar two crimes appeared, the closer they were to the behavior of the criminal. As Canter wrote in *Criminal Shadows*: "The comparison of behavioral profiles is a comparison of patterns, not the linking of one clue to one inference. The term 'offender profiling' does not appropriately draw attention to the configuration of the many points that a profile must have. One point, or one clue, no matter how dramatic, does not make a profile."

Early one morning in July 1992, the body of Rachel Nickell was found on Wimbledon Common, in southwest London. Her head had been nearly severed from her body, there were forty-nine stab wounds, and her two-year-old son was frantically trying to wake her. There was no forensic evidence, apart from a single unidentified footprint, and what could have been the murder weapon, a single-edged sheath knife, which was found nearby.

Passersby described a young man who had been seen washing his hands in a nearby stream, and, when the crime was reconstructed on the TV program *Crimewatch UK*, several people telephoned in to name Colin Stagg. He was an unemployed twenty-nine-year-old bachelor who lived only a mile away from the scene of the murder. Stagg protested his innocence—though he admitted that he could have known the victim by sight—and after three days of police interviews he was released.

Soon afterward, the police were shown a letter that Stagg had written two years earlier in reply to an advertisement in a "lonely hearts" magazine. It detailed a masturbation fantasy;

profiler Paul Britton was consulted, and asked whether he could suggest a covert operation to implicate "a person"—the only description he was given—in a police inquiry. Britton suggested that an undercover policewoman should contact this "person," and expose his deepest sexual fantasies by correspondence. The approach succeeded, and the policewoman later met with Stagg, and encouraged him to admit, into a hidden tape recorder, that he had witnessed Rachel Nickell's murder.

Although Stagg did not make a clear confession, he was charged with the murder, and his trial opened at the Central Criminal Court in London in September 1994. After a week's hearing, however, the judge ruled that the police plan amounted to entrapment and that all the letters and recorded conversations between Stagg and the policewoman were inadmissible as evidence. The prosecution withdrew its case, and Colin Stagg left the court a free man. The case proved to be a major embarrassment for psychologist Paul Britton, who was as a result called before a disciplinary hearing of the British Psychological Society in 2001.

Stagg has consistently denied his guilt, and in 2003 he made an application for DNA tests to establish his innocence. The killer of Rachel Nickell has so far not been identified.

ABOVE YOUNG MOTHER RACHEL NICKELL, WHO WAS VICIOUSLY MURDERED IN FRONT OF HER TWO-YEAR-OLD SON ON WIMBLEDON COMMON, SOUTHWEST LONDON, IN 1992. HER KILLER HAS STILL NOT BEEN IDENTIFIED.

LEFT THE ORIGINAL SUSPECT IN NICKELL'S MURDER, COLIN STAGG, UPON HIS ARREST. THE EVIDENCE OBTAINED ON PROFILER PAUL BRITTON'S ADVICE WAS DISALLOWED BY THE JUDGE AT STAGG'S TRIAL, AND THE PROSECUTION WITHDREW THEIR CASE. STAGG LATER WROTE AN ACCOUNT OF HIS EXPERIENCES, *WHO REALLY KILLED RACHEL?*, IN WHICH HE CLAIMED TO IDENTIFY RACHEL NICKELL'S KILLER.

GEOGRAPHIC PROFILING

Returning to his first success, in the case of John Duffy, the "Railway Rapist," David Canter also ventured an opinion on the identity of nineteenth-century serial killer Jack the Ripper,

which has continued to interest criminologists. A prime suspect is Aaron Kosminski, a Polish bootmaker who arrived in London in 1882, some six years before the Ripper murders. On a British TV program in 1988, John Douglas and Roy Hazelwood of the BSU agreed that Kosminski was most likely the killer. Postulating that "to maintain the optimum distance that balances familiarity and risk, you would have to commit your crimes in a circular region around your

CASE STUDY
JOHN DUFFY

RIGHT JOHN DUFFY, THE INFAMOUS RAILWAY RAPIST. THE PROBABLE LOCATION OF HIS HOME, AND OTHER DETAILS PINPOINTED BY DAVID CANTER, BROUGHT DUFFY TO THE TOP OF THE POLICE LIST OF SUSPECTS, AND TRACE EVIDENCE CONFIRMED HIS GUILT.

By February 1986, British police of three authorities were no further in solving twenty-four cases of sexual assault that had occurred over the previous four years. Professor David Canter, who read in a newspaper about the puzzle of the "Railway Rapist"—as the press had dubbed him because a number of the assaults had occurred close to railway stations—decided to draw up a table of the events. By coincidence, he was invited soon afterward to attend a high-level conference at Hendon Police Training College, as two murders, in addition to the assaults, were causing concern.

Forensic evidence, as well as certain unusual aspects of the cases, suggested that the rapes and murders had been committed by the same man. One body, of a nineteen-year-old girl, had been discovered in east London, and the other, of a fifteen-year-old, was found in a forest 40 mi. (64 km) north of London. Both the rape and murder victims had their thumbs tied together with a particular type of twine, and a specific blood type (this was before DNA typing had been widely adopted) had been found in the rape cases and on the body of the fifteen-year-old.

Assisted by two police officers, Canter began his work using a small computer that he had intended for market research. Very soon after the team was put together, a similar third murder was discovered, north of London. Canter decided to make maps for each year the relevant crime had taken place, drawn on sheets of transparent acetate: "Casually, I pointed to an area of north London circumscribed by the first three offences, and said with a questioning smile, 'He lives there, doesn't he?'"

Under pressure from the police to produce a preliminary profile, Canter summarized his current findings at the time in July 1986. The killer had lived in the Kilburn area, or nearby, since at least 1983, probably with a wife or girlfriend, but without children. He had a job involving weekend or casual labor, and had some knowledge of the railway system of London and its suburbs. Canter concluded that the man had been arrested sometime between October 1982 and January 1984, probably for an aggressive but nonsexual attack.

Professor Canter had heard no more for four months, when he received a telephone call from the senior officer in charge

of the investigation: "I don't know how you did it … but that profile you gave us was very accurate." One John Duffy had been arrested and charged with the crimes. The police had put together a list of nearly 2,000 suspects; Duffy was No. 1,505, but Canter's profile had bumped him to the top of the list.

Duffy, who was childless, was already known to the police, for an attack on his estranged wife, and he had trained as a carpenter with British Rail. At his mother's home, the police found a ball of the unusual twine he had used to tie his victims, and thirteen "foreign" fibers discovered on the clothes of one of the murdered girls matched those from one of his sweaters. Duffy was sentenced to thirty years' imprisonment on counts of four rapes and two murders— the evidence in the third murder being considered insufficient by the prosecution.

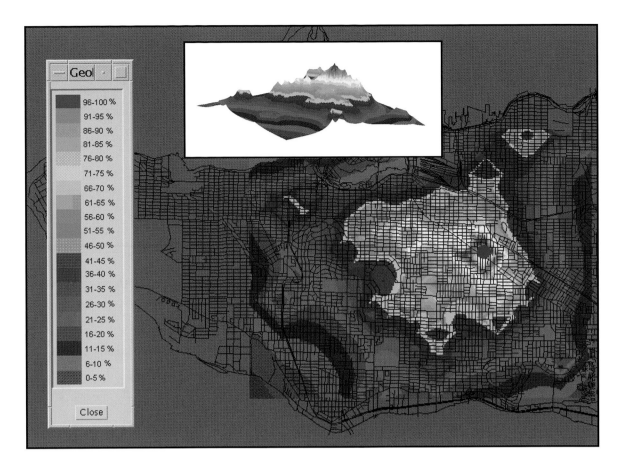

home," Canter drew up a map of the sites of the Ripper crimes. Kosminski's home lay roughly at their center. This type of approach to crime solving is now known as geographic profiling.

Clues to the location of a more recent "Ripper"—Peter Sutcliffe, the "Yorkshire Ripper," who was apprehended in 1981—were developed by an ingenious piece of computer-aided mapping. In *The Scientific Investigation of Crime* (1987), the late Stuart Kind described the outcome of a high-level conference at which he and other forensic experts considered the evidence available in the case. He wrote:

"Consider a map upon which we plot the positions of the seventeen ... crimes. If we mark each of these with a map pin and tie a piece of thread to it ... at which single location on the map could be placed an eighteenth pin, such that if we stretched the seventeen threads and tied each thread to the eighteenth pin, the minimum total amount of thread would be used?"

In the Yorkshire Ripper case, this calculation was carried out by computer, and it pinpointed a location close to the city of Bradford, "possibly in the Manningham or Shipley area." When Sutcliffe was arrested only a month later, he was found to be a native of Bradford, and residing in a district between Manningham and Shipley.

Geographic profiling has been developed to its most advanced stage by Dr. Kim Rossmo, a detective inspector with the RCMP in Vancouver, British Columbia. It is essentially a computer-based statistical approach to crime analysis, and is not directly concerned with the psychology of the offender. As an epigraph to his book *Geographic Profiling* (2000), Rossmo quotes John Douglas:

"Interview the subjects: what they'll tell you is, the thing that was really appealing to them was the hunt, the hunt and trying to look for the vulnerable victim. [Geographic profiling is, therefore, the discovery of] the spatial patterns produced by the hunting behavior and target locations of serial violent criminals. ... By establishing these patterns it is possible to outline ... the most probable area [the anchor point] of offender residence."

In association with Simon Fraser University in Vancouver, Rossmo and his colleagues have developed a "criminal geographic targeting" (CGT) computer program. Employing statistical formulas that determine the relative probabilities of the distances of the crimes from the anchor point, the program produces a

RIGHT DR. KIM ROSSMO, OF THE RCMP, WHO HAS DEVELOPED THE MOST ADVANCED FORM OF COMPUTERIZED GEOGRAPHICAL PROFILING. IT IS DESIGNED TO DETECT AND ANALYZE THE SPATIAL PATTERNS OF THE HUNTING BEHAVIOR OF VIOLENT CRIMINALS, WITHOUT REGARD TO THEIR SPECIFIC PSYCHOLOGY.

BELOW WHEN BRITISH POLICE SEARCHED THE HOME OF EDGAR PEARCE, WHO CONFESSED TO BEING THE "MARDI GRA BOMBER," THEY DISCOVERED THIS POWERFUL CROSSBOW. A PSYCHOLOGIST MIGHT WELL FIND A CONNECTION BETWEEN THIS WEAPON AND THE HUNTING BEHAVIOR OF THE VIOLENT CRIMINAL.

colored, three-dimensional "jeopardy surface." This can be superimposed on a district map—much in the same way as an ordinary relief map will indicate changes in elevation, or topography, with colored contours—resulting in a "geoprofile." The "high ground" on this map will be an indication of the locality of the offender's anchor point.

This "geoprofile" may, on occasion, indicate more than one anchor point. From 1994 through 1998 in Britain, for example, the "Mardi Gra Bomber" (so called for the misspelled message printed on the video cassette boxes containing six bombs sent in the first atack) planted a total of thirty-six explosive devices, mailed or otherwise delivered, at various targets in the Greater London area, accompanied by ransom demands. New Scotland Yard requested a geoprofile from Canada, which produced two anchor points: one around Chiswick in west London, and another in southeast London. After two brothers were eventually arrested, the police found that, while they both lived in the Chiswick area, they also had family in southeast London.

The use of geographic profiling has been increasingly adopted by law enforcement authorities in recent years. It has proved of value in more than one hundred investigations involving more than fifteen hundred incidents—

for the FBI, New Scotland Yard, and in a wide range of other countries. In Britain, geographic profiling is now available through the National Crime Faculty, based at the Police Staff College at Bramshill.

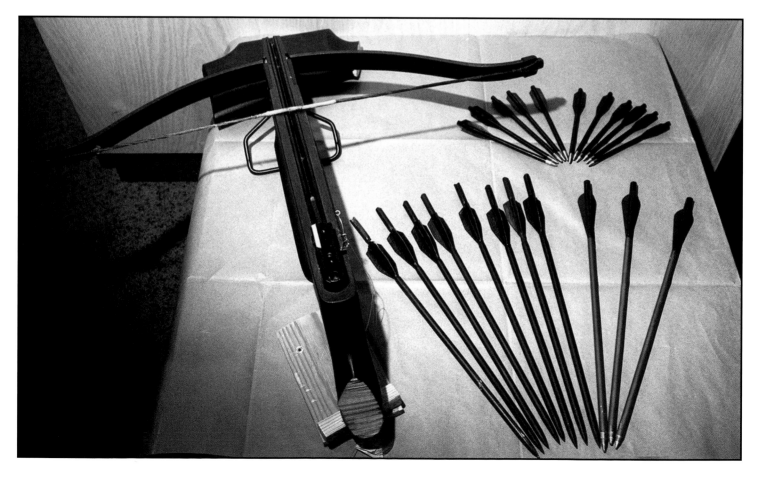

THE CRIMINAL WORD

The ways in which criminals express themselves can be as characteristic as their behavior. We all learn to recognize quite quickly not only the voice and speech patterns but also the handwriting of a person with whom we are in regular communication. Graphologists (or handwriting analysts, as they prefer to be called in forensic circles) have frequently been called on to give expert evidence that a piece of script was definitely written by the person concerned, but they have also long maintained that the form of the writing can be a good indication of the psychological makeup of the individual.

For many years, police regarded this aspect of graphology as little better than palmistry or phrenology, but recently greater interest has been taken in the subject. Graphology takes, indeed, an essentially forensic approach: the identification and comparison of specific letterforms. A few graphologists have even claimed—with some justification—that their psychological assessments are as valuable as behavioral analysis. It has to be admitted, however, that most graphological analyses that

LEFT A PORTION OF A LETTER WRITTEN BY SERIAL KILLER TED BUNDY, WHO WAS EXECUTED IN FLORIDA IN 1989. COURT-QUALIFIED HANDWRITING ANALYSIS EXPERT SHEILA LOWE HAS DRAWN ATTENTION TO THE CROWDED STYLE OF WRITING AND THE SHARP INITIAL STROKES, WHICH INDICATE AN INNATE DESIRE FOR POWER AND CONTROL.

RIGHT IN 1995, SUSAN SMITH KILLED HER TWO YOUNG SONS BY PUSHING HER CAR—WITH THEM STRAPPED INTO THE BACK SEATS—INTO A LAKE IN SOUTH CAROLINA. HER HANDWRITING IS PRACTICAL BUT IMMATURE. THE VARYING SIZE OF INDIVIDUAL LETTERS INDICATES A RELUCTANCE TO FACE UP TO HER ACTIONS.

have been successfully demonstrated so far have been performed on the handwriting of apprehended criminals, and therefore with a considerable degree of hindsight.

Indeed, as Patricia Marne, a leading British handwriting analyst, wrote in her book *The Criminal Hand* (1991), "No graphologist would describe a person as dishonest or criminal just on the strength of these give-away clues, any more than a physician would diagnose a particular illness without taking more than one symptom into account."

The comparison and analysis of handwriting can be a lengthy task. Graphologists begin by determining the relative heights and depths, as well as the sizes, of the written letters. Children who learn to write using copybooks are given three horizontal rulings within which to form their letters, but gradually they begin to express their individuality by deviating from these forms, and graphologists maintain that this individuality is clearly indicated by these deviations. Even stronger indications are most likely found in the handwriting of those who did not learn from copybooks.

A very formal, mannered hand, such as is taught in script classes, as well as handwriting that has been deliberately disguised, obviously presents greater problems in analysis, but even in these cases graphologists are able to spot certain giveaway clues. They point out that no matter how much

BELOW TED BUNDY (LEFT) LEANS AGAINST A WALL IN THE LEON COUNTY JAIL IN TALLAHASSEE, FLORIDA, BEFORE HIS INDICTMENT FOR MURDER IN 1978. HE APPEARED MOST UNLIKE THE POPULAR IMPRESSION OF A SERIAL KILLER. HE WAS TALL AND GOOD-LOOKING, AND CHARMING AND WITTY WITH YOUNG WOMEN, BUT HE EMPLOYED HIS ATTRACTIVENESS TO LURE HIS VICTIMS TO THEIR DEATH.

When I left my home on Tuesday, October 25, I was very emotionally distraught. I didn't want to live anymore! I felt like things could never get any worse. When I left home, I was going to ride around a little while and then go to my mom's. As I rode and rode and rode, I felt even more anxiety coming upon me about not wanting to live. I felt I couldn't be a good mom anymore but I didn't want my children to grow up without a mom. I felt I had to end our lives to protect us all from any grief or harm. ▓▓▓▓▓▓▓ I had never felt so lonely and so sad in my entire life. I was in love with someone very much, but he didn't love me and never would. I had a very difficult time accepting that. But I had hurt him very much and I could see why he could never love me. When I was @ John D. Long Lake, ▓▓▓ I had never felt so scared and unsure as I did then. I wanted to end my life so bad and was in my car ready to go down that ramp into the water and I did go part way, but I stopped. I went again and stopped. I then got out of the car and ▓▓▓ stood by the car a few minutes. Why was I feeling this way? Why was everything so bad in my life? I had no answers to these questions. I dropped to the lowest when I allowed my children to go down that ramp into the water without me. I took off running and screaming "Oh God! Oh God, NO!" What

the characters may differ from a "natural" hand, there are certain traits that will be unconsciously revealed; a right-handed person, for example, forced by injury to write with the left, will gradually develop the same characteristics as before.

However, there are two aspects of the personality that cannot be conclusively determined from handwriting alone: age and gender. Some persons write a less mature hand at age sixty than others do at twenty, and everyone possesses both male and female characteristics, in differing proportions.

The graphologist follows up an initial examination by considering such factors as the visual appearance of the writing, its apparent pressure and speed, the slant of the letters, and whether the lines run level, unevenly, or slope upward or downward. Next comes consideration of the formation and significance of individual letters: the capitals, and particularly the letter *I*, which represents the individual; the crossing of the *t* and the dotting of the *i*; loops; punctuation; and numerals. When analysis is complete, the graphologist is able to confirm that two specimens are by the same hand—and, it is maintained, can also provide an insight into the personality of the writer.

Acknowledging the significance of the psychological profiles provided by graphologists, the FBI has now begun to take a practical interest in the subject. A few weeks after four anonymous letters laced with anthrax spores had been mailed, in 2001, to Senators Tom Daschle and Patrick Leahy, to Tom Brokaw of NBC-TV, and to the *New York Post*, the FBI published a handwriting analysis and behavioral profile of the writer, stating: "It is highly probable, bordering on a certainty, that all … letters were authored by the same person."

In its release, the FBI drew particular attention to the use of enlarged first capitals in proper nouns; the unusual way in which the date was written; and the formalized figure 1. The bureau also pointed out that the name and address on each envelope had a noticeable downward slant.

However, FBI agents offered no psychological assessment of the handwriting, although their behavioral profile identified the writer as probably an adult male, a loner with a longstanding grudge, who possibly worked in a laboratory. Disappointingly, few analyses by graphologists have advanced the inquiry any further—although at least one has suggested that the letters were actually written by a child at the dictation of the offender.

Left The text of one of the "anthrax letters," supposedly mailed by the perpetrator.

Below Members of a biohazard team, in full protective gear, entering the Hart Senate Office on Capitol Hill, Washington D.C., in a search for anthrax contamination on November 6, 2001.

TEXTUAL ANALYSIS

Even when a handwritten specimen is not available—when the text in question is printed, for example—a great deal can still be learned from the words and phrases employed by the writer. Don Foster, a professor at Vassar, gained sudden fame when he identified the author of the novel *Primary Colors* (by "Anonymous") in 1996. Using computer analysis, he found a wealth of adjectives and adverbs, as well as unusual compound nouns, that proved typical of the columnist Joe Klein.

It was at this point that handwriting analysis proved especially important. Klein naturally denied that he was the author, but an article in the *Washington Post* in July 1996 reported that the corrections and notations on the original manuscript of the novel were clearly in his handwriting. He was eventually forced to

admit his authorship. Professor Foster's success attracted the attention of the FBI, and he was asked to advise the prosecution in the case of Ted Kaczynski, the "Unabomber," who was arrested in 1995. They wanted to know whether Kaczynski's writings could be admitted as evidence. Foster's analysis was, naturally, colored by hindsight; however, he was able to pinpoint much of the Unabomber's favored reading, and he suggested that this would have enabled the FBI to identify the research libraries in northern California that Kaczynski had visited—and even the dates on which he had consulted particular books.

In a related field, the study of how people communicate with one another is known as psycholinguistics. The FBI has recently taken a growing interest in this subject, on the grounds that an unidentified subject's use of language can be a valuable component of offender profiling. A paper in the FBI's *Law Enforcement Bulletin* stated, in part:

"One type of behavior overlooked, or underused, exists in the offender's actual language. The offender's written or spoken language can provide investigators with a wealth of information…. Both have features that may reveal an individual's geographical origins; ethnicity or race; age; sex; and occupation, educational level, and religious orientation or background."

money and hence d earlier ~~delivery~~ pick-up of your daughter. Any deviation of my instructions will result in the immediate execution of your daughter. You will also be denied her remains for proper burial. The two gentlemen watching over your daughter do not particularly like you so I advise you not to provoke them. Speaking to anyone about your situation, such as Police, F.B.I., etc., will result in your daughter being beheaded. If we catch you talking to a stray dog, she dies. If you alert bank authorities, she dies. If the money is in any way marked or ~~tampered~~ with, she dies. You will be scanned for electronic devices and if any are found, she dies. You can try to deceive us but be warned that we are familiar with Law enforcement countermeasures and ~~tactics~~. You stand a 99% chance of killing your daughter if you try to out smart us. Follow our instructions

American psycholinguist Dr. Andrew G. Hodges has put forward the concept of what he calls thoughtprints. He suggests that every action has a secondary, underlying motive, known only to the subconscious, which emerges detectably in the actual communication. "I look at each word for two meanings, not one," he wrote in his book *Who Will Speak for JonBenét?* (2000), in which he analyzes the "ransom note" left by the child's killer. Among his conclusions were that the killer was a woman, that she expected to be caught, and that the victim was dead before the note was written.

When O.J. Simpson set off on the road, apparently to avoid surrendering to his arrest, he left behind a long, rambling, and misspelled note, which suggested to investigators that he contemplated suicide. Professor Foster pointed out that the misspellings could prove significant. Simpson wrote that it was "tough spitting up" with his wife, but that the breakup was "murtually agresd." Psycholinguists such as Dr. Hodges might well suggest that *spitting*, as well as the echoes of *murder* and *aggression*, reveal the subconscious feelings of the writer.

LEFT THE MURDER OF SIX-YEAR-OLD JONBENÉT RAMSEY REMAINS UNSOLVED. HER FATHER DISCOVERED HER BODY IN THE BASEMENT CELLAR OF THE FAMILY HOME, IN BOULDER, COLORADO, BUT A PRELIMINARY POLICE SEARCH REVEALED NOTHING OF USE IN THE INVESTIGATION.

BELOW JOHN AND PATSY RAMSEY, THE PARENTS OF JONBENÉT, PROTESTING THEIR INNOCENCE OF HER DEATH ON CNN'S TELEVISION PROGRAM *BURDEN OF PROOF*.

PART 6

A HIGHLY EDUCATED GUESS

Agent Pedersen followed Officer Gregory to her office. As they walked, Gregory said, "Let's hear about the carpet first. That's physical evidence, the kind I like. Those profilers may claim a lot of successes, but that psych stuff seems more than a bit hit-or-miss to me."

"Right," said Pedersen, producing a fax from his briefcase. "Here's what we got on the carpet. First, Northwestern Carpet Corp., in Tacoma, Washington, manufactures it. It's from a batch they wove between May 1998 through May 2000. Not a big company—they only sell to dealers and carpet fitters in Washington, Oregon, Idaho, California, and Nevada. Soon as they've checked their records, they'll fax us here with a list of the outlets they sold that particular pattern to, and the dates."

"More waiting," groaned Gregory. "Okay, let's see what your mind reader in the big city has to say."

The report from the profiler read:

The UNSUB is most likely a white male, aged between thirty and fifty, probably married, or else in a relatively stable relationship. He is generally controlled and meticulous in his actions, precise in his business dealings. This was not a premeditated crime, but probably a genuine vehicular accident. It may well be that he picked up the victim with the intention of taking her to a hospital, and was appalled when she died in his vehicle. At that time, however, he remained in control, and took steps to carry the body as far from the scene as possible, and to remove all means of identification. This meticulous care—and the degree of cold-bloodedness involved—suggests someone of European origin; but not, I think, German. The perpetrator may originate somewhere further east, perhaps one of the Baltic states. This man is used to driving long distances, and he knows the roads all down the West Coast. He could be a sales representative for a medium-size company, but I rather think he is possibly the proprietor of a one- or two-man private operation. His partner in business, if he is at the upper end of the age bracket, could be a grown-up son.

Gregory let out a little grunt. "How the hell can he know all that?" she muttered.

"*She*, actually," said Pedersen, smiling. "Dr. Elizabeth Hansen. She does it by long experience consisting of one part training, one part wide knowledge of previous cases, and several parts expert intuition."

Gregory smiled back. "So what you're saying is that this is an educated guess."

"Do you want to talk to her yourself?" asked Pedersen.

Gregory nodded, picked up the phone, and dialed the number Pedersen gave her. Dr. Hansen sounded cross, and overworked. "Listen," she said. "This is an unusual case, and I've had to make a number of informed guesses, based on my study of violent crime. My report explained why I came to the conclusion that an immigrant was involved, rather than a local perp. He's almost certain to be male, and you've already established that the body was buried far from the victim's home, and probably well away from his usual area of activity. Reps usually work within a single state, so he's likely to be self-employed, and used to traveling all the way from his home base to Tacoma. Now can I get back to my work?"

Gregory put down the phone, and grunted again. "Just as I thought," she said, "no more

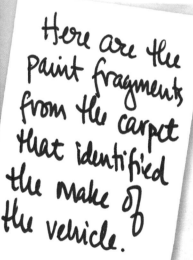

Here are the paint fragments from the carpet that identified the make of the vehicle.

than an educated guess." At that moment, a civilian assistant in the sheriff's office brought them a fax that had just come through. It was from Northwestern Carpet, and listed some forty companies that had ordered the carpet in question, over the previous two years.

"Are we going to need to have all these questioned and checked out?" asked Gregory with a note of despair.

"Not necessarily," Pedersen reassured her. "Let's start with the assumption that our UNSUB drove as far away from his home base as he did from the crime scene. That could place him somewhere like Vancouver or Portland, of course; but let's begin halfway between Longview and here, somewhere in northern California, and work outward from there." He glanced down the list, and whistled. "Well, what do you make of that? Stasz Pawlowski and Son—Polish name, yes?—carpet fitters, Sacramento. Collected three cut rolls from the Northwestern factory on August 14, 2000. Luckily for us, it's the only one that seems to fit the profile. I know it's well out of your jurisdiction, but how do you feel about a visit to our state capital?"

Around mid-afternoon the same day, Pedersen and Gregory presented themselves to Lieutenant Gary Keller of the Sacramento PD. He already knew of their case, the computer-reconstruction photographs having crossed his desk. Pedersen allowed Gregory to outline the latest developments, as well as the conclusions they had both come to on their drive north. "The way we see it," she said, "Pawlowski collected the carpet late in the afternoon, so it was dark by the time he reached Longview. Didn't see Anna, and ran her down. When she died in his van, his only thought was to get as far away as possible. It was only after he was well on his way to Sacramento that he realized his mistake, and so he carried on southward until he was too tired to go any farther. When he finally got home, he probably made up some story about a breakdown, about having to wait all night to get it fixed."

"Okay," said Keller, "let's have a look."

In his unmarked car, Lieutenant Keller led the way to the business premises of Pawlowski and Son, a modest establishment in a suburb of the city. As the two cars were pulling into the small parking lot, they noticed a burgundy-red Chevy van, with faint but unmistakable signs of a repaint job on the right front quarter panel. And, on guard in the passenger seat sat a fierce-looking German shepherd. "I think I'll just step inside the office," said Keller, "and ask Pawlowski if he'd like to accompany me to the nearest precinct."

At the station, Stasz Pawlowski readily confessed to the crime. "I'm glad to get it off my conscience at last," he said. Additionally, after processing Pawlowski's fingerprints, it was discovered that one of them matched the print on the wallet found at the scene. He was charged with manslaughter and concealment of a crime, released on bail, and scheduled to stand trial in February 2002.

CHAPTER EIGHT

IN THE COURTROOM

After the victim has been named, the cause of death established, and the perpetrator found, the work of the forensic experts is not finished. One or more will be required to testify to their findings in court, whether at preliminary hearings or at trial. Especially in United States courts, a trial is a confrontational process, and even in British courts—which frown on the aggressive examination of witnesses—it is the forensic scientist who has to face some of the most intense questioning on the stand. The exchanges that take place between counsel and witness can be among the most dramatic events in the courtroom, and can also occasionally provide humorous relief for all those in the court.

> *"The charge is prepar'd;*
> *the lawyers are met;*
> *The Judges all rang'd*
> *(a terrible show!)"*
>
> —JOHN GAY, *THE BEGGAR'S OPERA*

FACING PAGE THE JUDGE IS IN CHARGE IN THE COURTROOM, AND MAY BANG HIS GAVEL TO KEEP ORDER. THE WORK OF THE CRIME INVESTIGATORS WILL BE PRESENTED AS EVIDENCE BY THE PROSECUTION WHEN THE CASE COMES TO TRIAL. THE DEFENSE WILL QUERY THE VALIDITY OF THIS EVIDENCE, AND MAY EVEN ATTEMPT TO DISCREDIT THE EXPERT WITNESSES.

Forensic evidence must be made available to the defense, and the defendant's lawyers will exploit every legitimate means to discredit it. If, for example, they can establish that the essential "chain of custody" of evidential material has been broken at any point, they will contest it, on the plausible grounds that it could have been contaminated. They will query the professional standing of the expert, as well as his or her ability to make an unprejudiced assessment; they will raise doubts about the validity of the techniques employed. Frequently, they will call another expert—quite likely a respected professional colleague of the witness in question—whose opinion will flatly contradict the prosecution's submissions.

THE FRYE STANDARD

In the United States, the admissibility of forensic evidence was first defined by the Frye Standard, so named from the precedent established in the case of *Frye* v. *United States* in 1923. The evidence in question in that case was the use of the "lie detector," or polygraph, and the motion to exclude it was granted in the District of Columbia Trial Court, and affirmed by the D.C. Appellate Court. It was ruled that "the thing from which the deduction is made must be sufficiently established to have gained general acceptance in the particular field in which it belongs." The polygraph had been introduced only two years previously, and could certainly not be considered to have "gained general acceptance" at the time; however, to this day, polygraph results remain inadmissible as evidence—though they have proved a useful tool in the hands of investigators in a number of cases.

In 1975, a set of Federal Rules of Evidence was promulgated by the U.S. Supreme Court, and enacted by Congress. These rules defined a standard somewhat looser than Frye's, giving greater discretion to the courts. Then, in 1993, the Supreme Court rejected the application of the Frye Standard in jurisdictions governed by the Federal Rules. A new standard, named for the case of *Daubert et ux.* v. *Merrell Dow*, gives even greater discretion to the judge. The Supreme Court set the following guidelines in determining admissibility:

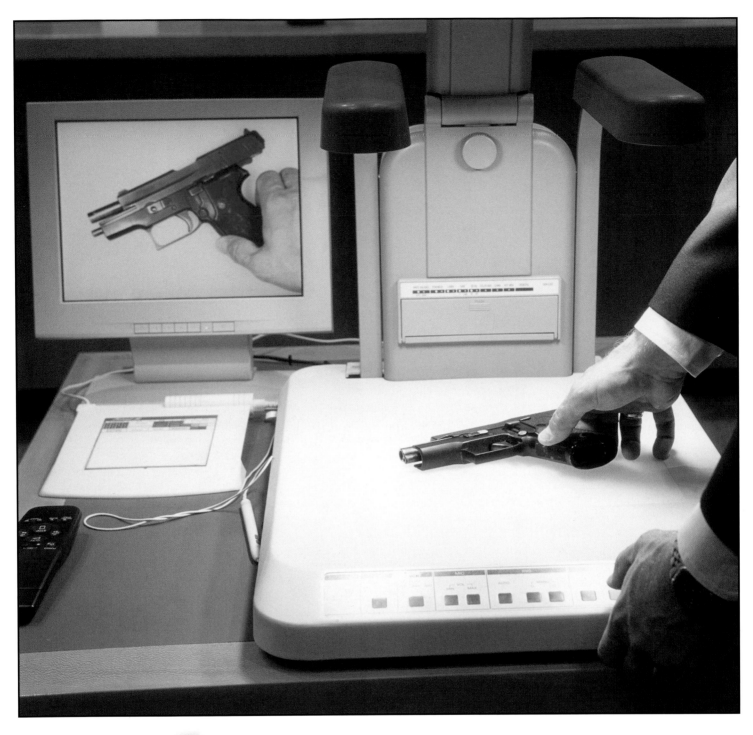

Whether the theory or technique in question can be (and has been) tested.

Whether it has been subjected to peer review and publication.

Its known or potential error rate, and the existence and maintenance of standards controlling its operation.

Whether it has attracted widespread acceptance within a relevant scientific community.

Some American states, notably California, continue to maintain the Frye Standard, but many are now adopting the Daubert Standard.

In Britain, the admissibility of evidence remains at the discretion of the judge, and becomes an accepted precedent, unless it is later rejected by the Court of Appeal.

As a British wit has put it, "The law presumes that everyone knows the law, except for Her Majesty's judges; for they have a Court of Appeal over them to set them right." Very rarely, appeals on a particular point of law of public importance are passed to the House of Lords, which remains the final stage of judicial appeal.

ABOVE THE AVAILABILITY OF VIDEO EQUIPMENT IN THE TRIAL COURT HAS MADE IT MUCH EASIER TO PRESENT VITAL FORENSIC EVIDENCE TO A JURY. IT IS NO LONGER NECESSARY FOR COUNSEL AND WITNESSES TO SHOW PHYSICAL EVIDENCE, SUCH AS THIS GUN, TO THE INDIVIDUAL JURY MEMBERS.

confirmed that there were no beech trees in the wood. Clearly, the body had been brought to the site from elsewhere.

Most important, however, were the maggots. The corpse, of a man, was already disintegrating, and the police supposed that it had been lying half-buried for six to eight weeks. But Simpson disagreed. "At least nine or ten days," he said, "but probably not more than twelve. It's astonishing how quickly maggots will eat up the flesh. I've seen a body reduced to this state in as little as ten days."

The maggots were bluebottle larvae. "The larvae I was looking at," wrote Simpson later in *Forty Years of Murder*, "were mature, indeed elderly, fat, indolent, third-stage maggots, but they were not in pupa cases. Therefore I estimated that the eggs had been laid nine or ten days earlier. Adding a little more time to allow for the bluebottles' getting to the body, I reckoned death had occurred on 16 or 17 June."

Because of the stage of decomposition of the body, Simpson decided to dissect it on the spot. He found a pool of blood over the left side of the voice box, and the small bones of the larynx were crushed on that side. One of the police officers suggested that the victim might have received something like a "karate chop" to the neck; Simpson agreed, and thought it probable that the man had died from bleeding into the windpipe as a result of the blow. Among persons recently reported missing was

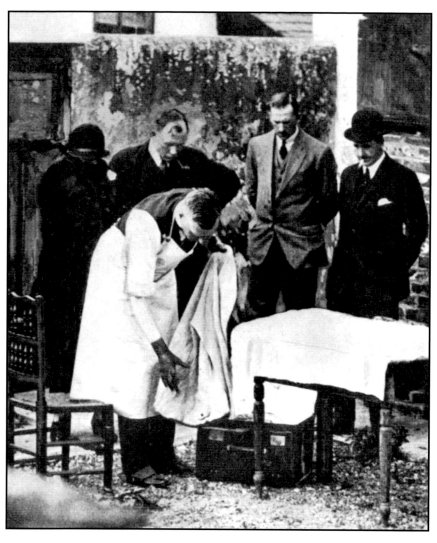

ABOVE THE YOUNG BERNARD SPILSBURY EXAMINES THE REMAINS OF EMILY KAYE IN THE MAHON MURDER CASE OF 1924. FOR NEARLY HALF A CENTURY HE WAS THE MOST FAMOUS PATHOLOGIST IN BRITAIN, AND FOR SOME TIME WAS THE ONLY EXPERT OFFICIALLY APPOINTED BY THE HOME OFFICE. WITH HIS FORMIDABLE REPUTATION AS A PROSECUTION WITNESS, HIS EXPERTISE WAS SELDOM CALLED INTO QUESTION.

THE TRIAL OF WILLIAM BRITTLE

Entomological evidence can also produce some entertaining exchanges in court, and the trial of William Brittle resulted in a classic example.

On June 28, 1964, two boys setting out on a fishing expedition were searching a patch of woodland in Berkshire, England, hoping to find a dead rabbit or pigeon infested with maggots that they could use for bait. They found a seething mass of fat maggots on a rough mound of turf, covered with beech tree cuttings, just a short distance off their path; but, pulling the turf aside, they were horrified to uncover a decaying human arm.

After local authorities were alerted, pathologist Dr. Keith Simpson was summoned at once, and he superintended the disinterment of the body, while photographs were taken at every stage. Simpson was puzzled by the presence of the beech cuttings, as the local police

RIGHT WILLIAM BRITTLE, FOUND GUILTY OF THE MURDER OF PETER THOMAS IN ENGLAND IN 1964. AT HIS TRIAL, THE QUESTION OF THE TIME OF THOMAS'S DEATH WAS SETTLED BY ENTOMOLOGICAL EVIDENCE, AND BRITTLE WAS SENTENCED TO LIFE IMPRISONMENT.

BERNARD SPILSBURY AND THE TRIAL OF NORMAN THORNE

During nearly forty years of the first half of the twentieth century, Sir Bernard Spilsbury was the leading British medical expert for the prosecution in many murder cases, and for much of that time he was also the only accredited Home Office pathologist. In more than one trial, he found himself in contention with Dr. Robert Brontë, who often appeared for the defense. Brontë was an excitable Irishman, of whom one judge wrote:

"At the time when people were saying that Spilsbury was 'laying down the medical law,' a so-called pathologist, Brontë, was frequently called on to contradict him in criminal cases. The only time I heard Spilsbury let himself go was on an occasion when an opinion of Brontë's was in question. 'I cannot believe,' he said, 'that any man with a knowledge of anatomy ever said that.' We got a celebrated surgeon to say ditto next day in the witness-box."

One of the critical appearances in which Spilsbury publicly disagreed with Brontë occurred during the trial of Norman Thorne.

Elsie Cameron, a London typist, disappeared on December 5, 1924, on her way to visit her lover Norman Thorne at his poultry farm in the county of Sussex. It was five days later that her father, having had no communication from her, alerted the police. At the farm, Thorne maintained that Cameron had never arrived; however, a month later, two men reported that they had seen her on her way there. A rapid search of the farm by the police soon unearthed her traveling bag, and Thorne then told a different story. Yes, Cameron had arrived, and declared that she staying until Thorne agreed to marry her. He then went out, to visit a new girlfriend, and upon his return he had found Cameron hanging dead from a beam in the poultry shed. Panicking, he had cut the body down, dismembered it, and buried the parts in his poultry run.

Investigating detectives observed that there were no rope marks on the beam, such as would have been caused by the jerk of a hanging body, and, indeed, the thick layer of dust on it was undisturbed. The implication was clear: Cameron had not hanged herself, and neither had Thorne, but he had almost certainly murdered her. The remains of Elsie Cameron were dug up on January 15, 1925, Thorne was charged with her murder, and two days later Spilsbury examined the body. It was interred on January 26, but a month later, on the application of Thorne's defense team, the body was exhumed, to be examined by Brontë in the presence of Spilsbury. At Thorne's trial, Spilsbury testified:

"I made a thorough search of the neck on 17 January…. There was no sign of any sort or kind of damage resulting from attempted hanging or actual hanging. It was therefore not necessary at that time to make any microscopic examination or to make slides. When the postmortem was conducted by Dr. Brontë on 24 February, the condition of the tissues was then such that no examination, microscopic or otherwise, would help. When the marks, which I say were normal marks found on most women's necks, were seen on 24 February by Dr. Brontë he made the remark, which I took

ABOVE NORMAN THORNE WITH HIS LOVER, OFFICE TYPIST ELSIE CAMERON. HE WAS FOUND GUILTY OF STRANGLING HER, THEN DISMEMBERING AND BURYING HER BODY IN HIS POULTRY RUN, IN 1925, AND WAS EXECUTED BY HANGING.

down at the time, that they were 'the normal creases in the skin.'… I took samples of the same parts of the skin of the right cheek and the right side of the neck that Dr. Brontë had, and I made slides from those examples…. It was quite impossible for me to identify the slides or the matter which was in the slides. I formed an opinion on 17 January that there was no sign at all of congestion of the brain."

There was also the question of contusions found on Elsie Cameron's body, including two about the head, one of which had pulped the tissues. Brontë claimed that some of these had been caused before death, others during death, and some after death. In a way, these injuries were irrelevant, however, as the principal question to be resolved was whether Cameron had hanged herself or not. During his examination by defense counsel, Brontë maintained that the cause of death was "shock following an unsuccessful or interrupted attempt at self-strangulation." He further denied that the creases were natural, and described them as "grooves." He also claimed that he had found evidence of the extravasion (rupture) of blood vessels in the neck. Spilsbury, however, had already testified that he could find no such evidence, in view of the state of decomposition of the body on February 24. The microscope slides taken by both pathologists proved inconclusive.

Speaking in his own defense, Thorne described how he had found Cameron hanging with her eyes open, but "screwed up." On the last day of the trial, Spilsbury made his final point: "Assuming unconsciousness had intervened, if not death, the eyes would have been in the condition of paralysis. That is to say, the eyes would not have been completely closed or completely open, [but in] a half-open condition, with flexive lids—certainly no puckering."

In his summary, the judge remarked, "Sir Bernard Spilsbury would be the first to disclaim infallibility in matters of this sort, but his opinion is undoubtedly the very best opinion that can be obtained." Norman Thorne was found guilty, and sentenced to death. This was one of the cases referred to the Court of Appeal, on the grounds that the judge's remarks about Spilsbury were "tendentious." In delivering the court's judgment, the Lord Chief Justice upheld the original decision.

THE TRIALS OF CLAUS VON BULOW

On December 21, 1980, socialite Claus von Bulow discovered his wife, Martha "Sunny" Crawford (von Auersperg) von Bulow, in a coma in their mansion in Newport, Rhode Island. This was not the first occasion. In December 1979, Sunny had been taken in a coma to Newport Hospital, where she was diagnosed as suffering from bronchopneumonia. After her recovery, her New York doctor, Richard J. Stock, discovered that she had a very low blood-sugar level, though not low enough to be considered life threatening.

Early in December 1980, in their New York apartment, von Bulow again found his wife unconscious. Sunny was rushed to Lenox Hill Hospital; her speech was slurred, and she had an injury to her head, presumably because she had fallen as she lost consciousness. Stock diagnosed "involuntary aspirin toxicity in the course of treating a severe headache." It transpired that Sunny had taken at least sixty-five aspirin tablets—a lethal amount.

Just three weeks later, Sunny was again taken to the hospital, in Newport. The emergency staff suspected an overdose of alcohol and barbiturates, but doctors at the hospital were puzzled by Sunny's low blood-sugar level. They put her on an intravenous drip—to raise the sugar level—then asked for an insulin assay. Insulin is normally produced by the pancreas to control sugar in the blood, and is therefore prescribed as a drug for those suffering from diabetes.

Confusion reigned over the analytical results. A laboratory in Boston obtained a reading of 0.8 units of insulin on the first assay, and 350 units on the second. A leading laboratory in California reported a level of 216 units—a possible result of the IV drip in Sunny, who remained in a coma.

Learning of this unusual amount of insulin in Sunny's blood, however, made her family suspicious. Her maid further reported that a "black bag" had contained a variety of drugs, several hypodermics, and a vial of insulin. When the bag was found in a locked closet at the Newport mansion, there was no insulin in it, but one of the needles had been used.

Claus von Bulow was charged with the attempted murder of his wife, and he went to trial. The prosecution maintained that the used needle was encrusted with insulin, but New York City medical examiner Dr. Michael Baden, who was consulted by the defense, later wrote in his book *Unnatural Death* (1989) that this was impossible: The outside of the needle would have been wiped clean upon its extraction from the flesh. Baden also drew attention to the amount of amobarbital in Sunny's blood—equivalent to ten or twelve capsules—and maintained that she had again attempted suicide.

Hired for the defense, Herald Price Fahringer nevertheless decided to base his case on the inconsistent blood assays. Those who had appeared to be his strongest defense witnesses, however, proved unconvincing in court. Dr. Milton Hamolsky of Brown University Medical School, for example, was forced to admit under pressure that he could not rule out insulin as the cause of coma. And Dr. Stock, together with other experts, testified that Sunny's coma in particular could only be the result of an insulin injection. Claus von Bulow was found guilty on two counts of attempted murder in March 1982.

Von Bulow appealed, and this time hired two other lawyers: Alan Dershowitz, a distinguished Harvard professor, who advised on legal shortcomings in the first trial, and prominent advocate Thomas Puccio. At the same time, writer Truman Capote appeared on television, gossiping about his friendship with Sunny. He said that she drank excessively, took drugs, and injected herself with insulin in order to lose weight.

At retrial, the prosecution hoped to rely heavily on the testimony of Dr. Jeremy Worthington, a neurologist at Newport Hospital, who claimed St. Edward's, Oxford, and the University of Bologna, Italy, as his universities. He was intended to describe contusions and scratches on Sunny's body—although, as Dr. Baden points out, these could easily have been caused during efforts to resuscitate her.

However, in a private hearing before the judge, Dr. Worthington admitted that St. Edward's was only a school in Oxford, and that he had taken just two forensic medical courses at Bologna; the judge ruled that Worthington was not sufficiently qualified to testify.

Puccio based his argument for the defence on an affidavit from Dr. Michael Baden, in which he argued that the evidence strongly suggested that Sunny had attempted suicide on at least two previous occasions. The jury returned a verdict of not guilty.

BELOW THE IMMACULATE CLAUS VON BULOW FACES THE ASSEMBLED PRESS DURING HIS TRIAL FOR THE POISONING OF HIS WIFE, SUNNY, IN 1981. AT RETRIAL, FOLLOWING HIS APPEAL, IT WAS ACCEPTED THAT SUNNY HAD PROBABLY COMMITTED SUICIDE.

one Peter Thomas, who had disappeared on June 16 from Lydney, Gloucestershire—more than 100 miles (160 km) away. The victim's body measurements, an old fracture of his left arm, his fingerprints, as well as a tailor's label in his jacket, established identification. A search of his home uncovered letters revealing that Thomas had lent £2,000 ($3,000) to a certain William Brittle, who lived less than 10 mi. (16 km) from where the body was found. And the loan was due for repayment.

When questioned, Brittle stated that he had driven to Lydney on June 16 and had settled his debt with Thomas, and a hitchhiker confirmed that Brittle had picked him up on Brittle's return home that same day. An intensive examination of Brittle's car further revealed nothing more suspicious than a single beech leaf found under the mat. There were a few small bloodstains on his jacket, of type O—which both Brittle and Thomas shared. The police did discover, however, that Brittle had learned unarmed combat while in the army.

Unfortunately, while work on the case was continuing, a man came forward to say that he had definitely seen Thomas in Lydney on June 20 (and, at the subsequent trial, two other witnesses for the defense insisted that they had seen him on June 21). If this were true, Thomas could not have been dead for more than five or six days when his body was discovered. "Is that possible?" the chief investigator asked Simpson.

"No, it isn't," the pathologist replied. "And I am ready to stand up to severe cross-examination on the point if it comes to trial."

Despite the reluctance of the Director of Public Prosecutions to take the case to trial because of this conflicting evidence, a coroner's jury took the unusual course of naming William Brittle as the murderer of Peter Thomas "on or about 17 June." The trial was heard in Gloucester in the spring of 1965.

The defense was led by Quintin Hogg, QC (Queen's Counsel)—later, as Lord Hailsham, he was made Lord Chancellor of England, the (politically appointed) head of the judiciary. Among the defense experts that he called was a distinguished entomologist, Professor Thomas McKenny-Hughes.

"Professor," asked Hogg, "can we agree about one thing? Let us suppose the bluebottle lays its eggs at midnight on the—"

"Oh, dear me, no!" interrupted the entomologist. "No self-respecting bluebottle lays eggs at midnight. At midday, perhaps, but not at midnight." There was a ripple of amusement in the court, and even the judge's face twitched.

Hogg pressed on, "At what period, then, Professor, would you expect the eggs to hatch?"

"Well, it all depends. You see, in warm weather—"

"Yes, Professor, we know it was June and quite warm. How many hours would have elapsed before the first maggots were hatched?"

"Well, I agree with Dr. Simpson," said McKenny-Hughes, apparently unaware of the effect of his testimony.

BELOW LEADING BRITISH PATHOLOGIST DR. KEITH SIMPSON ON HIS WAY TO COURT. SIMPSON'S FORENSIC EVIDENCE FOR THE PROSECUTION WAS ESSENTIAL IN MURDER AND OTHER CASES OVER A PERIOD OF SOME FORTY YEARS. WITHOUT HIS EXPERT TESTIMONY, MURDERER WILLIAM BRITTLE WOULD ALMOST CERTAINLY HAVE BEEN FOUND NOT GUILTY.

"And these maggots would settle down on the dead tissues at once?" asked Hogg, rather desperately.

"Well," said the entomologist, "maggots are curious little devils." He produced a matchbox. "Suppose this is a dead body. And suppose you have a hundred maggots here. Ninety-nine will make their way toward the body, but the hundredth little devil—he'll turn the other way." Those in court dared not look at one another, and the judge's face twitched again.

"No further questions," said Hogg, in despair.

The defense now turned on the evidence of those witnesses who were sure they had seen Peter Thomas as late as June 21, while prosecuting counsel tried hard, though with little success, to make them change their mind. Nevertheless, the entomological evidence stood uncontested, despite doubts, and the jury found Brittle guilty. He was sentenced to life imprisonment.

THE TRIAL OF O.J. SIMPSON

Few trials in recent years have attracted as much public interest as that of ex-pro football star O.J. Simpson. The court proceedings were viewed on television by millions of people around the world, and the jury's verdict depended, at least in part, on the admissibility of the evidence presented.

On June 12, 1994, the bodies of Simpson's estranged wife, Nicole, and her friend Ronald Goldman were found on the path leading to the front door of Nicole's home in the exclusive Los Angeles suburb of Brentwood, on the outskirts of Santa Monica. Both were covered in blood and had received deep knife wounds. Nicole's head was virtually severed from her body; the wound ran from the left side of her throat to just below her right ear, and was so deep that it exposed the spinal cord. Goldman had been stabbed at least thirty times.

When the victims were discovered, after midnight, they had been dead about three hours. Far too many errors were soon to be made in the initial stages of the investigation. The police left the bodies lying at the crime scene—covered with a blanket taken from Nicole's home—for several hours before allowing the medical examiner access. And the forensic pathologist who carried out the autopsies was forced to admit at trial that he had made up to forty errors in his examination of the bodies.

Even more important was the question of the blood spots on Nicole's bare back as she lay facedown—clearly visible in the crime scene photographs. It was obvious that someone had bled on her. In transporting her corpse to the morgue, however, the coroner's team had turned it over—the usual practice—while zipping it into the body bag, and the blood from her neck washed this vital evidence away. Forensic blood expert Dr. Herb MacDonell was particularly concerned about this problem, and carried out a number of experiments to replicate the spot pattern, but when he gave testimony

(for the defense) in court, he was not examined about this research.

O.J. Simpson's behavior during the hours following the murders, and later, was deeply suspicious. Between 9:36 and 10:56 p.m., his movements were unknown. He claimed he had been at home, but he had made a telephone call at 10:03 p.m.—not from his home, but from his Ford Bronco. At 10:56 p.m., a limousine driver waiting to take Simpson to the airport for a flight to Chicago saw him enter the house. A few minutes later, he emerged with his luggage, including a small black bag, which was no longer in the limousine when the airport was reached.

When he returned from Chicago the following day, Simpson was interrogated at police headquarters. They particularly noted an open cut on his hand, which he was unable to explain fully. The interrogation lasted a mere half an hour, the details of which were not introduced at the trial. Moreover, when a warrant for his arrest was issued, Simpson took off in another Bronco driven by a close friend, which was soon followed by a line of a dozen police cars, together with helicopters carrying news photographers and TV cameramen.

In the car, found when it eventually stopped, were Simpson's passport, $8,750 in cash and traveler's checks, a loaded gun, and a false beard and moustache. Behind him, at his home in Benedict Canyon, he had left a long note to a friend, which seemed to indicate that he was considering suicide. On the other hand, it was suggested that he had been planning to flee to Mexico. Neither the note nor the possible escape attempt was placed before the jury.

When Simpson's trial opened, on July 22, 1994, he pleaded "Absolutely one hundred percent not guilty." For 133 days, with Judge Lance Ito presiding, the proceedings were transmitted live on TV; the prosecution called seventy-eight witnesses, the defense, seventy-two. Simpson's defense was soon dubbed the "Dream Team." Led by Johnnie Cochran, a "hot-shot" L.A. attorney who had successfully defended Michael Jackson in the 1993 child-molestation case, it included renowned counsel Robert Shapiro; the famous defense doyen F. Lee Bailey; Barry Scheck from the Innocence Project; and Harvard professor Alan Dershowitz, and totaled eleven in all. The prosecution team, led by Assistant District Attorney Marcia Clark, numbered nine. They were confident of obtaining a verdict of guilty, but would prove no match for the Dream Team.

Three weeks of the trial were taken up with detailed testimony concerning the DNA typing of blood samples. Tests revealed DNA consistent with Simpson's in seven traces at the murder scene; a blood-saturated glove found near his home matched with both of the victims'; a sock recovered from his bedroom was stained with blood that matched Nicole's. Blood drops on Simpson's driveway, in the foyer of his home, and found in his Bronco were consistent with his own DNA. But, though most of the blood samples taken from his Bronco were also shown to be his, three small smears, discovered just six weeks later, matched not only Simpson's DNA, but also that of Nicole and Goldman.

Barry Scheck, however, remorselessly attacked criminologist Dennis Fung, who claimed responsibility for the collection of the blood samples. On the stand for nine days, Fung was forced to admit that many of the bloodstains had actually been swatched by his assistant, "under my direct supervision."

Scheck also pursued the question of the time that had elapsed before Fung arrived at the crime scene; he was gradually working up to the implication that some of the evidence had been planted, and much of it contaminated. At a crucial point in his cross-examination, Scheck made his intentions clear:

"In terms of the custom and practice of your laboratory and its workings with detectives, would it have been improper if either of these detectives had kept the blood drawn from Mr. Simpson on June 13 overnight in their personal possession, and then delivered it to you the next morning on June 14?"

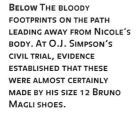

BELOW THE BLOODY FOOTPRINTS ON THE PATH LEADING AWAY FROM NICOLE'S BODY. AT O.J. SIMPSON'S CIVIL TRIAL, EVIDENCE ESTABLISHED THAT THESE WERE ALMOST CERTAINLY MADE BY HIS SIZE 12 BRUNO MAGLI SHOES.

A minor scandal then occurred in the courtroom when Robert Shapiro later handed out fortune cookies "from the Hang Fung restaurant." He was compelled to make an apology to the court.

Leading forensic scientist Dr. Henry Lee was called as a witness for the defense. Scheck asked him about photographs of blood spatter at the crime scene, and led him to agree that the absence of a ruler in the photographs was a serious lapse of procedure. Lee was then asked about his examination of two socks from Simpson's bedroom, which had both been put into the same paper bag, and therefore possibly cross-contaminated.

Scheck asked, "Is there any significance in terms of this examination that you were not wearing a lab coat or a hairnet?"

To which Lee replied, in his broken Chinese-English, "Doesn't matter what I wear, spacesuit, body armor. Still contaminated."

F. Lee Bailey cross-examined Detective Mark Fuhrman about the finding of a knitted watch cap, together with a single glove that allegedly matched the one in Simpson's bedroom, close to Ronald Goldman's body. Fuhrman proved a poor witness when persistently asked to recall details of meetings he had had with the prosecution lawyers, and Bailey then returned to the attack: "Did you anticipate, based on what you had been told, that some sort of attack might be visited upon you with respect to alleged racial slurs?"

This line of questioning was to prove a crucial point in the trial. Marcia Clark had endeavored to blunt the defense's attack on Fuhrman, but writer Laura McKinny testified

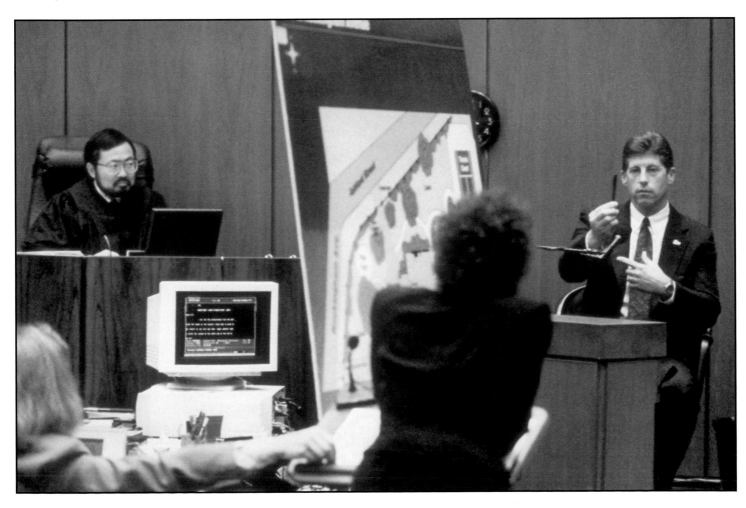

ABOVE ADA MARCIA CLARK IN COURT, WITH A STATEMENT OF THE MEANING OF "REASONABLE DOUBT" PREPARED FOR THE ASSISTANCE OF THE JURY. FORENSIC EXPERTS ARE REQUIRED TO ESTABLISH THE DETAILS OF A CRIME "BEYOND REASONABLE DOUBT."

that, in taped interviews that she had made with the detective over the course of ten years, he had used the "N word" forty-two times. When Fuhrman denied under oath that he had ever used such an expression, he was revealed as a perjured witness, and the defense was quick to imply that he had also planted crucial evidence. Indeed, on one tape played in court Fuhrman not only used the "N word" several times, but also admitted that he had at times planted evidence to secure a conviction.

Despite the prosecution's calling of experts to explain the importance of DNA in simple terms, it soon became clear that not only millions of TV viewers but also the jury were confused and bored by the lengthy scientific discussions. More important, it seemed, were the doubts raised concerning the chain of custody of the evidence. It transpired that a vial containing a sample of blood taken from Simpson had mysteriously decreased in volume. Two defense experts who had examined the socks taken from Simpson's bedroom two weeks after the murders testified that they had seen no bloodstains, and the prosecution admitted that the stains were not reported until four weeks later.

There was an unsubstantiated allegation that extracts from the socks, sent to the FBI

laboratory, had shown the presence of the preservative added to Simpson's blood samples. There were also signs that reference vials of the blood of Nicole and Goldman had become contaminated with Simpson's DNA—which raised serious questions regarding practices at the LAPD laboratory. Dr. Lee famously commented, concerning this evidence, with the succinct (but bowdlerized) remark, "Something wrong."

In the face of these admissions, other incriminating evidence—such as the glove, as well as the bloody imprint, at the murder scene, of what was probably one of Simpson's size 12 Bruno Magli shoes—faded into insignificance. On October 2, 1995, after only three hours of deliberation, the jury found Simpson not guilty.

After the trial had ended, several members of the Dream Team were at pains to stress that they had appeared for the defense not because they necessarily believed Simpson to be innocent, but to illuminate points of law—and in particular to highlight the carelessness with which the blood samples for DNA typing were handled by investigators. Ronald Goldman's family subsequently brought a civil suit against Simpson, in which he was found guilty of "wrongfully causing the deaths of Ronald Goldman and Nicole Brown Simpson."

LEFT WAYNE WILLIAMS
SPEAKS AT A PRESS
CONFERENCE FROM JAIL AFTER
HIS CONVICTION AS THE
ATLANTA SERIAL CHILD
MURDERER. DESPITE
AN APPEAL AGAINST THE
CONVICTION, THE ORIGINAL
VERDICT WAS UPHELD BY THE
GEORGIA SUPREME COURT.

A knowledge and understanding of criminal psychology can also be of great value in the examination of defendants and witnesses in the courtroom. When Wayne Williams was brought to trial in 1982 for the Atlanta child murders in Georgia, the prosecution realized that—despite a wealth of physical and circumstantial evidence—they would have difficulty in persuading the jury that he was capable of committing the crimes with which he was charged. Williams was mild mannered, well spoken, and disposed to be cooperative; he wore thick glasses, and his facial features were far from coarse. He lived with his parents, both retired schoolteachers, and he protested that the accusations brought against him were solely racial in origin.

The prosecution did not expect Williams to take the stand, and were surprised when his attorney announced that he would testify. For more than a day the attorney repeatedly drew attention to his physical appearance: "Look at him! Does he look like a serial killer?… Look how soft his hands are. Do you think he would have the strength to kill someone, to strangle someone with these hands?"

FBI profiler John Douglas had earlier provided his expertise to the investigation. He and his colleague Roy Hazelwood had opined that the perpetrator of the Atlanta killings was black— that fact alone very unusual for a serial killer—single, and aged twenty-five to twenty-nine. And "I was betting on something

to do with music or performing," Douglas later wrote in his book *Mindhunter* (1995). (Williams described himself as a music-biz talent scout.)

For this reason, Douglas was invited to attend the trial. When Williams was due for cross-examination, Douglas advised Assistant District Attorney Jack Mallard: "You've got to keep him on the stand as long as you can—you've got to break him down. Because he's an overcontrolled, rigid personality … and to get to that rigidity, you have to keep the pressure on him, sustain the tension by going through every aspect of his life." Finally, Douglas suggested, Mallard should move in close, violating Williams's personal space, physically touch him, and ask in a low voice, "Did you panic, Wayne, when you killed those kids?"

After several hours of piercing questions, Mallard did what Douglas had advised. Weakly, Williams at first replied "No"— then he burst into a towering rage. He pointed to Douglas and shouted, "You're trying your best to make me fit that FBI profile, and I'm not going to help you do it!" Williams ranted on, describing the FBI as "goons" and the prosecution team as "fools." It was the turning point of the trial, as the jury realized that the violent side of Williams's personality had so far been concealed from them—but was there all along. He was found guilty, and sentenced to life imprisonment

NATIONAL EDITION
Sacramento Tim

VOL. CLII...N0. 52,475   SACRAMENTO, THURSDAY, FEBRUARY 23, 2002

Sacramento Man Found Guilty of Manslaughter

FBI INVOLVEMENT AFTER INVESTIGATION CROSSES STATE LINES

Victim's Family Disappointed with Verdict

By BRIAN INNES

The Library and Courts Building, Sacramento, was the scene of a manslaughter trial

SACRAMENTO, Ca., February 22 — At the opening of the trial of Stasz Pawlowski, a carpet fitter from Sacramento, Assistant District Attorney John Meyer called for a verdict of second-degree murder yesterday. Pawlowski pleaded not guilty before a packed courthouse presided over by Chief Justice Frank Carson at the Library and Courts Building.

Opening his case with a presentation of evidence, prosecutor Meyer praised the investigative and forensic skills of both the police and the FBI in identifying the victim, Mrs. Anna Jepson, 24-year-old daughter of Mr. and Mrs. Ahmad Razak, of Longview, Washington. The FBI had been called in because the evidence showed that though the victim's skeleton was discovered in a shallow grave in southern California, her body had been transported across two state lines to the burial site. Many hours of patient analysis, including digital facial reconstruction and DNA typing, resulted in the positive identification of the remains as those of Mrs. Jepson. Additional analysis

of the carpet in which the victim was wrapped, as well as vehicular trace evidence found at the scene, eventually led investigators to Pawlowski, whose fingerprint was matched from a discarded wallet, also discovered at the scene.

Defense counsel Rachel Weinberger, in her opening address, stated that the evidence that was to be presented was entirely circumstantial. She did not propose to question the identification of the victim, but there was nothing to connect her with the defendant. He lived a long way from the location where the remains were discovered, and an examination of his sales and travel records would show that he worked only in the northern area of California and in Oregon. Evidence could be presented that at no time had he fitted carpets in the Razak home, and there was no suggestion that he had been acquainted with the victim. Pawlowski was known as a scrupulously honest, hard-working artisan, and witnesses could attest to his character. He was, said Ms Weinberger, incapable of the heinous crime of murder.

Buried Skeleton Discovered

The first prosecution witness, Deputy Jose Rodriguez, described the discovery of the remains, on October 20–21, last year. Ms. Weinberger questioned him on the precautions that had been taken in their initial recovery. "We had all the necessary experts there at the

scene," replied Rodriguez. "I am not qualified to express an opinion, but they were meticulous in all the standard procedures, and the chain of custody was carefully logged."

Assistant Medical Examiner Dr. Jane Kurosawa then detailed her examination of the skeleton, and testified that the injuries sustained indicated the deceased was the victim of a vehicular hit-and-run. On cross, Ms. Weinberger questioned

Continued on Page A20

ear Officer Gregory,

February 24, 2002

anted to take a m
terday's
nd
n ca

sed
tior
dica
g oi
ire

y,

zale
olic
Poli

e Sacr
roperty

SEVENTY-FIVE CENTS

Courtesy California State Library

day.

Sacramento Man Found Guilty of Manslaughter

Continued from Page A1

Dr. Kurosawa's professional quali-fications, and asked: "Could these injuries have been caused by other means? By blows from a blunt instrument, for example?"

"I have seven years' experience of some thirty auto-accident deaths," said Kurosawa, "and these distinctive fractures, and the impression in the skull, are typical of such incidents."

Officer Tamara Gregory, crime scene investigator, then detailed the various examples of trace evidence that had led to the apprehension of Pawlowski. The first indication that the victim came from out of state was the discovery of seeds from a plant that was not native to California. She referred briefly to the technique of facial re-construction, which would later be described in detail by a representative of the FBI. Gregory then described the dog hairs, together with fragments of glass and paint from a Chevrolet van that were obtained from the carpet. Finally, she told how a fingerprint on the inside of a wallet, recovered at the scene, had been positively identified as Pawlowski's.

"I won't contest the print on the wallet," said Weinberger, "but couldn't it have been Pawlowski's property, lost during his business trip? Where is the evidence that connects it to Mrs. Jepson?"

"With the cooperation of Mr. and Mrs. Razak," said Officer Gregory, "fingerprint experts from Seattle were able to obtain

comparison prints from a number of their daughter's personal possessions. These confirmed the identity of other prints on the inside of the billfold as the victim's. The photographs are entered as evidence items 12 and 13." Mr. Meyer then indicated that four expert witnesses for the prosecution were in court, and could be called. Judge Carson: "I am so far satisfied with the testimony of the police witnesses. Further experts can be called, on both sides if necessary, after we have heard what Ms. Weinberger has to say."

Speaking for the defense, Weinberger stressed the use of the word "accident" in Dr. Kurosawa's testimony. While the evidence as yet presented appeared to implicate the defendant, there had been no suggestion of any intent to kill. The victim was unknown to Pawlowski, and his subsequent behavior was that of a man panic-stricken at what he had done, and filled with remorse.

Surprise Development

Both attorneys then approached the bench, and spoke privately with Judge Carson, following which he announced that a plea bargain had been struck: the charge of murder would be withdrawn, and Pawlowski would plead guilty to manslaughter in the second degree. The jury was discharged, and the judge retired. Sentence was later pronounced: three years in a state

©HIRB/Index Stock Imagery

Defendant Stasz Pawlowski was convicted yesterday of second degree manslaughter and sentenced to a three-year prison term.

correctional institution, with possibility of parole.

Speaking on the steps of the courthouse after the trial concluded, Mr. Meyer read a statement from the parents of the victim. "Nothing can ever bring our beloved daughter Anna back to us, and our grandson has lost a beautiful and loving mother, but at last our minds are set at rest concerning her dis-appearance and death. We are pleased and grateful that the police and FBI have finally identified the perpetrator of this horrible crime, and that he is to receive due punishment. However, we consider the sentence wholly inadequate in the circumstances." Mr. and Mrs. Razak were not available for further comment.

FURTHER READING

Ainsworth, Peter B. *Offender Profiling and Crime Analysis.* Portland, Oregon: Willan Publishing, 2001.

Baden, Michael. *Unnatural Death.* New York: Ballantine, 1989.

—, and Marion Roach. *Dead Reckoning.* London: Arrow, 2002.

Bartol, C. *Criminal Behavior: a Psychosocial Approach.* Toronto: Prentice-Hall, 1991.

Bass, Bill, and Jon Jefferson. *Death's Acre.* New York: Putnam, 2003.

Beavan, Colin: *Fingerprints.* London: Fourth Estate, 2002.

Blackburn, Ronald: *The Psychology of Criminal Conduct.* New York: John Wiley & Sons, 1993.

Block, Eugene B. *Fingerprinting.* New York: Franklin Watts, 1969.

Britton, Paul. *The Jigsaw Man.* London: Transworld, 1997.

—.*Picking Up the Pieces.* London: Bantam Press, 2000.

Brussel, James. *Casebook of a Crime Psychiatrist.* New York: Simon & Schuster, 1968.

Canter, David. *Criminal Shadows.* London: HarperCollins, 1994.

Cook, Stephen. *The Real Cracker.* London: Fourth Estate, 2001.

Cooper, Paulette. *The Medical Detectives.* New York: McKay, 1973.

Douglas, John, and Mark Olshaker. *Mindhunter.* New York: Scribner, 1995.

—*Journey into Darkness.* London: Heinemann, 1997.

—.*Obsession.* New York: Scribner, 1998.

—.*The Anatomy of Motive.* New York: Scribner, 1999.

—.*The Cases that Haunt Us.* New York: Simon & Schuster, 2000.

Erzinçlioglu, Zakaria. *Every Contact Leaves a Trace.* London: Carlton, 2000.

—.*Maggots, Murder and Men.* Colchester, UK: Harley Books, 2000.

Evans, Colin. *The Casebook of Forensic Detection.* New York: Wiley, 1996.

Fisher, Barry A.J. *Techniques of Crime Scene Investigation.* New York: Elsevier, 1992.

Fisher, David. *Hard Evidence.* New York: Simon & Schuster, 1995.

Foster, Don. *Author Unknown.* New York: Henry Holt & Co, 2000.

Godwin, J. *Murder USA.* New York: Ballantine, 1978.

Green, E. *The Intent to Kill.* Baltimore: Clevedon, 1993.

Hare, Robert D. *Without Conscience.* New York: Pocket Books, 1995.

Hastings, Macdonald. *The Other Mr Churchill.* London: Harrap, 1963.

Henry, Sir Edward. *Classification and Uses of Fingerprints.* London: HMSO, eighth edition, 1937.

Holmes, Ronald M. *Profiling Violent Crimes.* Newbury Park, C.A.: Sage Publications, 1989.

Innes, Brian. *Bodies of Evidence.* Leicester, UK: Silverdale Books, 2001.

—.*Profile of a Criminal Mind.* Pleasantville, N.Y.: Reader's Digest, 2003.

Jackson, Janet L., and Debra A. Bekerian (eds). *Offender Profiling.* New York: John Wiley & Sons, 1997.

Jeffers, H. Paul. *Who Killed Precious?* Boston: Little, Brown, 1991.

Joyce, Christopher, and Eric Stover. *Witnesses from the Grave.* London: Bloomsbury, 1991.

Kind, Stuart. *The Scientific Investigation of Crime.* Harrogate, UK: Forensic Science Services, 1987.

Lambourne, Gerald. *The Fingerprint Story.* London: Harrap, 1984.

Lane, Brian. *Encyclopedia of Forensic Science.* London: Headline, 1992.

Leyton, Elliott. *Compulsive Killers.* New York: New York University Press, 1986.

—.*Men of Blood.* London: Constable, 1995.

Lyman, M.D. *Criminal Investigations: the Art and the Science.* New York: Prentice Hall, 1968.

Maples, William R. *Dead Men Do Tell Tales.* New York: Doubleday, 1994.

Markman, Ronald, and Dominick Bosco. *Alone with the Devil.* Boston: Little, Brown, 1989.

Marriner, Brian. *Forensic Clues to Murder.* London: Arrow Books, 1991.

Miller, Hugh. *Traces of Guilt.* BBC Publications, London, 1995.

—.*Proclaimed in Blood.* London: Headline, 1995.

—.*Forensic Fingerprints.* London: Headline, 1998.

Norris, Joel. *Serial Killers.* London: Arrow, 1988.

—.*Walking Time Bombs.* New York: Bantam Books, 1992.

Nickell, Joe, and John Fischer. *Crime Science: Methods of Forensic Detection.* Lexington: University Press of Kentucky, 1999.

Owen, David. *Hidden Evidence.* London: Time-Life, 2000.

Parry, Eugenia. *Crime Album Stories.* Zurich: Scalo, 2000.

Paul, Philip. *Murder Under the Microscope.* London: Macdonald, 1990.

Ragle, Larry. *Crime Scene.* New York: Avon Books, 1995.

Ressler, Robert K., Ann W. Burgess, and John E. Douglas. *Sexual Homicide.* New York: Lexington Books, 1988.

Ressler, Robert K., and Tom Schachtman. *Whoever Fights Monsters.* New York: Simon & Schuster, 1992.

Rhodes, Henry T.F. *Alphonse Bertillon.* London: Harrap, 1956.

Rhodes, Richard. *Why They Kill.* New York: Knopf, 1999.

Rossmo, Dr. Kim. *Geographic Profiling.* Boca Raton, FL: CRC Press, 2000.

Rudin, Norah, and Keith Inman. *An Introduction to Forensic DNA Analysis.* Boca Raton, FL: CRC Press, 2002.

Sachs, Jessica Snyder. *Time of Death.* London: William Heinemann, 2002.

Scott, Gini Graham. *Homicide.* Los Angeles: Roxbury Park, 1998.

Sengoopta, Chandak. *Imprint of the Raj.* London: Macmillan, 2003.

Simpson, Keith. *Forty Years of Murder.* London: Harrap, 1978.

Smith, Sir Sydney. *Mostly Murder.* London: Harrap, 1986.

Smyth, Frank. *Cause of Death.* London: Orbis, 1980.

Söderman, Harry, and John O'Connell. *Modern Criminal Investigation.* New York: Funk & Wagnall, 1935.

Stern, Chester. *Dr. Iain West's Casebook.* London: Little, Brown, 1996.

Stockdale, R.E. (ed). *Science Against Crime.* London: Marshall Cavendish, 1982.

Turvey, Brent. *Criminal Profiling.* San Diego: Academic Press, 1999.

Ward, Jenny. *Crimebusting.* London: Blandford, 1998.

Wecht, Cyril. *Cause of Death.* New York: Dutton, 1993.

—.*Grave Secrets.* New York: Penguin, 1996.

Williams, Judy. *The Modern Sherlock Holmes.* London: Broadside, 1992.

Williams, Katherine S. *Textbook of Criminology.* New York: Oxford University Press, 2001.

Wilson, Colin. *Written in Blood.* London: Grafton Books, 1990.

—, and Donald Seaman. *The Serial Killers.* London: Virgin Books, 1996.

Wynn, Douglas. *On Trial for Murder.* London: Pan Books, 1996.

PICTURE CREDITS